# BETWEEN ROCK AND HARD PLACES

# BETWEEN ROCK AND HARD PLACES

## A Musical Autobiodyssey

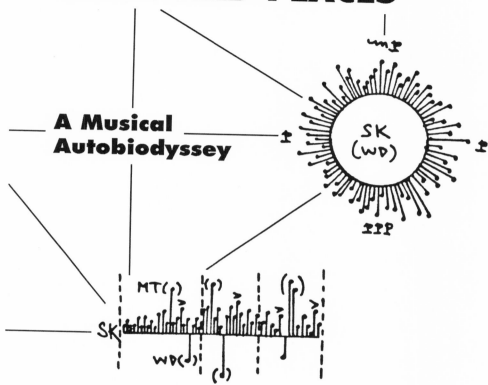

# Tom Constanten

**HULOGOSI**
Eugene    1992

PUBLISHED BY HULOGOSI, P.O. BOX 1188, EUGENE, OREGON 97440

LIBRARY OF CONGRESS CATALOGING-IN-PUBLICATION DATA:

Constanten, Tom.
   Between rock and hard places : a musical autobiodyssey / Tom Constanten.
      p.   cm.
   Includes bibliographical references.
   ISBN 0-938493-16-7
   1. Constanten, Tom.   2. Rock musicians—United States—Biography.
I. Title.
ML410.C752A3   1992                                    92-7064
780′.92—dc20                                              CIP
[B]                                                         MN

# CONTENTS

ॐ

Hanging out with T.C.

There is                          NARY

A Dull Moment
Master Musician
                    AND
                        Story Teller
    Tom's Words
        AND
        Music
Dance to an irresistible intergalactic Beat
        That

                ONLY            Will Not
    Delight    Old    Trippers

                            but Also
            Young Souls
Who would Like to Savor with
        This Co(s)mic Taskmaster
A Journey
        That Has
                    Fallen        into
Some of the More Interesting Cracks of
                Life.

22 II 92                        Terry Riley

*For Ginny, who dreamed it possible*

# PREFATORY RAMBLE

JUST what the world needs. Another relic of the sixties cashing in on the simple fact of having survived. Good ol' American exploitation. Actually, I never set out to write a book. Honest. Steve Goldstine loaned me a personal computer and I figured it was a good chance to organize all these scraps and snippets of protoinformation I had collected in (and sometimes on) paper bags. Before I knew it, I had 64 pages of draft assembled, and there was no turning back.

Neither a daunting Babel of political correctitude nor a rags-to-riches comic book story, it's not a lurid exposé of life in the jet set world of Rock stars, either. For as interesting a segment as the Grateful Dead adventure was in my life, it remains only a segment, just one of several musical worlds I've explored. As for the other elements in the triangle, sex and drugs – not that there are a whole lot of them, but there are people around who'd just as soon not be implicated by my anecdotes, colorful though they may be.

What it is, though, is an earwitness account of musical realms ranging from the wild and woolly Julys of Woodstock to the august cynosures of Broadway and Hollywood, with all due elbow-rubbing. You can't cross as many borders as I have without it influencing the way that you think, write, and speak. I recall, for instance, a conversation during my student days in Europe. When I mentioned Berkeley one person saw fit to 'correct' me: "Oh, *we* say 'Barkley.'" I thought to myself, "The nerve of this guy, telling me how to pronounce the name of the place I came from!" Since then, I've been sensitive to local pronunciation and spelling of proper nouns. If my onetime neighbors know their home towns as Bruxelles or Köln, well, that's good enough for me.

Nor will you find me a slave to foolish consistency in this regard. If I drop the final 'o' in Milan, I hope that the natives will think of their winning football team, unless of course they're loyal to Inter, the crosstown rivals. Across the globe, Chinese has a pronoun (*ta* in

Mandarin, *kéuih* in Cantonese) that is indeterminate of sex. In my judgment, the restrictively sexist 'his' is more objectionable than the merely formal consideration of disagreement in number. Not finding much to choose from among a curse of contrived epicenities, I will go ahead and use 'they' and 'their' instead when speaking generically. Let anyone who might cavil know that it's not I who am defective, but the English language.

It's a Great American Fantasy – how successful one could be if sufficiently capitalized. It hasn't exactly been raining money on me, but there are those who have been helpful in a substantial way. It's with a very light heart and great pleasure that I express my appreciation of the support it's been my privilege to enjoy: from Stephen Goldstine, who, it seems, has usually done something for me recently; from (in alphabetical order) Bill Bolcom, Phil Lesh, Bob Moran, Terry Riley, Terry Ryan, and Bill Walker – friends since the early sixties, who've always been there for me; from Henry Kaiser, a benefactor by any name; from Peter Dybwad, the right man at the right time; from Tim Fox, a gentleman and a Texan; from Meredith Tromble, the Roving Painterly Eye; from the relentlessly good-looking urban geographer Bonnie Loyd and the articulatious Sedge Thomson; from diligent archivists like Dale Anderson and Ken Hunt; from Willy Legate, Mad Trapper of the Frozen North; and from the vicars of the Lexical Edge, Robert Hunter and Alan Trist.

If you count your wealth in friends, and I do, I'm rolling in it.

*Tom Constanten*
*Las Vegas, Nevada*
*January, 1991*

# PART ONE/ LIFE AMONG THE MXNXTRXNDXNRS

# I/ PLEASED TO MEET YOU
## hope you can spell my name

**A**lien from any angle, that's how it looks.

As I hold this biodesic tome – the 'story of my life, up to now' – at arm's length, and imagine how it might appear to the populex at large, it seems like an irrational number, or a puzzle diabolically designed so as to be unsolvable.

The events don't array themselves neatly. Household names and everyday concepts in one realm will be 'hoozits' and 'whazzats' in another. Thing is, I can no longer tell which are which. A chameleon feels at home in any color. Furthermore, my musical philosophy has been noncompromist for too long not to impact my verbal expression as well. So – no limbo dances beneath anyone's mindset!

There's no telling if it's anything more than coincidence, my winding up with the names of an Apostle and of a Roman emperor, both of whom had to be *shown*. Spiritually an anarchist and politically an agnostic, I've an innate skepticism of the need for more than one birth per lifetime. In my case it was in Long Branch, New

Jersey, a stone's throw from the Atlantic Ocean, to a family practically fresh off the boat from Europe.

March 19, 1944. St. Joseph's Day, the date the swallows return to Capistrano – just about that corner of the month where the lion turns into a lamb. The front pages of the New York papers that day featured a photo of a B-25 dive-bombing a Japanese gunboat. I'm told that I was born with a caul, which was sold to a sea captain. Legend has it that a ship with one aboard will never go down. Now and again I wonder how that particular ship fared against the U-boats.

Lilian Sture, my mother, had come with her family from Bergen, Norway. She'd met my father-to-be, Thomas King Hills, in the New World. He was named after his godfather, Thomas Edison, an associate of his father. Don't know if any of that brilliance rubbed off, but my parents delighted in telling of how they took me to see Albert Einstein when I was two or three years old, and I wet my pants while sitting on his lap. Talk about leaving an impression.

We lived in a house near the ocean in Deal, New Jersey, and briefly in an apartment in New York City, but the most enjoyable time was spent with my maternal grandparents in Elberon, New Jersey. 'Bestemor' and 'Bestefar,' as they were known to me, lived in a big but cozy house. Doting grandparents of the finest sort, they would take me to nearby Asbury Park, and treat me to rides on the little train at the boardwalk, or walks along the beach.

Those times seem so far away now. It was the era of cellar doors, coal chutes, and ice boxes, of Mercury dimes and buffalo nickels. Busy intersections in town would more likely have a traffic cop than a stoplight. I remember Bestefar coming up the driveway in his brand new '49 Buick station wagon, a maroon woody. It was so *modern* – like, there were no running boards, and the hood opened in front!

Television hadn't yet caught on, so in the evening we'd gather upstairs and 'watch radio.' The comic one-upmanship fest *Can You Top This?* was a particular favorite of mine. We'd also tune in the (time warp – it's still on the air!) Metropolitan Opera broadcasts. Once in the late forties I blew my elders' minds by singing a line from *Carmen*. "Where'd he get that!?" they marveled (a phrase that was to recur in less marvelous contexts later on).

Precocious may not be the word. By the time I arrived at school age I was practically bilingual, perhaps a bit more comfortable på norsk. I'd read an overview of 'world' history up to the end of W.W. II by my fifth birthday – about as much of it as there was then – and was preparing to dive into Gen. Omar Bradley's book *A Soldier's Story* when the inevitable happened: Kindergarten. Whatever it was, I knew I wanted no part of it. A relatively sheltered upbringing may have hampered my development of social skills somewhat. On the other hand, I became adjusted to the idea of being an outsider wherever I went.

My parents split up when I was but four years old, and in 1949 my mother married Frank Constanten (accent on the 'tan' as in 'swimming'), a captain of waiters at the Copacabana in New York. Earlier he'd been saluted as 'The Combat Hero of the Savoy Plaza.' D-Day veteran, Bronze Star, Purple Heart. Put *that* on your chest, General! I remember him bringing me in to work one afternoon to introduce me to Jimmy Durante. At first it was a shock – there was a pair of glasses perched on that immortal schnozz! – but I was duly awed nonetheless.

He also took me to that great temple of urban America, Yankee Stadium. Someone once asked Joe DiMaggio why he put out so much effort and energy day after day, game after game. He replied that on any given day, there might be a kid up in the stands who'd be seeing him for the first and only time in his life. One sunny afternoon in the summer of '51, when the Yankees were hosting the White Sox, that kid was me. It blew me away to see that much open field in the middle of the Bronx asphaltitude. Even in suburban New Jersey we'd usually wind up drawing home plate on the pavement with chalk. A pile of rocks was second base, and first or third could be either the fender of a '48 DeSoto or a telephone pole.

It's been said that the ancient Greeks had all the dramatic plots down, but the ancient Greeks didn't have baseball. Subtler than Sophocles, æsthetic as Æschylus, and meaner than Menander, baseball is unexcelled in generating new and unforeseen possibilities. Like they say, on any given day, you might see something you've never seen before. Still, there are those who simply cannot see the fascination in watching a couple dozen 'grown men' making such a fuss over a little white ball, and no amount of explanation will change their point of view. For me, having been indoctrinated at such an early age, no explanation was ever necessary. And what an indoctrination! Included was that other temple of the sport, Ebbetts Field, fabled in song and story. Snyder. Hodges. Reese. Robinson. Furillo. I even remember the numbers they wore.[1]

Major League ballparks still had that narrow path cut out between home plate and the pitcher's mound, as if the catcher needed help to find the way. At the end of the inning, players would take off their mitts and toss them onto the field instead of taking them back to the dugout. The cigar smoke...the fedoras and Homburgs...the way hot dogs were prepared to your specifications before your very eyes...the vendors' cries of "Cold beer here!"...all these things colored the atmosphere in the stands. I remember the way the fans would yell 'swish' as the Phillies' Bill Nicholson swung and hit nothing but air...the way the Brooklyn Sym-Phony would play a derisive march as strikeout victims made their way back to the dugout, punctuated by a bass drum blort as they sat down. Once Bill Howerton, an outfielder for the Pirates, thought to avoid the latter by going over to the drinking fountain instead. The wily musicians, not to miss a trick, burst into "How dry I am!"

My first National League game, actually, was the Braves versus the Giants – Boston at New York. The first Giant I ever saw come to bat was a scrappy second baseman, wearing number 12: Eddie Stanky. Games at the Polo Grounds were frequently bizarre because of its unusual lozenge shape. Short home run 'porches' – yet I can recall watching Sal 'the Barber' Maglie shave 'em close and dress 'em down.

After the game, the ushers, dressed like Uptown doormen, stood around the skin part of the infield, and they opened the gates to let us exit the park through the center field gate. Once we had got to about where the centerfielder stands when Bobby Thomson ran by us on the way to the clubhouse. I knew it was him by his number.[2] Whitey Lockman was another favorite of mine. Perhaps because of the time an engineer waved to me from the cab of his locomotive and said "Hi, Whitey!" – I was a towhead at that age. That was at the train station back in Elberon, where President Garfield paid the ultimate price for an imperfect employment policy. More on this later.

[1] 4, 14, 1, 42, and 6.        [2] 23.

We lived six miles across the George Washington Bridge from New York City in a comfortably dull northern New Jersey bedroom community called River Edge. Definitely not at the 'edge,' and nowhere near any river, although I enjoyed exploring a sunken creek that ran behind the houses across Mohawk Drive. After a couple of years we began to feel settled in, but in 1953 Frank Constanten was offered a job at the fledgling Sands Hotel in Las Vegas, and on September 11th of the following year the rest of us joined him there.

Three days out of Penn Station by rail, we were exhausted but ecstatic when the train pulled into Vegas. The station (alas, it's long gone – there's a hotel there now) was right at the head of Fremont Street, so the ride to our new home went straight through the heart of Glitter Gulch. Above the doors of the Pioneer Club, Vegas Vic's luminous arm was swinging in the night air, inviting you to come in and lay your money down. They've become grander in design and dimension with the intervening years, but the neon signs and displays were already an eyeful then.

There was still a 'wild west' flavor to Las Vegas when we moved there. The *Territorial Enterprise*, 'Mark Twain's newspaper,' was on sale at the local drugstore. 'Hoot' Gibson, star of the Saturday movie matinées, was virtually a neighbor, living around the corner on Smoke Ranch Road. There was a part of town where people ate, lived, breathed, and sometimes even resembled horses. And kids like me could find pre-Disneylandic bliss at the Last Frontier Village, cavorting on genuine antique autos, trains and wagons.

The climate amounted to some kind of a change from what we'd been used to on the Eastern Seaboard. Arriving in early autumn might've softened the blow. Maybe it's the altitude, maybe the low humidity, but after you've been in Las Vegas for several years it's hard to find anywhere else that gets hot enough for you. You can feel the electrifying crispness in the air. The openness. The surrounding countryside has a primordial beauty, perhaps an acquired taste, and the showbiz neon circus that takes place there is at least interesting, verging on intoxicating. There's a strength that accrues to those that stand on the Devil's doorstep, yet don't pass through.

Or vice versa. I recall 'dust devils,' mini tornadoes that would sally across the desert, across lawns, streets, occasionally through

the house – with amusing results. Desert storms can be very com-
pactly localized not only in space, but in time. Once I was driving up
Fifth Street (it had not yet been rechristened Las Vegas Boulevard)
on one of those days when it was so hot you could barely touch the
steering wheel, when out of nowhere came this torrential rainstorm
so heavy that visibility was reduced nearly to nil. So there I was,
facing this choice: open the window and get drenched, or close it
and roast. As I recall I think I cracked it a little and took a sauna.
Fifteen minutes later, it was clear and sunny again!

The colorful sunsets, the panoramas of clouds and mountains –
the place would be spectacular even without the bedizened stage
extravaganzas. The weather, too, has a knack for the flamboyant. I
drove into town once in the late seventies during a combination
flash flood and electrical storm. As we sped through the pouring
rain, bolts of lightning were hitting close enough to the car for us to
feel their impact through the ground. Getting off the highway to
seek lower ground, we found ourselves driving up the Strip, past
the most gaudily lit hotels. The parking lots at Cæsar's and the
Flamingo were the lakes they often become during such downpours
– they're set in the middle of Flamingo Wash, a dry gully that
occasionally aspires to riverhood. The sight of all those flashing
neon signs reflected in the windows of floating VW bugs was
nothing less than surreal. Arriving at our friends' house on the far
side of town, I commented on the ferocity of the storm. "What
storm?" they said.

But I'm getting ahead of myself. Back in the fifties Vegas had
more of an open, spacey feel to it. Views of the surrounding
mountains were highlighted. West of town there's a ridge that, in
the right light, looks like a frog sunning himself. If you're driving
out West Washington Avenue, it should be right in front of you.
Diametrically opposite, to the east, Sunrise Mountain rules the
horizon. The silhouette of peaks and sky imprints itself on your
being, until it's as familiar as the proverbial back of your hand.

KA-WHOOOM!!!! Oh, I almost forgot, the jets, at first F-86
Sabrejets, later F-100s, flew training missions out of Nellis Air Force
Base, just north of town. When we moved there, they still were
allowed to fly over Las Vegas proper. Often you'd see them before
you'd hear them. Time to brace for the sonic boom. Wake up

America with technology. And if that wasn't intense enough for you, you could get up before sunrise and watch the bright flashes from the A-bomb tests at Yucca Flat, some two hours up the Tonopah Highway.

This was before the orgy of development that was to come in the ensuing decade. When the Riviera Hotel opened in the mid-fifties, it was heralded as the 'New, new high in the Las Vegas sky' – all seven storeys of it. Until the Fremont Hotel trumped it with eleven floors (seven – eleven. Get it?), it was the tallest building around. Few places in Nevada had an 'upstairs' or, for that matter, a 'downstairs.' Cellar, basement, whatever you call it – they didn't call it anything in Vegas because there weren't any. Sage and sand notwithstanding, the water table was too high. As a result, homes and schools were at most split level.

Hotels, casinos, and a few public buildings had air conditioning when we moved there. It's since become omnipresent. But by and large, in private residences and in the public schools, it was the heyday of the old 'reliable' swamp cooler. Based on the principle of a fan blowing through a wet sponge, they'd be switched on every spring, when it started to warm up enough for them to become useful. In the schoolrooms, you could count on them to deposit half an inch of sand everywhere – all over desks, floors, and books – the accumulation of a windy winter.

And there was a generous supply of sand all around. More than vacant lots – we were surrounded by the desert. Wild, unmanicured, and untamed. Here I didn't have just traffic to watch out for. There were scorpions, tarantulas, and...rattlesnakes. It lent an air of adventure even walking or riding a bike to school. The route usually involved going where the roads didn't yet, through gullies, past sage and yucca, often along a thin lane worn by the passing of many bicycle tires. Desert byways beloved by kids and detergent manufacturers – they'd fill us with fresh air and sunshine enough to fortify against the tides of scholastic ennui.

Everyone at school – classmates, teachers...everyone – seemed relieved that I hadn't moved there from California. In those years students transferring from California to Nevada were automatically set back a year. New Jersey wasn't quite as well known a quantity in Nevada, so I got the benefit of the doubt. Not that I had any trouble excelling. In the Spring of 1956, I was chosen as the Red Rock School candidate for the county spelling title. The final show-down was on KLRJ-TV, Channel 2. Since then it's moved to Channel 3, changed its call letters to KORK, and then to KVBC (wonder why), but it's still at the same location. Somehow, it seemed a lot farther out of town back then. It was my first introduction to the pressures of the lights and cameras, and I wound up placing second. I'll never misspell the word I missed again for as long as I live. I put one too many "i's" in 'indispensable.'

Even during classes there were reminders that you were in Vegas. Like the time the P. E. instructor was describing the positions taken by a basketball team, and one of the students said, "Oh, like 'five' on dice." But in general public school was pretty much a bore. I'd started exploring Latin and algebra on my own in sixth grade, and looked about hungrily for other candidates for Consuming Interests. Someone on high might have noticed my impatience with the standard pace, because halfway into seventh grade I found myself going through a battery of aptitude and psychological tests. After the Xmas break, instead of returning to seventh grade at Red Rock School, I went to eighth grade at Crestwood School. Skipping a grade in midstream, as it were.

High School in the fifties was still a four-year proposition – none of this 'Junior High' nonsense – and Rancho High School was where you went if you lived outside the Las Vegas city limits. Since there was 'nary another building between my house and the mountains, that meant me. Kids were bussed in from as far away as Goodsprings, Moapa, and Pahrump.

Thanks to my speech at the campaign assembly, I *was* elected Student Council treasurer my senior year, and I *did* place fifth in a class of about two hundred (3.818 grade point average), but still I wasn't your typical walk-on character from *Happy Days*. Like, I wore a slide rule on my belt, strapped to my leg with a piece of rawhide to facilitate quick draws. Thirty three scales – decitrig – log/log…

Those calculations occasionally found applications on the physi-cal plane. After the final bell one school day, two of my classmates collaborated with me in driving my car, a two-tone green '55 Olds Holiday. Frank Kirk, whose father Jess was maître d' at the Sands, got down on the floor and worked the pedals. I was prone on the front seat, where I could control the steering wheel; and the mechanically precocious Jim Hrudicka, son of Charlie, the trumpet player, sat in the back seat and called the shots. So what you'd see was this car going merrily along, with *no one* in the front seat, and a lone passenger in back smiling contentedly with his hands folded behind his head.

We were just getting the hang of it when we were stopped. By the Principal, Paul Arenaz. "Who's driving this car?" he questioned sternly. Frank was the first to find the courage to speak. "Well...we *all* are." Chalk it up to Dumb Luck, or maybe I really do have a Guardian Angel, but Mr. Arenaz just turned with a chuckle and told us to cut it out. We thought we'd actually seen a silly grin on his face as he walked away. Later on we found out that that very week the results from the National Merit Scholarship Test had just come in, and the three of us were the school's top three scorers.

Not all of my calculations came out as 'planned,' though. On one of several charmingly zany walks with Frank Kirk through the Municipal Golf Course, I lost a ball on a putt. One of the greens on the back nine was banked wickedly, you see, and I'd misjudged the angle. It was a matter of inches, but the ball started rolling in a totally unplanned direction, gathering speed and momentum until it bounded off into the rough.

For a while I was heavily into astronomy. It was supposedly what I'd be going to college to study. My fascination with the lore and lure of the sky went back to grade school field trips to the Hayden Planetarium in New York City. It was a kick to check out how much you'd weigh on the Moon, Jupiter, Mars, or even – ouch! – the Sun on their specially recalibrated scales. One particularly memorable show highlighted the total solar eclipse of June 30, 1954, visible from upstate New York.

Using Elger's map of the Moon I became familiar with its landmarks, sketching a few that caught my fancy. Craters Maurolycus, Cassini, and Gassendi...meetings of mountains and maria near Archimedes....craters of the Southern highlands. At the old library building in downtown Las Vegas there was a meeting to start an astronomy club. Lord Buckley was there, his nattily waxed mustache glistening by the fire in his eyes. When the subject of picking a name for the group came up in the meeting, he suggested 'Star Diggers,' but, alas, they weren't ready for him at all. It was through a founding club member, however, that I was able to acquire a telescope at low cost. Nick Carter had put a 3 1/4 inch Jaegers object lens on a machined tube, and then put that on a Unitron equatorial mounting.

The mounting sported Vernier calibrated setting circles, which made it easier to locate interesting deep sky objects. All I had to do was look up the coördinates, and point the telescope where the numbers indicated. A great boon, because until you know where to look and what to look for, an instrument of such modest size won't show you much by way of cosmic spectacle. Galaxies and star clusters don't look anything like those time exposures from Mt. Palomar, and you won't see any canals on Mars. But after a while the subtleties begin to emerge: the reticulately festooned belts of Jupiter... exquisite double stars, like Albireo (ß Cygni): one blue and one gold, as if to show each other off to best advantage...spectacular anomalies like the Straight Wall on the Moon...

During one sidereal season, mainly with that telescope, I tracked down all of the objects in the Messier catalog. Charles Messier was an eighteenth century French astronomer whose greatest discovery, it seems, was that the first person to report a sighting of a comet would have it named after him. On all too many occasions, however, what he'd hoped would be his ticket to fame and immortality was yet another hazy patch that was somehow every bit as permanent as the 'fixed' stars. He was thus motivated to compile a list of objects that might be taken for comets, but weren't really. This catalog, numbering some hundred odd celestial wonders, includes the likes of M(for Messier)17, that floating check mark in the sky; M31, the Andromeda galaxy – the farthest the unaided eye can see from the surface of this planet; and M45, the Pleiades, or Seven Sisters (can you make out the tiny dipper formation?). It's understandable how he might have missed Omega Centauri – it's so far south – but I've always wondered at the omission of the great double cluster in Perseus, included in Herschel's catalog (but that's another story). Ironically, a couple of objects on the list are not to be found at the coördinates he prescribed, and may well have actually been comets! Sorry, Charlie!

CATHARINA
August 10, 1959
4h, 15m UT
S — 9   T — 5
3.25" refractor, 96x
Colongitude 342.8°

TRANSIT OF MERCURY

November 7, 1960
Egress
1st. Contact: 19h, 11m, 20s
     (Uncorrected)
2nd. Contact: 19h, 12m, 12s
     (Uncorrected)
1st. Contact: 19h, 10m, 25s
     (Corrected)
2nd. Contact: 19h, 10m, 17s
     (Corrected)

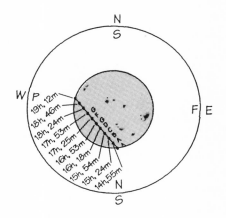

REGION OF HAAS AND PICO

July 15, 1960
10h, 15m UT
5 — 6   T — 4
12.5" reflector, 303x
Colongitude 196°

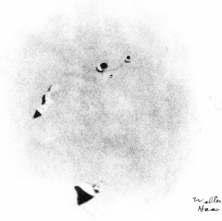

Walter
Haas

I became a member of the Association of Lunar and Planetary Observers (the A. L. P. O.), in whose magazine, *The Strolling Astronomer*, drawings, observations, and even an article of mine appeared. Next I hooked up with the American Association of Variable Star Observers, checking variable stars' brightness against those grand old blueprint charts from the Harvard College Observatory. I dabbled in astrophotography. One shot of mine, a ten-minute time exposure, showed the spiral structure of the Andromeda galaxy. I got as far as having my observations included in the report of the November 7, 1960 solar transit of Mercury in *Sky and Telescope*.[3]

A lasting benefit of my sky sojourn was the discovery of my internal clock. I could 'set myself,' I discovered, to wake up at a certain time, say to observe a star emerging from behind the Moon. Meteors, especially, are better after midnight. And some of the best views of Mercury and Venus are to be had before dawn, when the desert air is at its stillest.

In Las Vegas, of course, 'stars' has another meaning. What with John Bromfield (television's 'Sheriff of Cochise') and Connie Francis visiting our high school – Shecky Greene even came to talk at an assembly – nobody had to be told that growing up there was a bit 'different.' And the 'difference' wasn't confined to the incandescent architecture. Compared to nowadays, it was a golden age of entertainment. Each major Strip hotel (and even some of them Downtown) had a dinner show, usually *cum* house orchestra. Even a lounge here or there would have an amazing assemblage of musicians appearing 'nitely.'

Morry King's[4] Magic Violins serenaded 'em at the Dunes. The group included players like Ennio Bolognini, who was Toscanini's first chair 'cellist and would do things like play Wieniawski's *Scherzo Tarantelle* for violin on his 'cello – *untransposed*; and Mischa Violin, who used to conduct at the Roxy in New York and would regale me with stories of friends of his like as Moriz Rosenthal, who worked out with weights like an athlete and whose piano teacher was Franz Liszt. A favorite pastime of mine in those days was to listen to orchestral pieces with the score in front of me. At first it was

[3] Vol. XX, No. 6 (December, 1960, p. 384), and Vol. XXI, No. 1 (January, 1961, p. 19).
[4] Whose son Michael and I were finalists in the music section of the *Las Vegas Sun* Youth Forum – 1960.

disappointingly demystifying, then it turned fascinating. When I first followed along in the score of *The Rite of Spring*, it was from Mischa's copy. Mischa was married to a remarkable woman named Jeannette Violin (yes that's their real name, and what's even more incredible, it had been her maiden name!) who had been First Violinist of the Amati String Quartet.

The showrooms created a demand for quality musicians, and turned what would have been a desert outpost into a rosin-scented Oz. There were the British 'cellist Joseph Pacey; violinists Louis Pressman, Lewis Elias, and Robert 'Frenchy' Spokany; and violist William Gromko, who soloed on exploding paper bag at the legendary John Cage concert at Town Hall[5] in New York.

As you might well expect from the self-styled 'Entertainment Capital of the World,' there were all kinds of jazz players around. I ultimately wound up hanging out with them more as time went by. Maybe it was the smaller age differential, maybe just local geography, maybe the hours we kept, but for whatever reason the gravitation was there.

Drummer Don Farr was one year ahead of me at Rancho High. We even rode the same bus to school. 'The Dimpled Troll' once described himself as the kind of person his mother wouldn't want him to hang around with. When he wanted to clear the house of all but his friends, he'd put on the John Coltrane album *Ascenscion*. In the creative burgeon of the mid-sixties the Troll started to write some really strong, evocative poetry.

Those were magical times. One night we drove the entire length of Charleston Boulevard in his English Ford (the 'Don-Farrmobile'), from well past the Boulder Highway to Decatur (as far as it went back then) without hitting a single red light. To understand how miraculous that was, you have to know how perverse the lights in Vegas are. In the wee hours just before sunrise, when there's scarcely another car around, they'll turn red just in time to make you wait. Time and again. And won't turn green until a car comes the other way. Just in time to make *them* stop...and wait.

There were drummers around town like Jimmy Manone, son of the famed and beloved Wingy, and Bob Haney, who'd been with the Vegas psychedelic group, the Scatter Blues. In the mid-sixties he

[5] The '25-year Retrospective Concert of the Music of John Cage,' on May 15, 1958.

joined with others in my ken to form the pioneer fusion band BZZXA, which, had they been based in New York or L. A., would have got a lot more recognition. Steve Douglas's solos would certainly have made an impression. Since then, however, Bob moved to Los Angeles, changed his name to Rhio Hirsch, and has switched from bold rhythmic explorations to a 4/4 country beat.

Even before he joined BZZXA, Terry Ryan's keyboard prowess and imagination had astounded me. Frank Kirk, my driving (but not putting) collaborator from high school, introduced me to him in 1959, as the redoubtable leader of a group called Terry and the Pirates. T. R. always knew when I'd be dropping by, even in the free and easy early sixties, when you never called. You just showed up. It was telepathic, like we'd known each other for thousands of years. Once he invited me to come to hear him play in a lounge show called, appropriately enough, 'The Las Vegas Strip,' and with no planning or forethought, we dressed as 'negatives' of each other. He was dressed all in black for the show, and I'd decided – completely independently – to wear all white. Even our glasses fit the pattern! Backstage, bassist Seth Kimball compared us to Sergio Aragones's 'Spy vs. Spy!'

There were creative 'types' abounding in Southern Nevada, if you knew where to find them. Loosely gathered around the University was an interesting (to say the least) artist community: The magical potter, Bill Bradford; the pen-and-ink philosopher Jerry Pfaffl; the unclassifiable Farrell Walback – his 'rainbow' series is breathtaking – like many other paintings of his they seem superficially abstract-expressionist, yet have an organic feel, a 'placeness' to them; and the exstounding and outmazing multitalented artist, Bill Walker, who a few years down the road was to do the cover for *Anthem of the Sun.*

Bill assembled a book of poems and pen and ink drawings called *Constellations.* A powerful package, in the manner of St. John Perse or Charles Olson, full of vivid images and associations. He said he just shuffled the pages and bound it the way it came out, in the one copy he made. Who knows where that copy is. I wish I did.

It was also my good fortune to know the remarkable Bill Willard. A writer, painter, woodcarver (some finely carved doors of his are on display at the Hacienda), radio personality (a pioneer in bringing not only jazz, but the 'classics' to Las Vegas), and political campaign savant – in sum, a giant standing in a hole.

Time and again, Las Vegas has proved fallow ground for 'culture,' with many fine efforts amounting to little or naught. Musicians who paid their bills by working the showrooms by night would get together by day to play Bach and Mozart *gratis* to sparse audiences. But there was also a wide open spirit, a desert emptiness. Instead of being saturated by precedent, the place offered a *tabula rasa* unbounded by convention. The rowdy frontier exuberance was not inconsistent with the feeling of being 'out there.' In that spirit Bill Walker and his delight of an aunt, Nancy Gunter, took me out on Lake Mead in her boat, and we slept on a tiny island by the light of the full Moon. The classical cause of Lunacy, it is said, but by then it seemed a mere formality to us.

### TWO WINTER HAIKU

Misty blue mountains -
Your gentle coolness lifts you
Up into the sky.

Even in the cold
Of the middle of winter,
A summer sun shines.

### TWO SPRING HAIKU

Look up into the sky.
The grey clouds.
Can you see the rain coming down?

I not being unlike
Can hear your kindness voice and
Notice noticings.

# 2/ MUSIC REARS ITS HEAD

*"Nothing is so totally lost
as a day in which you've not laughed."*
Mexican saying, attrib. Yrrah Revilo

**M**y parents sent me off for my first piano lessons in New Jersey in 1953, from a woman I knew only as 'Mrs. Biggs.' Once a week I'd trudge down Kinderkamack Road from Cherry Hill School to her musty-smelling house. Not exactly an auspicious beginning, nor did things look to get much better for quite a while.

There followed a parade of what could charitably be called a mixed bag of instructors. I never felt like practicing for any of them. What might ultimately have saved me is that I would practice anyway, even if it wasn't what I'd been assigned to do in the lesson. It taught me a lot, though, about ways to turn your students off music.

After we'd moved to Las Vegas, there was Betty Sherlock, who was an accompanist for tenor John Mowbray. I've lost track of her, but he since became Chief Justice of the Nevada Supreme Court. She was followed by Charles John Lauria, who introduced me to the wonders of Hanon and Czerny. "If you can do it once," he told me, "you can do it again – and if you can do it again, you can make it a habit." Later there came a 'Mrs. Singer,' whose perfume could kill bugs at twenty yards, and Gene Feher, who was the organist at Temple Beth Shalom.

I finally got enough nerve and chops together to appear 'publicly' performing at the piano at a Rancho High School talent assembly.[1] I played a piano impromptu of my own creation, and the reaction of my listeners – several hundred of them – was warm enough to insure my being bitten by the 'footlight-ning' bug.

I took violin lessons from Frank Iddings, who directed the All School String Orchestra, and was the universally beloved music man of Las Vegas.[2] Each one of his students felt that they were his favorite, and not one of us would hesitate for a moment to follow him through precipitous and craggy paths of Mozart, Beethoven, and Tchaikovsky. He invited me to play in the orchestra, encouraged me in my interest in writing for the ensemble, and even programmed the resulting *Serenade* on one of the orchestra's public concerts. It was on January 16, 1961. The *Las Vegas Sun* gave us a nice writeup – it tickles me to think that when I first made headlines as a composer, the president of the United States was named Eisenhower. Less than a week was left in his term, but like the casting director said about the Algerian actor, that's close enough for a Moroccan rôle.

For composition and counterpoint instruction I went to Howard Chase. Aside from being the *de facto* entire music department (there was no one else!) at the local university, he had a studio on Lewis Street, where he gave music lessons. For his doctoral thesis at the University of Michigan, he'd analysed the harmonic idiom of Beethoven's middle Piano Sonatas, and with a powdered wig on, he could pull off a good J. S. Bach impression. But he didn't have a whole lot to tell me about what had been going on in music since 1900, which was where my real interests were.

One afternoon, at one of the lessons at Lewis Street, Dr. Chase asked me, "How commercial do you think you can get?" Antonio Morelli, Music Director at the Sands, was planning a 'Pops' concert on the theme 'Musicians of the Future,' and was looking for a work by a young composer. Morelli was very 'old school' in his musical outlook, and Dr. Chase knew that I'd have to write something a bit

[1] May 13, 1960.          [2] Unless you were a wind player, in which case it was Ted Vesely.

more down to earth than was my wont, hence his question.

There were two grand pianos in his studio, and I remember the thrill of playing a Mozart concerto (the K. 449) with him. As much fun as that was, though, being accompanied by a second piano seemed far less exciting than performing with an entire orchestra. So I put together a *Conversation Piece* for piano and orchestra, and got a few licks in, in the bargain: systematically but subtly breaking every counterpoint rule I could think of, adding an extra beat to the occasional measure, and such.

There followed a few meetings with Morelli. A brusque, intense, white haired man, he cut an imposing figure, and was usually awash in *4711*. I remember him inviting me to his mansion on Country Club Lane, pouring me a glass of Galliano, and regaling me with maestrific pronouncements on all things bright and musical. His views were colored by years in the theater orchestra trenches.

Another time I met him backstage at the Sands. As Morelli was going over my score, a few feet away Jerry Lewis was preparing for the evening's proceedings, and doing an uncanny impression of a real human being. The things they never tell you in the trades! Morelli introduced me to J. L.'s Music Director, Lou Brown, whose encouraging words were like wind to my sails.

Those were amazing years. Let's see…there were the Las Vegas Symphony, the Las Vegas Philharmonic, and the Southern Nevada Festival Orchestra – except they were all the same musicians! The name was determined by whoever got it together to put on the concert. This time it was Antonio Morelli's show, so it would be the Las Vegas 'Pops' Orchestra.

Finally the date for my début as composer/pianist arrived: May 28, 1961, at the Las Vegas Convention Center. Sharing the Las Vegas 'Pops' stage with me were Darlene Gray (who has since distinguished herself with the San Francisco Symphony) performing Massenet's *Meditation* from *Thaïs* and the first movement of Edouard Lalo's *Symphonie Espagnole*; flutist Paul Fried, a fine player from a highly musical family, playing a Mozart concerto; and Greg Butcher, later known as Greg Pepetone, a fine pianist and a good friend in the ensuing years, playing the opening Allegro from the Bach D minor concerto. There was a sizable crowd at the Convention Center Promenade that afternoon, and it made for an exciting, if slightly glitzy, event.

As conventional a piece as I thought I'd created, though, Morelli still found it kind of far out – "fragmentary," he called it during our preparatory meetings. Talking about me in his introductory remarks during the concert, he said, "He's probably really going to be an astrologer *(sic)*, and his head is up in the clouds *now*." After the performance he commented to the audience that it caused them some concern the first time they'd played it, but by the third time, they'd grown to like it "rather much" (his words). I had to chuckle – little did the audience know that the performance they'd just heard *was* the third time!

An educational experience, all in all, but after the concert those newfangled sounds were still there in my ears, and there were yet other areas a-beckoning. Instead of 'future shock,' it was a case of 'future thirst.' *Horizon* magazine came out with an article on contemporary music. I remember trying out the example from Stockhausen's *Klavierstück XI* on my piano, and being enthralled by the intricate, crystalline sonorities on the 'other side of dissonance.' Whether I knew it or not, my omnivoracious curiosity was in full stampede, and there was no turning back.

But where does one whose head has been turned by Cage and Stockhausen go when the academic orthodoxy is tuned to Hindemith and Piston? Books and recordings of the new music were scarce. In retrospect I suppose the wonder is that there were any at all. Miraculously, I found a recording of the Schönberg *Violin Concerto* at a downtown music store. The New York Philharmonic programmed each of the two Boulez *Improvisations sur Mallarmé* on its broadcast concerts. When Eugene Ormandy and the Philadelphia Orchestra came to town[3], they performed some of Alban Berg's selections from *Lulu*. A local critic didn't like them, but I thought the lush, sensual Ormandy sound, coupled with Berg's salacious orchestration, was a magical combination. About that time, Robert Craft's records of everyone from Schönberg to Stockhausen started appearing, Dr. Chase found me a copy of Ernst Křenek's twelve-tone primer, and I was off and exploring.

This is by no means to say that I listened to contemporary music exclusively. Not only were there the usual hot rocks on the airwaves, but the family record collection had all the usual sympho-

[3] June 9, 1962.

nies, concertos, and sonatas performed by such as Toscanini, Rubinstein, and Heifetz. We even subscribed to the Max Goberman (Library of Recorded Masterpieces) issues of Vivaldi and Corelli. These were outstanding series – for the benefit of the likes of me, the scores were bound in, and each disc had four to six 'new' pieces to investigate.

But once you leave the museum, it's 'today' outside, and in the meantime pieces of the puzzle were coming together for me. BMI was sponsoring a contest for student composers. Dr. Chase 'helped' me prepare an entry, a stupefyingly cerebral (no oxymoron, this) *Double Quintet*, matching modern instruments with their Renaissance counterparts. Cast in an overwrought serial idiom, it never stood a chance in the competition. But I found out who won and got in touch with him. Since known and feared as 'Blue Gene' Tyranny, Robert Sheff did me the honor of playing some of my *Sketches* for piano in concert in San Antonio[4]. An amazing talent. I know he'll go far. He in turn put me in touch with Philip Krumm, and then with La Monte Young.

La Monte Young was one of the prime movers in a very exciting New York scene – a group later called 'Fluxus' – that included Ray Johnson, Dick Higgins, and Yoko Ono. When I told him that my college plans involved going to the San Francisco Bay Area, he suggested I get in touch with a composer/pianist who was playing ragtime at a nightclub called Gold Street in North Beach. A guy named Terry Riley.

I believe that if you were around Terry long enough your soul would get a tan. His is an exothermic, solar personality – he radiates positive energy, and has an ever active imagination. I love the way his mind works. Visiting him at his Butchertown (an area of San Francisco) digs, I heard a recording of his *String Quartet* ("Don't wait for the fast part," he told me), and then I remember the two of us experimenting with Bach at the upright piano in his studio downstairs. The word 'wise' fits him, but it's not the wisdom of accumulated years of experience. He was always that way, 'least as long as I've known him.

I'd come from Las Vegas to U.C. Berkeley in the fall of 1961 with dutiful intentions, but my first (and only) semester of college was rainy and unfulfilling. R.O.T.C. was compulsory, but I had the good

[4] June 30, 1962.

fortune to be in the first class in a hundred years never to march. It
was too rainy…day after day…after day…after day.

One thing that kept it from being an unqualified washout was the
opportunity to hear so much exciting music in live performance.
The Merce Cunningham dance troupe came to the University of
California in late February, 1962. On tour with them to provide
music were none other than John Cage and David Tudor! I found
their Wheeler Hall performance of *Antic Meet* lovably zany. Elsewhere on campus, at Hertz Hall, I watched William Bolcom perform
his flamboyantly Boulezist *Fantasy-Sonata*; an ensemble including
Morton Subotnick on clarinet perform Henri Pousseur's *Quintette à
la mémoire d'Anton Webern*, a scintillatingly colorful glose.

Ralph Kirkpatrick played a feast of harpsichord recitals – both
books of *The Well Tempered Clavier*, a powerful C minor fantasy, and
oodles of Scarlatti. Even earlier music was performed by the Antiqua
Players. John Dowland's *Come Again! Sweet Love doth now Invite*
brought the house down, and its courtly message was scarcely
wasted on a seventeen year old like me. Meanwhile, across the Bay,
the Tape Music Center was giving its first presentations at the San
Francisco Conservatory, where I was treated to the remarkable
electronic tapestries of Richard Maxfield.

There were also the terpsichorean adventures of Ann (later
'Anna') Halprin. Her *Three-* and later *Four-legged Stool* was a high-
light of my first year in San Francisco. With musical assistance from
Terry Riley, it was a marvelous indulgence in Non-Sequi Tourism.
It was mounted at a theatre at the foot of Hyde Street, at the end of
the cable car line. Their intermittent bells colored the soundscape.

I'd taken some of my pieces to Morrison Hall to show to U. C.
professor Seymour Shifrin – my first 'real live' composer. He let me
down fast if not gently. "Even a Beethoven bagatelle has development," he ruminated disapprovingly over one of my piano sketches.
With sails thus duly trimmed I went to try the entry level exams for
the music department.

During a break I got caught up in a conversation about music in
general with Margie Panofsky (yet to attain distinction in Early
Music). A rather intense discussion was joined by a third party.
When I said, with teenage conviction, that music might've stopped

in 1750, but it started again in 1950, this blond-haired guy spontaneously reached across and heartily shook hands with me. He subsequently invited me to share his apartment, a block off the U. C. campus. Compared to my humble room in a house in the Berkeley hills, it seemed too good a deal to pass up. His name was Phil Lesh.

Phil introduced me to a fascinating array of music and people. As a volunteer at KPFA, he had access to the latest tapes of European festival performances of Stockhausen, Boulez, and more. Accompanying him to the peninsula (I had the car) I met characters like Bob Hunter, Willy Legate, and Jerry Garcia. One eventful evening we were visited by his friend, the troll poet of the open road, Bobby Petersen.

With an infectious smile and a disarming laugh, Petersen was a brilliant soul of the dearest sort. One day the two of us hiked the length of Strawberry Creek through the U. C. campus. Suddenly, a different world, so close to the concrete and pavement, and yet... There was a transcendent quality to his vision, both in and out of his poetry. I'd vote for him for God. Isn't it time for a change?

I don't believe in miracles. I rely on them. And transcendent skill is no match for dumb luck. Phil and I had just got the recording of Berio's *Différences*, and the fact of his appearing virtually in our back yard had an air of the miraculous about it. We signed up for his class (at Mills College) forthwith, possibly even thirdwith. And what a class it was! Among the students were Steve Reich – he was into a Gunther Schuller/Lukas Foss (understandable – we encountered both of them at that year's Ojai Festival) third stream improvisation sort of thing – the phase pieces were nowhere in 'sight;' Robert Moran – that groovy maniac of the pandæmonic scores for dozens of automobiles, dancers, and radio stations…in varying configurations; and Shirley Wong, who joined me in the première[5] of my *Three Pieces for Two Pianos*, and has since become expert at the harpsichord, as well as Chinese classical music as a founding member of the Flowing Stream Ensemble.

Earthy yet exalted, Berio smoked strong cigarettes (Picayunes) as he lectured. Evidently he couldn't find Gitanes in California. I remember him pointing out a part of a student's composition and saying, "You should devil up this here." I thought to myself, "Well, all right! *Now* we're out in the wild and woolly *avant garde!*" Later

[5] May 27, 1962. Mills College Concert Hall.

I found out that that was the way he pronounced the word 'develop.' He turned out to have his feet more firmly planted than many of the 'traditionalists.' It was as if the same penetrating intellect that broke the surface tension leading to the future would extend equally as well into the past. His ideas were well thought out – he once told me, "Never do something of which you're not convinced." His thoughts on instrumentation were nothing less than a revelation. Still...he never approved of my work 'inside' the piano.

We gave a performance at the Mills College concert hall of the Winter Music of John Cage, using thirteen pianos[6]. Some sort of obscure record, possibly. The score allows for as many as twenty. Berio was joined onstage by Robert Moran, and the rest of us were scattered throughout the building. Phil and I were sequestered up in the practice rooms. I remember in particular figuring out one of the more massive icti and playing it with great gusto – triple *forte*. The resulting sound was considerably more remarkable than I'd anticipated, and I thought I'd check how it sounded with Phil. Running out into the hall, what should I see but Phil, coming at me from the other direction, like a mirror image. It seems we'd thought of doing the same thing at the same time! Bobby Petersen, who was there, said that he heard the sound in question and saw Berio turn his head and grin – or wince.

In early May a group of us from Berio's class went down to a 'Composers' Symposium' at U.C.L.A. The concert[7] featured a performance of a 'collaboration' piece, with a section composed by each of us in the class. Later in the month we went to the Ojai Festival, where concerts and seminars featured the music of Mozart and of the four invited guests: Milton Babbitt, Luciano Berio, Lukas Foss, and Gunther Schuller. The evening of the same day[8] that Laraine Youngsten and I performed the second of my *Three Pieces for Two Pianos* was an amazing outdoor concert, opening with Eric Dolphy playing Edgar Varèse's *Density 21.5*, continuing with two John Cage works: the *Winter Music*, performed by Luciano Berio and Lukas Foss on two limousine size pianos, the *Aria* with *Fontana Mix*, featuring the astounding vocalizations of Cathy Berberian, and then moving on to Berio's *Différences*.

The second half of the program was devoted to Gunther Schuller's

[6]May 1, 1962.    [7]May 5, 1962.    [8]May 19, 1962.

explorations of the Third Stream. So many musicians had played in both the jazz and classical traditions, there had to be a way, they figured, to combine their loves. Tracing the history of twentieth century music year by year, Schuller's radio program, which was carried by KPFA in Berkeley, was a wonderful and illuminating introduction to a broad spectrum of new music. For as much as I admired his guided tour, however, something just didn't sit right with me about Third Stream music. It seemed like an Esperanto of musical forms – an artificial attempt to reach some sort of ecumenical consensus. As Lord Buckley put it, "They didn't know where they was going, but they knew that where they was, wasn't it." So many attempts to mingle musical styles have led to less than convincing results. Like, I'm not so impressed by the *Jazz Symphony* of John Glaas as I am by Bob Graettinger's *City of Glass*, which was recorded by the Stan Kenton Orchestra. Not only is it clear that its composer had heard the likes of Berg and Varèse, but his treatment of instrumental color groupings presaged works to come in the following decade by such as Berio and Stockhausen.

But the problem remains: you can't *unknow* the music you've heard. Maybe therein, ultimately, lies the solution.

Across the metaphorical river, a lot of jazz purists were expressing similar reservations about the viability of a 'Third Stream,' citing the potency of the genuine article. I remember a time when Miles Davis was appearing at the Jazz Workshop on Broadway in San Francisco. His drummer, Tony Williams, was under age, so there were no alcoholic beverages for sale that night. It also meant, however, that my being under age wouldn't be a problem for me when it came to getting in. It was one of their better gigs. That is to say, Miles showed up. For all of that kind of rigamarole, however, my ear was already in the Space lane – even jazz players that I've since come to respect seemed too *tame* for me. Five-four time? Three keys at once? Plucking the strings of the piano? So what.

By the time I heard Cecil Taylor I thought, "How quaint!"

Meanwhile Phil's and my apartment in Berkeley had become an avant garde music factory. He was working on a piece for four orchestras, called *Foci,* using the same sixty-stave paper he'd used for his earlier serialist piece for mammoth orchestra that Berio had smiled over as he turned the pages: "Nice!" Over in my corner of the room I was working on a piece for chamber orchestra – twenty three instruments – called *Phrases*. Based on a combinatorial series (much in the manner of Webern's Op. 24, but with three groups of four notes instead of four groups of three), it too won Berio's approval: "A real galaxy!" he called it. The center of the 'galaxy' was a twelve-note chord about half way through the piece. Up till then the texture was a network of four note 'phrases,' fashioned out of the patterns in the series. Afterward the instruments were more filtered, more 'arrayed.' Berio put special emphasis on orchestration – one of his many strong points. New and exciting groupings, startling contrasts, mellifluous transitions – all marked the Berio style and method.

It was during this time that I wrote my *Three Pieces for Two Pianos*. Heavily influenced by the piano idiom of Boulez, these pieces represented three different directions in the exploration of twelve tone technique. The first was originally written for solo piano, but was recast as a duet when Berio said something to the effect that I had to be kidding, to expect one pianist to do all that. The second was an eerie, melancholy fugal treatment, with melodic strands lacing the two pianos together. Pitches, rhythms, and intensities were serially determined. In other words, a melancholy lover's lament. In the third piece, precision manifested itself in the form of a stop-watch. Titled *Saros*, after the cycles of solar eclipses, it represented a deteriorization of the serial factor as a formal element.

There was also a *Sonatina* for solo piano, which I wrote for Phil's twenty-second birthday. Somehow it didn't go over as well with Berio as the pieces for two pianos, even though I'd taken care to delineate the forms and structures more clearly and objectively, all the while exploring the coloristic effects of extreme registers (à la Boulez).

The plan had been that on the way to Darmstadt, self-proclaimed capital of the New Music world, Phil and I would stop off in Las Vegas. In the euphoria of digesting all the wondrous experiences of the past year, though, I'd spaced out on the situation at home. Around the house, communication was *to* or *at* me, never *with* me, and *forget* about from me. Instead of a sharing, whether of the wonders of life or its caveats, it was usually, often transparently, manipulative. 'Discussion' consisted of threats and ultimata. And here I was coming back, after a most unusual school year, with a head full of new ideas!

It must have been something truly horrendous that my natural father had done, to judge from the way that my reconstituted parental unit tried to enforce the fantasy that he'd never existed. They obviously, and erroneously, were counting on my being too young at the time of his departure to remember him. If getting a passport didn't require a birth certificate (with my born name on it, wouldn't you know) I'm sure that they would have been quite content to blithely continue the pretense. So at the age of seventeen, I was legally adopted into the family I'd been living with since I was five.

Obviously there's a difference between biological parents and those who care for you, provide for you, and share their lives with you. The fact that they never had the faith in me to be able to make that distinction is something that I don't think I'll ever be able to forget. Not to say that I didn't enjoy any of their upper middle class largesse, but it always came with strings attached, and was in lieu of, rather than along with confidence and fellowship. By my tenth birthday I'd figured out that opening up to them was hazardous to my emotional health. Any triumph I'd want to share was no big thing, while any setback became another opportunity for them to say "I told you so!"

The way my attitudes and opinions on art, politics, culture, and religion clashed with theirs was in mid-gallop by the late fifties. And it had extended to music. I remember on Christmas Eve, 1960, the twenty-fifth anniversary of the death of Alban Berg, listening to his *Violin Concerto*. Later, on the violin, I groped for the 'Ich habe genug' melody quoted in the second movement. It was beginning to come clear when my mother walked into the room, tearfully exclaiming "That was beautiful!" and then going on to demand how I could torture her by doing what I was doing. By then I knew better than to ask what that might be. I had no read on where she was coming from, and scant cause to expect it'd be worth the effort to find out. That it might have been a moment of some meaning to me was something that I knew better than to even bring up.

Perhaps it was too disillusioning for her to go from violin lessons with Albert Spalding to playing in Phil Spitalny's All Girl Orchestra, but she had already peremptorily decided for me that music was to remain an avocation[9]. Beyond that, at an age when I was getting my bearings and sorting out my views and ideas of the world, I was getting all sorts of conflicting and disrupting messages from them. Things came to a rifty head once when I was at home, listening to a favorite Schönberg recording. The family gathered around, each one in turn saying how there had to be something wrong with someone who actually enjoyed this kind of music. When my brother Skip[10], the white sheep of the family, joined in, it was more than I could bear. Something snapped in me. I lashed out at him, and stormed out of the room. My mother was hot on my heels, screaming: "That was *brutal!*" Ill advised, immature...yes, perhaps, but the word 'brutal' rings truer than any other in describing the emotional tiger cage they expected me to call 'home.'

'Home.' The ice blue cinder block house, what with the antique furniture, the chiaroscuro paintings on the walls, and the superfine crocheted tablecloths, felt more like a cross between a museum and a morgue. I really should have known better than to lead Phil into this pit. The rigid adherence to conventionality that kept my parents from throwing me out into the street didn't shield him. I remember dropping him off at Bill Walker's house ('The Snake Ranch'), putting a silver dollar in his hand, and telling him I wished it could be a lot more. He asked me if I really meant that, and I said "Yes," but there was no way to express how helpless I felt.

If it had been their avowed purpose to smother any budding sense of self-worth, indeed to break my spirit, I don't know how they would have gone about it any differently than they did. To my knowledge, no one in the family has attended any musical presentation that I've been involved with since 1961. When I drove to Las Vegas for Bestefar's funeral a few years later – he had died of diabetes – they gave me a five pound sack of sugar to take back home with me. But I'd already got the message. I could go on – I've only scratched the surface – but it wasn't just them. It was the whole scene there.

[9] At least she didn't make me write with my right hand, like the nuns did to her.
[10] Carl Philip Constanten. Seven and a half years younger than I – our birthdays are   six months apart in either direction – he had already figured out that the appropriate attitudes toward me around the house ranged from condescension to contempt.

As much music as was going on in Vegas at the time, it was clear that if I wanted to get anywhere, I'd have to go somewhere. Everyone who was anyone in music there had distinguished themselves elsewhere first. Besides, since the fire at the old El Rancho Vegas the place just didn't *feel* the same. Howard Hughes megabucks were paving over the green felt jungle. Through my telescope, set up in front of our house out past the Municipal golf course, you used to be able to read the time and temperature off the sign on top of the Sahara Hotel. In the summertime the numbers would shimmer in the thermals. That view and many others were rapidly disappearing. Meanwhile, The Road beckoned. And, ready or not, my feet were already in motion.

## AFTER AUGUSTINE

...but what do I love, when I love thee?
Not beauty of bodies,
  nor the fair harmony of time,
  nor the brightness of the light,
    so gladsome to our eyes,
  nor sweet melodies of varied songs,
  nor the fragrant smell of flowers,
    and ointments,
    and spices...

None of these do I love...
...and yet I love a kind of light,
  and melody,
  and fragrance,
  and flesh,
  and embrace,
where there shines what space cannot contain,
  and there sounds what time bears not away,
  and there smells what breathing disperses not,
  and there tastes what eating diminishes not,
  and there clings what satiety divorces not.

This is it which I love, when I love thee...

# 3/ JOURNEYS TO THE EAST

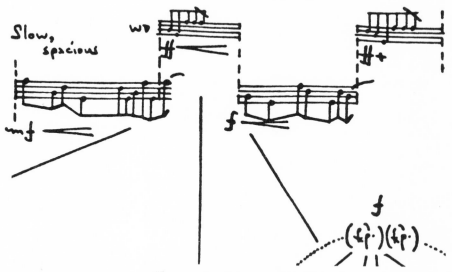

*"Le monde existe pour aboutir à un livre."* Mallarmé

The socio-cosmic force field between East and West has an elemental, primal aura to it. Whether in the Hessian sense, or simply referring to geography, there are tides, jet streams, and under-tows that can pick you up and take you with them. I've gone East to learn...I've gone East to earn... and usually returned overstuffed with food for thought.

Actually, my first trip eastward from Las Vegas wasn't in connection with music but with astronomy. But then, again, it wasn't as far East, in any of several senses, as many a trip that was to come. In the summer of 1960[1], Pan American College in Edinburg, Texas invited some thirty high school students from around the nation to come and wallow in space science for six weeks. This 'Institute in the Astro-sciences' consisted of classes, social gatherings, and Texas style field trips.

A high point for some was the firing of a solid fuel rocket that had been assembled in class. It took the rest of the afternoon to find

[1] June 7 to July 16.

where it landed. Tito, our bus driver, finally found it, much to everyone's delight. What excited me more was having the use of the College's main telescope, a 17-inch reflector. One night we set up the Cassegrain focus at 975 power and pointed it at Saturn. The Cassegrain, like the Maksutov and Schmidt optical systems, bounces the light back and forth in the tube a couple of extra times, thereby multiplying the effective focal length. Since magnification is a quotient of focal lengths, it can make a perceptible difference, and it showed the planet in its amber majesty, glowing big as a beach ball.

One of the professors running the show was already familiar to me as the Director of the A.L.P.O. A delightful, kindly man, Walter H. Haas was a famous selenographer. That is, his specialty was the Moon. How famous? In the region on the Moon near the mountain Pico and the crater Plato there is a crater named after him! Recognizing it as an opportunity too good to pass up, I sketched the area, using his very own telescope (a 12-1/2 inch reflector), and asked him to autograph it for me.

Professor Haas paid me the further compliment of comparing me with a colleague of his in New Mexico, Clyde Tombaugh. Heady stuff, even being mentioned in the same breath as the only person this century to have discovered a planet in our solar system (he is credited with the discovery of Pluto in 1930), but it wasn't as an astronomer that I was being touted – it was as a punster. Derided by the philologically inept as 'the lowest form of humor,' the pun will one day regain the respect that is its due as the venerable art form that it is. It takes a haiku seventeen syllables to convey an image, but a well-fashioned pun can reveal new facets and reflections for decades. I can't remember a time when I didn't enjoy wordplay. I still can recall Bestemor telling me how in her French class at school, they taught her to say "Vive la reine!" which, to a Norwegian ear, sounds a lot like "Vi ville ha regn (we'd like to have some rain)."

The program included a field trip to surpassingly bucolic Mexico to visit the site of their observatory-to-be. In collaboration with the Instituto Tecnologico of Monterrey, Pan American College was sponsoring an observatory on a mountain not far from Linares: 10,392 foot Infiernillo Peak. And every one of those feet was in shoes. Like, there were no roads. But the view from the top was magnificent, well worth the day long trek. Looking through Gary Kraus's 8 inch reflector, you could see the 15th magnitude star in the center of the Ring Nebula in Lyra. Even with the unaided eye, the panorama was overwhelming. I'd never seen the Southern Cross before; nor Alpha Centauri, another stunning double; nor the Milky Way so clear and *massive* looking.

By late 1961, however, it was clear that my career as an astrophysicist wasn't much longer for the rails. The Muse was already demanding – but She was also delivering. With Berio's assistance, I was able to arrange a veritable Grand Tour of my dreams, beginning with the two-week festival of lectures, classes, and concerts that took place every July in Darmstadt, Germany.

Darmstadt – 'Gut City' – it's difficult to overstate what a Mecca for new music it represented at the time. Like a surfer anticipating a good wave, you can feel the momentum, the surge, the excitement of being at the edge, the *avant garde*. The electricity is almost visceral, and carries along even those who aren't fully aware of how it's working – maybe I should say especially. Before there's a bandwagon to hop onto, shaping activities that in retrospect will seem inevitable, the gathering forces are exerting their magnetism. One need only glance through the programs at Darmstadt and Donaueschingen, as later on the posters of the Fillmore and the Avalon, to see the waves of new names and ideas arising as if out of nowhere.

Still, as ready as I felt for what was to come, I found out that, once over there, I wasn't anywhere near as ready as I'd anticipated. At first, much of my effort and attention was devoted to the problem of getting along in the language. The first time in Stockhausen's class I was struggling to catch all the words I could. When I came back the following year (1963) it was much easier to follow what he was saying, and it probably wasn't he who had improved.

Stockhausen waxed poetic describing how, on a tour of the U. S., each time the airliner took off, time seemed to stand still ("Die Zeit steht still. Es ist wunderschön!"). Someone in the class must've taken the lesson to heart because, later, when Stockhausen asked to know the time, in French, "Quelle heure est-il?" he got a quick reply: "Die Zeit steht still. Es ist wunderschön!" How quickly your words can come flying back! And a rhymed couplet, no less! Here it was, the summer of '62, and ol' Karlheinz was already telling me that space is the place!

In his '62 class Stockhausen expounded on musical parameters. From the five 'classical' parameters: pitch, duration (which includes rhythm), intensity, timbre, and location in space; to his five new ones: number, proportion, quality (by which he meant degree of newness), movement, and, as a marvelous catch-all, the 'organic.' Here was a calculus to go with Webern's algebra. This addition of dimension to understanding not only affects the creation of new music but our understanding of the old. Composer Paolo Castaldi told me how he was once asked, at a seminar, "You mean if we knew more about music, the new music wouldn't bother us as much as the old?" "Au contraire," he replied, "If you knew more about music, the old music would bother you *just as much* as the new!"

It wasn't exactly a surprise, but the class with Henri Pousseur was a total delight. I'd read his articles in Die Reihe and liked his lucid style. An unassuming apostle of music, Pousseur composed intellectually engaging works which nevertheless had a succulence, an organic feel to them that many of his colleagues' lacked. His way of rising above accepted formulas to examine the effects they create – often something gets lost in the translation between method and result – also sets him apart. I can still picture him driving off in his Deux Chevaux. Un vrai chevalier!

Sharing a room with me at Darmstadt was the German composer Helmut Lachenmann, who had driven up from Bavaria in his '35 Mercedes. Very tall, très aimable, he seemed to be able to put on the Teutonic stiffness when the situation called for it, but beneath it all was a very sensitive and sensible human being. He also practically owned me on the chess board. His explorations in music paralleled mine and I found a good example in his experiences. His Echo-Andante for piano, which he performed at Darmstadt in 1962, was almost hypnotic with its 'recollections' of earlier material.

We were boarded at a Seventh-day Adventist seminary at Marienhöhe, in the woods south of town, towards Pfungstadt. Across the road a tent had been set up, to serve as an ad hoc watering hole. In some ways, it's where the show really was, what with all the musical types hanging out there. Here was Frau Stockhausen telling the story of the cricket chirping along during a performance of her husband's *Klavierstück VI* ("unvorstellbar komisch" were her words); there a heated discussion about the latest musical heresy. There were card games, and other kinds of games as well. Connections were made, discussions, plans, all over a beer under the canvas. Each table would tend to have its own language, and when someone would move from one to another (say, to visit with a friend) they would then switch languages!

I shared a drink with Herbert Brün, who was there for a performance of his *Third String Quartet*. He'd delivered a stimulating lecture on the new music the previous year at the U. C. Berkeley music department. Among other examples, he played a recording of Györgi Ligeti's *Atmosphères*. It was amazing how 'electronic' it sounded – he had to emphasize that it was "the same orchestra you can play a Mahler symphony on." There at the table in the German summertime, I mentioned to him how impressed I'd been by his presentation in Berkeley, and commented on how a couple of the U. C. profs' questions struck me as no more than ignorance costumed in critical condescension. He replied, "If you thought *those* questions were stupid, you should have heard what they asked after everyone else left!" Not wishing to test whether the fine local beer tasted as good coming up as it did going down, I didn't query him further.

The concerts at Darmstadt were a veritable fountainhead of new music in those years. Not only the 'classics' were featured – Bruno Maderna opened the proceedings in '62 conducting the Schönberg *Kammersymphonie*, whose assertive rising fourths were the 'Motif' of that year's festival; Pierre Boulez directed performances of *Pierrot Lunaire* (with Helga Pilarcik 'sprechstimming'), the Webern *Symphony*, and his own *Le Marteau sans Maître* – and dutiful obeisances to monuments of the past by such composers as Landini, Debussy (a sublime *Sonata* with flutist Severino Gazzelloni, harpist Francis Pierre, and Michel Wales, violist of the Quatuor Parennin), and Stravinsky – but new and exciting works were coming from every quarter. The Quatuor Parennin gave the première of Part III of the Boulez *Livre pour Quatuor*, and the LaSalle String Quartet premièred the first quartet of Krzysztof Penderecki at Darmstadt in 1962. It created something of a sensation (as did Michael von Biel's quartet the following year) with its novel approaches to getting sounds out of those grand old instruments.

Two dizzifying weeks, and it was time to move onward. Henri Pousseur invited me to come visit his studio in Bruxelles, so I hitched a ride with the Italian composer Niccolò Castiglioni in his DAF. In a small car like that, you really pay attention when the signs on the Autobahn say "Wind!" At a roadside eatery, I was amused to note the way the Germans would hold a Würstchen in one hand, and a piece of bread in the other, taking bites out of them alternately. Like it never occurred to them to slice open the roll and insert the sausage. Saves a napkin that way, too.

We stopped overnight in Köln, and visited the electronic music studio at WDR (West Deutscher Rundfunk, or radio Köln). As Stockhausen's bailiwick, it was the proverbial 'state of the art' in equipment, with huge speakers and imposing Telefunken tape machines. The technology even extended to their moving elevators, turning the trip 'upstairs' into an adventure in nimbleness.

In Bruxelles I got to know Leo Küpper – an eccentric genius – of a different cut of eccentricity than I, but we still got along. He was working on an electronic mobile (Pousseur influence, no doubt) composition during the time I shared room, board, and ring modulators with him. Our room was directly above the studio APELAC (never did learn what that stood for), in a building on the Chaussée de Vleurgat that still showed signs of damage from the Great War. Borrowing a line from John Cage, Leo said, "An old shoe would look good in this room." Our abode was austere, but the thrill of exploration more than made up for it. I got an extra kick out of hearing some of the really fine works that came out of there (Pousseur's *Trois Visages de Liège*, and *Rimes pour différentes sources sonores*, for example), knowing that I was working with the same equipment.

That equipment consisted of essentially the same components that would later be assembled into a box and called a 'synthesizer.' Only on the Chaussée de Vleurgat it pretty much filled the room. Tone and noise generators, processors, filter banks, all wired to the ever present, ever daunting patch bay. In this oasis of Mid-Tech, tape splicing became a delicate art. There could be as many as a few dozen segments of tape, some wider than long, flashing by in less than a second. Stretches of silence would be measured out on leader tape for safety's sake.

In August I left Bruxelles for a fortnight in England – at Dartington, in Devon. I took the train down to Paris to meet Berio and the author Umberto Eco *(quel raconteur!)*, with whom I motored up to Boulogne, and thence across the Channel. The doings at Dartington were much like Darmstadt, only not as exclusively *avant garde*. In Berio's class, we assembled another dragon parade of a collaboration piece. As for the concerts, Vlado Perlmuter, who had been a student of Ravel, gave several memorable performances at the piano. His renditions of Debussy's *L'Isle Joyeuse* and Schumann's *Etudes Symphoniques* blew me away.

There was a Luigi Nono première[2] *(Canciones a Guiomar)* featuring Cornelius Cardew on guitar and a whole slew of crotales surrounding a lone soprano. After the cold, stiff, wooden acoustics of the Darmstadt Stadthalle, the old hall at Dartington seemed to cradle the sound in velvet. Justin Connolly conducted the Webern *Concerto for Nine Instruments*, and was set to join me in an unscheduled performance of my *Three Pieces for Two Pianos*. *Ad hoc* or not, it would have been my European début, had it not been for my first bee sting in fourteen years – on the hand, *faute le mieux!* Justin was noble in consolation, though, even putting me up in London overnight between the festival's end and the train/ferry ride back to Bruxelles.

There followed a few pleasant side trips out of Bruxelles. We went to Ghent for a Flanders Festival concert[3] featuring Berio's *Différences* and Pousseur's *Rimes* – both perfect examples of the kind of music I was there for. *Rimes* was an ambitious piece, one of what Cathy Berberian referred to as Pousseur's 'juicier' works. Instead of stage front, the conductor faced the audience, so he could be seen by the two groups of players in the balcony. I sat next to Pousseur, who minded the knobs and dials of the electronic playback.

Between the rehearsal and the concert was enough time to walk across the Plâce St. Bavon to see the Van Eyck panel, *The Lamb of St. Bavon*. The centuries-old reds and golds glowed in the late afternoon light. It was for things like that as well, I realized, that I was there.

The lighting was also noteworthy on the day I took the tram out to the battlefield at Waterloo...where Napoleon was blown apart. Amid the blues and grays of an overcast afternoon, the sky seemed to reflect the patchwork pattern of the fields. All the touristy trappings abounded, but the old buildings and fields were still able to evoke times and deeds gone by. Walking back to the tram

[2] August 11, 1962.          [3] September 11, 1962.

terminus, I stopped by the strangely deserted farm 'Mont St. Jean,' used by Wellington as a hospital. The ride back to Bruxelles found me in a nineteenth century sort of *M*A*S*H* frame of mind.

As fall fell, I went southward, there to reconnect with Berio in Italy. I remember a beautiful sunny morning's train ride through the meadows, lakes, and snowy peaks of Switzerland. And so immaculate! It reminded me of the model train layouts at the F.A.O. Schwartz toy emporium in New York that I fairly drooled over as a kid.

There was scarcely time for me to get my bearings after I got off the train in Milan when Berio said it was time to hit the *autostrada*. With but the foggiest notion of our destination, I accompanied him on a scenic ride to Turin. There, across the street from F.I.A.T., we lunched with Eduardo Sanguineti, Berio's collaborator on the music drama commission he was completing for *La Scala*. Then we went down precipitous roads through incredibly gorgeous country. Woodsy in a more rugged way than the serene Alpine forests, it reminded me more of California than Switzerland. Berio stopped near Cuneo to pick up some lavender from a roadside vendor. Turning westward at the Mediterranean, it wasn't much longer before he took a side road leading back up into the mountains. I'd been on the brink of a quandary, wondering whether I'd be able to choose between mountains and ocean, but by the time we arrived at our destination, I realized that I wouldn't have to.

The next few months found me studying with Berio in Linguegletta, a tiny village on the Italian Riviera, along where the mountains meet the sea. The village was so small, cars had to be parked at a central courtyard – all traffic from then on was on horse, goat, or foot. Situated between the Maritime Alps and the Mediterranean Sea (well, technically the Ligurian Alps, and the Ligurian Sea, but nobody quibbled in the Cisalpine sunshine) the Italian Riviera seemed suspended between two worlds. People there seemed more spiritually akin to southern France than to southern Italy. Monte Carlo and Nice were less than an hour's drive away, and in the local dialect, the numbers and the days of the week would bounce back and forth between French and Italian.

There I rejoined fellow Berio student Bernard Rands – we'd met at Dartington. An immensely likable fellow, and a composer of likable music. We didn't see eye to eye on every little thing, but no matter – his heart, mind, wallet, and watch were all in the right places.

We were all staying in Berio's sister's house, the last one down the hill towards the shore. It was said to be the oldest house in the village, dating back a thousand years. As a result of its location, there was a beautiful view of the terraced hills, and the sleepy resort town San Lorenzo al Mare nestled on the water. Bells from neighboring villages echoed through the valley in the sunny mornings. All about were stone walkways that seemed little changed from the time of the Cæsars. In this setting Berio was completing his opera, *Passaggio*, sometimes even enlisting Bernard and me, Renaissance fashion, to help measure and draw lines in the score.

Everyone in the village knew everyone else, and pretty soon so did I. It got so I couldn't walk up Via Discesa to get some bread and cheese without someone calling to me through their open door, inviting me to come in and try some of their wine. Wine bottles didn't have labels in these parts, nor did anyone need a label to tell whose wine they were drinking. Olives and carnations were the other main 'industries' of the place. Anyhow, you know how put out they can get if you decline to try their wine, so....

Marino and Fifina Sartori ran the Osteria Littardi Giuseppina, where I took my meals. These were usually multi-course feasts, and the table company was always interesting. I'd often arrive early, and watch Fifina make ravioli the painstaking, old-fashioned way, or polenta, or rabbit. Kind of like chicken but tastier, I thought. Marino saw to it that I had my own flask, and instructed me in the location and operation of their wine cask. Such fine food, such generous portions, and my last night there, they wouldn't even hear of accepting any payment from me.

As the only eating *or* drinking establishment in 'town,' the Osteria was its social center. There I learned card games like *scopa* and *briscola*, and was regaled by the colorful banter of the *paesani*. One of the village's two television sets was set up in a large room adjacent to the dining room, and every evening villagers would gather there to get their taste of electronic culture. It was amusing to note that most of the 'crowd' would be sure to get there in time for

*Carosello,* the parade of commercial announcements that opened the evening's fare.

Marino still knew enough German from a few decades earlier to be a valuable connection for me. It softened the shock of assimilating yet another language. One evening after dinner, after we'd translated for one another all of the spiciest words our curiosity could get us to ask about, Marino was describing the way the locals were treated by the occupying German army. "Sonofabitch!" I exclaimed, setting off an explosion of laughter in the cantina.

Having got comfortable with Vegas musicians' hours, I'd usually be up till the wee hours reading or composing. I'd understood that 'Buona sera' meant 'Good evening,' but I noticed that the Linguegliettans used the expression when the sun was still high in the afternoon sky. I asked Marino about this. He paused for a moment, and finally explained it to me: "As soon as you get up, it's time to say 'Buona sera!'"

Uniquenesses abounded. Tetrahedral milk cartons – you could open any corner. A five lire coin that, in a stiff wind, could well blow out of your hand. And then there was shopping. A curious institution in Italy, the tobacconist was also where you'd go to buy salt or postage stamps. Book matches were unknown. You'd either get *Svedesi,* boxed wooden matches, or *Cerini,* those tiny wax matches in the little box with the scenic pictures. La Tabaccheria was also where the village's public phone was. There were only two other stores there. One of them had fresh bread every morning that, with a wedge of *Bel Paese,* was to die for. But you had to be careful not to get there *too* early, or you'd get last night's leftovers! They would put your purchases on a flat piece of brown paper and then crimp up both sides with their hands to make a sack for you. I'd watch them closely, time and again, but never could figure out just how they did it.

The warm hospitality the natives showed me matched the Mediterranean sunshine. Giovanni Re, who was about my age, took me out with his family when they went to harvest olives. First they'd spread sheets under the tree, then climb up into it and shake all the olives off the branches. Finally they'd gather up the sheets, and in a few moments would have several baskets filled to the top.

But most of all there was Berio. A fountain of insights and an education to watch, he also put up with me at the breaking crest of my adolescence. With wisdom, patience, and humor. In awe and gratitude I remain forever. Occasionally we'd motor down to the water and then up the coast to Imperia, Berio's home town. Imperia actually consists of two communities – Porto Maurizio and Oneglia. It was the latter that Berio was from. There I met his parents. His father, an organist, didn't take to his son's musical style at all. "When music deserts tonality," he told me emphatically, "it is no longer music."

One eerily moonful night I was walking near the central plaza in Linguéglietta, and heard them singing in the *parrocchia*, the centuries old church. It had a haunting effect on me. Partly because of the simple country living conditions, but mainly because of the theoretical nature of my studies, the only music I'd been listening to was inside my head. Here, undiluted, in its native abode, the full, primal flavor came through. As missiles were setting up in Cuba, here I was an ocean away, safe in another century.

For all the splendor of 'Indian' summer on the Costa Azzurra, I was really ready for it when we packed it up for Milan. At first I lived there in a *pensione* on Via Ariosto, run by a silver-haired character who had been an officer in the *Wehrmacht* under Rommel. I never did know his name, but everyone called him 'l'ingegnère.' His wife was a sassy and succulent Jugoslav redhead who adorned him much like the jewels with which he adorned her. The dinner hour brought forth a full range of characters. Several shoe design students were living there, and it fell to me to be the interpreter for a young man from Bavaria. One time one of the students was displaying her newly acquired English, counting right along for us "one, two, three…" When she paused at "six," I prompted her: "seven," and several heads turned my way in surprise – "Ohhh…you know English, too!" Sometimes a little bit goes a long way.

Unlike German, Italian seemed to soak in osmotically, effortlessly. Tending towards the taciturn in the boondocks, I was much more venturesome in conversation in the city. That was partly because of the increased social activity, but mainly because my vocabulary had grown enough to be serviceable for everyday use. I'd brought an Italian textbook with me, but it was months before I opened it. And then it was just to say "Yeah, that's the way it is," and close it again.

Listening to a recording of Bach's cantata, *Christ lag in Todesbanden*, in Berio's apartment in Milan, amounted to breaking a fast. The city's cultural life fairly glowed in contrast to the quiet pace of Liguria. Here was the chance to make up for lost time. Names that I'd only seen in books or on record labels were turning up almost every night in the concert halls. Rene Leibowitz led the Teatro Nuovo Orchestra in the Schönberg second *Kammersymphonie*.[4] His association with the composer lent an authoritative air to a smooth performance. When Hermann Scherchen conducted the Vivaldi *Gloria* in the RAI (RAdiotelevisione Italiana) broadcast concert series[5], for his final curtain call, he went to the podium and held up the score, to get its share of the applause. Nice touch.

An especially savory series at the *Angelicum* the first three Mondays of April, 1963 featured the music of Monteverdi. If I had to pick a single 'favorite' composer, it might well be he. Setting aside for the nonce his single-handedly moving music from the Renaissance to the Baroque and his revolutionary harmonies such as the world wouldn't hear again until Wagner, there's a piquance to his melodies – especially in the madrigals – that usually isn't confined to the lead and bass voices. His poignant, soul piercing suspensions can still make me shiver.

With other concert series at the Palazzo Durini and the Ambrosiano (at the cathedral of St. Ambrose, home of Ambrosian chant, a building dating back to the Middle Ages), there was many a hard choice for the evening's entertainment. But some of the most memorable music was far from the crowds. There could scarcely have been a half dozen of us in the loft – the 'music room' – above Berio's apartment the afternoon that Cathy and he ran through the *Seven Popular Songs* of Manuel de Falla. *Nana* was particularly stunning.

On the ground floor below the pensione was a cafe. At first I came in for a fair share of good natured ribbing, as the new *giovanotto* on the block. I'd go in and ask for a "cappuccino," the hood of steamed milk decking the coffee like the cowl of the monks after which the drink was named. "Oh, you mean a 'cappuccio,'" they'd correct me.

---

[4] February 16, 1963.          [5] April 5, 1963.

Next day I'd go and order a "cappuccio." "Eh – eh. You mean a 'cappuccino!'" they would reply. All in good fun – and it tasted great whatever you call it.

Robert Moran stayed at the *pensione* when he came down from his studies in Vienna for a few weeks. At the time he was composing these remarkable graphic scores – pieces that looked as amazing as they sounded – and one evening a stray droplet of ink flew onto an open area in a page he'd only just begun. Time to call it a night! But when he'd finished the page, you couldn't tell where it was, and he hadn't erased it. The score evidently had grown around it.

For a while a fellow Berio associate, the Australian Harry Redner, stayed there. We'd met before at Darmstadt, and rode together with Castiglioni to Köln. I ran into him again at Dartington. Our differing backgrounds and viewpoints gave our frequent discussions the air of cordial sparring matches. Sometimes after hours I would hang out in the kitchen with Carlo, the chef, and Giordana, the chambermaid, of the delightfully spicy voice and sweet smile. I'd never had anyone make my bed before – with me in it! It was a sad day for me when she moved back to Trieste.

There was one fellow living there that Bob Moran and I dubbed 'Doctor Orbit,' who would pick up the phone in the lobby just to listen to the dial tone, or stare at a point on the dining room wall for minutes at a time. A charming menagerie, all in all, but when a place turned up at a fraction of the cost, I went for it.

In the haze of Italian springtime I moved to a room in a sixth floor apartment, located a short distance away on Via Mario Pagano. There was one of those grand old black wrought iron elevators, but I often opted to race up the white stone stairs that wound around it. Next door to me in the same apartment lived another Berio student – the Dutch composer Louis Andriessen. Coming from a veritable dynasty of composers, he was very traditionalist in many ways, but he was capable of cutting loose on occasion. One manic afternoon we 'collaborated' on a piece for piano four hands. We laid a large page of manuscript paper out on the floor, and proceeded to assault it, at first with pens, but soon with brushes, nails, string, and who knows what else. Each of us concentrated on one half of the page – one pianist's part. Before the ink dried, we folded it in half so that each side would imprint on the other. We then gave it its one and only performance at the piano in his room.

There was a concert at the United States Information Service in Milan that showcased three of Berio's students[6]. Bob Moran and I were joined by Paul Epstein, whom we'd met in Berio's class at Mills. At the same time Epstein had been an acolyte at that Temple of Philistia, the U. C. Berkeley music department, studying with Roger Sessions. A couple of students from the Milan Conservatory were lined up to play our pieces. Violinist Glauco Talassi and pianist Pierangelo dal Seno (Bob and I called him 'Mr. Breast') were waiting for us for a pre-concert meeting to go over the program. Dal Seno gave a tautly precise reading of my *Sonatina*, missing only a handful of notes in the entire piece. His training and practice must have been quite rigorous, because, come concert time, he played it exactly the same way, mistakes and all, just as if there'd been no meeting at all.

Another of my pieces on the program was *Dimensioni*. It was my first exploration in the use of a four dimensional hypercube – a tesseract – as a compositional base. That is, the music was all on one large page, with musical segments at each of the sixteen vertices of a projected four dimensional supercube. Having four dimensions to work with, one could array musical events according to varying parameters at will. For instance, as one moves from left to right across the page, the music would get faster. Front to back, louder. Earlier that week, on the upright piano in Louis Andriessen's apartment on Via Mario Pagano, Bob Moran had made a recording of it, which was played at the concert.

It was a short walk from my room to the *Cenacolo Vinciano* – the *Last Supper* of Leonardo da Vinci. I'd often go there on a Sunday, when admission was free. Not far away, the Cinema Orchidea, showed all the Eisenstein, Antonioni, Bergman, and Fellini films – and I was in town for the Milanese opening of *8 1/2*. On the lighter side, it could be terribly amusing to see an American film, dubbed for the locals. Watching Walter Brennan get all a-flustered – *in italiano* – added a comic touch I'd never imagined as a youngster at the Saturday matinée.

A few times I met Berio at the Studio di Fonologia Musicale, the electronic music studio that he had set up on the top floor of the RAI building on Corso Sempione. As loose as things were at APELAC in Bruxelles, they were uptight here, what with security checks, calling upstairs to verify my 'appointment,' and all. John Cage had just

[6] March 26, 1963.

been there, and declared it "not artistic." He then took the engineer, Marino, on a tour of the city to record a few reels of environmental sounds. After being so careful to get the highest possible 'Fi,' Marino just about fell off the floor when Cage went ahead and started to measure and shuffle the tape segments without even auditioning them! Another subtle but palpable victory of art over red tape.

Suddenly I found myself in Opera Heaven. The same price as the movie house – about fifty cents – got me in for standing room for nearly every opera I wanted to see at La Scala that season. And if you got there early enough, you didn't even have to stand. Both balconies had a second row of unnumbered seats for whomever got there first. Not only did I see *Lulu* three times, but one afternoon Berio and Cathy took me to a rehearsal. Berio deposited us in one of the lower boxes and went off, presumably to take care of some business regarding *Passaggio*. On stage they were rehearsing the scene Dr. Schön gives Lulu a pistol, and tells her that the only honorable thing to do is to shoot herself. She thinks for a moment, and shoots him instead. Toni Blankenheim's stage fall accidentally started a domino like chain reaction among the furniture. The clatter of tables and knick-knacks provided a mirthful tension lightener.

At the break Berio took us backstage and introduced me to Nino Sanzogno, the 'house conductor' at La Scala. His looks reminded me of Morelli, but Morelli would'nt've been caught dead conducting Alban Berg. For his part, though, Sanzogno didn't want for affability. His personality was a big change from that of his predecessor, Gianandrea Gavazzeni, in whose presence people had been known to fear for their lives. The bearlike Gavazzeni carried on in the Toscanini tradition of periodically tearing the phone off the wall during supposedly musically motivated fits of rage. By comparison Sanzogno was serene.

During Bob Moran's visit we went to see *La Bohème*. The production featured Mirella Freni, who then looked like a blonde Annette Funicello. After one of her well deserved thunderous ovations started to die away, we were amused to note that conductor Herbert von Karajan had held the beat, as if to say to the audience, "Puccini wrote it. You should hear it!" The orchestra then went on to finish its part, and the ovation for la Freni was immediately reprised. We also enjoyed her delectable Zerlina in *Don Giovanni* (alongside of Leontine Price (Donna Anna) and Elizabeth Schwarzkopf (Donna Elvira). Hermann Scherchen's leisurely tempi unnerved Bob, however. He had a train to catch. Literally. Back to Vienna!

My own travels took me to Venice for the Biennale. *Esposizione*, a Berio collaboration with the dancer Ann Halprin, was the featured work one of the evenings[7] at the *Teatro La Fenice*, site of the premières of *Rigoletto* and *La Traviata*. A choreographic setting of the Pousseur *Visages de Liège*, called *Gardens without Walls*, opened the proceedings. I shared a first tier box with the composer Sylvano Bussotti and Heinz-Klaus Metzger, the much touted post serialist modern as tomorrow music theorist. During intermission, Bussotti's eyes glowed like a choirboy's with unctuous solicitude as he explained to me how there was something about the American approach that rubbed him the wrong way.

Even Berio seemed a bit out of his element. As calm and controlled as *Passaggio* was, *Esposizione* was wild and unbridled. It began innocuously enough, with some exquisite electronic music in the best Berio manner, but very soon things started to get promisingly out of hand. Dancers appeared in the boxes, shining flashlights and madly gibbering. Yet more strode up the center aisle carrying a trunkful of old clothes, which were soon flying about everywhere. The audience was ready to revolt, but a marvelous sense of helplessness set in when they realized that whatever they did *just became part of the event!* A deep voice in one of the lower boxes warned a dancer high on the netting on stage: "Attenzione che non casca!" ("Watch out you don't fall!") but the riot had already been defused.

Another *La Fenice* evening[8] showcased the *Hannover Landestheater* production of the three Schönberg mini-operas, ranging from the intensely psychodramatic *Erwartung* and *Die Glückliche Hand* to the sitcomical *Von Heute auf Morgen*. There was an interesting Xenakis première[9]: *Stratégie*, 'a musical game for two conductors.' Supposedly Bruno Maderna defeated Konstantin Simonovic, but I sure couldn't tell from the music.

Returning to Milan, it was back to city life *all' italiano*. There was a spicy game of Scrabble at Umberto Eco's apartment on Corso Sempione with the Berios, where by agreement only dirty words

[7] April 18, 1963.          [8] April 21, 1963.          [9] April 23, 1963.

were permitted – but in any language! Beyond that, I made new and interesting acquaintances – like composers Franco Donatoni and Angelo Paccagnini, the electronics wizard Alfredo Lietti, musical theorist Luigi Rognoni, the British composer David Bedford, and the remarkable American pianist/composer Fredric Rzewski.

When Berio's *Passaggio* was mounted at Piccola Scala[10], it was on a double bill with Purcell's *Dido and Aeneas*, with Teresa Berganza in the title rôle of Dido. Having seen her performance of *Pierrot Lunaire* at Darmstadt, Berio had wanted Helga Pilarcik for his sole onstage protagonist. Then he saw her *Lulu* and changed his mind. I managed to get to four of the five performances of *Passaggio*, and had an idea of what to expect, having seen the score. But the opening, with the speaking (as opposed to the singing) chorus distributed among the audience, in total darkness, was magical. Unrivaled for his intuitive grasp of the melos, Berio infused his works with a deep and genuine polish that few others approached. And while not as overtly political as Luigi Nono's, his works usually display a thought-provocative streak.

The reaction of the staid and stodgy Italian audience ranged from philosophical ("Bisogna avere le cose brutte per capire le cose belle") to incensed ("Questa è La Scala di Verdi, di Puccini, di Bellini!"), but the night of the third performance, instead of whistling and misbehaving like usual, they were as quiet as church mice. With waters thus unmuddied, the piece was free to work its spell best that night. Then, just as strangely, it was back to the traditional idiocy the next performance.

May brought a monumental *Ring* cycle. Birgit Nilsson, Regina Resnik, Hans Hotter – Andre Cluytens conducted the La Scala Orchestra and an all star cast. In June an attempt was made to revive Cherubini's *Ali Baba*. A fine cast and stunning sets failed to resuscitate the score. There was an intriguing Stravinsky double bill at *Piccola Scala* in late June, with *Oedipus Rex* and *The Flood*, with Igor himself conducting the former, and Robert Craft the latter. But as the weather warmed it became time to move on. With the summer I went northward again.

Darmstadt the second time around was entirely different. Help-

[10] The first performance was on May 6, 1963, with Giuliana Tavolaccini as the lone singer on stage and Berio conducting. He must have liked it, because he went on to direct the four repeats as well, instead of turning the baton over to Bruno Maderna, as was the plan.

ing me to feel 'at home' were quite a few of my newly made friends. There was Louis Andriessen playing *A Night in Tunisia* (exactly like he'd practiced it in Milan) at the old upright piano in the Rathskeller – a favorite gathering place after the concerts at the Stadthalle – while at our table Terry Riley was chuckling, "Every time I buy a car, I lose my pen!"

Through Berio's good offices, I'd been corresponding with Alfred Schlee, head man at Universal Edition of Vienna. They'd be interested, he wrote me, in publishing my chamber orchestra piece *Phrases*. All I had to do was let them know the date of its performance, so they could verify for themselves that the piece 'worked.' Unfortunately there was no such date scheduled, despite my chasing after a fistful of leads. Playing on the pragmatism of size, I had better luck with my *Three Pieces for Two Pianos*. Pousseur had assembled an ensemble for a tour of Scandinavia, winding up at Darmstadt, and was kind enough to include my pieces in the program.

That concert[11], one of a few in the Darmstadt series that were broadcast live by Hessischer Rundfunk (Radio Frankfurt), showcased an ensemble assembled by Pousseur, whose *Répons pour sept musiciens* was the featured work. *Répons* is virtually a musical dice game enacted before your very eyes and ears. Every so often one of the musicians would get up and rearrange the game board on stage, thereby determining (or at least influencing) the music to follow. Its patterns and textures reminded me of those curious critters one encounters in Yves Tanguy paintings. To highlight its 'mobile' nature, it was performed both to open and to close the concert, so that the listeners might compare the two performances. Completing the program were *Hodograph* by Earle Brown, a *Cassation* by a fellow Pousseur student, the Belgian composer Philipp Boesmans, and my piano duet, performed by Pierre and Francette Bartholomée. With some trepidation I'd showed the score to the pianist Aloys Kontarsky, whose pronouncement: "it looks well," delighted me as much as the brilliant and upbeat performance of the Bartholomées.

Although better known, the Luigi Nono choral work *Cori di Didone* didn't impress me as much as did his *Ha Venido*, a pointillist gem sung *a capella* by seven women. Bernard Rands's *Actions for Six*, which he'd been working on while at Linguegglietta, was given a

---

[11] July 25, 1963.

sprightly performance and was well received. The ninth and tenth of Stockhausen's *Klavierstücke*, each in its own way, pointed out the composer's determination to be a trend setter, not a follower. And, most vividly of all, I recall some scintillating moments in the *Structures II* of Boulez, which was performed by the famous piano duo Aloys and Alfons Kontarsky. Completely unlike its predecessor, the hyper-Cartesian[12], totally serialized *Structures I*, this work was less abstract but every bit as adventurous. Thunder and lightning, shimmering colors, jagged glistening atonal peaks dominating an Antarctic soundscape.

Stockhausen's class in '63 included guided tours through *Gruppen* and *Kontakte*. "You can't miss it!" he said, as he explained the structural significance of the *sffz* chord in the winds of all three orchestras at 'Bar' 160 in the score of *Gruppen*. In *Kontakte*, we were treated to a treatise on form. Boulez mainly read from his own writings in the newly published *Darmstädter Beiträge zur neuen Musik*. There were a lot of impressions to sort through. It took some time after my studies at Darmstadt before I was able to unclog my brain and get back on track again, as far as writing music was concerned. Those were the latter years of the ascendancy of 'serial' technique, wherein a single basic idea, or *Grundgestalt*, would replicate and ramify throughout a composition at every level. Works were appearing in incredible profusion, many of them mindblowing blockbusters that redefined our perceptions of music in fundamental ways. A dream of those times was to define an entire composition parametrically, just as the blueprint of an organism is contained in its chromosomes. Pierre Boulez's two piano work *Structures I*, like earlier experiments by Messiaen and the Belgian composer Karel Goeyvaerts, was an attempt to apply that concept musically. It thus became thinkable to generate throughly serialized pointillist wallpaper *ad surditatem*. Lava lamps for Olympus.

In today's ever more pluralistic *milieu*, it's questionable whether a *reductio ad absurdum* as egalitarian-to-a-fault as serialism, whether conceived as an expression of democratic or socialist ideals, was ever meant to function as a universal operating principle, either artistically or socially. It appears that this 'serial' ideal (it turns out, after all, that it *was* invented and not discovered) is just as much a dinosaur as the older models it sought to replace.

[12] It can be contended that the voice of French philosophy was hoarse before Descartes.

For one thing, to assume that only the most strictly controlled shapes will be perceived as related bespeaks a very low estimation of the expressive qualities of sound, whether considered as information content or Dionysiac rapture.

For another, who needs models and systems, anyway? In Las Vegas there's a saying, "You've got a system? Our doors are open to you. A *surefire* system? We'll pay your way!" The most effective of Schönberg's compositions – the *Five Pieces for Orchestra*, Opus 16; the Opus ll and Opus 19 *Klavierstücke* come to mind – were written *before* his method-of-composition-with-twelve-tones-related-only-to-one-another had congealed into a solid system, and thereafter his imagination was needlessly shackled. It seems the serialists found themselves unwilling, or more likely, unable, to deal with the wealth of harmonic connotation unleashed by post-Wagnerian adventurism, and this "system of barbed hooks" (Herbert Eimert's phrase) allowed them the chance to dodge the issue altogether.

The most pressing issue confronting me was more mundane. My string ran out after the second summer at Darmstadt, and it was time to return to Nevada. The coffee on the flight back was so weak, I could see the bottom of the cup! It was just as if there were a printed message taunting me: "Welcome back to America!"

### WORDS WITHOUT SONG

Everything's hunky-dory with Mr. Gruntny-Groily
(trilled Schottish rrr's, if you please)

Straw hat, rolled up sleeves, walrus mustache,
Obesely obsequious obstinacy,

"Crack you a whip, Mr. Free!
Whatright happiness when workingman company-toil
& you leech just sit
& live off bloodearned gravy
(bringdown footonground cigarsmoke in yr eyes like
stormclouds blocking Springsun)!"

Deathmud (why else does he need someone to hate?)
vainly
raising cane
to quench
Firelife

# 4/ WILD, BLUE, AND OTHER YONDERS

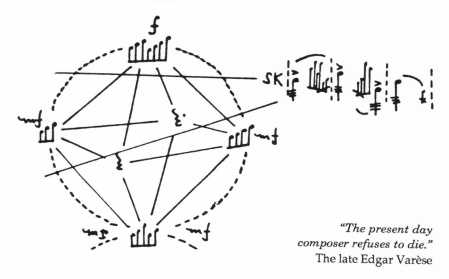

"*The present day composer refuses to die.*"
The late Edgar Varèse

**S**oon after my return to the States, in late summer, 1963, I reconnected with Phil Lesh. We'd been corresponding all along during my European sojourn, and I rejoined him in Palo Alto, where we shared the hospitality of then Stanford graduate student Howard Hersh. Phil and I had encountered Howard at the Ojai Festival the year before. Later known for his erudition as program annotator for the San Francisco Symphony, he first impressed me with his uncanny simulation of the sound of a siren. This was displayed to greatest effect when he was riding in the back seat of a car. With his dark beard, I could easily imagine him in a turban. He had a cat named 'Kmir.'

Meanwhile, our Berio classmate Steve Reich had become involved with the San Francisco Mime Troupe, contributing an appropriately impudent score (performed on kazoos) for their production of *Ubu Roi*[1]. He invited Phil and me to participate in four 'Music Now Koncerts[2],' to be given at the Mime Troupe's theatre located in

[1] Premièring December 10, 1963.  [2] May 21, 23, 29, and 30, 1964.

the since demolished church at Twentieth and Capp streets (nowadays it's a playground). There were four performances of a wide
ranging program, featuring ensemble improvisations with Steve at
the keyboard, Jon Gibson on clarinet, Georges Rey on violin, Gwen
Watson on 'cello, Paul Breslin on bass, and myself occasionally
inside the piano. Phil contributed a piece for the group, including a
jubilantly eruptive prepared piano solo for me, called *6 7/8 for
Bernardo Moreno*. In the true, adventurous aleatoric spirit of the
times Phil shuffled the segments anew before each performance.
One of many things I've admired him for. The first half of the
program closed with Gwen Watson playing a Bach suite, and I
opened the second half with a prepared piano plus tape solo called
*Piano Piece Number Three*.

Like *Dimensioni, Piano Piece Number Three* was a 'tesseract' score,
giving me enormous latitude when it came to designing each
individual performance. Steve Reich had just acquired a new 'toy,'
a Sony 777 two-track tape recorder. He helped me prepare a tape
with a separate version of *Piano Piece Number Three* on each track,
distinguishable from each other and from the live performance by
subtle variations among the piano preparations. The plan for the
premiére was for me to start playing, to be joined by the tape after
thirty seconds or so.

The opening night of the series was punctuated by the sounds of
the judo class that met upstairs. Coming on right after intermission,
I found them hard to ignore. Rather than consider it an interruption,
though (like, what am I going to do – go tell a roomful of black belts
to knock it off?), I simply found a place in the multi-dimensional
road map of a score that could be interpreted to fit the sounds of
bodies being thrown to the floor (ceiling, to us), and took it from
there. The way things meshed together in the ensuing performance
worked beyond my wildest imaginings. Sounds on the tape would
seemingly imitate what I'd just done live. Crashes on the low strings
would turn into the sound of passing cars outside. Splashes in the
high register would turn into a spatter of coughs among the audience. I'm not clear as to *how* or *why* it works, but I've seen *that* it
works.

The most satisfying version was at the third concert, where the
tape was started immediately and I dived right in 'balls to the wall.'

If only Tamara Rey had let us borrow the tape recorder one more night. Steve Reich picked up on it right away, quoting the soft drink slogan: 'You like it, and it likes you!' Even in the dark green woodsiness of Northern California he marched to a Manhattan tempo. The sign on the mirror at his Bernal Heights home said "Are you a bore?" He drove a taxicab in San Francisco at the time, and was putting together a *musique concrète* tape piece out of recordings he'd secretly made in the cab.

His rap has changed but little since those days. 'Bach, Bebop, and Stravinsky' are as pertinent to his approach today as ever. Although interested in improvisation, he wasn't as willing as I to go along with some of the post-Cage developments, but we did agree on the preëminence of Earle Brown in that circle. Therein, perhaps, lies the point, that something intangible is involved. Others go through the motions with results that are about as interesting as bashing rocks together, but an Earle Brown or a Steve Reich can do things that seem transparently simple, yet make the sparks fly.

The new music was starting to make inroads, such as they were, into the more standard concert venues. Josef Krips held his breath and took the plunge, conducting the San Francisco Symphony in the *Passacaglia*, Op. 1, by Anton Webern[3]. It was a big step for him. Across the Bay, Gerhard Samuel not only led the Oakland Symphony in a creditable performance of the concert suite from Alban Berg's *Lulu*[4], but also programmed Terry Riley's *In C* in the main concert series. Now, *that* was a major step.

The Tape Music Center had moved out of its attic at the Conservatory and into a new home, sharing 321 Divisadero with Ann Halprin's dance company. Continuing its remarkable series of presentations, the Tape Music Center featured new electronic works and performance pieces from the cutting edge of the American *avant-garde*. There was a fabulous set of five concerts with John Cage and David Tudor at 321 Divisadero in late March/early April 1964. Programs I and IV were the same, as were II and V, but with this kind of music it's always new anyway. David Tudor gave an electrifying performance of Cage's *Variations II*, as well as a hypnotically ethereal Toshi Ichiyanagi piece. Cage's *Music Walk* parted the Curtains of Chaos in a whimsical way. 'Backstage,' Bob Moran did me the

[3] January 15, 16, 17, 1964.          [4] February 14, 15, 1964.

honor of introducing me to the Great Man. John Cage's humor put
me at ease right away – he mentioned having heard of our *Winter
Music* blizzard at Mills – and made it seem quite unlike your typical
first meeting.

At another 321 Divisadero event, Pauline Oliveros' accordion
was heard in Ramon Sender's *Desert Ambulance* ("This is a cultural
desert," she said, "and we're coming to rescue you!"). The music
was accompanied by a light score (as billed in the program) by Tony
Martin, who was later to bring his art to places like the Avalon
Ballroom.

A few doors up Divisadero, on the same side of the street, was the
Magic Theatre for Madmen Only. The Wolf of the Steppes was
already at large and stalking minds in San Francisco. One of the
shop's proprietors was a friend and neighbor of mine (at whose
house I saw the Beatles début on the *Ed Sullivan Show*) named Mike
Ferguson. He'd turn up again later as the keyboard player for the
Charlatans.

Phil, Bill Walker, and I had rented a house in San Francisco, but
things were moving too slowly for us. Steve Reich moved back to
New York. Bill Walker moved to Utah, and I finally moved to Las
Vegas, there to open for another extended run at the Post Office. In
San Francisco I'd worked at the Ferry Annex, a dusty, grimy
building straight out of Upton Sinclair. Located at what is now
Embarcadero Plaza, the building has long since been demolished.
One of the old timers told me that it was old and dirty when he
started working there – in 1922. Just down the Embarcadero was the
greasiest spoon I ever did slide into, where I once ordered a bowl of
chili and a cup of tea – and could scarcely tell them apart!

Then they moved our operation to Rincon Annex. I remember as
if in a misty, Molochian dream working there side by side with
Danny Rifkin. One night we were sorting flats – trucking bills, as I
recall – and he turned to me and said, "What does America move
on?" "?" said I, and then he showed me the blurb on their postage
meter: "America moves on rubber wheels." I never would have
guessed. When I next encountered him, he was in the Grateful Dead
management tower, and still inclined to play with people's heads.

This time it was to be the Bonanza Annex in Las Vegas. I suppose it's a useful talent sometimes to have an encyclopædic knowledge of a city's streets, but somehow it wasn't my idea of a stimulating situation. Events were in store, however, that would in effect take things out of my hands for a while.

Namely, the U.S. Air Force. I'd received my draft notice – the circus was going full tilt in Vietnam in 1965, you'll remember – but it was still possible to avoid an appearance in Center Ring by enlisting, and I figured I'd rather program a computer for the Air Force than a potentially malfunctioning M-16 rifle for the Army. It seemed like a reasonable choice at the time.

Lackland A.F.B., Texas. Site of Basic Training. A preselected (and you know how painful that can be) cross section of Americans – Japanese from Hawaii, Blacks from Alabama, Latinos from Arizona, Italians from New York – all of us 'rainbows' were in for a program carefully calculated to render us the same color: Air Force blue. Wearing pith helmets to protect us from the Sun, we had a lot of marching to look forward to. My platoon was led by a Staff Sergeant Huggins and a colorfully expressive Airman First Class Brown from North Carolina, who'd keep the laggards in line. "Hey, ditty bop, let's see you dig in those heels! Get in step, sealbean! Stand up! Lean back! Steady! Steady! Steady!"

Just as the rain gave me a reprieve in Berkeley, the heat and humidity of June in Texas did its part to keep us off the parade grounds. They'd put up a red flag when the mercury got too high, and all outdoor activity came to a sweltering halt. Still, six weeks of drill, twice through the obstacle course ('combat confidence course,' they called it – ha!), a trip to the Alamo – it seemed like a boy scout outing compared to what was to come.

I was assigned to learn computer programming at Sheppard A.F.B., near Wichita Falls, Texas, on a UNIVAC 1050-II drum system. 'Tech School' was where they dished out in abundance what you thought they were seeing how much you'd take of in Basic. At Lackland we had the dubious honor of being marched around by NCOs. A platoon leader might even be a master sergeant. At Sheppard we saw scarcely anyone but other rookies. The meanest and toughest of the students were given a gold rope to wear on their shoulders, and put in charge of a barracks full of recruits. We were 'instructed' to say "Yes, Rope!" instead of "Yes, Sir!" to them.

Especially the Red Rope who was in charge of the whole squadron.

Second in command to the 'Rope' was the Assistant Barracks Chief, to whom we said "Yes, ABC!" There can be little doubt but that the heat and the regimentation are *designed* to get to you. Once on a cleanup detail ('squadron beautification' they called it – ha!), being seized by an attack of Texas thirst, it occurred to me that in the barracks around which we were 'policing' was a drinking fountain. Arriving in a mild stagger, I found the device and proceeded to take a drink. During which the first thought, "Gosh, I'm thirsty!" returned. It was followed immediately by the second: "Hey, there's a drinking fountain in that building." A moment of mild consternation set in when I realized I was taking a drink at the time! To resolve it, I had to consciously decide to take the second drink without interruption.

It could have been worse. I got out of the rest of a week of K. P. when, on the second day working in the mess hall, the mop I was operating dislodged a light fixture, which landed on my hand. It left a crescent shaped scar over my left thumb. Unless you were bleeding profusely or comatose, the Air Force regarded you as a malingerer. At Lackland I'd made the mistake of actually wearing the G. I. prescription glasses I was issued, and wound up getting intense headaches from the eyestrain. But 'Sick Call' wouldn't even give me any aspirins, simply because I didn't have a headache at the time I reported. This time, though, I qualified in spades, and fortunately my finger agility wasn't impaired. Not that they'd've cared.

At Sheppard we used shoe polish on the floors, and floor polish on our shoes. No lie. Cordovan shoe polish was applied to the floors by us poor schleps on our hands and knees. And a cotton ball dipped into Glo-Coat added the finishing touch to a spit-shined pair of brogans. Despite these and other bizarrities, I finished first in my class, and it was Air Force policy to try to place top finishers in bases of their choosing. My first choice was Hamilton A.F.B. – Marin County, literally next door to where the Grateful Dead rehearsed. It was not to be, but I did get my second choice: Nellis A.F.B., Nevada – back to Las Vegas again! And the ice blue family 'mansion.'

Nellis was a TAC (Tactical Air Command) base, more like what the Green Berets would refer to as 'wash and wear' than 'spit and polish.' It also meant that they used IBM 1401s. By this time, I felt, "What's another language, anyway?" and promptly picked up SPS, Autocoder, and even (gulp) machine language. After a few more travels (like to IBM at L.A.) I was up on COBOL, FORTRAN, and ferreting out goodies about the then newly unveiled IBM-360. Their top of the line model had a 128K central processing unit. The consensus among programmers was – who would ever need that much!?

The computer system at Nellis would have filled most people's living rooms. It makes me feel like a barnstorming biplane pilot to describe it, but one time I repaired the program that printed the military payroll checks. I mean, it doesn't get much more important than that! An intricate operation, entirely in machine language, it might possibly have had something to do with my making Nellis A.F.B. Airman of the Month. That was in October, 1966 – and the Base Commander put me up for Airman of the Year!

One of the benefits of working in a technical field is the opportunity to take advantage of other people's ignorance. The higher their rank, the more pleasure we took in it. We programmers at Nellis informally awarded one another the 'Silver Polar Bear' (occasionally with 'Eskimo Pie Cluster') for a snow job above and beyond the call (and occasionally above and beyond belief!).

Just being in the military service at all during the Vietnam misadventure was good enough for the first of my three 'real' decorations. The 'National Defense Service Medal' was essentially a door prize. Then there was the 'Good Conduct Medal,' or 'N.B.C.' medal (for 'Never Been Caught'). For the third, well…I did shoot 70 out of a possible 60 for my expert marksman's ribbon, but somebody else was helping by shooting into my target. After all, in high school R.O.T.C., I'd dis- and reassembled the M-1 rifle so atrociously that the instructors didn't know what to do. They had to send it back to the factory to have it repaired.

A more apt symbol of my military career involved the Decon team I got stuck on. 'Decon' stood for 'decontamination.' Our *raison d'être* was to wash off planes that had flown through radioactive clouds. Fortunately we never had to do that, but one time they decided they'd teach us how to fight brush fires. So after a few 'classes' with somebody from the Bureau of Land Management, they bussed us out into the desert, and set one for us to put out. A real challenge. After a couple of gratuitous desert breezes it became too much of a challenge. They ended up having to call in the real firefighters to contain it.

By this time William Gromko had a series of concerts going at the university with a string orchestra he'd assembled from the best musicians on the Strip. He was kind enough to invite me to write something for the ensemble, and furthermore wasn't wearing the same 'old school' blinders as Morelli. Feeling thus unfettered, I went and arranged for string orchestra segments from my *String Quartet*. The piece was begun in mid-1963 as my last student piece for Berio, continued in San Francisco, and completed in Las Vegas in October, 1964. The original was in proportional notation as 'developed' by Berio – the players don't count a beat, but take their cues from each other's parts. I'd been unsuccessful in my quest of a quartet gutsy enough to give the piece a go, and I was curious to hear how some parts of it would work, so the idea of an arrangement had its appeal. It was clear, though, that I'd need to transfer it to mensural notation for the larger group of instruments.

Billed as *Sinfonia*, the work was performed on the campus of Nevada Southern University by the University String Orchestra, William Gromko conducting[5]. William Baffa, writing in the *Las Vegas Review-Journal*[6] said it "seemed to reflect what we might hear if a sound recording unit were strapped to one of our space ships." and called it "both exciting and interesting." The performance was pleasing enough, but the real difficulties I'd gotten myself into, compositionally speaking, had to do with the unwieldiness of the system I was using. It had evolved out of a method similar to Pousseur's, wherein interval proportions were more directly controlled than is possible with the inflexible application of serial technique. Wouldn't it be nice if I could somehow get the use of a computer...

There was a story going around Nellis about a unit that requested five hundred pieces of blank paper from the Base Duplicator Office. Their request was denied, but Base Duplicator said that they *would* photocopy a blank page five hundred times for them. Military 'logic' takes some getting used to, but you figure out early on that

[5] June 12, 1966.          [6] June 19, 1966, page 24.

as long as you at least look busy, they tend to not hassle you as much. As a systems analyst (AFSC 68750) I was entitled to access to the computer for the purpose of sharpening my programming skills. I simply used my allotted time on the machine to write and debug a musical composition program to handle the 'busywork' aspects of my harmonic system, thereby liberating me to concentrate on the more expressive side of the work. In the original version, the program even made instrumentation choices among Flute, 'Cello, and Piano. It was to be a trio, but when the opportunity came to do another piece for the string orchestra, it didn't take me long to adapt the program.

The resulting work was blessed with not one but two performances[7]. The second is often harder to achieve than the first! Called *Propagations*, it was performed both times by the University String Orchestra, William Gromko conducting, on the Nevada Southern campus. There was greater exploration of stereophony among the instruments – a sound texture would snake its way across the stage, being passed from instrument to instrument, to meet and cross paths with a different one coming the other way. And strangely tonal implications were starting to show up more – already in the *String Quartet*, near the end, there was a tantalizing hint of a lazy A-flat suspended chord, dissolving like an image seen in a cloud. Indeed, towards the end of *Propagations*, there was a spirited 'chorale' segment that first saw the light of day as the 'Old Smuggler Chorus' in one of my communiqués from Europe to the Snake Ranch.

Meanwhile, in the realm of electric music, Don Farr and Ron Gougé had gone to San Francisco with a short-lived but remarkable group called The Möbius Band. Their experience there must've been a little one sided, too, because they regrouped in Las Vegas as The Dæmon, with Bob Haney on drums. One memorable evening in 1967 at the Nevada Southern Student Union, they invited me to sit in with them – my one and only adventure as a bass player. I was just getting my bearings when my thumb started to get numb. What a blister! My fingers made me promise never to treat them that way again.

---

[7] July 30, 1967 and April 6, 1968.

It was thenabouts that a friend of a friend came back from Texas with a truckload of peyote, which started to circulate among people I knew. About a half hour after gobbling down the cactus gastric misgivings often set in, and you'd wonder whether you'd done the right thing. But in another fifteen or twenty minutes or so, the Door to the Infinite opens a crack, and the light shining within removes all doubts. My first experience with the cactus was at a friend's house in the desert south of town. The freeway hadn't been built yet, so the subsequent ride home took me right up the heart of the Strip. The neon blended right in.

There was also acid, yet to be discovered by the media, the Mafia, and most importantly, the legislators. The waters had not yet been muddied by horror stories or chemical impurities, and batches were affectionately dubbed 'Blue Lagoon,' 'Brown Renown,' 'Plum Pretty,' and 'Startling Burgundy.' A friend in the Prankster circle scored some small transparent capsules from Sandoz. They worked wonderfully well, but the caps looked suspiciously empty, so they naturally enough became known as 'The Emperor's New Clothes.' After a few excursions up the psychedelic mountain I got a bit of a reputation as a 'guide,' someone to have along on a trip so it won't go sour. Clearly a field where the more you know, the less you know – and vice versa.

Tripping soon began to resemble a proto-yuppie weekend entertainment, like skiing or going to the lake. On some of the more interesting jaunts out in the desert we'd combine 'fuels,' sometimes with remarkable results. One clear, moonless overnighter found me gazing straight into the eye of Canis Major, an awesome and serious matter. Looking directly at the constellations, I was impressed not only by their mythic associations, but also by their propensity for movement. After all, this point in time is like a freeze frame, as far as the stars are concerned. None of these shapes are permanent. A thousand years isn't much time in the Cosmic scheme of things. These shapes are in mid-gesture, so to speak, on their way somewhere else. Those vectors, as well as the 'ancient' associations, were all there to read in that vertiginous moment.

I remember going through tableaux, as if playing recordings left by departed life forms. A jack rabbit's life story held my interest for a while. Somehow I could tell when the end of the 'reel' was coming.

Evidently the bunny had gone to a river to drink, and was done in by a hunter. It was caught totally by surprise, so there was no view of the hunter, nor even an inkling of the weapon used. But as my eyes opened, the image faded – dissolving directly onto the constellations Lepus, the Hare; Eridanus, the River; and, as I turned to face it, Orion, the Hunter!

Taking it a step further, consider that mere parsecs away, the relative positions of the stars would be substantially altered. What numinous *Gestalts* might cultures there evolve, connecting the celestial dots as they see them from their neck of the Galaxy, I wondered. It is said in Zen: "Everyday life – that is the Way." Could that be a cryptic hint of the view from beyond the miraculous?

Wondrous books were coming out in those years – like Alan Watts's *The Joyous Cosmology*, and Aldous Huxley's *The Doors of Perception* – after which a rock band was named. And many of the original Asian texts were becoming available: the collection *Zen Flesh, Zen Bones* of Paul Reps and Nyogen Senzaki; *Hekiganroku (Blue Cliff Records); Tetteki Tosui (The Iron Flute);* the *Platform Sutra* (alluded to by Cage); the *Hundred Thousand Songs of Milarepa;* and (a favorite) the *Diamond Sutra* (watch out for those arbitrary conceptions of phenomena!). These were Guidebooks to the High Country. Truths not revealed by the conventional sources. Useful descriptive information about our Situation – rather than a bunch of conditions that outrage your (God-given, no?) sense of logic and/or fairness which, if you buy them nonetheless, you'll be introduced into some sort of cosmic knitting circle.

While I might not express it as bluntly as he, I concur with Bakunin that the primary focus of organized religion is political rather than spiritual. To paraphrase Pascal, Evil has no more devoted servant than religious fervor. The bitter sectarianism and brutal chauvinism of the megacults gives the lie to their pretentions to representing Universal Truths. Any God who made any of us, made all of us. Those folks across the river who trim their nails (or whatever) differently weren't put there for target practice.

The reality of our nature exceeds in beauty and wonder all of the 'ancient' metaphors. Indeed, the very term 'ancient' needs to be qualified. To a God who made the mountains and rivers, the Moon and the stars, what's a measly five or ten thousand years?

From John Cage I'd learned of the *I Ching* – by the mid-sixties I'd practically memorized it, and even used it to model parts of my string orchestra piece *Propagations*. More useful than any single oracular revelation were the insights it provided on the interaction of event and situation – how the former can initiate change in the latter. Or, to put it another way, more valuable than any of the answers it gave me was learning how to formulate the right questions.

Not that the answers were always what a young guy would hope for. From the pretty blonde daughter of the singing emcee of one of the Strip hotels who caught my eye in sixth grade, I'd had a predeliction for musical types. A flutist I knew in high school could, in a single gesture, evoke a sultry Carmen or a delicate Cio-Cio San. In fact, Carmen was her middle name. She played Debussy's *Syrinx* in her senior recital. Alas, I'd already graduated and had gone to Berkeley by then.

During my Air Force days one person started to take up more and more of my attention. I'll call her 'Mona Moore.' Her father, an affable Venezuelan, looked like Artur Rubinstein. He had the same birthday as I, and treated me like a son. Her mother, a Ukrainian Jew *via* Philadelphia, was cordial but reserved. Anyhow, 'Mona' and I went out together – to movies, concerts, dining , dancing – and I'd come to call at her North Las Vegas home, where we played Chopin *Ballades* for each other at their blond Acrosonic. I admired how she played, the way it revealed an earnest, questing spirit. I remember her eyes, the mole on her upper lip, kissing her goodnight like I meant it, which I did. She reminded me of the bittersweet second theme in the opening movement of the Chopin *First Piano Concerto*. At the time I thought to give her comfort and encouragement. As it turned out, it was she who helped me feel better about myself.

*Enfin*, I don't know if I was too fast, too slow, or too blond. It must have been disorienting to be in a household where I felt welcomed instead of shunned. With reliable guidance from neither parents nor peers, I blundered along on my own, learning step by painful step. And of course just being around her tensed me up more than any piano teacher could've. Maybe it was just another charm for her bracelet, but in those dark moments when my heart sighs, it hears her name reverberating like a stinging mantra. Don't even ask me to pronounce it.

Hearts aren't broken. They're torn. It seems to hit harder in the teens and twenties because it's a bigger future you're missing out on. This on top of the mix of feelings and emotions that goes along with being stationed at a military base in your own home town. Having your friends around helps a great deal, though I'm sure that the Air Force never meant for it to work that way. They'd as soon keep you disoriented enough to believe them when they tell you which way the wind blows. It didn't take a weatherman or an oracle to tell me that there was a storm on the horizon, and that it constituted a clear and present danger to my cozy situation. Starting in early '68, lots of orders were being cut, sending people to Tan Son Nhut A.F.B.

Vietnam. Clearly, *this* trip was not necessary. Another job for my Guardian Angel. The first step in the process of shipping you across the Pacific consisted of getting you a Secret clearance. All I had to do, as it turned out, was let it slip in conversation with the 'wrong' officers that I'd been to Communist rallies. True enough, but they were in an open air plaza in Italy, and anyone passing through on the way to where they were going, like I was, could've made the same claim. I took a few afternoons off work to explain it to those nice folks at O.S.I. (Office of Special Investigations), and they decided that it'd be a much better idea for me to serve out the rest of my term right here at home.

There was a chance for me to become a warrant officer in the Army, but it involved a transfer to Fort Huachuca, Arizona. Somehow not quite attractive enough to get me to re-up. Besides, changes were brewing, and (Hooray) my separation date from the Air Force was approaching. They wouldn't be calling me 'Sarge' much longer. What on earth, I wondered, could lie in store...

SONG LYRIC
*On the flight back from the 'Woodstock' Festival*

In the tentacular web of Ulysses Sleaze
    all's the same, and disagrees.
Twittering caldron falls off the shelf,
    subtracts your mind and adds up to itself.

"'Who's to say?' you say," say I
    (slithering ocean to fragile sky...)
The weight of the obvious crushes dispute,
    as primordial slime juggles repute.

Time watches crystalline fish in a school,
    as stone lizards cue up for entropy pool.
Galaxies twine in astral mentation,
    imposing monoliths beyond demonstration.

Whither you wander, dancing through faces,
    Cereberus in line going through his paces.
The buzzing of bees, sunlight on the heather;
    How sweet it can be when you get it together.

# 5/ REALLY MOST SINCERELY DEAD

*"When I hear the word 'culture', I reach for my gun."* Hermann Göring

The FIGMO calendar on my desk at Nellis had started counting down the days until my discharge from over a thousand. FIGMO is one of those military 'folk' acronyms in the tradition of SNAFU and (a favorite) FUBB. It might be delicately rendered as 'Forget it! I Got My Orders.' A transfer to another unit or separation from the service, not to mention promotions, would inevitably involve the 'cutting of orders.' That's 'cutting,' not 'printing.' These are one time limited edition jobbies, so the plates are presumably G.I. sharp.

And these orders are not merely oral commands, mind you, but signed official documents, in black and white, real as the Washington monument for all to see. The consensus was that someone who wouldn't be there for the fan's distribution of whatever might hit it was legitimately presumed to be apathetic even beyond normal G.I. standards. There was a TAC saying: "What is urgent today will be urgenter tomorrow." Usage: "Don't give him the job. It'll never get done – he's FIGMO."

Well, you see, in the Fall of '68 I was FIGMO. The attraction for civilian life is something that lifers will make a point of telling you that they just can't understand. Often in as many words – you can tell when it's the deep end of the pool, as far as their vocabulary's concerned. Among the career military people I met during my hitch, I can count the ones who weren't total jackasses on my fingers, and still have enough left to play *Für Elise*. A few months before I got out (they were threatening me with an Article 15 because my hair was too long) the squadron First Sergeant squawked, "I don't know what's wrong with you young troops. You think all we expect of you is for you to do your job!" As your time gets short, however, military tradition allows you the prerogative of not caring about such things.

Appropriately enough, my separation from the Air Force oc- curred on St. Cecilia's Day, November 22, 1968. FIGMO fever was in full force. The next forty eight hours didn't do anything to break the spell, either. My real and metaphorical bags were already packed, and after a few hours in the air (on commercial airlines – I never did get a lift from the Air Force, in any sense of the word) I was in Columbus, Ohio, joining the Grateful Dead on tour. The next night was my first at the organ with them, at the University of Ohio at Athens.

The trail that led me there started back in the pristine, pre-Dylan, pre-Beatles sixties, before Rock had reached the roots of a generation's collective unconscious and acid still came in sugar cubes. It started slowly, and then exploded into a multicolored geyser! One could sense the gathering winds. The times, they were about to change, acting on people trying to reconcile what they'd learned in and out of school with what they saw around them. "It's not that my heels are dug in – it's just the way I was standing when the wind hit." How many inquisitions arise from the conflict of evidence with precon- ception!

Florence Nathan, Phil's lady at the time, described being in the Grateful Dead extended family as like living on a block where all the kids were like you. It was definitely a *karass* and not a *granfaloon*, in the sense Kurt Vonnegut meant in *Cat's Cradle*, whence came the name of the band's publishing arm. The feeling shared was that the question was not "What is the world coming to?" but "When is the world coming to?"

The question of hair length arose. Now, if that's the way you distinguish between the sexes, it reveals some serious gaps in your upbringing and education. It never felt like a rebellious statement as far as I was concerned, for all it was taken as such. After years of crew cuts, pants that buckled just below the armpits, nerdy glasses; in short, being made to look and feel ridiculous, I welcomed the chance to explore and develop my own æsthetic, to see what *I* wanted to look like. The immediate results are guaranteed to look gawkish, but you have to spread your wings before the feathers can dry.

Peer pressure never was much a factor to us. It was a big factor, though, to our elders, who turned it every which way according to their purpose. It it was something they approved of, it was "Johnny Jones eats his broccoli. Why don't you?" If it was something they didn't, it was "And I suppose if Johnny Jones jumped off the Empire State Building, so would you." This adversarial posturing belied a tragic lack of trust. Telling your kids about the facts of life doesn't necessarily mean that they'll draw conclusions that you disapprove of, but that seemed to be the presupposition of a great number of American parents, to judge by the zeal with which they tried to conceal, distort, and mislead.

The persecution of youth culture dates back at least as far as ancient Greece. No doubt Socrates's crime was revealing to the youth of Athens the clay feet of the so called authorities: that those in charge were just older, not necessarily wiser. For one egregious example, in several decades of living on the outskirts of the seamier side of society, I've yet to observe so much as a single solitary instance of anyone whose life was seriously damaged by the 'demon weed,' except as a result of someone else's opinion. And I've yet to hear a single reason for its prohibition that boiled down to anything more than some 'authority' saying "Thou shan't!" It should be pointed out in this connection that there are those who can watch television in moderation. The enforcement of counter intention without adequate explanation is the very essence of totaliarianism. Despite reports commissioned from Mayor LaGuardia to President Nixon, there are those whose minds are made up, and won't be confused by facts. Unfortunately, they're in 'charge.'

Part of the social function of the rock bands was to give coherent expression to the very same street wisdom that our elders had been warning us against. The bands gave form and substance to the mounting instinctive rejection of the 'acceptable' surrogates for thinking for oneself. That, more than any lurid lyrics or loud noises, was the 'danger' of rock 'n' roll. Meanwhile, rock music was banned here and there, on the flimsiest and most specious of pretexts. It was profoundly dishonest, the way that they felt they had to fabricate some other reason to keep us from playing. If they'd had a cogent, convincing argument, why didn't they use it? And if they couldn't be up front about what they were trying to shove down our throats, what can it be worth?

The rock concerts broke the intersocial surface tension, evolving a sense of community out of what had been a scattered array of 'scenes.' In concerts, on record players, over free form radio – there had evolved an electrified version of the *I Ching*. The song lyrics would reflect the Moment, sometimes with startling clarity and immediacy. Beatle and Dylan songs proclaimed they'd 'been there,' to a psychedelicized audience ravenous for new experience. Subjective experience became objectified through synchronicity.

The first Mothers of Invention album, *Freak Out!* gave me the same sense of *avant garde* that I'd found so thrilling in Europe a few years earlier. Truth to tell, fifties rock 'n roll never grabbed me. I-IV-V...it all sounded the same, and all so simplistic. But in the early sixties people my own age were getting into the act, and more interesting things were starting to happen. Phil and Jerry started playing in a band called the Warlocks. I managed to slip away from the Air Force and catch them at the 'In Room' on the Peninsula. But it turned out there already was another band called the Warlocks. Not a bad name, actually, but I've yet to run into anyone who said that Grateful Dead wasn't a change for the better.

Bill Walker and I made the drive from Vegas to San Francisco for a benefit concert for LeMar, at which the Dead were joined on the bill by the Charlatans. California Hall, Memorial Day weekend, 1966. The Charlatans dedicated a tune to the uniformed onlookers: *We're not on the same Trip*. Long jams, a raucous *Dancin' in the Street* – it was a memorable evening, even factoring in my blue and cheery mood (appropriate to the holiday, I suppose). Bill and I just about glowed all the way up Route 101 to the Olompali ranch, just north of Novato, which was the band's residence at the time. After a couple of days staying with them, it was plain to see that the guys in the band were having the time of their lives. Mime Trouper Tom Purvis described Phil: "He blew his non-flower mind!"

Using a three day pass I'd won as Airman of the Month I managed to join them in Los Angeles during the recording sessions of *Anthem of the Sun*. The prepared piano and electronics work that I did on that album was my first real musical collaboration with the band. It seemed to come naturally out of what I'd been doing before, and their musical explorations were challenging, to say the least. So I didn't feel any decompression, polarization, or *anything* unusual in the transition from 'serious' to 'pop.' Aside from the inherent absurdity of such categories, it seemed simply a case of musicians of like mind pursuing paths of interest to them. Back up on street level after some sessions at Columbus Recorders in San Francisco, Jerry turned to me and said, "I think we can use you."

Jerry Garcia is one of the remarkable men of our times. So inventive, so assured, so alert, so amazingly aware in and out of musical contexts. He takes the responsibility personally, that the music should unfold interestingly. He doesn't need much help in doing it, but that also means that he doesn't leave much room. He's a thoroughly professional musician, with the accent on 'musician.'

The drummers, on the other hand, are as thorough in their accent of the word 'professional.' Bill, almost blasé in his steadiness, and Mickey, acrobatic and energetic beyond anyone's expectation, would shine in whatever they chose to do. But that it should be music doesn't seem to be the imperative for them that it is for Jerry.

Bob Weir is the easiest person I know of to underestimate. He possesses a wonderful sense of the ironic. His descriptions of road manager Jonathan Riester: "We hired him – to boss us around!" and extended family member Barney, Shane of Wertzplurg: "The only person I know who can misspell words he makes up!" are typical of his inciteful style. At the house he and I shared in Ross, we fought it out to a draw in Indian leg wrestling. A lot of fine guitar technique only got displayed when Jerry broke a string. I'm glad to see that he's had more of a forum for his talents since. He did me the honor of accompanying me to Las Vegas for the performance of my *Invocation of the Sun,* for soprano solo, chorus, and orchestra. For a few years I wore his prescription glasses. We'd noticed our specs were interchangeable, so I just asked him to order an extra for me. We also noticed that Jerry's, Phil's, and Owsley's optometry weren't far off from ours, either.

The feeling on meeting fellow keyboardists was almost always one of friendliness, rather than the iciness of professional jealousy. I remember an appropriately philosophical discussion with John Locke, my counterpart with the group Spirit. In the hotel room at the 'Woodstock' Festival, I enjoyed looking on as Pigpen and Nicky Hopkins talked about their musical idols with wild eyed, almost childlike enthusiasm.

Pigpen and I usually shared a hotel room on the road, and among the various pastimes we got into was chess. The 'Pig Bag' packed one of those peg-board portable chess sets. We brought our chess mania home with us, but there were other diversions as well. I recall a 'friendly' game of cutthroat (pool) with Marty Balin and Ron Polte at the Airplane house. I can't recall who won, which means it probably wasn't me.

Pigpen made Led Zeppelin awfully nervous with his six-shooter once at a photo session, drawing a bead on weather vanes and cupolas visible from Herb Greene's San Francisco loft. Didn't hit anything, but he *looked* so mean…it had to crack you up if you knew him. How much he deserved, yet how little he got out of this life. He sang the blues with the power and conviction of a prince. I hope that he's being treated accordingly this very moment.

During one of the sessions at Columbus Recorders, Pigpen was overdubbing a vocal track for *Alligator.* One of the takes started to click *so* well, was *so* compelling was *such* an evocative – I daresay perfect – word painting, that all of us in the control room were rolling on the floor in cackles and howls. Pig saw us through the glass and started chuckling, too. In the effervescence of our jollity we neglected to save the take. Besides, we figured he knew what he was doing, and could come up another one just as good anyway. We figured wrong. After you've seen the spark, it's not too hard to tell when 'it' is no longer there. So what wound up on the album was an assemblage of three solo vocals. Here's a sigh for the 'one that got away.'

The first time I heard the music through the headphones, while laying down the piano tracks for *Alligator*, it was as if I could sense the sound coming out of all the speakers that would ever play the record – from portable transistor to Dolmen Dimension sound system. I came to take things in stride that I'd find out later were unique to Grateful Dead recording sessions. Instead of hearing 'testing...one... two...three' for sound checks, there'd be Robert Hunter reciting the opening pages of *Finnegan's Wake* – by heart.

Live performance was something else again, though. Seeking relief from being positioned stage right, directly in front of four Jerry Garcia twin reverbs turned up to 10, I moved across the stage, there to be greeted by Mickey's cannons.

Life on the road can be bizarre, exhausting, frustrating, and more. But the lure remains. Like at no other time there's the feeling that *this* – playing music – is what you do. And doing that much of it is the best thing for your chops. One performance can achieve things impossible in a dozen rehearsals, in that so much attention is *focussed*. After every gig there'd be a gathering in one of our hotel rooms to check out a recording of that night's performance. Kudos, queries, and other libations flowed freely.

On the road you're surrounded by your act, if only because of how tightly your time is segmented. There's a 'merry band of rogues' sort of camaraderie that arises in this strangely insulated existence. When your path crosses that of another band, especially if you know them, it can be like a letter from home. The burden of road weariness gets a bit lighter.

We were always coming up with ways to beat boredom on the road. One week it'd be cooking up huge batches of bacon in the hotel rooms, another it'd be bottle rockets. Chalk it up to scientific curiosity if someone wants to see how high a Super Ball® would bounce if thrown from a third floor balcony onto the pavement. During one phase there was a run on Buck® knives. Even I got one. Only 'used' it once, though. One summer afternoon at home at Ross, as Weir's amour of the nonce was giving Phil a haircut, Bob was sitting on the couch, contemplating who should be the next victim of his water balloon arsenal. All I had to do was steal up behind him, give a single poke with the Buck knife...and a lapful of water signaled an end to his contemplation.

After a week or so of a routine that consists of hustling from performance to hotel to airport to another airport (they all have this 'timeless' and 'placeless' atmosphere to them, anyway) to another hotel, and finally to another performance, the band becomes your boogie board. Nothing else is stable – only your comrades in rhythm are there, day after day. Everything else changes – people, cities, buildings...the climate. Things you might ordinarily consider important and substantial get lost in the haze. An extremely hectic schedule can make it all seem like some sort of hazy 'Anytown, U.S.A.'

To find out the time of day in San Francisco, you'd dial P-O-P-C-O-R-N...in Los Angeles, try U-K-E-L-E-L-E...in New York it's N-E-R-V-O-U-S. When you travel a lot you start noticing 'types' and 'patterns.' You notice what towns have the same kind of buses or taxis. You notice television anchorpersons hundreds of miles apart who must've been in the same class at broadcasting school. You notice what brands of beer and potato chips are available in what states. Then you notice that it's a quarter past ungodly in the a.m., subfreezing outside, you've got an hour to make your flight, and the hotel's seemingly flaked out on your wake-up calls.

February, 1969 started with the second night of a two night stand at Aaron Russo's 'Kinetic Playground' in Chicago. The ensuing week took us to Minneapolis, Omaha, Kansas City, St. Louis, and wound up in Pittsburgh. Not much time for sightseeing. I had to borrow Iron Butterfly's Vox organ for the shows in St. Louis and Kansas City. Similar to the one I'd used earlier with the band (I much preferred the Hammond B-3, when it was sufficiently amplified), except this one was set up high, so you had to play it standing up. Subtracting the foot needed to work the pedal, it quite nearly left me without a leg to stand on. But there were rewards as well. For the show in Pittsburgh we shared the bill with the Fugs, and the emcee was Paul Krassner, no less.

Returning to St. Louis in early April several of us in the band went to one of its ritzier restaurants. The kind where potatoes inspire the chef to sculpture, and the waiter lights the dessert at your table. Silver tongued thespian Jon McIntire, traveling with the band as our road manager, was from there, and arranged everything. "No, sir. They are a famous Rock band. They don't even *own* neckties." The decorously decorated staff were eyeing us nervously the whole while, but we were on our best behaviour.

Later that night found us down by the river, at the base of the Gateway Arch, looking up and wondering if we could scale it if 'they' were after us. To be sure, we represented a viewpoint that was extremely unpopular with the powers that be in some places. There were needless and mindless hassles with supposed bastions of 'order' that were obviously expressions of as much hostility as they felt the law would let them get away with. The way the cop in Omaha put it, just the way we looked – in and of itself – amounted to 'asking for it.'

Another social phenomenon involved the necessity to be careful about what you drank at the gig. Once at the Fillmore West four or five sly elves decided to spike the apple juice – unbeknownst to one another. I remember Janis venting her high dudgeon at Owsley backstage that night – her trumpet player had got dosed. Poetic injustice – O. had nothing to do with this one. When it came time for us to play, Phil's bass was loosely draped over his shoulders and he was pushed onstage, muttering the while about the Fall of the Roman Empire. The scene reminded me of a Hieronymus Bosch painting. I found Robert Hunter painted onto the stairs on our way out the back door. He and Pete Grant were then decanted into their respective back seats for the ride back home across the Golden Gate Bridge.

I was careful then, but there were other times I wasn't so 'lucky.' Like the time at Bullfrog Lake in Oregon. Pigpen was singing *Easy Wind*, and suddenly I had that old familiar feeling: 'Here we go again!' It being an outdoor concert, the power came from on site generators. I was playing a Hammond B-3 at the time, and the fluctuations in the electric current affected its 'sense' of pitch. So on occasion it'd suddenly be in C-sharp, or B. And that was with Owsley taking time from among his other activities to monitor the generator's output, to keep it on or about sixty cycles.

And then there was the time in Chicago, where we achieved sonic saturation. The screens for the 360° light show had to be reinforced – fire regulations they told us, and as a result bounced the sound right back in your face with a vengeance. The 'Wall of Sound' made the music a tactile as well as auditory experience anyway, but this one really loosened my eardrums.

New York City. The complete yellow pages. Population saturation, communication nexus, geopolitical serendipity, event space density – whatever the reasons and like it or not, it was always a special place to play. There's something you can feel in the air, the exhilaration of performing for a critical but approving audience. Even the lights feel warmer. I remember several magical *Dark Stars* at the Fillmore East, even aside from the April 28, 1971 show when I sat in with the band. That one occurred during the *Tarot* project, and so I happened to be in town. The previous night, the Beach Boys sat in with the band, and Bob Dylan was in attendance. Guess which evening got written up in *Rolling Stone*.

I remember a musically warm afternoon at the Central Park bandshell; joyous, reckless abandon at the Cafe a GoGo. Once we did *Hey, Jude* as an encore at the Fillmore East. Pigpen did the vocal, and so it was modeled more on the Wilson Pickett than the Beatles version. We'd been on the lookout for 'cappers,' like *I Bid You Goodnight*, and thought we had one here. Didn't work, though – they still wanted to hear more. Or, rather, M-O-O-O-O-R-E!!!

"St. Stephen!!" the yells would come. Jerry once pointed out that if they wanted to hear that tune, it was available on two albums. One night at the Fillmore East, after who knows how many encores at the end of the first of our usual two shows, Jerry went to the microphone and said we had to stop playing, that it was house policy to clear the house for the second show. Back around upstairs in our dressing room, we were hanging out waiting to go on again when Bill Graham exploded into the room: "I never said it was policy to clear the house. You could've played one more number!" Satisfied he'd made his point, he deploded out of the room, after which Jerry said, "That was nothing. I was gonna say 'If you don't like it, don't come to places like this.'"

It was New York without walls at the 'Woodstock' Festival. The name should be qualified in that, although the original plans were for the 'Aquarian Music and Arts Fair' to occur near Woodstock, New York, the city fathers there said no go, so it was moved to a cow pasture near White Lake, New York. But the name stuck. The sheer numbers of people there was overwhelming. Larger than some cities, yet unified around the exuberant electric testimony in sound.

Los Angeles, city of dreams and illusions, sprawls like a superannuated imperial capital, with a view of everything and contact with nothing. In 1967, while there recording *Anthem of the Sun*, we had the opportunity, along with some of the Airplane folk, to have an audience with the Maharishi Mahesh Yogi. It was in the house where the photo was taken that wound up on the back of the *Gift from a Flower to a Garden* album of Donovan, who was also there that week. The Maharishi didn't especially like the band's name. "Oh, no," he said, "You should call the group 'Everlasting Life,'" through his infectiously good-natured chuckle. He gave us each a personally selected mantra[1], and as he made his grand exit, handed each of us a rose.

Another Hollywood adventure took us to Television City for an appearance on *Playboy After Dark*. The bookshelves on the set filled with mindless books not even worth stealing, other inane façades like the phony high-tech sound system behind 'my' harpsichord, the stifling *hyperformatted* work situation – all tinted the experience. Sid Caesar was the main guest, if I'm to judge by the amount of time 'Hef' spent with him. Also on that particular show was the astrologer Sidney Omarr, who ran off this marvelous spiel about rôles and personæ, ultimately boiling it down, as he put it, to the question, "Who are we?" Dramatic...persuasive...but that didn't stop the director from fading out some thirty seconds before the end.

We were supposed to be the band in the movie *Zachariah*. It got as far as touring the M.G.M. back lot, getting fitted for costumes, and impacting the script, but no farther. The band even went horseback riding as a group a couple of times out at Mickey's ranch in Novato. They found a sufficiently comatose mare named 'Peace' for me.

Part of the Alchemical equation is that not every project you get involved with will be blessed with glowing success. I met Timothy Leary at the 'Big Rock Pow-Wow' in Florida, on a Seminole reservation just north of Miami. He was running for governor of California at the time, and invited us to play at his inaugural ball. Now, *that* would have been interesting!

---

[1] The mantras are simple to intone, and different ones can put you in different places. But be it ever so hummable, there's no place like 'Om.'

Altamont might stand out as another example, but there are yet others. We were hired, for instance, to play at the 1969 Black and White Ball, an annual benefit extravaganza for the San Francisco Symphony. The original idea was to dress up in those black and white striped prisoner outfits made famous in the old time movies, but that proved impracticable. The ones we settled on weren't too shabby, though – Jerry was a pirate, Mickey was Zorro, and I had an eighteenth century bell ringer costume complete with three cornered hat. All this in black and white. It would have been a smashing success, if only the P. A. system could have been ready a few hours sooner. Like, by curtain time.

In the preparatory meetings with the Symphony people, Phil and I suggested the possibility of a musical collaboration between the band and the orchestra. I'd envisioned (enauditioned?) a latter day concerto grosso with plenty of interaction among the sonic forces. They all but laughed in our faces. So much for orchestral dreaming. A couple of years down the road the Symphony did a Bill Russo number featuring Corky Siegel. Vapid. Unimaginative. Dull. A duel between the blues and the classics with both contestants leaving their weapons at home. At the time I hadn't realized what a playground for cretins symphony management was.

As much fun as I had in the making of *Aoxomoxoa*, I wasn't as much of an influence as some might think. It's easy to overlook the fact that the band members' tastes already tended toward the far out. I've mentioned Phil's propensities, but Jerry had broad tastes as well. He had kind words for my *Sonatina* and a tone clustery *Cadenza* that I played for him in 1962. And then there was the evening Bill and I tuned in the radio to John Cage's *Variations IV*, which made everything after it sound like a continuation.

*What's Become of the Baby* was mainly Jerry's project. The trans-Moogrifications and pre-echoes of the vocal track, the freely-freaking accompaniment – in its original form it's a bit busy in places, not necessarily 'my' style of experimental, but I still like it, and don't make any apologies. It was a legitimate development of *Barbed Wire Whipping Party*, which struck me as a bit nihilistic at first but has since grown on me.

Everyone in the band was/is his own individual, and interests vary, but that's not to say there wasn't a fair amount of interplay. Jerry turned me on to the *Urantia Book*, and I in turn loaned him the volume of Hazrat Inayat Khan's *A Sufi Message* that deals with music. If you figure that two heads are better than one, seven should be close to critical mass!

There was a give and take of ideas musical and otherwise. Phil and Jerry had suggested the descending F major scale I played on *Alligator*, and the 'nah, na-nah' figure on *China Cat Sunflower*. Contrariwise, if you were to check the older concert tapes you'll hear the organ playing what later became a guitar lead-in to the bridge of *High Time* on *Workingman's Dead*.

It's supremely enjoyable for a band not to have to be an android jukebox. The extended improvisations in tunes like *Dark Star* and *Lovelight* were often where we and the audience alike got off the most. Much of what happened was nailed down during our extensive rehearsals, but a lot was left flapping to the breeze. Rehearsals were also the place to try out new songs and experiment with new material. There was a slow ten figure that we'd run through from time to time, like some sort of conceptual chewing gum. It was amusing to notice it later in the middle section of *Playin' in the Band...* which I no longer was by that time.

Why that was had a number of causes, not all of which are clear even now. Scientology is mentioned. Even as I was touring with the band I was completing the Dianetic Auditor's Course at the San Francisco Org (the H.S.D.C. – while logging the auditing hours for my certificate I accumulated enough material for a science fiction anthology). Certainly it was no help, but there were other factors that deserve consideration.

William S. Burroughs exhorted us to "try and make it without any chemical corn," and I figured that if ever there were a chance to put that to the acid test (so to speak), this was it. What people put in their own bodies is their own business, and I make no judgment on it, but throughout my entire stint with the band I never intentionally partook in any of the psychedelic sacraments. Still, as far as drugs are concerned, I'm pro-choice. The Ninth Amendment mentions rights accruing to the people. Wherefore this zeal to dam them at the State level?

Of more immediate importance was the matter of the instrument I had to play. Or didn't have. About the same time as I joined the band full time the Hammond organ that Pigpen had been playing got repossessed. Problems with banks prevented me from getting a piano on three occasions. The third was a heartbreaker. I had an opportunity to buy a nineteenth century vintage Bösendorfer grand for under a thousand dollars. A Swiss woman had to sell it because she was moving. An appeal to the Grateful Dead office for assistance was to no avail. I could have paid off an advance in a matter of weeks, but their indecision was final. The whole time I was with the band I had no instrument at home to practice on. The mismatch of desire and opportunity is perhaps the cruelest trick Nature plays on us.

On stage, I was chronically underamplified. As a result, my dynamic range consisted of *triple forte, double forte,* and (anything below that) inaudible. Consequently I was never able to find a comfortable platform amid the band's texture wherefrom to express anything cogent. The pulse of the music is a very real, perceptible thing, but usually I felt as if I were groping for it in the dark. Like overdubbing a track while sequestered in a separate room, I felt baffled, remote, unable to get a fix on even my own contributions to the mix.

Considering the fact that the sometimes truculent directions I got from the band members were often mutually contradictory, and comparing the problems more experienced players, like Vince Guaraldi and Howard Wales, encountered in interacting with the band, I began to suspect that some of the band members themselves didn't have that clear an idea of the keyboard's rôle in a guitar band context.

Not that I did, either. It seemed that the basic rock trio – like Cream or the Jimi Hendrix Experience – pretty much covered the territory. Even Weir had to stay alert for openings to place his rhythm guitar patterns. Beyond that is garnish, quite nearly in the Fugsian sense. It was gratifying for Jerry to tell me to play "more like a source and less like a sideman," but as Pigpen had already demonstrated, when the keyboard assumed a more active rôle, the mix became something else. My 'thing' wasn't developed enough yet to stake out its territory in the texture, and it was becoming increasingly clear that that break wasn't coming.

I'd played before large crowds in Vegas, but I still felt like a rookie joining a championship team when I joined the band. There's a reluctance to mess with a winning formula. I figured that this configuration deserved nothing less that an original groundbreaking approach, such as Phil was doing with his bass work. Slowly – too slowly, some might contend – that was what I set out to do at the keyboard. One of the band members suggested that I'd've been better advised to imitate someone who was already 'doing it.' Aside from any philosophical disagreement I might have with the premise it was based on, I couldn't make that advice work. Patterns I'd 'appropriated' from Gregg Rolie or Garth Hudson wouldn't fly in rehearsals.

It was unsettling enough for Phil to pointedly remark how much he preferred Howard Wales's playing when he sat in with the band. But what really hurt was his apparent insensitivity to the fact that Howie's system was driving twice as many Leslie speakers as mine. Still, I can't come down too hard on Phil. For one thing, despite his occasional autocratic high-handedness (he'd expressed admiration of that quality in the likes of Richard Wagner and Herbert von Karajan), I've never been able to stay mad at him for long. Four years and four days my senior, he was the older brother I never had, an elfin, playful soul one counts oneself blessed for having known. For another thing, I could sense the disappointment in his voice – he was one of a handful of people in my life who'd believed in me, and translated that belief into action. It's not too hard to imagine band discussions in my absence where Phil's was the lone voice taking up the cudgel on my behalf.

It was quite another matter, however, for Owsley to serve up the warmed over homily "a good worker never blames his tools" when I tried to explain that I couldn't get behind the sound of the Vox organ they had for me to play when I first joined the band full time. An identical instrument served Terry Riley's purposes eminently well in *A Rainbow in Curved Air*, but in the context of electric guitars it came off as thin and nasal sounding. Setting aside the fact that every major keyboard player since Bach has asserted that the instrument you play *does* make a difference, it's inconsiderate, even *stupid,* to disregard the performer's own preference, even if based on nothing more than subjectivity.

I wish I could have seen more of the artistic and philosophical side of the man, but I remember little else of Owsley than interpersonal gamesmanship and power trips. That and the Gospel of Red Meat. No doubt my metabolic recalcitrance must've rubbed him the wrong way, but some have explained his actions as being rooted in a desire to be one of the members of the band. He's been called a 'super-groupie.' As low man on the totem pole, I must have represented a safe target for him. If it had been either Phil or Jerry saying simply "I like this axe better," not only would he have raised no objection, no doubt he'd have fallen all over himself coming up with reasons to agree.

Perhaps it's inevitable, a post-revolutionary disillusionment syndrome, but it was profoundly disturbing to see the same closed-minded old 'I'm right, you're wrong' attitude that's the badge of fundamentalists of every stripe. Each of us vows not to repeat the mistakes of the past, but who knows whether by that very same process we perpetuate the aberration?

All the same, the meeting in the hotel room in New Orleans where the plans for our musical parting of the ways were drafted was as cordial and supportive as anyone could imagine under the circumstances. And as Phil said, it didn't preclude interesting intersections in the future...

# 6/ LIFE AFTER THE DEAD

*"...our lot is to be hurled into inconceivable new worlds."*
don Juan Matus

**M**ardi Gras. New Orleans. Ingredients such as these should make for an eventful weekend, and we certainly weren't disappointed. Our hotel was right on Bourbon Street. *Vieux Carre*, the wrought iron, the narrow streets. Pigpen and I felt like kids again wandering through the antique gun shops on Royal Street the afternoon before our first show.

And the music! Downstairs in our hotel, Earl 'Fatha' Hines was playing in the lounge. Within a short walk was a gourmet's gamut of Southern Fried Jazz. Ironic, then, that it should be my last gig as a member of the band. But that story suddenly found itself taking the back seat to a heavier one: the 'Great New Orleans Bust.'

Pigpen and I had already called it a night by the time that the police broke down the door. If they'd have come to our room first instead of last, there might not have been a bust at all. We were totally clean. They found it hard to believe, but it was true. In any case, that left us free to get on the phone back to California to try and get things back to abnormal.

It wasn't as if there hadn't been any warning, contrary to what you might have heard in *Truckin'*. The Airplane had just taken the same tour, including the trip Downtown where they take your picture and all, and Pigpen was even stopped and given a friendly admonition in the hall by the house dick: "We're watchin' you!" Nothing like Southern hospitality. So next day the band was back on the street, and in true bar-the-door-after-the-horses fashion, moved to a much less atmospheric place comfortably closer to the airport.

And I never got to hear Earl 'Fatha' Hines.

After the discussion about my leaving the band I went to the gig anyhow through sheer force of habit. In the onsetting numbness I remember little more than standing behind the amplifiers until Jerry beckoned me to the keyboard with his eyes. The second night I didn't even go.

Still, it wasn't as if they were casting me adrift in musical Limbo. There was another project a-brewing where there'd be more for me to do. More room to stretch out on my own. I hadn't been getting off like I knew I could in the context of the band, and it couldn't help but be noticed. Moreover, it may have been a smaller pond I was moving to, but I'd get to be a bigger fish.

I found myself rehearsing what was to become *Tarot* with musicians like Peter Rowan, Richard Greene, and Mickey Hart. There were even a few gigs around the Bay Area, playing behind the show's driving force, mime Joe McCord (a.k.a. The Rubber Duck, and later Dolphin the Mime). Ron Wilson and David Garthwaite (brother of Terry) managed to find time off from the Joy of Cooking to join us a few times. Don Buchla even sat in with us, with his 'Buchla box' synthesizer, one night at Mandrake's in Berkeley. By late fall, 1970, the show was ready to take to New York – there was a commitment from the Chelsea Theater Center in Brooklyn to mount it. The East was beckoning yet again.

Before we hit the road there was an invitation from the Incredible String Band, extended through Peter Grant, to work on the album of their mime show *U*. Coincidence strikes again. I'd met Robin Williamson on the grassy runway of the White Lake airport, while we were awaiting our helicopter rides into the 'Woodstock' Festival. After a few meetings with him and Mike Heron I prepared a chart and brought it to Pacific Recorders in San Mateo for the session. This was familiar territory to me – some of *Aoxomoxoa* had been done there – but as chaotic as Grateful Dead sessions could be (especially mix-downs), these were serene. Producer Joe Boyd achieved a creditable balance between keeping things moving along and staying out of our hair. I conducted the ensemble in my arrangement as we added it to the tracks already recorded, and then overdubbed a piano track of my own.

Sea and I had been living together for a couple of years before we made it official. Pigpen had been both 'father of the bride' and 'best man' at the ceremony. She and I had met in the sixties when she was living in one of those houses in the Haight that was like a nonstop psychedelic party. Our first meeting was typical of the times: I was in the tub with Bill Walker and a young lady when Sea walked into the large Victorian style bathroom where the party was happening at that moment.

There was the matter of a few months between moving out of our house in Novato and starting the rehearsals in New York. Pigpen said we could stay in his new place, a few miles away in another part of Novato, while the band went on tour. It was a weirdly built house, one where you had to go through the bathroom to get to the bedrooms. But suddenly the tour was cancelled, and we had to pull up stakes again.

David Driscoll, one of the more personable and helpful people I'd met in Scientology, had set up a candle factory with his lady Clementine in East Oakland, and offered to put us up at their house in Alameda. Another weird building – Dave once estimated that he could kick it apart inside of forty-eight hours. No hammers, tools – nothing but a good, sturdy pair of boots. Ideally, the house should have been razed, and a new one built on the site. According to current building code, however, it was situated on a lot that was too small to build a house on, so that would have been illegal. Unsafe as it was, however, the house violated no laws.

As a last resort we went to Las Vegas for a few icy weeks. My last memory of my mother was her shoving a magazine in my face, listing shows opening in New York that season, and demanding to know how come *Tarot* wasn't on it. It seemed as if she thought she'd 'found me out,' that I'd made up the whole thing about there being

a show at all with some ulterior, no doubt questionable, motive. My
failure to recant my 'heresy' aggravated her all the more.

One thing that made the whole visit worthwhile, though, was the
chance to visit Mr. Iddings again. As friendly and encouraging as
ever, he invited me to his house on Pyramid Avenue where I played
him some of the numbers from *Tarot*, and he played me some of his
own favorites. Now and again he'd complain about how his technique wasn't 'there' for him anymore. I didn't make much of it at the
time. Neither of us knew he had just a week left to live. How glad I
am I got to see him.

The musicians that went East to do *Tarot* included Gary 'Chicken'
Hirsh, of Country Joe and the Fish fame, and in whose Berkeley
house I was married for the first time; Paul Dresher, guitarist/
flutist/sitarist/and musician extraordinaire – it's been a delight to
watch his career unfold since; Wes Steele, bassist, since then moved
'upstairs' at Lawrence Berkeley Laboratories; Jim Byers, a Michael
Lorimer guitar student; the peripatetic violinist, Art Fayer; and
myself on keyboards. The troupe was known as the Rubber Duck
Company, so naturally enough we were the Rubber Band.

Since I'd come from there to begin with, this amounted to yet
another trip *back* East. Already my directions were getting confused.
One Saturday shortly after our arrival I was on the way to an
audition (we were in the process of assembling the cast) blissfully
unaware of the fact that subway schedules – even the routes certain
lines took – changed on the weekend. Later on, after I'd got to know
the system, I still couldn't figure how I'd got to where I got to.

We'd been invited to stay with 'friends' – potential musical
collaborators, in fact – in a brownstone apartment overlooking
Tompkins Square Park. That turned out to be one of those shallow
showbiz pleasantries with nothing behind it, so the first opportunity that presented itself we moved to the building in Brooklyn
where most of the band was housed. It was closer to the theater
where the show was happening, but still our basement apartment
was far from a honeymoon suite. Equally distant (I paced it off) from
four different subway stops, the house was in a Haitian neighborhood. Things were dicey enough that, as a precaution, Paul Dresher
would bring the battery of his truck into the house every night.

Frank Constanten.
T–Sgt., U.S. Army. 1946.

Tom Constanten in the mid-forties.
Deal, New Jersey.

Lilian Sture. Early 1940's.

Tom Hills. 1940's.

Bestefar in the garden. Late 1940's.

Tom Constanten
at 11 years.
5th Grade class photo,
West Charleston School,
Las Vegas. Nevada, 1955.

'Home' in the Las Vegas
Desert. Late 1950's.

The mountains of
northern Mexico.
July, 1960.
Photo by T.C.

T.C. at the piano with
the Las Vegas 'Pops'
Orchestra, Antonio
Morelli, conductor.
Las Vegas Convention
Center. May 28, 1961.
Photo by Pacey.

With the Grateful Dead,
Novato, California. 1969.
Photo by Rosie McGee.

With Luciano Berio,
Lingueglietta, Italy.
Fall of 1962.
Photo by Bernard Rands.

On the Paisley Tea
House with Jan Wooley.
Channel 20,
San Francisco.
September 26, 1972.
Photo by Mark Van
Amringe.

At the Old Waldorf club,
San Francisco.
June 19, 1983.
Photo by Ed Perlstein.

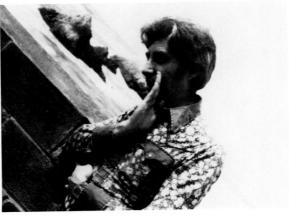

At Point Lobos,
San Francisco,
1983. Photos by
Christopher
Coppola.

*Village Voice* reviewer Carman Moore came to see *Tarot* during the run in Brooklyn (with Berio, whom I remember faintly applauding) and described the mix as 'magical.' As house lights dim and incense flavors the air, a turtle character crawls toward the stage, making his way through the audience seated on the mats up front. Joe McCord delighted in the fact that the cheap seats were closest to the stage – on the floor like the 'old days' in the Haight. The turtle climbs onto the stage and...the show is on!

The run at the Chelsea Theater Center was for a fixed duration, but there was some interest generated in moving the show to Manhattan. What that meant to us was a series of showcase performances (for potential backers), and a few reprises of the mime *cum* music show. Once at the Village Gate we were billed between a rock band called Farmer John and one called The Factory. I couldn't resist commenting – I announced the numbers as well as played the piano – on how proletarian it made us feel to be appearing between an agricultural and an industrial organization.

Just when it looked like we were all set to move the show into the Circle in the Square on Bleecker Street – almost exactly across the street from the Village Gate – one of the major backers suddenly and inexplicably pulled out. The remaining producer, Richard Fields, using all his ingenuity, got United Artists Records to make up the difference as part of an 'original cast album' deal. It still wound up being a pretty lean winter. How lean? Our Xmas tree was drawn in crayon and thumbtacked to the wall.

One good thing that came out of that basement apartment in Brooklyn was the chance for me to finish the score to *Idyll of Sea and Mountains,* a symphonic piece that I'd begun at Novato. An elaboration of some of the material from *Invocation to the Sun,* it was eventually performed at the University of Nevada, Las Vegas by the University Chamber Orchestra, G. Keith Moon conducting[1].

There were a few other opportunities to pursue. Richard Fields put me in touch with a Belgian playwright named Andre Ernotte. He had a brief appearance in the film *The French Connection* as an interpreter. He was from Bruxelles, so naturally enough we got into the 'Oh, do you know so-and-so' thing and – what do you know – we knew everybody! He'd come up with an outline for a play about six failed suicides, a fifteen-year-old girl, a twenty-five-year-old

[1] March 5, 1972.

man, a thirty-five-year-old woman, and so on. I met him a couple of times at this luxy flat in the eighties, overlooking Central Park. They had an original Rembrandt hanging in the hall. That kind of place. Nothing came of it, but it was fun while it lasted.

New York, of course, is a great place to network, to make connections, to get things done. Weeks went by, filled with meetings and signings in plush midtown offices belonging to United Artists, or one of several attorneys. We were represented by Robert F. Levine, whose office was reached by your typical Madison Avenue astronautical elevator ride. There we were initiated into arcane mysteries, like 10% of 90%. Back in the days of 78 r.p.m. records, you see, they assumed that 10% of them would break in transit. So they factored that into computing the artist's royalty. Fascinating. But we began to get antsy to get back to playing music.

*Tarot* had evolved quite a bit during the run in Brooklyn. A lot of dead wood was cut out, and new ideas, when they worked, were kept. One of the members of the troupe, actor John Proctor Parriott, gave me my first view of the depth and breadth of which the acting craft is capable. During the course of both runs, he played most of the major rôles, and was a major factor in defining them. One major change in the show that moved to Manhattan was the complete absence of words. The earlier version was graced by the sleek vocalizations of Yolande Bavan. Strange, but true, there were actually two songs – complete with words!

A lot of encouraging portents were coming together, but even doubling the box-office week after week wasn't enough. The Equity stake ran out and that was that. Having played the music for lo those many weeks, though, we were able to put down all the tracks for the projected two-record set in four six-hour sessions at Electric Lady Studios. Built by Jimi Hendrix for himself, the studio was lavishly equipped and psychedelically appointed. Some of the staff even reported having encountered his ghost in the halls. In these plush surroundings we recorded the material that had become so familiar to us in the past few months. *The Moon* was done on the first take, and none of the other numbers took very much longer. Well...*The Mystic Carpenter* took twenty-eight tries, but at least half of them had to be scrapped because the tape machine developed a problem holding to proper speed. And the record button was lamentably off during a monumental Paul Dresher guitar solo for the Fool's encounter with *The Star*.

The experience of doing *Tarot* helped the band, renamed Touchstone for the Manhattan run, to jell, and we packed it up for Southern California with good intentions and great expectations. Michael Butler, the producer of the enormously successful show *Hair*, had come to see *Tarot* in New York. He had a rock musical version of *Frankenstein* in the works and signed me to do the music on the strength of what he'd heard in *Tarot*. He ultimately went through five scriptwriters, none of whom could come up with a script that grabbed him. Meanwhile, there we were in West Hollywood, trying to scare up what leads we could, waiting for things to 'happen.'

There was theoretically an option for a second Touchstone album. We certainly had the material, and there were details – cover photos and such – to be wrapped up on the *Tarot* project. But dealing on a day to day basis with a record company proved to be an eye opener. I never was so naive as to figure that they were in the business to promote the music – they're only in it to make money. But it was something of a surprise to find that they didn't do *that* well, either.

As a teenager tooling down the Las Vegas Strip, listening to my car radio, I thought I had a fairly good idea of what it took to make a hit record. But as I got closer to the centers of production, a thick fog seemed to cloud everyone's mind – including mine. Mike Stewart, then president of United Artists Records, told me in almost as many words that they'd have been more interested in our band if we'd had some flack in there hyping us to them at the record company. An amazing number of records are released every week, and the usual practice among the industry was not to get behind any album (especially a 'first album') unless it grew legs and took off by itself, and fast.

It wasn't as if we didn't have the credentials. By current Industry standards, we had a legitimate claim to Supergroup status, seeing as I'd just left the Dead and Chicken had been a Fish. But in the absence of full time (or at least hotshot) management the band's relationship with the record company began to deteriorate. Friendly A. & R. man Eli Bird was replaced by Dan 'Tell Them I'm Not In' Burguoise. Patti Johnson, who'd signed us in New York, was canned – an ominous sign. What had been our tightly conceived two record package suddenly had to be cut to one. I suppose I should be thankful they gave us the choices of what to axe. And even that wouldn't've been released had not Richard Fields threatened to sue the record company for breach of contract.

The band's relationship with Richard Fields didn't end up as idyllically as it could have, for all that he did for us. Without naming names, it seemed that someone saw that things weren't going to go their way, and wasn't above trying to make sure that 'our way' wouldn't work, either. I sometimes wonder whether, as a result of that backbiting, Richard Fields ever had any intent to come out West and help the band get established, as he'd assured us he would.

Coincidentally, in the next apartment building from where we were living there lived a band with a few Richard Fields stories of their own. He'd managed them in New York as well! One evening I found one of them hanging out in front of their place. "How are things?" I asked. "Pretty bad..." was the cheery reply. "You don't seem too broke up over it." "Well, you know...they're pretty bad...until they're pretty good." He went on to explain that they'd had an album in the can and ready to move. Unfortunately, on the very day that it was to be released, the record company folded.

Our apartment was one of those egg crate affairs so common in West Hollywood. Even at that it was much more like a real abode than the swampy cellar in Brooklyn, and as such it was Sea's and my first place together. About then she decided she wanted a dog, and Cheri Cleland, a high school friend from Las Vegas and Bill Walker's cousin, volunteered to find us one. By the time she called: "Well, I found you a dog...real sweet personality...but...well, you see...it's blue and it has no tail," it fairly blended into the SoCal circus. So we welcomed in a female Australian Shepherd named 'Quillybung.'

Virtually around the corner from our place was the statue of Bullwinkle, a longtime idol of mine. Street and place names fabled on the silver screen and in Frank Zappa songs were everyday sights. The excitement of Sunset Strip was a few short steps from our door.

Often, the action would come to us, like the time our next door neighbor almost blew up the building. There were two explosions, forcibly punctuating what would have been just another lazy Los Angeles afternoon. The first one almost knocked me off my feet, and we realized right away that it'd be a good idea to get outside post haste. A smart move, because no sooner were we out when the big one came – it blew out the windows of his apartment both front and back!

A call brought the Fire Department promptly, and when they went in to check the damage we found out how incredibly lucky we'd been. Turns out this guy was in the explosive commodity business. After the sheriffs took him away it took four of them four hours to unload the place. There were hand grenades, cyanide (luckily the firemen didn't hit it with the water), and some fifty-sixty thousand dollars in cash. A veritable munitions warehouse, and it had been but a few short yards from where I lay me down to sleep every night! The landlady was baffled: "I can't understand it. He was such a nice, pleasant boy. Always paid his rent on time – sometimes he was even early."

Another interesting project that amounted to a spectacular fizzle was the film version of Carlos Castaneda's saga – life with the brujo don Juan. I was all but signed to do the score. It got as far as discussing musical possibilities and special effects with the show's would-be producer, Mark Silliphant (son of Stirling, of *Shaft* fame). There was talk that Victor Jory would be cast as the old magician. Evidently Carlos tired of Tinseltown, felt there was another book (or six) to write, or something, because abruptly interest in the project vanished.

By this time it was clear that it'd be one uphill battle after another. Out of ten (your mileage may vary) outlines, one becomes a treatment; out of ten of those one becomes a script; even fewer of those ever get shot; and then the product has to be completed, released, and distributed – with hazards and hassles at every turn.

Schönberg once composed an *Accompaniment to a Cinematographic Scene* – it's his Opus 34 – but he didn't have any particular movie in mind. His philosophy was, "I'll write the music and then you fit the picture to it." I'd like to think that my approach is a bit more flexible than that. The music is, after all, only part of a multidisciplinary whole. But that doesn't justify the contemptuous manner with which musicians are often treated. Even the textbooks stress how 'established' composers had better be ready to see their work butchered.

The ludicrously overrated film *2001 – A Space Odyssey* has revived the practice of cutting and pasting stock – in this case 'classical' – musical selections like so much aural wallpaper. You may say that you can't argue with the results[2], but I submit that anyone with tastes as finely developed as a film director can go to his record library and pick out ten albums at random. Seven will fit any given scene 'asking' for music. Three will fit well enough to uncork the champagne to celebrate an inspired choice! Even composers of 'original' music tend to be slavishly derivative. Once upon a time the rage was Franck and Rachmaninoff. The current recipe would have you start with a base of hearty Holst stock, stir in some Wagner for flair, add a dash of Stravinsky for spice, and *voilà!* Prime cut movie music!

On the other hand, I've also seen what can result from a director working with a composer toward a common, handcrafted goal, unique to their purpose. Thanks in no small way to my longtime chum (we were classmates at Rancho High in Vegas in the fifties) Rick Kaczmarczyk, I had the occasion to score (and record) music for a Jeremy Paul Kagan feature length film project. Jeremy is something of an anomaly in 'Hollywood' in that he is both sensible and sensitive musically – extensive brain racking turns up no other examples in my memory. Of either. Evidently they're as rare as equilateral trapezoids.

This in that zoo which is Hollywood. Before long you see certain specimens recurring: the junior exec who doesn't know diddly but is IN CHARGE of the recording session; the coddled quasi-stars who look right through you; the patronizing publicists who talk right through you; the go-getter promoters who walk right through you; the overqualified Art Director who'd be head of a national museum in his home country, if he could go back.

Jeremy's film was titled *The Love Song of Charles Faberman* (replacing an intriguing working title of *Palindrome)*, and was an oasis of sanity. For the first time I can remember, it was a completely open creative relationship. Rather than fearing to express an opinion – the

[2] One of the lessons of Watergate is that success not only can, but on occasion *should* be argued with.

'yes man' mentality – I felt free to tell him what I thought. More often than not he was thinking along the same lines already. We saw eye to eye about virtually everything, and planning the musical scoring was a pleasure. We scheduled two days of recording sessions at the American Film Institute's Doheny mansion. 'Greystone,' it was called, and the old place in the hills above Sunset Boulevard was the scene of many an intense drama – and not always for the cameras.

The first day's session involved a string quartet including Yukiko Kamei and Milton Thomas (he was on my first Boulez record!) Among the pieces of mine that we did was music for a scene at an Italian restaurant, and some 'imitation' Mozart...or was it Schubert? They'd rented a drippingly classy Neupert two manual harpsichord for me to play. Yielding to temptation, I laid down some Bach and Scarlatti tracks 'to check the sound.' The next day Touchstone, now with George Suranovich on drums (he'd been with Arthur Lee's group, Love), recorded.

It was the only film I've worked on where I had the opportunity to see the final result screened, and a festive occasion that turned out to be. It was shown in the same hall at A.F.I. where we'd made the recordings, and most of the cast were in attendance. John Cassavetes was there, and had some kind words for the film, but alas that's about all that came of it. It was shown, I'm told, at the film festival in Mannheim, Germany, but was never 'released' in the U. S. A.

About that time George Suranovich started playing behind Eric Burdon, in a group called Tovarish (a 'Gollywood' transliteration of the Russian word for 'comrade'). Their keyboardist was none other than Terry Ryan! It was great to share some time with him again amid our respective treadmills. Playing guitar for them was a tremendously talented guitarist named John Sterling. One time after another, on the verge of one form or another of success, he'd have his plans upended in midstream. Some sort of karmic autodestruct. . . gives me pause to contemplate.

One great opportunity that I'm glad didn't fall through was the chance to participate in the piano master classes with Mario Feninger. These were held at his house, up Nichols Canyon just below Mulholland Drive, and I wound up going regularly the entire summer of 1971. Possessor of secrets and powers, he provided a shining example of how 'music' and 'magic' differ by only two letters. To know him is to understand how virtuosi like Liszt could have been regarded as demigods. A onetime student of Edwin Fischer, he'd worked out his ideas on the physiology of playing with Raymond Thiberge in Paris, and generously shared the many subtleties he'd mastered. He in effect returned control of my hands to me. From that point on I knew that the only thing between me and any music I wanted to play was a finite amount of work.

Not since the karate lessons my last year in the Air Force had I learned so much about playing with authority. But for all the thrill of taking a talent and polishing it up, there were precious few opportunities to trot it out and show it off. Touchstone moved back to the Bay Area, going through a series of drummers before settling on Gene Reffkin (who still performs with Paul Dresher). It might have been all those tunes in 'odd' meters: 10/8, 7/8, and even a rock fugue of my own composition in 17/8. But after all too few appearances the band essentially biodegraded. Our last gig was in the fall of '72 – a benefit for the McGovern campaign up in Boonville, California.

It was a muddy, rainy night. Ah, the rain again. I'd bought tickets for the A's game against the Minnesota Twins on September 25, 1972 so far in advance, they were in the front row, right next to the Twins' dugout. Monday nights were half price, so a good crowd was guaranteed, even in the Finley years. They hadn't even got an inning in before it started pouring. Somewhere I read that I was privileged to be at the first Oakland Athletics game ever to be rained out (there have since been others, but those are other stories). It would've been great to cash in my rain check the next night. The seat location wouldn't've been anywhere as choice, but the promise of a twi-night doubleheader made up for it some: two games for the price of one-half.

But we had plans for the next night. Touchstone were the featured guests on the *Paisley Teahouse* on KEMO-TV, Channel 20 in San Francisco. Among the commercial breaks, the show consisted of six six-minute segments. Three consisted of the band playing. In between was your proverbial rappy snappartée between me and the show's host, winsome Jan Wooley.

As it turned out, Tuesday night in Oakland was rained out, too, so I got my twi-nighter on Wednesday (the A's won both games in extra innings on RBI singles by Sal Bando), but there wasn't too much happening for me the next few years, except for another extended run at the Post Office, this time in Oakland. Other than planting the seeds of my solo piano act by playing Sunday after-noons at the Sweetwater Saloon in Mill Valley, there wasn't much to write home about, until I was rescued by an invitation to join in the fun at the Center for the Creative and Performing Arts at the State University of New York at Buffalo. Winter like I'd never known...the notorious 'lake effect'...losing a yardstick trying to measure the depth of the snow...a white Easter...all these things awaited me and still I was looking forward to it.

Based at the State University of New York at Buffalo, the Center for the Creative and Performing Arts was ostensibly a performing ensemble (flexible in size and make-up) specializing in new music. We put on concerts monthly at that massive architectural contradic-tion in terms overlooking the Scajaquada Expressway, the Albright-Knox Art Gallery. Even the name has a split personality. In addition there were numerous presentations at Baird Hall on the Main Street S.U.N.Y. campus. Among its directorate were Lukas Foss and Lejaren Hiller.

Back in the fifties in Las Vegas, I'd heard some of Lukas Foss's compositions on the New York Philharmonic broadcast concerts. There was a delightfully witty mini-opera, Hellos and Good-byes. The entire work, running eight to ten minutes, consisted of the host and hostess greeting their party guests upon their arrival, and then felicitating them on their departure.

On another broadcast, in advance of its appearance on disc, they performed his *Time Cycle*. It was curious how much interest the serialists had in rendering the most precisely controlled image possible, yet how little they had in what it might be an image *of*. The way that some in the Darmstadt camp would, for instance, number all the notes in their Webern scores according to their place in the tone row seems an exercise in futility. Like, nobody hears these relations. Webern himself indicated his apprehension of that fact by his predilection for combinatorial series. A twelve note pattern would consist of three or four smaller patterns, in various orienta-

tions. The additional reiteration, Webern reasoned, would aid comprehensibility. Foss eschewed all that hypermeticulousness in *Time
Cycle* and went straight for the wondrous sonorities that the better
new pieces were revealing. The result was a far more faithful setting
of the texts than was possible with the strict cookie-cutter style
application of serial technique.

Though there were purists who shook their heads, I enjoyed his
flamboyant style – the double length baton, the grand gestures, the
finely sculptured phrase. Those who abide in the ivory towers of
academe may well decry acts that are all glossy exterior with no
content beneath, but it should be pointed out that it's possible to err
in the opposite direction as well. Lukas Foss never lost sight of the
fact that the great works are great not only because they uplift but
also because they entertain. A pianist and conductor with an appreciation of showmanship, he nevertheless struck me as a paragon of
scholarly thoroughness. I remember a wonderful concert at Ojai's
woodsy outdoor amphitheatre where he joined Andre Previn and
Leo Smit, each of them playing and conducting, in turn, a different
Mozart piano concerto[3]. What a bouquet of interpretative styles!

I'd encountered him at the U.C.L.A. Composers' Symposium
and at the Ojai Festival in 1962. He was kind enough to praise my
piece for two pianos for its 'lucid sonorities.' One thing that he said
in Buffalo will always stick with me: "You can't be a genius every
measure." Just keeping that in mind can work like a talisman against
writer's block and other stresses. Bach and Mozart, for example,
didn't build their reputations on their recitatives.

I'd read Lejaren Hiller's article in the December, 1959 issue of
*Scientific American*, and remembered his fascinating but rudely
received lectures at Darmstadt[4], so I was really looking forward to
meeting him. I discovered a sense of humor – in the music as well as
in the person – that belied the professorial image. His *Fourth String
Quartet*, also known as the *Illiac Suite*, was the subject of the *Scientific
American* article, and remains the most rigorous, yet most accessible
example of computer-assisted composition that I know of. His
doctorate, incidentally, is in chemistry.

The Buffalo String Quartet gave an animated performance of the
Hiller *Sixth Quartet* that season[5]. It was clear that there was more

[3]May 18, 1962.          [4]July 17-18, 1963.          [5]June 16, 1975.

LIFE AFTER THE DEAD

going on in this piece than the usual maxicaphonic babble so fashionable in academic circles. There was sweep, movement, direction – *Zweck*, as they say in German. There were many amusing moments in his electronic one-act opera *Cuthbert Bound*. It's sort of a *Waiting for Godot* among the Bound family, who spend the whole time fretfully awaiting a relative named Cuthbert.

The nouveau Boulangeriste Yvar Mikhashoff was kind enough to put me up my first few days there. His sparkling performance of the Ives *Concord Sonata* was one of the highlights of the concert season. I would, and have, voted for him for President. Yvar's roommate, the pianist Neal Hatch, helped us to find an apartment, a third floor flat near Delaware Park, and to get settled in. When we bemoaned not being able to find any Mexican food in the area, Neal, a Texan, said "No problem. We'll just drop by Bells market and pick up a can of tortillas." Yup.

The university was also the home base of Morton Feldman. This refugee from the garment district reminded me of nothing so much as a Dick Tracy character. His career was scarcely more than a ride on John Cage's coat tails, and if his music is incredibly dilute, the sleaziness of his personality certainly wasn't. "Find a string and pull it" seemed to be his motto, both personally and artistically. He was clearly not so much into composing as 'composering.' It was apparent that if he didn't think you'd curtseyed deeply enough, or were of some use to him, he'd make as if you didn't even exist! When I tried to congratulate him at the Buffalo Philharmonic's première of his *String Quartet and Orchestra* , all I got by way of reply was a stare and (maybe – I'm not sure) a grunt. This was in stark contrast to the disarming openness of John Cage and the warm matter-of-factness of Earle Brown (in him they are no contradiction in terms).

Among my fellow Creative Associates was the outstanding pianist Joseph Kubera. A diligent exponent of Cage, Hauer, and ragtime, he was the first other than myself to perform my post-rag pieces. In fact, he was in on the action so early, when he played the *Green and Gold Take the Cakewalk* on his WBFO 'Breakfast Concert[6],' the final strain hadn't been written yet.

On Election night, 1974, he invited me to participate in a marathon performance of Satie's *Vexations*. That performance, which went on for twenty hours and involved more than a dozen pianists

[6] February 24, 1975.

(playing in half hour shifts), was broadcast live. I recall setting my clock radio to the concert on WBFO. I then played my shifts – two-thirty to three and three-thirty to four in the morning – and headed back home to fall out. When I awoke the next day...it was still on the air!

It was also thanks to Joseph Kubera that I participated in another monster performance of the Cage *Winter Music*, this time involving eleven pianos[7]. No record breaker, but a festive event nonetheless. Thomas Putnam, the reviewer for the *Buffalo Courier-Express*, found me at my offstage post and we discussed the piece, *during its performance!* The page I'd been dealt resembled a desert landscape, so there were plenty of wide open spaces of time among the cacti and icti.

The percussionist Donald Knaack brought a finely tuned mania to the ensemble. He and his wife Peggy came to our Hallowe'en party dressed as rivets. He gave some memorable performances of Cage, Castaldi, and Duchamp. Two of the works that I wrote there – *A Giraffe of Wyne (and Thou)*, and *When You Get to the* *, benefited from his timely touch. Flutist Eberhardt Blum's most remarkable performance, curiously enough, wasn't on flute, but was the spoken *Ursonate* of the Futurist Kurt Schwitters, dating from the twenties. Violinist Ben Hudson tempered his virtuosity with a lovable zaniness that kept things interesting for us throughout the winter.

Working with a hastily assembled but resourceful group of local musicians, I put together a concert in early October, 1974 consisting mainly of numbers in Touchstone's repertoire. We did *You Know, You Know* from the Mahavishnu Orchestra – it was amusing to note that one of the critics who was there that night 'knew,' and one didn't.

As part of the promotional preliminaries for the concert, Dale Anderson, the Rock expert for the *Buffalo Evening News*, was dispatched to interview me. He turned out to be one of several people I met there who was awake and aware in a way that utterly belies the backwater image that places like Buffalo often suffer from. As 'Dempster Bucks,' he reported on the Rock scene on a local FM station, and according to the polls, Dale and Dempster were the two most popular Rock reviewers in town. That is, until his cover was

[7] June 11, 1975.

blown by the rival *Buffalo Courier-Express*, which has since gone out of business...hm...

One wintry day, soon after the blizzard that stranded two Niagara Frontier Transit buses in front of our house for several hours, I was walking along Summit Avenue and suddenly thought to myself, "Hey – it's colder than a *refrigerator* out here!" As if that represented some sort of absolute. In fact, people there will use a handy window or door to the outside in just that way – you just can't beat the great outdoors for storage space! A lot of 'absolutes' looked less absolute to me after that winter.

The heater in my car, a powder blue '65 Dodge Coronet, didn't work the entire time I was in Buffalo. That didn't make as much difference as you might think, though. By the time the engine would be warmed up enough to be a source of heat, you'd have arrived where you were going, anyway. More to the point was learning to cope with the motorboat effect, as you take a corner in the powdery snow. Too much speed at the wrong time could lead to very distressing consequences. It got so I'd prefer it to stay below freezing, so the snow wouldn't melt and then refreeze as ice.

In mid December we flew down to New York City to do a concert at WBAI's Free Music Store[8]. Donald Knaack was featured as percussion soloist in my *A Giraffe of Wyne (and Thou)*, another tesseract piece. As at the Buffalo concert[9], the live performance was accompanied by two prerecorded versions, made with differing percussive 'kitchens.' The same magic was working as in my earlier *Piano Piece Number Three* – torrents of xylophonic pyrotechnics crisscrossed the temporal dimensions among live and recorded realms, as exotic-sounding bird calls on wood and temple blox were seemingly answered by the speakers. Outside, there was snow on the ground, but strangely the Big City didn't seem as cold as my memory of it, coming as we were from Buffalo. The cold came in January, when I found out that there wasn't the funding to keep me on as a Creative Associate.

This time it was Hiller who manifested the miracle that saved my bacon. He'd been contacted by a film company about doing a computer synthesized soundtrack, and I'd be the likeliest candidate for a research associate. The film was to be an animated version of

---

[8] December 11, 1974.          [9] December 8, 1974.

a half dozen of Ovid's *Metamorphoses*. So far, so good. I'd read Ovid
in the original Latin back in my school days, knew my way among
the studios and offices along Sunset and Hollywood Boulevards,
and was into computers to boot. The meetings with the people from
L.A. were most cordial, but by this time I was pretty much frozen
into *rigor dubitantis* in regard to film and/or record companies.

Hiller was no dummy. His motivation for the project was to fund
some acquisitions to upgrade the university's electronic music
studio. There already were some fine devices there: a twenty-two
channel vocoder, built by Bob Moog, who lived up the street in
Williamsville, a frequency analyzer, and a PDP-8 computer that we
used to digital-to-analog convert tapes we'd get from the Control
Data 6400 up at the Ridge Lea campus.

We had a Music V (that's 'Music Five') program, with which I
worked a great deal those ensuing months. What it would do is
solve wave equations according to your specifications, allowing
you to describe sound forms in great detail and with great control.
The output tape would then be taken to the PDP-8 and be D-to-A
converted as mentioned above. That tape, then, could be played on
any garden variety tape recorder.

We were discussing possibilities like Risset tones[10] for Orpheus's
descent into Hades when the plug was pulled on the project.
Goodbye, Kitty. But the explorations in digital sound manipulation
made it far from a total loss. Furthermore, thanks to the good offices
of Betsy Cohen, I was able to visit Bell Laboratories in New Jersey.
What an amazing array of equipment they had there! Computer
complexes in virtually every room – and projects ranging from
computer-generated animation to artificial voices. I met Joe Olive,
who was putting together an opera for talking computers; and Hal
Alles, who was working with digital filters and would eventually
help figure out how to do what Music V could do in real time. As we
were doing it in Buffalo, a minute of music could easily take an hour
of computer time.

Not all of the explorations at the studio in the basement of Baird
Hall, on the S.U.N.Y. Buffalo Main Street campus, involved computers. We did elaborate cross fades on the vocoder, experimenting

[10] After Jean Claude Risset, whose algorithm we modified for our researches. Like an audio
Möbius strip, it is a sonic pattern that moves up (or down) one octave, to become itself! The
result sounds like an eternally ascending (or descending) glissando. Ascending it reminds
me of a motorcycle that just won't quit.

with sound effects records and various genres of music. One of the more effective setups involved overlaying Bob Dylan's *John Wesley Harding* onto Palestrina's *Missa Papae Marcelli*. Every single word of the Dylan song came through loud and clear, but the underlying texture and harmony were pure Palestrina.

Coincidental with my departure from the Creative Associates was an offer to do a weekly musical program on WBFO-FM, a public radio station on campus. Conveniently enough, it was located in the student union building, across the campus road from Cooke Hall, the music building. A journey well known to me already, what with all the C.A. events that had been broadcast. So Walter Gajewski, who was getting on the C.A. train just as I was getting off, volunteered to help me with studio production, and *Ad Astra per Asparagus* was on the air.

The radio station, housed on campus as it was, fielded an intramural softball team. The 'WBFO Bombers' weren't really hard nosed, but we weren't embarrassingly inept, either...well, most of the time. Electronic genius Mitch Tannenbaum, the station engineer, confused 'em from the mound. Former New Christy Minstrel Steve Mann, who followed my show Wednesday nights with a feast of vintage folk music, gobbled 'em up at shortstop. Don Knaack was one of two switch hitters in our lineup – I was the other. I remember hitting .500 overall – better power from the left side, but better average from the right.

Meanwhile, back in the real world, Terry Ryan passed through Buffalo on tour with Louis Prima. To help him fight off the road doldrums, I decided to take him to Niagara Falls. Along for the ride with Terry were bassist Seth Kimball and drummer Joey Vespe, who was supposedly from there. He was the one on this tour who was always introduced as coming from some small town near wherever they were playing. To Bostonians he was from Cohasset, in Chicago he was from Highland Park. So here he was a native of Niagara Falls, New York. The crowds ate it up.

So anyway here we were driving back into the U.S.A. across the Peace Bridge, after a pleasant afternoon listening to the Great Lakes being poured downriver. What to our wondering ears should appear on the car radio but Wally Gajewski, moonlighting as a D.J. at WBUF! And as we drive up to the customs inspector, what should come out of the speakers loud and clear but Wally's voice, saying, "On the subject of marijuana..." Just what we needed. An extra half hour delay while they looked the car over. A fruitless search as it turned out – I may be crazy but I'm not stupid!

The mathematical wizard, John Myhill, invited me to assist him in his computer/sound research. The summer of 1975 was an interesting time for me, musically. There's the exhilaration of hearing a sound you've designed that, in all likelihood, *no one has ever heard before*. For as deeply as I was into the music, though, my hands never touched a keyboard nor did I have occasion to use five-lined paper. Much of my time was spent at one or the other computer, or in the Math library, sifting through logarithm tables and plotting graphs.

John Myhill proved to be not only a brilliant thinker and a fascinating man to work with – he seemed to have fallen out of a Dickens novel – but he was a big help in my being able to return to California. We were living out of suitcases the entire time in Buffalo – we'd never thought of it as a permanent move. So thanks to his introductions, and after a few more months of overworking my Guardian Angel, I was 'back West,' under contract to the San Francisco Art Commission.

ODE TO GREGOR SAMSA

The prayers that a mantis says
Are nothing like what a Bishop prays.
More like eef eek eet
And eckle ockle ickle.
Why, a mantis couldn't tell the Host from a pickle!
But the bugs that like only bugs
Can bug you,
Are like Nature's way of saying 'Fug you!'

# 7/ OCCAM'S SHAVING CREAM

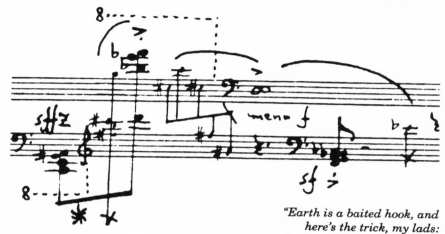

"*Earth is a baited hook, and
here's the trick, my lads:
Let's see you snap up all the
bait and not get hooked!*"
Nikos Kazantzakis – *The Odyssey:
A Modern Sequel* (Book III, lines 581-2)

**E**ven in the waning summertime, it was great to be back on the West Coast. More than the weather, I'd missed the California tempo. As Dr. Watson put it, "there's no pace like Holmes.'"

There was an opportunity for me to check out at the Exploratorium, the unique science museum located at the Palace of Fine Arts. I'd done science fairs back in high school, but walking through the exhibits there on the way to my interview with Frank Oppenheimer, I realized that this was the major leagues. He showed me to the grand piano they had on the premises, but in playing it I might have made it too clear that I'd evolved in a different direction from my high school days. It was just as well, though, because I was fortunate enough to catch on with the Neighborhood Arts Program, under the auspices of the San Francisco Arts Commission, as a sort of musical handyman.

John Myhill had introduced me to the program's director, Stephen Goldstine. If there can be pillars of society, this man is a ganglion, a

connector with such zeal and zest for creativity himself as to make
for exceptional sensitivity. He'd entertain at his house in the Berkeley hills; lavish affairs with room after room, floor after floor of
visiting East coast intellectuals, U.C. classics professors, musicians,
and poets. When our mutually bizarre schedules permitted, I've
found him a capable four-hand partner at the piano, joining me on
forays through Mozart, Schubert, and Bizet. Ah, but were there
more like him!

My official title was 'Music Librarian,' but my duties extended to
playing at convalescent homes, dance classes, workshops for the
'disturbed,' and more. During this period I created and performed
music for productions of plays by Brecht, Ionesco, and Pinter. A
variety of projects saw me working alongside the likes of the concert
whistler Jason Serinus and the actor Peter Coyote who, like John
Parriott earlier, impressed me with the depth of his knowledge of
his craft. But what really made me feel like I was back in showbiz
was playing piano for L. O. Sloan's *Three Black and Three White
Refined Jubilee Minstrels*. Rollicking songs, great dancing – it at-
tracted a marvelously mixed audience, and everyone was laughing
together by the time in the second act that one of the white guys sang
"Coon, coon, coon, I wish my color would fade." Above and beyond
its historical significance, and the way it exposed the sources of so
many racial stereotypes, it was an enormously entertaining show.

If you find him doing three things at once, you've caught him on
a slow day – Leni Sloan is not only a gifted dancer, but also an
inspired director and choreographer. He's also proficient on the
management end. In fact, his being capable of excellence both as
creative artist and administrator has occasionally confronted him
with the dilemma that, with the time demands that each end of the
business can make, one area or another can suffer from neglect if one
person tries to do it all. Of course, it's not always easy to find
someone capable enough to fill in for you, especially with standards
as high as his.

One of the actors in the show – Lester Jones, who portrayed 'Mr.
Tambo' as well as can be done – was to work with me on other Art
Commission projects, including Harold Pinter's *The Collection*, which
he directed and I did music for. *Jubilee Minstrels* got him into singing,
and eventually he was doing vintage songs with me at the piano. We

billed ourselves The Asbestos Players (as in, "We do asbestos we can"), and gave a couple of concerts in San Francisco.

I was with the Art Commission for several years, and the stability it brought allowed other interesting things to happen as well. In 1977 Bob Moran invited me to bring my piano act to festivals in Portland, Oregon and Lockport, New York.

The *Through Cloud and Eclipse* festival in Portland featured a multi-media Moran work of the same name. A shadow puppet show, among other things, it was an irresistible blend of ancient wisdom and Moranic mischief. I loved the giants Turalura and Turalay. Another Moran piece featured children's voices narrating a fanciful history of America. My presentation then, as at the *Blaze of Glory* festival in upstate New York, consisted of a piano recital featuring my recently completed suite called *The Syntax Collector*. Furthermore, Moran had induced C. F. Peters, the music publishing house, to produce a set of newly commissioned waltzes, and the New York festival marked the première of my contribution to the set, *Dejavalse*. In a sense, the piece's first performance was, as provided for in the score, a round. I played it on July 3, 1977 and Joseph Kubera entered promptly three days later.

*The Waltz Project*, as it came to be called, toured Austria and Yugoslavia in May of 1978, and I was invited to tag along. It can be hard to pick out the high points of a European concert tour. There was the thrill and awe of performing waltzes in Austria – land of the 'Waltz Kings' – such as Scott Joplin's *Augustan Club Waltz*, and my own *Dejavalse*; or the way they laughed in the right places at the Innsbruck concert, as I did my usual introductory raps – *ganz auf Deutsch*; or the Bösendorfer *Imperials* they had for us in Austria, which allowed me to play the extra low notes in *The Syntax Collector*; or the looks on their faces in Eastern Europe after I'd given them some Pop Rocks®!

The border crossing into Hungary lived up to its billing. It was like *Mission: Impossible* – not one but several checkpoints, each manned by soldiers with automatic weapons on their backs. I handed over our passports to the guard at the first one, and he looked at us and then our pictures, back and forth, real hard. They 'let' us wait in the car while they checked out our visas, then had me open the trunk, and sent us on our way. Once inside the 'Iron Curtain' it was like another world. An artificial Depression – you could see it on everyone's faces. Not infrequently, an oxcart would hold up traffic on the two-lane highway to Budapest. Finally getting a chance to pass, what should I see but an assholic Mercedes passing me at the same time! But hey– in a police state, there's *always* a cop when you want one. And in the Brezhnev era Eastern Bloc countries, they didn't chase you in a beefy squad car – they'd radio ahead, and an officer walks into the oncoming traffic holding out his hand. Those automatic weapons again – the Mercedes were (this happened twice) ever so coöperative, pulling over right away.

Budapest also lived up to its billing. We dined at a place a block off the Danube, complete with a Gypsy band playing the sort of music that sounds corny anywhere else, but *right* there. A meal that eclipsed even my glitsy memories of travel as a Rock star, at a tenth of the price! From there I drove to Zagreb, there to meet our most gracious host, Nikša Gligo. Nikša had warned me: "The road to Beograd is killing so forget it at once!" and so had arranged for tickets for the flight to Beograd for our first concert.

Jugoslavia struck me as Italy through the looking glass. The mood for the Beograd concert[1] was surprisingly open and cordial. Someone showed up dressed as the American flag: a blue shirt with white stars, and red and white striped pants. That show turned out to be good preparation for what was to come, because it was clear that the audience that awaited me at the Student Center of the University of Zagreb was hungry for some high-spirited music. The evening of waltzes at Zagreb preceded an evening of rags, my one solo recital of the tour. Even though it was to be televised, the concert[2] was sold out two weeks in advance. Following Nikša's suggestion, the hall had been redecorated as a saloon, complete with beers and candles. For the classic rags of the first half of the program, they had an appropriately skeletal upright piano for me. For the newer pieces, including the European première of *The Syntax Collector*, as well as the first performance anywhere of Bill Bolcom's *Fields of Flowers Rag*, there was your standard concert grand. I never got to see the tape, but it stands out in my mind as quite the warmest reception I received the whole tour.

A stopover in Venice for a twilight gondola ride, and it was on to

[1] May 22, 1978.     [2] May 24, 1978.

Innsbruck, for the next leg of the tour. Our hotel was not far out of town in a medieval village called Hall-in-Tirol. The moving clouds revealed ever changing views of the snow-capped mountains through the balcony windows. After the concert at the Innsbruck Conservatory[3], it was on to Graz, to record the waltzes for ÖRF (Austrian Radio)[4]. Stopping on the way to refuel at an *Aral* station in Mittersill, my thoughts ran toward Anton Webern – it had been his home town.

Graz was situated in lower climes than Innsbruck. The snowy peaks of the Großglockner and the Hohe Tauern were well behind us. Still, the place had a lot of charm. The birthday cake buildings in the old part of town, a shop jutting into the street like a fine armoire, the chubby clock tower – one could easily imagine elves and witches walking these corridors. But it was a twentieth century taxicab that took me to the recording studio, a one story Vegas kind of building, where I joined John Cobb for piano duo versions of *Dejavalse* and the *Modern Love Waltz* of Philip Glass. A big change from the rock n' roll universe – there was even someone reading along in the score in the control room as we played. Like, *they* decide when it's a take!

After the recording sessions I made my way up to Amsterdam for a few days to visit my friend Leigh Landy, who had become Professor of Music at the University of Amsterdam. Personable and quick-witted, Leigh had been my colleague working for Hiller at S.U.N.Y. Buffalo. As an ethnomusicology student at Columbia University, he'd assembled a tape collection of nearly fifty shelf feet, containing recordings from all over the world. Every kind of music you've heard of, plus quite a few you haven't, was represented – Eskimo vocal music executed on a gold miner's pan, Ethiopian armpit choruses, a kazoo orchestra from Malawi, and of course the Legendary Stardust Cowboy. His musical explorations ventured into popular realms as well. He'd performed on the *Arthur Godfrey Show* with a group called Our House.

It was by dint of my old friend Dumb Luck that I was able to stay on with the San Francisco Art Commission for as long as I did. I'd had enough seniority to weather the cutbacks in the wake of Proposition 13, and had been with them a few years past that before

[3] May 27, 1978.     [4] May 29, 1978.

they decided to put an upper limit on your term. So my situation changed with the decade.

It's arguable that the musician's path is purer than the priest's, in that for the former the vow of poverty is superfluous. This is not so flippant a remark as it may seem. There's the story, quoted by John Cage, where Ramakrishna advises a musician to stay with his art rather than to become a devotee, saying, "Music is a rapid means of transport to life everlasting."[5]

I ultimately found relative shelter from the storm at the Community Music Center in San Francisco, where they welcomed me aboard as an instructor of piano and music theory. It was pleasant to contemplate that once upon a time Steve Reich and Joseph Kubera had taught there. There's something about teaching that solidifies your awareness of your art like nothing else. Maybe it's having to drag all those concepts into the light of day so you can explain them to someone else.

In between was a period of several dry months, during which I was as frantically busy as only the unemployed can be. As usual, the most interesting and productive offer came completely out of the blue. One Wednesday evening in March, 1980 the phone rang. It was my old friend Omar (formerly Rick) Kaczmarczyk, calling from New York. Would I be interested in another film score, he wondered. After my normal three tenths of a second pause – you don't want to appear too hot to trot – I said, "Sure," and Friday morning found me arriving at Heathrow Airport, London, England.

There to meet me was Omar – he'd flown over from New York while I was traversing the Great Circle from San Francisco. The film, as he explained to me during the cab ride into London, was a project of Bertha Dominguez, wife of Alexander Salkind. The producer of enormously successful movies such as *Superman*, Salkind had a gangsterly look and demeanor that made me feel quite at home, in a Vegas sort of way.

The film, directed by and starring Mme. S., was called *Maya* – Hindu illusion and ancient Yucatan allusion in one tidy bundle – was the story of a Central American immigrant in New York. After a week of screenings, long hours at the moviola machine, and discussions about what music should go where, we were ready to record. Rather than wade through the U. K. red tape, however, it

[5] Pandit Pran Nath, as quoted to me by Terry Riley: "Music is the easiest way to approach The God."

was deemed more practical to go to Paris to do the sessions. Salkind had a thing about flying, so we were booked on the night train out of Victoria station. A very choppy Channel crossing made for a sleepless night for me.

The recording studio in Paris, interestingly enough, was also named 'Maya.' It was a thrill and surprise to discover that I was functional in French. No small help – I'd learned about the vicissitudes of being both producer and performer during the *Tarot* sessions. There's a cultivated schizophrenia you have to get into: as the producer, I'd be worrying about optimizing the use of time, how to minimize setup interruptions, and the like. But once I walked through those big thick doors, and sat down at the keyboard, I had to put all of that out of my mind.

The film never made it to a general release (surprise, surprise), but did make something of a splash at Cannes. Bertha Dominguez's 'tantrum' was the high point of the festival, according to some reports. But by then I could scarcely care. It turns out that they had 'commissioned' at least three different people to score the film. And then on the last day of recording in Paris, Mme. Dominguez brought in an Andean harpist she'd discovered playing in the Metro. Never having seen the final cut screened, I've no idea whether any of my material was used at all.

Back in the U. S. A. again, I started at the Music Center that September. Playing with the American Ragtime Ensemble (formerly the Take One Ragtime Ensemble) helped me keep my fishing pole in the river, so to speak, as far as performing ragtime is concerned. Violinist/Leader David Reffkin is the brother of Gene, onetime drummer with Touchstone.

I gave a concert[6] at the Music Center wherein I soloed on harpsichord, piano, and prepared piano. Starting out on the harpsichord, I played a sonata I'd discovered in my researches, composed in 1759 by William Herschel. His pieces deserve better than the inevitable accusation of dilettantism, inasmuch as he is mainly remembered as the discoverer of the planet Uranus. My performance was in commemoration of that event's bicentennial.

On the Steinway, I did some of my own pieces, some rags, and played for the first time anywhere the first two movements of what

[6] August 15, 1981.

was to become Terry Ryan's *Parallax,* a suite that I've had signal success with since. The pre-prepared piano came into play in the much-awaited (by me at least) first performance of *Cedar Tavern* by Leigh Landy. A multifaceted three movement piece, it was a colorful homage to some of the more interesting New York artists of the fifties.

It was lamentable that I couldn't find more time to practice such a savory and ambitious program. For a few years there was only the illusion of weekends. It was about this time that Sea's career as 'Zooti the Clown' started to blossom. She would do children's birthday parties, company picnics, Xmas shows – she even did a television commercial! After a few years at it she was, in my admittedly prejudiced view, quite the best around at what she did. And there was the volume of business to prove it. There were a lot of repeat customers, but she had enough material, magic tricks, and all to show even old friends something new. Every Saturday and Sunday, after a work week as a music teacher, I would become the clown chauffeur. Before long we'd navigated the length and breadth of the Bay Area, from Vallejo to San Jose – sometimes there would be three or four gigs scheduled for a given day.

Margaret Fabrizio[7] heard *Dejavalse* at the Art Institute of Chicago and contacted me about writing a piece for harpsichord. She took the resulting work, *Sonata Desaxificata,* with her on a European concert tour, premièring it in Paris[8]. Following up a lead from Hiller, I made contact with David Harrington of the Kronos String Quartet. They've been kind enough since to program several of my pieces, even inviting me to join them as composer-in-residence at the 1982 San Luis Obispo Mozart Festival.

They played my *Lignified Rock Episodes* at four different venues during the festival. At the end of the suite, a rhythmically driving number called *Kentucky Chaconne,* violist Hank Dutt put his instrument on his lap and led the audience in a clap-along. The music then goes on to dissolve beneath the beat, leaving the audience to carry it. The way it further dissolved into enthusiastic applause was especially effective. Several people told me that they heard the ensuing Mozart quartet differently as a result of having heard mine.

The Mozart Festival turned out to be a hot ticket. So much so, in

[7] Described by composer/critic Charles Shere, with a decorous pause, as...'special.'
[8] September 6, 1981.

fact, that their restrictive seating policies combined with lack of planning to turn what would've been a peak experience for me into a nadir. At the last performance, at the Cal Poly auditorium, an officious ticket manager was 'magnanimous' enough to let me hear my own piece from the back of the hall. I'll never forget the helpless feeling as I watched David Harrington beckon for the composer during the applause. The 'ouch' that I couldn't restrain took the form of letters, one of whom wound up on the table at a meeting of the California Arts Council. There were a handful of Maestro/ Apprentice grants left to hand out, before the new administration's cuts would take effect. However it got there, my name was on the table, and I could scarcely believe my good fortune when Steve Goldstine (by then on the Arts Council) called me with the news.

My apprentice was a film student at the San Francisco Art Institute named Christopher Coppola. Son of August, nephew of Francis. He'd go by his middle name, Rémy, to frustrate those classmates who'd ask him to work on their project just to get the Coppola name on their list of credits. His brother, an actor, even changed his name in response to that sort of tackiness. He'd taken a photo of me that was to be used in a magazine interview, and I told him I'd credited it 'Christopher Rémy,' in hopes of making *that* name a hot property. His inimitable sly smile let me know he appreciated the gesture.

I'd got along without the California Arts Council for years without realizing how good a preparation that was for getting along *with* them. All the red tape you'd expect from a state agency, and twice the inertia. You've got to figure that the cutbacks in the eighties would be enough to push an overworked understaff over the line from disinterested to uninterested. What little relating they do is primarily with other bureaucrats. Plainly and simply put, their attitude toward the artists sucks. We were treated like some sort of migrant labor force beholden to faceless pencil pushers ruling over paper fiefdoms. It's like they were saying to us, "Well, we don't see any value in what you do, but maybe we can find some way you can talk about it in one of our institutions."

Once during my term with the S. F. Arts Council they yanked us in at 9 a.m. for a 'seminar' on finding employment. People who'd been performing past midnight the night before were tumbled out of bed before eight to attend this charade. Far from treating us like professionals, they conveyed the impression that they considered us shiftless, worthless peons. And here they were being so 'considerate' as to 'help' us find a 'real' job. Not since school days opened with the Lord's prayer had I felt so degraded by an institution purporting to have my best interests at heart. Larry Pisoni protested vocally, carrying it to the point of leading a walkout. Did us proud, he did.

The last Monday of every month was payday at the Art Commission. While at the office to pick up our checks, we had to fill out a weekly schedule, telling them where they could expect to find us on any given day. Now, my work took me to some two or three dozen places, so my schedule was a flea circus. There was no way to reduce it to a consistent weekly pattern. As a result, from time to time my pay was docked because I wasn't where I was 'supposed' to be. Once again, the individual pays for the shortcomings of a screwed up system.

It takes God millions of years to turn a lump of coal into a diamond, but a Monet, a Mozart, or a McCartney can do the equivalent (in terms of human valuation – and that is after all what we're talking about) in mere decades. There remains, however, the problem of sticking around to collect the royalty checks. Bridging this gap is a worthy task, but one for which state institutions are perhaps unsuited by nature. For as wasteful as most of them are, they shy away from copping to it directly.

Wasted time and effort are inevitable, perhaps necessary components of an enterprise. You know, the things that you don't know don't work until you give them a try. It's what experimentation is all about. The blind alleys that lure you to explore them. That gritty patience that keeps you going, until you're satisfied you've tried it every which way, looked at it from every angle. If he'd been funded by Arts Council money, Edison would've been so nettled with idiotic, irrelevant paperwork that he'd've never got around to inventing the light bulb.

The only art form that flourished in the eighties was grant proposal writing. All the others were to some degree distorted or perverted by contact with political compromise and pragmatism. The name Zhdanov comes to mind. It was a refreshing contrast when, thanks to the help of Dennis McNally and Lou Tambakos, I was able to do a solo piano performance at the Old Waldorf in San Francisco in June, 1983. My repertoire by then was beginning to include more new pieces. In addition to a growing fold of Bill Bolcom and Terry Ryan numbers, I started to play pieces by Joel Forrester, another former Community Music Centrist who has since moved to New York. For a while it appeared as if the log jam were about to break, and my musical career might actually start to go somewhere. The Fall of 1984 brought me another professorship, teaching the history and methods of twentieth century music at the San Francisco Art Institute.

Van Williamson, a guitar instructor at the Music Center, was one of the members of the Electric Guitar Quartet. Not only did they perform some of my string quartet pieces, but on September 19, 1984, at the Julia Morgan Center in Berkeley, we put on a concert together, collaborating on the first movement of the Mozart Sinfonia Concertante, K. 297b, with a synthesizer for my keyboard.

It was a timely shakedown cruise for my material, in anticipation of the next month's concert tour of the urban Northeast. Robert Kleinman, a college chum of Lou Tambakos, offered to line it up for me. A few more blind alleys and wild goose chases since the Old Waldorf show had rekindled my skepticism, but this time it seemed to be for real. As much playing as I got to do that October (fifteen shows in twelve cities in twelve nights) had, has, immediate, per-ceptible, and positive effects. By the end of the tour, as far as being on the stage was concerned, 'there' felt much more like 'here' to me.

When I came back from the tour, the momentum of my life was going so well that even splitting up with Sea was a relief and not a trauma. It was surreal. She just packed up and moved to Florida, where she'd been visiting relatives while I was on tour. Even before she was diagnosed as diabetic, it seemed she was bent and deter-mined to have a horrible time of it in this life. It was when I protested being taken along for the ride that things began to get sticky. The net result of her departure felt like the lifting of a huge burden.

Aside from there being no one around to yell at me and keep me reminded as to what a miserable excuse for a human being I was, it represented a windfall of practice time. The *I Ching* says to turn within in times of adversity[9]. "How good I'll be by the time they discover me," I thought. Bestemor liked to quote a Mark Twain saying that every day we should do at least one thing that we don't feel like doing. This represented a rather Puritanical view of duty to me, but doing something that one ought to do, on a consistent basis, seemed like a good idea. Well, one thing became a dozen, which became two dozen, which became three...and I became a mad lister. The high point of many a day was the crumpling up and tossing out of a completed 'things to do' list. "Do everything you can think of, and think of as much as you can!" Procrastination can wait till tomorrow.

On the business front, I made calls, wrote letters, and followed every lead I could dig up. All with scant result. After three meetings with an arts consultant that someone recommended to Lester Jones, the total sum and substance of his advice was that we needed a logo. Another one told me that my flyer didn't look 'professional' enough. You bust your buns practicing and performing and you feel you're about to break through to a new level. But no, it's take a number, get in line – it's shrink wrap time – you're chopped liver again.

The torrent of tours and parade of performances that I was hoping for didn't materialize. There was the Septovember Disremember 'tour,' that started out as a two week traipse through state universities in New York and promptly got unfunded. Then the Febmaraprimaybe tour, a springtime swing back eastward that got postponed to death. I was set to play an after hours spot at the Aladdin in Vegas after a Grateful Dead show. I was mentioned in connection with a Hot Tuna tour. Two film score possibilities had my phone ringing. Yes...well, no. Changed our minds. As the villain said, when his challenger chose the wrong weapons for the duel, "Foils! Cursed again!"

Meanwhile, my rent was doubling while my earnings were halving. These were the initial stages of the government's 'Just Say No!' policy, which first was applied to federal sponsorship of the Arts, humanities, education, and human services, eventually extending to anything that didn't benefit the established investocracy. I can remember when I had money, and no time; and then other times I had time and no money. In the eighties it became possible to have neither.

[9] Cf. the Images to hexagrams numbers 9, 36, 39, 46 and 51.

As far as I was concerned it meant a decade of getting trickled on. Taking on every offer, however lame or demeaning, just to pay the bills. The disculturation was pervasive. It was depressing enough that I hadn't been able to buy a ticket for a regular season San Francisco Symphony concert that I wanted to hear since Josef Krips was the conductor, but I couldn't even afford to get out and hear the work of my colleagues. There was a list of some dozen or so composition projects I'd hoped to get to. I wound up throwing it away because it was too depressing to contemplate the fact that there was no hope of freeing up the time.

The value of adversity, though, is that it reveals who your real friends are. Through the good offices of Ivan Tcherepnin, I was invited to come and demonstrate my music at Harvard University in April, 1986. An Arcadian week at the Lyceum. I inquired about returning to go for an advanced degree, perchance to advance my economic status above the snorkeling level. But it came down the same old problem, that ever present *argent provocateur* – money. Pursuing more local leads at Stanford, I came up against their systemic prejudice against 'older' students. Whether I have a degree or not is academic, but I can lay claim to a Master's from the College of Hard Knocks.

One hangover of a weekend in June, 1986 must have been the low point. As I lay dreaming, we were backstage at a rock club. Socializing, hanging out, and all. Then this huge, beefy security guard comes around, demanding to see everyone's 'papers.' I didn't know from any papers, permits, or anything, so my friends and I were shown the door. As it closed behind me I woke up, and was struck immediately by the irony of the situation.

I had just been thrown out of my own dream.

Nature abhors a vacuum, and I've got the feeling She's not too thrilled about me, either, whatever state of emptiness I've attained. Albert Einstein said that he couldn't believe that God 'plays dice' with the Universe. I can, but it doesn't especially bother me. We've been told to expect life to be unfair, and after all is said and done, my only claim to fame might well be as the Wally Pipp of Rock 'n Roll. One of the most bewildering things about performing can be the apparent absence of a direct connection between how well you feel you did and the kind of feedback you get – whether you get thunderous applause, rave reviews, or laid. It all seems to be at least partially a game of chance[10].

The Razor's Edge is more than a metaphor. On the shiny side, the future looks bright, and the past is a parade of triumphs. On the flat side, the future promises ever deeper shades of gray, and the past is a litany of disappointments. What appears from afar to be a pinnacle of achievement may on arrival only reveal a frustratingly clear vista of what might have been. The delight in the consonance of the one is matched by the pain in the assonance of the other.

Once back at Lingueglietta we trapped a rat. Berio's mother brought me a bucket – as the 'man around the house' that afternoon, it fell to me to drown it. I remember the poor animal frantically racing around the cage searching for a breath of air. When it pushed the trap's door open, and made for the surface, I had to beat it down with a stick. Until it came up no more. Some will say that my lack of success is my own damn fault, but I'm beginning to feel like that rat. So many paths I've tried have proved to be blind alleys. So many vehicles have broken down. So many plans have come to naught.

So what's the point – what's the lesson in all this meandering? Is my only success to be a bad example for others? Phil Lesh maintains that any art, to be valid, must be viable in its own time. There's enough of my stubborn Norwegian carpenter grandfather in me for me to want to pay my own way. Many a time I felt like quitting music, either out of disgust with my playing or despair at ever getting my career off the ground, but the Muse wouldn't quit me. Either a word of encouragement from a valued colleague or an audience's warm reception would touch me and change my mind.

Once I'd figured suicide would be superfluous, I adopted a more relaxed attitude. Not that it's a matter of honor or ethics – I never felt cut out for the greed stampede – but it's always seemed that a bright future lay ahead, if only I could survive till then. As somebody's left-handed brother, I'm not sure what I'm entitled to expect. There have been those whose proverbial 'overnight success after years of prepa-ration' was more than they could handle. Should such an updraft ever come my way and provide some lift, I'd hope not to be another Icarus...I'd be more grateful to be Dædalus.

---

[10] Cf. Jorge Luis Borges, *The Lottery in Babylon.*

# 8/ EPILOG –
# HEART BEFORE THE COURSE

Nel Modo Furibond'e Pazzesco

*"I'm so hip I can't stand it!"*
Mike Dixon

t was a dark and stormy night. A record setter, in fact. First it
eclipsed the downpour of 1961 that I'd remembered so gratefully for keeping me off the R. O. T. C. parade ground. Then the
weather archivists kept reaching farther and farther back for a
deluge to compare it to. Finally they ran out of comparisons. Friday,
Valentine's Day, 1986, turned out to be the onset of our rainiest
weekend in history. But that didn't stop some five dozen friends and
well-wishers from showing up at the Josef Marc/Amy Wallace
house in the Berkeley hills to witness my marriage to Virginia
Morgan. Not only would it be a romantically easy date to remember,
it was a year to the day from the date of my divorce decree. The rain
didn't bother one bit.

That afternoon I'd received a call from Sedge Thomson. There'd
been a last-minute cancellation on his radio program *West Coast
Weekend,* and he wanted to know if I'd be interested in filling in. So
next day Ginny and I made our way to the studios of KQED-FM, San

Francisco's principal public radio station. We arrived in fine shape, but the storm had knocked out the station's transmitter. The show went on anyway, with the tape set to be broadcast at a later date. So I was on but the station wasn't. Under the gun, but knowing it wasn't loaded.

Well, one thing led to another and...well, I was invited back to appear on the show on a regular basis. Soon thereafter the mailbox and the phone both rang, and it was Henry Kaiser, dressed as a frogman, inviting me to a musical repast. I don't go in for seafood, I told him, but coming up on a half dozen CDs and who knows how many performances later, my metabolism hasn't registered any complaints. An admirably wacko guitarist, Henry has come out of what must have been an extraordinary 'upbringing' with the coolest attitude going. A poster on his wall reads: "Problems are opportunities in work clothes." Playing in his band was a deliciously rewarding experience. An instrument at home for practice, an instrument on the gig whose sound I felt good about, and the confidence and credibility of my colleagues – never before did I have all three of these, and the results are happily there to be heard.

For a variety of reasons, this narrative cuts off about the mid eighties. There's always an element of caprice in deciding where to draw the line. Among other factors affecting the decision is the fact that musical projects have started trickling through again. Carl Weber, of the Stanford Drama Department and onetime collaborator of Berthold Brecht, followed up a lead from Bill Bolcom and contacted me to do the music for his revival of a mid-nineteenth century Eugène Labiche farce. Much fun. Terry Ryan helped me produce a couple of cassettes. Robert Hunter has booked me on tours for which there are no maps, as well as those for which there are. There's a difference now: I don't know what tomorrow might bring, but for once that's good news.

to Luciano Berio

# String Quartet

Tom Constanten

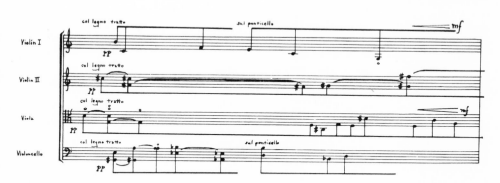

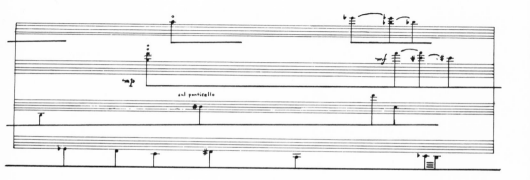

to Phil Lesh
on his 22nd birthday

# Sonatina

Somewhat Faster

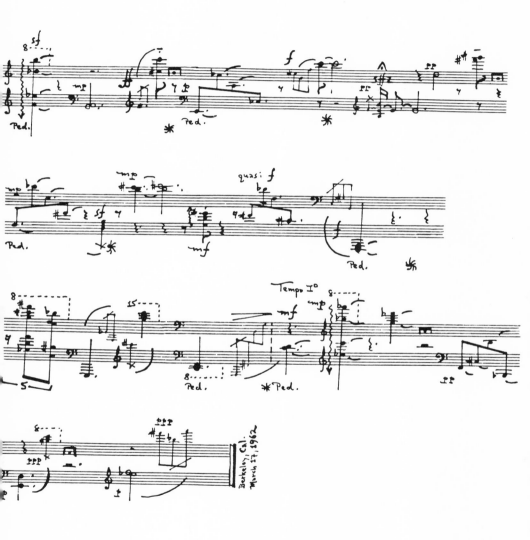

N.B. An accidental influences only the note it *immediately* precedes.

122

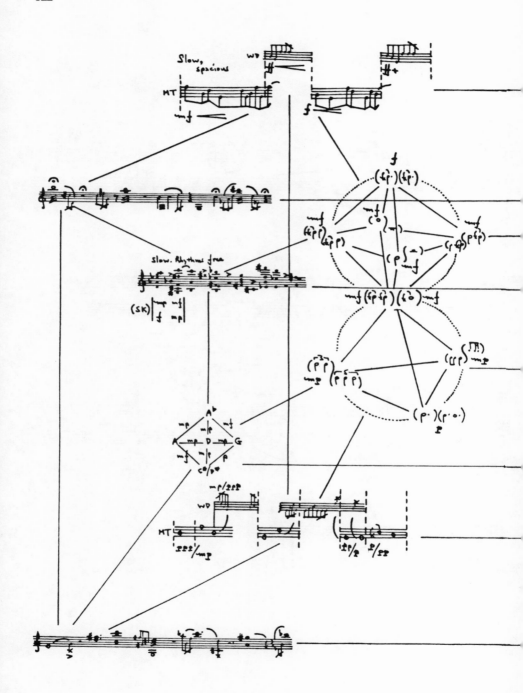

123

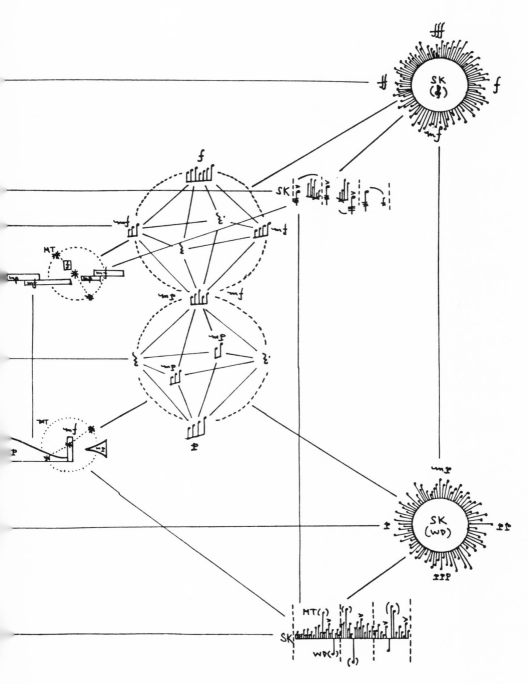

A Giraffe of Wyne
(2nd Thou)

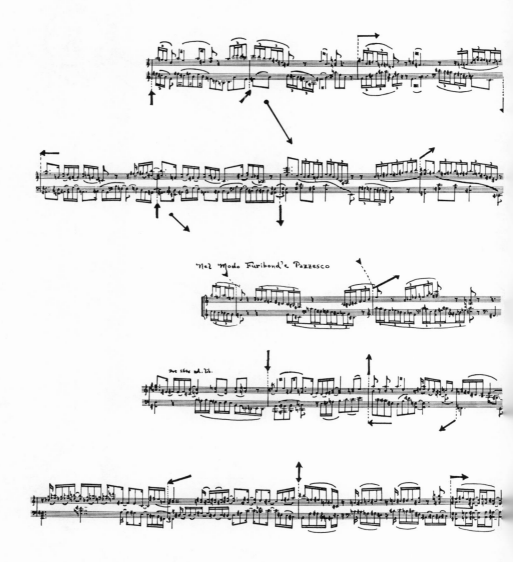

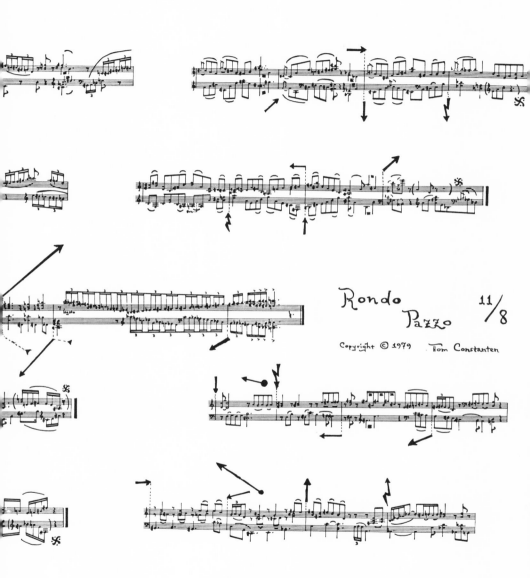

Rondo Pazzo  11/8

126

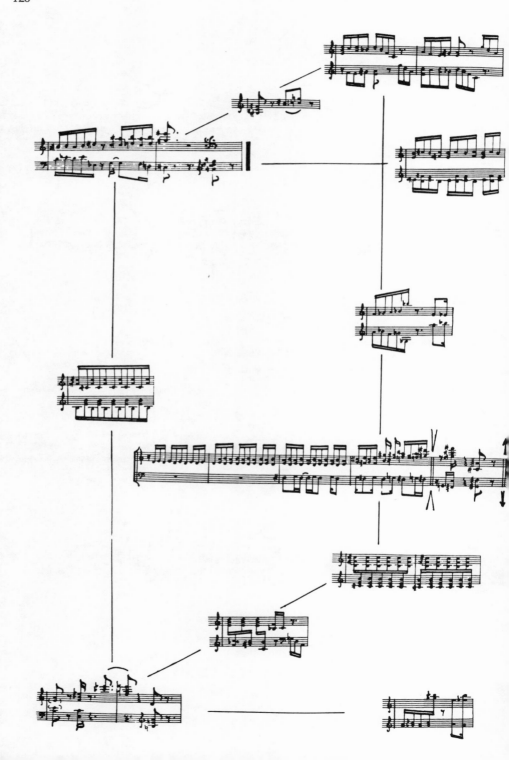

**Rondo Pazzo** 11/16

# The Disco Delius Banjo Bash

*More Khan artistry (but that's Machaut biz) to a hearty Burgundian cadence. (Don't forget to wah-wah)*

*All.º petulante all'afroamericano*

Tom Constanten

# Part 2/ MY FOUR BITS

Two each on two different subjects

THE FOREGOING should hopefully offer some insight into the genesis of the opinionations to follow. There remains the possibility that some of the topics addressed might be too specialized in scope for some.

Chapter 9, *History and the Composer's Dilemma*, might presuppose too much familiarity with contemporary music. Chapter 10, *Pumping Ivory*, may, in spite of my best efforts, be too technical or esoteric. It is in any case written specifically for keyboard players, although *aficionados* of other instruments may well find principles that apply to their own practice. My advice to the reader is, if it gets mucky, skip it. We're not all interested in all the same things. An Englishman's fish is a Frenchman's *poisson*, no matter how you distribute it.

# 9/ HISTORY AND THE COMPOSER'S DILEMMA

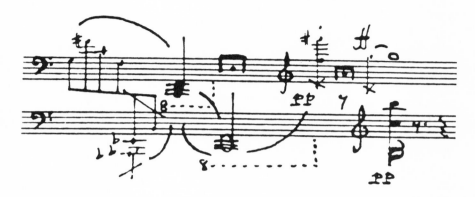

"Put your nose into the wind,
and the message will come to you."
Lord Buckley

t could be argued that Mozart had an easier time of it, in that he didn't have to labor under his own shadow. To be sure, there were standards an eighteenth century composer had to measure up to, but it's equally true that a few long shadows have been cast since his day. So what is a self-respecting late-twentieth century composer to do? What sort of music should it be our business to be creating?

We live in an age of both shadow and light. Creative minds have opened up new possibilities as well as exhausted old ones. The era of liquefaction of information has arrived. We've seen forms and systems arise which are non-linear. Ideas – information – like the points in a computer's memory, have become instantly referable one to another. This tends to remove the constraint on any aspect of a work to have anything in particular to do with any other.

The electronic collages of John Cage demonstrate that, in this *milieu*, discontinuity is impossible: the fact that an event occurs is reason enough for it to be there. The style of certain authors and composers can make for difficulties in placing a specific idea, image, or item in the sequence – it seemingly 'could be anywhere.' The associative strata, as in a well-written screenplay, run in all directions.

This is not to say that there aren't cogent and coherent relations implicit in the material. On the contrary – there is a surfeit of them! Enough to create the effect of a Jackson Pollock drip technique painting. In terms of music, often you can't tell just by listening whether it's a hyperquantified serial piece or a totally loose aleatoric work.

Aleatoric and modular scores do, in their fashion, indicate what the performer is to do. This harks back to tablature notation, which tells the performer what actions to take, rather than what target notes to hit. What is gone, however, is the predictability of the result. You can't follow along in the score of *Atlas Eclipticalis* the way you can in a Mozart symphony. Yet I have no difficulty imagining either John Cage or Wolfgang Amadeus, respectively, joyfully accepting the applause for their part in creating the work. It is as if composers in this century have realized that their choices needn't be graven in stone. As if to carry on the great tradition of composer/performers, ever greater latitude is being given in the interpretation of works.

This doesn't necessarily indicate an abrogation of responsibility on the part of the composer. For one thing, the choices might well be from among equally valid musical expressions. For another, the performers are not being asked to do something *that* far beyond their ken. They too, it might be presumed, have spent a great deal of time and effort in learning how to get the best results possible from their instruments, so why not invite them to apply what they've learned? It's curious to note how people innocent of any knowledge or experience in Copyright law, publishing, or recording will wax indignant with proprietary concern over who gets credited for what.

A thornier question is raised by computer composition algorithms. Now that both composers and performers can be replaced by machines, the question arises, what's the difference in the results? How can we tell there's a person at the other end of an expression? Dare we hope that beyond all Skinnerian constraints there'll still be loose ends flapping in the breeze? Likely as not, the answers are not in machines or systems but in ourselves. Rather than the Turing 'Test,' in this context it's more proper to talk of the Turing 'challenge' (like the Kremer Challenge). The legacy of computer technology may well be connection with powers that will render that and other technologies vestigial[1].

So what's a composer to do? We might do well to take another look at the composer's product: the musical text. There are two distinct ways in which one can take the word 'text.' A performance text, whether a musical score or theatrical script, represents a contract, or compact between author and performer, to the effect that if the latter accurately follow the indications prescribed, the result should correspond reasonably well to the intent of the former. It should be presumable that the score has been gone over well enough to insure that its faithful execution will be rewarded by an equally faithful rendering of the composer's intention.

Beyond that, however, the term 'text' can also be taken to mean the 'shape' or 'idea' of a work. Someone whose musical awareness isn't enhanced by a facile familiarity with the symbology might not perceive the music the same as its creators, but they can still be said to have made out the drift – sometimes in great detail. That message, that the composer hopes the listeners will get from the music, is the body of this 'text' – what the piece is about, where the action is. The Premise of the work, its metaphysical topography, its 'natural habitat,' – this must be comprehensible to the audience. For a composer to ignore that fact is at least inconsiderate, and artistically suspect as well.

(This is not to rule out the possibility that the artists may be on to something, despite a contrarily disposed audience. The tendency is to dismiss the *avant garde* on the basis of its superficial resemblance to something known – 'a child beating on the keyboard' or 'antiquated triadic tonality.' The word 'experimental,' in either the arts or sciences, can be taken to mean the exploration of possibilities perceived but as yet undemonstrated. This gets especially interesting if the existing way of looking at things has to be extended, altered, or amended in order to reveal its pattern.)

---

[1] The pioneering science fiction author, John Campbell, explored this possibility in his short story 'Forgetfulness,' collected in *Adventures in Time and Space*. (Healy & McComas, eds. New York: Random House, 1946).

In referring to 'natural habitat' I mean the realm wherein the music seems the most 'at home.' There is much music, alas, whose natural habitat is the two-dimensional page. Many of the best virtuoso works, for another example, can be said to 'lie well' for the voice, or hands. Ideally, of course, the best 'habitat' for a musical composition should be on a concert stage or in a dance hall, before a legitimately appreciative group of listeners.

This concept also extends into the finer planes. Beethoven directed his *Missa Solemnis* 'to the heart.' Schönberg maintained that there are intimate connections between 'heart' and 'brain' that can make their results hard to distinguish from each other. Existing as it does in the minds of the listeners, the more subtle 'text' behaves in an organic fashion. It grows, shifts, changes as each passing year's revelations cause us to reinterpret it. There arise 'classic' ideals, to explain how certain works endure the way time turns them all about, showing ever new facets and angles.

If a hallmark of a 'classic' is that it passes the test of judgment in varying contexts, should we then presume that a work should 'work,' however viewed? What about a work that won't 'work' unless certain viewpoints are deliberately avoided? There is that leap of belief that a film or a play asks us to make, to conjure images of another place or time. To achieve this they often appeal to prevalent stereotypes, rather than seeking to represent reality. Too large a dose of *verismo* can shatter the spell.

Theatre is a metaphor for life, but music has only itself. In many senses unique for its purity, music is nonetheless in one sense quite impure. Its models have from time immemorial been borrowed from other disciplines. Since in so many cultures music arose as song, it became natural that the structures of poetry would mold the music. Nearly all Native American music is vocal, and the influence extends to instrumental examples like the African 'talking drums,' which take advantage of the semantic importance of rhythm.

The bardic tradition of European antiquity is, obviously enough, essentially vocal in nature. In pre-Gutenberg society, the tunes funtioned as aids to memory. The strophic imprint on musical form has given us concepts like 'phrasing.' One could say that, in expecting a piece of music to 'say something' or to 'go somewhere,' one is attributing qualities more appropriate to the essay or narrative, respectively.

As the technology of instrument building advanced, however, people began to contemplate music for the instruments alone. The problem then became how to express oneself coherently in terms that were 'purely' musical, without the amplification of meaning that words bring. The listener demands – quite legitimately – to hear something glisteningly new, yet at the same time comfortingly familiar. 'Tell me something I've never heard before that I know already,' is how it goes.

To come up with an answer to that musical conundrum, musicians necessarily had to resort to subterfuge: a family of alphabet soup type forms based on controlled repetition. As in the time-honored 'song' form, A-B-A, where each letter stands for a section of the melody, these forms have worked because if the listeners haven't figured out that what they are – quite legitimately – demanding is a blatant contradiction in terms, they also won't notice that the a-a-a-ah of recognition after the bridge, when the A section returns, is because they're hearing something that they had heard in the same piece a minute or two earlier.

Repetition can assume significance in a musical context in a wide variety of forms as well. In many of the musical cultures of Africa, Gamelan, and Occidental process music[2], immediate repetition with little or no variation lends the work solidity. At the macro end of the scale, one may contemplate the many hearings one has had of a given piece. As long as it takes Tristan to get on with it and die, life is in fact longer than art (there's the after hours socializing, &c).

The erosion of attention to repeat signs in European classical music can be traced to this phenomenon. As the works gained in acceptance the audience's familiarity with them increased to the point where they didn't need to hear the exposition of a sonata movement twice in order for it to 'stick.' In the earlier sonatas even the second part was repeated, but by Beethoven's time, they'd stopped writing repeats for the 'B' section, in accordance with performance practice. Significantly, in minuets and scherzi the repeats are traditionally disregarded in the reprise of the 'A' section. In all these instances, macro- or micro-cosmically speaking, the repetition is front-loaded, to aid comprehensibility.

The concept of repetition is not unique to music. From quarks to

[2]There are correspondences in cyclic patterns that cross cultural boundaries. The forty-eight beat basic pattern of Shona mbira music, for instance, seems to have a wealth of cousins: from the Montunas, steel drums, and reggae of the Caribbean to the twelve bar blues.

galactic superclusters, repetitive patterns abound throughout Nature. Thusly, in the twentieth century we've seen increasing interest in areas beyond the safe womb of Literature. The consideration of repetitive patterns leads naturally to the visual arts. Terms like 'impressionist' and 'expressionist' show up equally well in the context of music or of painting. The connection of the term 'Rococo' to the music and decor of the eighteenth century might be cited as a precedent.

As Picasso was influenced by 'primitive' masks, so theatre and ritual have been important ingredients in compositions by Luciano Berio, Mauricio Kagel, and Paolo Castaldi, whose *Tendre* is a virtuoso *tour de force* of sardonic humor. The more solid art forms, like painting and sculpture, have their analogues in works like David Tudor's *Rainforest*, which one may enter and leave in progress like an art gallery.

The uninitiated often vaguely associate music, especially that of Bach, with mathematics. Most likely this is due to the consistent sixteenth note underpinning to the typical Bach Allegro texture, which gives the impression of a dot matrix background to the musical patterns, hence digital. It's true enough that the time-honored 'song' form – A-B-A – looks veritably algebraic, and it is of course possible to appreciate the æsthetic effect of a printed circuit without knowing its function, but there are examples in contemporary music where composers have consciously used mathematics to clarify the form of their music. Henri Pousseur has invoked geometric models. His mobile-like scores, such as *Caractères* for piano and *Mobile* for two pianos, project a realm of parametric matrices, wherein are revealed possibilities inherent in the material's permutations and combinations. Palindromes have been given musical expression by composers from Machaut to Berg and Webern. Hiller's *Illiac Suite* for string quartet has a segment based on Markov chains, or shifting probabilities.

In the face of a musical order wherein multiples and powers of two predominate (the octave itself, musical phrases, groupings of instruments, *et al.*) there are interesting instances of *arithmetic* progressions – as in the additive and subtractive aspects of the opening of the fourth movement of Beethoven's *First Symphony*, or the B subject of the A section of the Scherzo of his *Seventh*, or the beginning of the rousing finale of Hector Berlioz's *Harold in Italy*.

Furiants and other examples of hemiola point out the possibility of generating rhythms through the friction between periods of different lengths. The theories of Josef Schillinger explore this in detail, finding expression in ragtime and the music of George Gershwin. Other musical/numerical relations have been revealed by Ernö Lenvai in his analyses of the importance of the Fibonacci series in the music of Bartók.

From mathematics it's but a short step to physics, and musical wonders have been wrought simply from the expressive tendencies implicit in the sonic material itself. Seemingly wrought over the most elemental parts, many of the later works of Bach and Beethoven come to mind as examples, not to mention the exuberantly abrasive music of Varèse, and more recent explorations of processes that sound like aural analogues to Moiré patterns.

Even chess and astronomy have been appropriated for musical purposes. The direction has been toward ever greater conceptual elasticity. The Platonic ideal of phenomena in the world of the senses as being but reflections of transcendent archetypical forms or ideas (as expounded by Heinrich Schenker in his musical analyses) has itself been reëxamined and reëvaluated. Underlying forms themselves have become subject to change, just as Sarastro seems to metamorphose from villain to hero in *Die Zauberflöte* (but was it he who changed?).

Of particular interest are patterns that further listening elucidates: melodies that start out by contradicting their underlying metres, like the openings of Prokofiev's *Second Violin Concerto* and Schumann's *Rhenish Symphony*; Bob Weir's rhythm guitar opening *Cumberland Blues* on the off beat – these invite the listener to interpret and interact rather than passively accept whatever happens.

I can hear the principal themes of the last movements of Beethoven's *Violin Concerto* or Haydn's *Trauersymphonie* accented either of two ways. And the way I choose to hear a given performance will color the musical experience. It's like chancing upon a familiar piece on the radio, but on the off beat. There's a moment of fascinated bewilderment until you figure out what music it is.

It's been interesting to note the rise and fall of critical estimation of works by Purcell, Haydn, and Beethoven as they were de- and reauthenticated by musicological research. The music itself never changed, but many listeners found it alternately charming or mediocre, depending on who they thought wrote it.

When I finally got to hear works of Moscheles, Hummel, and Kalkbrenner, I discovered that much of what I'd regarded as Beethoven's style was merely the musical argot of the times. By factoring out those points in common, a much clearer idea of Beethoven's real individuality emerged. Like an astronomer's blink comparator, the process highlighted features otherwise recondite.

The listener's imagination, moreover, is an important ingredient in the effect created by pieces of music that simulate, or parody, a given personal or national style, or even a specific musical instrument. To start with national styles, one might mention the *English* and *French Suites* of J. S. Bach, as well as the *Italian Concerto* (the list goes on). The intervening years may have obscured the fact that when Mozart and Beethoven were writing 'alla Turc,' they were alluding to an imported style of music (Janizary) that was familiar to their audience. There are the Spanish simulations of non-Spaniards like Bizet, Lalo, Rimsky-Korsakov, and Ravel; and the bold and refreshing explorations in this century of such as Henry Cowell, Harry Partch, Alan Hovhaness, and Lou Harrison.

Pursuing this line of thought inevitably leads to instrument simulation, inasmuch as certain musical instruments carry strong national associations: nods to Indonesian gamelan in the music of Debussy (*Pagodes* is an obvious gamelan 'take'), Leopold Godowsky (*Gamelan*, from his *Java Suite*), Colin McPhee, and the early prepared piano pieces of John Cage; the cimbalom's understandable influence in works of Liszt and Bartók; likewise the guitar in piano pieces of Albeniz, Granados, and Turina; and of course Gottschalk's *Banjo*.

The pipe organ is depicted by Busoni on the piano (he and also Liszt and Tausig made transcriptions of some of the more flamboyant Bach organ works) and, some say, by Anton Bruckner and Cesar Franck in their orchestration. Artur Schnabel[3] has suggested that Schubert was simulating the lute in his famous *Serenade*, and one can't help but wonder if Schumann didn't have snare drums in mind in the opening of the scherzo of his Opus 41, Number 1 *String Quartet*.

[3] Wolff, Konrad. Op. Cit., Chapter 11: "The Means of Regulating Sound." Page 156.

Of personal styles there's no dearth of interesting examples, either: Schumann's images of Chopin and Paganini in *Carnaval;* Mozart's *Overture in the Style of Handel,* K.399; Paderewski's near parodies of Mozart and Scarlatti; Ravel's piano piece 'in the style of Borodin.' Closer to our time, there's the influence of Charlie Parker on bebop pianists, and the impressions by the Beatles of the styles of some of their contemporaries *(Back in the USSR* – The Beach Boys/ *Honey Pie* – Tiny Tim/*Maxwell's Silver Hammer* – Herman's Hermits/*Helter Skelter* – Jimi Hendrix/and possibly also *Blackbird* – Donovan). The song *Memories* from the Andrew Lloyd Webber musical *Cats* even seems to out-Puccini Puccini.

Beyond mere allusion, some composers have gone so far as to quote one anothers' works – on purpose! Handel got caught with his fingers in others' musical cookie jars literally dozens of times. The most flagrant example involved the wholesale appropriation of a *Magnificat* by a composer named Erba. Bizet shamelessly lifted the *Habanera* in *Carmen* from *El Areglito* of Sebastian Yradier. Opera goers of today might readily associate the *Marche des Rois* with *L'Arlesienne,* but Bizet himself was counting on his contemporaries' recognizing it as a centuries-old Christmas song. Wagner's opening bars of *Tristan und Isolde* have been parodied by Debussy (*Golliwogg's Cake Walk)* and revered by Alban Berg (*Lyric Suite* for string quartet) and Shostakovich. Bartók in turn tweaked Shostakovich's nose in his *Concerto for Orchestra,* as Stravinsky had Lanner's in *Petrouchka.*

The penchant of earlier composers toward programmatic representation, from battle scenes by Beethoven, Tchaikovsky, Heinrich Biber, and James Hewitt to storms invoked by Mozart, Rossini, Berlioz, and many others, has flowered in the twentieth century. There have been the evocations of trains by Honegger and Villa Lobos, as well as Aleksandr Mossolov's literal sounding *Iron Foundry.* Certain works of Prokofiev inspired a new term – 'motoric.'

At the other extreme there have been twentieth century musical Audubons such as Olivier Messiaen who have fashioned entire compositions out of bird songs. Respighi's *Pines of Rome* might be cited as a precursor. Looking further back to the turn of the century, there is a report of a bird call showing up in the Dvořák Opus 96 *String Quartet,* and yet further back, there's an ornothological chanson by Clement Janequin. There are paeans to larks by Haydn and

Vaughan Williams; nightingales by Weelkes, Couperin, Granados, and Stravinsky; and cuckoos ever since sumer's ben icumen in. Hunted by Papageno, understood by Siegfried, birds could scarcely have been ignored by musical ears.

There are composers who take limitations of 'reality' as a challenge, as witness the remarkable player piano works of Conlon Nancarrow, or the flirtations with transcendent trickery of Liszt and Rachmaninoff. Some mid-twentieth century composers have irrationalized rhythmic values (dividing, rather than multiplying a basic unit), enforcing aperiodicity – already implicit in their music harmonically – to the extent of rearranging the metric niches whereon the notes were to be placed. These and others have created works which accentuate, even exacerbate the dichotomy mentioned above in connection with the term 'text.'

Increasingly, music is becoming conceptually as well as contrapuntally polyphonic. A composer can do more than one 'thing' at a time. That is, more than one form may apply concurrently. For example, *Don Quixote* of Richard Strauss is simultaneously a tone poem, programmatically alluding to the Cervantes original in some detail; a set of variations 'on a theme of knightly character;' a concert showpiece for 'cello and, to a lesser extent, viola; and (this is clearer in live performance than from a recording) a fascinating study in the interaction of orchestral styles and textures.

As you go toward the front of *il duomo* – Milan's grand cathedral – the architectural style advances from Gothic to Renaissance. There are several noteworthy instances of similar overlays in music. An entire period just before Stravinsky's Neoclassic phase is marked by pieces – *Pulcinella, La Baiser de la Fée* – which are essentially reconstructions of earlier music – Pergolesi and Tchaikovsky in these cases. One might cite also the 'Baroque' suites of Grieg, Tchaikovsky, Debussy, Ravel, and Richard Strauss. A substantial portion of Respighi's music consists of reworkings of older music. Lukas Foss's *Baroque Variations* is a similar rethinking of earlier material, but one that explores the subject far more deeply, if at least partially as a result of musical revelations that Stravinsky and others were to make since Neoclassicism. Paolo Castaldi's *Anfrage, for two pianos* is assembled completely from clippings of other people's music. The composer proudly announces that *there is not a single original note* in the entire piece! And of course my ideal of song writers, Tom Lehrer, did a nice take on *Spaghetti Rag* of Lyons and Yosco in his own *Vatican Rag*. Ave Maria (now, there's another example[4])!

It goes as far as cannibalism. Several twentieth century composers have gone back and revised or reworked their earlier pieces in their later years. Conductors like Mahler, Furtwängler, and Toscanini freely rescored Beethoven and Schumann. Bruckner and Mussorgsky suffered one indignity after another at the hands of well-meaning souls who were sure they knew better than the poor 'undereducated' composer. I know of at least half a dozen versions of *Pictures at an Exhibition*[5]. My favorite arrangement is still for piano solo.

Syllogism suffices for theatre but not for engineering. In both instances, however, it's possible to be right for the wrong reasons (or to be misunderstood correctly). Everyone must decide for themselves how to design their own art, in the face of a world in flux, and pseudo-mentors who are usually No Help. Like Sirens the Isms beckon. From highbrow space musicians that seek to extrude half an hour out of twelve seconds of material, to the Uptown Wuornout school of highly polished imitation middle Stockhausen designers. Periodicity was 'out' in the sixties, now it's 'in.' It's as capricious as the seasonal rise and fall of hemlines. Furthermore, a lot of the resulting works are little more than glorified 'show n' tell,' more fashionable than significant.

Various vogues may parade by with the years, but throughout them all there'll be artists at play with their audiences, creating and nurturing expectations in order to alternately fulfill, exceed, or frustrate them. Sure, you can point out structural, even geometric designs in the music of Bach, Mozart and Beethoven, but what makes the music work is that you *care* about what you hear. There's an involvement that transcends Euclidean definition. The way musical ideas imprint on our minds, for example, would possibly make a valuable study. How is it that people will tend to prefer the first performance or recording they hear of a composition, whether it is the best (or even 'correct') or not?

[4] Bach-Gounod, if you have to ask.
[5] In addition to the well known Ravel orchestration, all or part of the suite has been arranged by Touschmaloff, Rimsky-Korsakoff, Sir Henry Wood, Leonida Leonardi, Sergei Borshchakov, Leopold Stokowski, and Vladimir Ashkenazy – not to mention Keith Emerson.

A little investigation reveals the arbitrariness of many of our assumptions. For example, the schism between 'serious' and 'popular,' 'art' and 'folk' musics hasn't always been the same as it's been in this century. Adam de la Halle and Josquin des Pres wrote songs to which such categories are meaningless. Even original melodies of the Viennese classicists have a genuine *Volkslied* flavor. Perhaps it was in homage to that melodic gene pool that Schönberg included a reference to *Ach, du lieber Augustin* in his *Second String Quartet*. And it is probably no coincidence that some of the most interesting and effective concert pieces of the last hundred years come from composers – Dvořák, Bartók, and Berio come to mind – who have devoted a lot of attention to 'folk' sources. When his music seems to be at its wildest and craziest, it's exactly where Bartók is at his most faithful in rendering some eastern European folk nuance. The intersections of musical cultures can be particularly interesting, as for example the elaborate *rapprochement* of the oral African cultures with the hyperlexic European traditions, influencing both 'serious' and 'popular' music profoundly.

Interesting explorations are being made in the realms of style – often derided because so easily perceptible to the untrained[6]. Or perhaps it is because the 'trained' equate the subjective with the unreal, so as not to have to confront it. I'd define 'style' as the aggregate sum total of one's choices, decisions, and considerations about 'how to do it.' The viewpoint of those involved can be very different from what is perceived externally. It's like coral – collectively, they create a certain form, yet individually each polyp is just attending to its business as it sees fit[7]. In the various corners of the world, the 'way things are done' will vary considerably. Yet to the natives, notions of 'local style' dissolve like mist in a Hegelian sunrise.

A number of musical cultures around the world attach special significance to music emanating from the dream state. The Xmas songs *In Dulci Jubilo* and *O Little Town of Bethlehem* both come with stories of overnight inspiration. There's the famous story of Tartini and the Devil, of course – but the twelfth century Persian musician

[6] Alexander Salkind once remarked to a technician at a screening: "I don't know what you talk. I don't know nothing. I only hear what I see." There can be little doubt that his success as a film producer comes more from his ability to 'hear what he sees' than from knowledge of any particular technical details.
[7] Cf. Schönberg: "The artist...does what he finds necessary."

Ziryab[8] is said to have composed many of his songs in his dreams, and according to Frances Densmore, in Native American culture there were fewer sources of a song, chant – or in fact anything – more authoritative than receiving it in a Vision.

I've composed – and lost – two operas, a symphony, and a volume of keyboard music in my dreams. Fortunately, there have been a few pieces that didn't get away. Still, what works in the realms of the imagination might not go over in the 'real' world. The pristine 'what ifs' and 'how abouts,' even those of wakeful origin, have to run a gantlet of pragmatic questions of music theory, perception, and performance practice.

Whatever their origin, the question arises of how long to mull over ideas before committing them to paper. At one extreme, it can be frustrating to think of the ones that got away – they were so clear and obvious last night, but in the morning light they're nowhere to be found! At the other, there's the impulse to let an idea stew, to let it solidify free of the distortions that can come in the process of relating it to a symbology. The image of drop forging, to let the ball achieve maximum sphericity, free of gravitational distortion, comes to mind as a comparison. Of course there are choices in between the two extremes. Even a generalized and nonmusical description can be a start in that it will tend to accumulate related ideas like a fishnet.

Mozart mentioned glimpsing an entire symphony in a single flash. Even if everyone might not do it in comparable detail, this is not an uncommon ability. When you think of two compositions, or two different performances of the same one, do you not behold two instant images, like distant cities appearing on the horizon?

An inevitable difficulty lurks in that bottleneck of getting ideas – verbal or musical – written down. Aside from the torrential speed with which they can inundate your mind, you have to divert your attention *from* the part of the brain that generates them, and *to* what is essentially a clerical procedure.

Furthermore, an idea, once transubstantiated to the physical universe, might be a 'different animal' than it first seemed – just like the way that things that may be normal in a dream may be absurd in the waking world. Like, Siegfried wasn't expecting anything like Brünnhilde! There's always an element of surprise in hearing a

[8] Starkie, Walter. *Spain: A Musician's Journey through Space and Time.*
  Geneva: EDISLI, 1958. Page 33.

performance of a work that's only existed in your mind until then. The test of the composer's art is whether that surprise be a pleasant one.

Debussy once said that he felt that composition should remain an arcane art, and composers shouldn't reveal all that they're doing. Indeed, a dramaturge may describe a theatre piece in detail and only obliquely allude to the plot. But this doesn't necessarily mean that 'art' consists of fooling the audience: "What you can get away with," as someone once put it. Despite any hocus-pocus gyrations that practitioners may go through to tout the importance of their work, a suprapattern will eventually emerge, for all to see. Therein will be revealed not only the intended meanings, but factors that are so much a part of the artists' make-up as to be invisible to the artists themselves.

Debussy's concern was in all likelihood misplaced. The intuitive apprehension of the musical process can neither be taught, nor can it be learned. The finest definition and codification emerges as futile as trying to make a 'definitive' map of the clouds. It's the difference between a native speaker's purview of the context and a student's translating word by word out of a lexicon.

Symbols, whether verbal or musical, may be confused not only with tangible objects they represent, but intangibles such as ideas as well. Idea is senior to symbol – it's the direct synaptic connection that makes it possible to think and communicate in any number of languages without mentally translating. History has tended to be kinder to those who were in control of, rather than tangled up in, the symbols they're invoking.

One of the results of proliferating technologies is that Time appears to pass by more rapidly. There are those, however, who would make this apparency of escalation a pretext for artistic judgment. It is an attitude summed up by Stockhausen when he brushed off a student's idea with: "We've been doing this since years." (Note the German usage amid the English vocabulary). The vehicle was moving faster and faster through the pages of history, and composers were vying with one another to be the hood ornament. The paradigm seemed to consist of inventing systems and techniques *in order to* make them obsolete!

There can be little doubt but that Karl Bach and Josef Haydn would have considered it only fitting that the symphonic form they helped define should have been made use of so often, and by so many. In the twentieth century, however, forms have become so totally identified with their content as to tend to make further realizations redundant. It is as if the composers were being asked to reinvent their music with every ensuing piece. Instead of being kept around as useful, forms and models had become eminently disposable.

It's natural to assume that increased complexity of *métier* implies increased complexity of structural and formal considerations. Held up as a paragon in this regard, the works of Anton Webern nevertheless seem distilled to molecular simplicity rather than saturated with information content. In praising him for "expressing a novel in a sigh," Schönberg might well have been admiring an achievement that he himself had been seeking. It's not unlike the tyro's assumption that the more notes per unit time, the better the playing.

While *métier* may change with the years, many of the trappings do not: the manifestos, polemics, theatrical postures – all the sociological affectations of post-adolescent enlightenment. When Gunther Schuller, in his seminar at the 1962 Ojai Festival, 'complimented' William Kraft's perform-ance of Stockhausen's *Zyklus* by referring to it as "his own (that is, Mr. Kraft's) composition," it seemed that he was being gratuitously catty. I mean, if the result is musically viable, why should anyone care? What's more, there are a lot of pieces much more deserving of his scorn than this work. He'd scarcely complain about a jazz drum solo, which is far less rigorously defined than the Stockhausen spiral bound piece. And how is William Kraft, the redoubtable percussionist/composer, to feel? Did he waste his labors on what was to serve as a negative example, or was he being slighted for his choice of repertoire?

Truth is, there's no style one can adopt without arousing the scorn of some captious faction or other. Some may find it reassuring to be told by some authority what kind of music to write, especially those not quick-witted enough to see the possibilities for themselves. One may perch in a cage made by Satie, or lounge in a settee made by Cage. Berio compared music to language. It's there awaiting us at birth, yet we interact with it as time goes by.

But at root language is arbitrary. Words are explained in terms of
– earlier words. Like a giant conceptual ball of yarn, the syllogism
ultimately unravels. As does one's sense of rationale. To make any
value judgment – especially artistically, since an artistic principle
need not be correct in order to function – is to invite its opposite. In
the inner cities, 'bad' is now 'good,' and in living memory 'hot' and
'cool' have approached synonymity. One person's reason *to* do
something could be another's *not* to[9].

In one of his more lucidly cynical moods Bill Walker said that the
only reason to do anything is because something's wrong. Action is
response, an attempt to return to an imagined 'same old used-to-be,'
to restore equilibrium. But when you get there, and you are then free
to design your next work with a clean slate – what then? There's the
'Desk Top Illusion,' the idea of getting totally and permanently
caught up, so you can actually see the top of your desk. Even on
those occasions when it's possible to be temporarily on top of things,
the resulting feeling is often not one of achievement but of emptiness. Model Subject Number 28 of *The Iron Flute* compares those
who reach the 'Ultimate Stage' to 'burglars sneaking into a vacant
house.[10]' It's a state worth working toward not so much because it's
so intrinsically full of grace, but because it enables you to tackle fresh
projects without distraction. There will always be that next hill on
the horizon.

It becomes a question of being comfortable enough in one's own
knowledge to feel secure in making judgments for oneself. The way
it seemed to me as a teenager in Darmstadt was that if everything
had been done, there wasn't anything left for a young composer to
do. The way I finally turned it around was to figure that, well, if
everything had been done (a spurious premise anyway) I could do
whatever I pleased! John Cage quoted Vergil Thomson on how to
write American music: "First, be an American. Then, do as you
wish!" The same may be said to apply to writing 'contemporary'
music – just to be alive today should be enough. But many are too
deeply imprinted by one discipline or another to ascertain what it is
they really want. It's like 'trying to relax.' For all the inexorable

---

[9] While recording *Mountains of the Moon*, Phil Lesh wanted the instrumental accents ('fol-de-
rol-de-rid-dle') swiveled opposite their counterparts in the words, rather than doubling
them, the 'standard' way.
[10] Senzaki, Nyogen and McCandlass, Ruth S. *The Iron Flute*. Rutland, Vermont and Tokyo:
Charles E. Tuttle, 1964. Cf. also *I Ching*. Hexagram Number 46. Third Line: "One pushes
upward into an empty city" (Wilhelm/Baynes translation).

inevitability posterity may infer from their traces, the prime movers (Igor Stravinsky, Bob Dylan, for example) are often the least predictable, and if such an attitude has worked so well for them, it should be at least worth a try.

## ANNOTATED BIBLIOGRAPHY

ABELL, ARTHUR M. *Talks with Great Composers.* Garmisch-Partenkirchen: G.E. Schröder Verlag, 1964. The impressions of Brahms are especially engaging.

BERLINER, PAUL. *The Soul of Mbira.* Berkeley: University of California Press, 1978.

CHERNOFF, JOHN MILLER. *African Rhythm, African Sensibility.* Chicago: University of Chicago Press, 1979. Approaching Carlos Castaneda in style, these books reveal much not only about the music and musicians, but also about the social impact and function of music. May there be more such – Africa is a big continent!

BLESH, RUDI AND HARRIET JANIS. *They All Played Ragtime.* New York: Alfred Knopf, 1950. For the longest time this was the only book on the subject. An encyclopædia or a bible, depending on whom you ask. Does its billing justice, though.

CAGE, JOHN. *Silence.* Middletown, Ct.: Wesleyan University Press, 1961.

_____. *A Year From Monday.* Middletown, Ct.: Wesleyan University Press, 1967. Every time I settle into the simplistic attitude that John Cage is a composer whose impact will ultimately be greater as a philosopher than as a music man, I hear a new piece of his that takes my head off. These, and his subsequent books, however, are a treasure trove of ideas, images, and stories well nigh guaranteed to lift you off your moorings.

COWELL, HENRY. *New Musical Resources.* New York, London: A. A. Knopf, 1930. The ideas of an American musical pioneer, straight from the source. It is not only his loss, but ours, that he didn't have more people of like mind to talk to.

DENSMORE, FRANCES. *Choctaw Music. Northern Ute Music. Papago Music. Pawnee Music. Teton Sioux Music. Yuman and Yaqui Music.* New York: Da Capo Press, 1972.

_____. *Chippewa Music*. Washington: U.S. Government Printing Office, 1910-13.

_____. *Seminole Music*. Washington: U.S. Government Printing Office, 1956. Landmark studies, with lots of musical examples, of a fascinating culture that was still flickering with life at the time of these investigations. They were originally published (in most cases) under the auspices of the Bureau of Land Management or the Smithsonian Institution.

Eco, Umberto. *Opera Aperta*. Milan: Casa Editrice Valentino Bompiani, 1962. The questions opened by John Cage made interesting problems for the European *avant garde's* need to rationalize its every move. European 'open' works were essentially road maps among prescribed choices rather than truly aleatoric chance processes. It seemed as if, for as far as they had come, they were still tethered to Platonic precepts of control. It would be a while before a Stockhausen could bring himself to write anything as loose as *Spiral*, or *Aus den sieben Tagen*. Earlier such procedures were rejected as "unrigorous and æsthetically unacceptable," to quote from Andre Hodeir. The first glimmers of awareness were in this study of 'Open Form' by Umberto Eco, and in Heinz-Klaus Metzger's article *John Cage o della liberazione*, which appeared in *Incontri Musicali* and was reprinted in *Die Reihe*.

Einstein, Alfred. *The Italian Madrigal*. Princeton: Princeton University Press, 1949. A paragon of musicology. Numerous musical examples – the third and final volume is chock full of them – and a great deal of historical and theoretical background as well. An engrossing study in how music evolved in a little over a century.

Erickson, Robert. *Sound Structure in Music*. Berkeley: University of California Press, 1975. Professor Erickson's presence on the faculties of the San Francisco Conservatory and U. S. San Diego made for a golden age of music in each case. The San Francisco Tape Music Center arose under his ægis, and La Jolla was a haven for such as Pauline Oliveros and Bernard Rands. In this book the good professor lays out his insights in an entertaining way. Webern will never sound the same again.

Harrison, Lou. *Music Primer*. New York, C. F. Peters, 1971. Useful information....mind fulminating ideas...gorgeous calligraphy...I'd give it a '10.'

HILLER, LEJAREN A., AND LEONARD ISAACSON. *Experimental Music.* New York: McGraw-Hill, 1959. A more extensive development of the material in the article in the December, 1959 *Scientific American.* Hiller, aside from being one of the pioneers of computer music, manages to blend thoroughgoing scientific objectivity with manic creativity. This book concentrates on compositional algorithms, specifically those used in the *Illiac Suite.*

HODEIR, ANDRE. *Since Debussy, a View of Contemporary Music.* New York: Grove Press, 1961. Making the best of his reputation as a jazz critic, Hodeir fashioned this book as a pitch for his crony Jean Barraqué. Simply because there were scarcely any other books on Boulez, Stockhausen, *et. al.,* it attained to a significance far beyond its merit. Barraqué's music is not bad – kind of a softer edge Boulez – but I don't see any monumental works such as might eclipse the other modern masters that Hodeir rates so far below his pal.

LANDY, LEIGH. *At a Fork in the Way.* Amsterdam, 1980. Eventually serialized in *Ear* magazine in the early eighties, this is an insightful overview of the European contemporary music scene – reflections of a voraciously inquisitive mind that I can only admire.

MATHEWS, MAX. V., ET AL. *The Technology of Computer Music.* Cambridge, Mass., and London: The M. I. T. Press, 1969. Unlike Hiller's above-cited book, this one gets more into sound synthesis, specifically by means of the Music V program, developed by Mathews at Bell Laboratories.

MESSIAEN, OLIVIER. *Technique de mon Langage Musical.* Paris: Leduc, 1956. A landmark work by the teacher of Boulez and Stockhausen.

PARTCH, HARRY. *Genesis of a Music.* Madison: University of Wisconsin Press, 1949. Looking back to Cowell, and forward to Lou Harrison, this is the kind of book whose significance grows with each passing year. It is a work that, to paraphrase Schumann's description of Brahms, will take generations of Pharisees to decipher.

ROUGET, GILBERT. *Music and Trance.* Chicago: University of Chicago Press, 1985. Mickey Hart turned me on to this book. A refreshingly analytical examination of an area where subjectivity has wreaked havoc. As with any musical question, no matter how far you trace the whys and wherefores, it comes to a point where all you can say is "that's just the way it feels."

SCHÖNBERG, ARNOLD. *Style and Idea.* New York: St. Martin's Press,

1975. A revelation of Schönberg's mind, and how he was able to impress Berg and Webern so much. Not so much nuts and bolts talk, although there are plenty of musical examples, as passionate investigations of the more subjective aspects of music. "An apostle who does not glow preaches heresy," he said, and the light these essays generate reflects well on their author. Personally, this was one of the three documents I encountered in my late teens that impressed me the most profoundly[11].

SCHONBERG, HAROLD C. *The Great Pianists, from Mozart to the Present*. New York: Simon and Schuster, 1963. I might have listed this book after the chapter on piano playing, but its historical and theoretical import is even greater than its technical. It brings into focus a wide range of greater and lesser luminaries. Who studied with whom. What who thought about whomever. The hows, whys, and wherefores of their music. Some books you skim, some you savor. This one I chug-a-lugged. Eminently readable for all its four-hundred-plus pages, it's still a whirlwind tour that suffers here and there for want of a little more research.

Some points are minor (even diminished). My facsimile of the Couperin work on keyboard performance *does* say "1717", as Schonberg dates it, but further examination reveals it to be a reissue of a work that had appeared the previous year. Couperin evidently had already made the discovery that nothing aids proofreading better than publication! Later in his book Schonberg drops an 'I' from Bella Davidovitch, and then compounds his error by commenting on the masculine sounding name!

But these are mere quibbles. More telling is his mention of how advances in technology allowed nineteenth century pianists to be more expressive, followed by his curt dismissal of Hans von Bülow's descriptive programs for the Chopin *Preludes*. I find Schonberg's suggestion that such an anti-idiosyncratic martinet as von Bülow was indulging in frivolous flummery hard to swallow. Even in our times, who is so abstract of mind that they've never imagined fanciful images in connection with a piece of music? Movie composers even encourage the association. The immense popularity of Walt Disney's *Fantasia* is *based* on it!

That any given piece of music may convey any number of different images to different people is immaterial. Adolph Kullak

---

[11] The other two being the Parable of the Talents in the New Testament and Emerson's essay on self-reliance.

(Op. Cit. pp 324-327) relates no fewer than eight different scenarios to imagine along with Beethoven's *Moonlight* Sonata! The very epithet 'Moonlight' comes not from the composer, but (most likely) the early nineteenth century music reviewer Heinrich Rellstab. But it really doesn't make any difference. The existence and accessibility of a coherent feeling 'behind' the notes is the important point, no matter how incomplete and inadequate a verbal description of it must inevitably be[12]. In this connection Schonberg reveals himself as the mid-twentieth century clinician.

He quotes Beethoven's license with his sonata movments, and then, like Alfred Brendel in his otherwise excellent book (Op. Cit.), tries to rationalize it away. What about all of those interchangeable Bach movements? Or Mozart's 'assembled' sonata (K.533-K.494, with the second movement – bars 8-10 – anticipating Mahler)? Or the 'Haffner' complex (K. 250/385)? A twist here, a turn there, and before your very ears a serenade turns into a symphony, a cantata into a concerto, with all the ease of a menacing looking toy robot transforming into a shiny jet plane. What about the *Große Fuge*, removed and set aside like a vacuum cleaner attachment that was too large? Who's to say that our sacred *Urtext* editions are the *only* possibilities that their composers might have dreamed of?

How valid, after all, is the assumption that one single version alone carries the composer's blessing? What of the decisions he didn't get around to making – or *decided not to make*. A composer/performer, especially, has reason to keep the options open! Within these pillars there is a lot of room to navigate. Comparison of recordings of Chopin by pianists whose knowledge of the music was closer to first hand – Karl Mikuli, Moriz Rosenthal, Ferruccio Busoni, and Josef Lhevinne – reveals a soaring image untrammeled by any imperatives of uniformity. Early recordings of their own works made by composers such as Debussy often differ substantially from the printed scores, and the disparities don't sound like mistakes!

This spirit of adventure, so crucial to the Romantic movement, has been strangled to death. A quarter century ago, when Glenn Gould attempted his bold experiments with the Beethoven G major and Brahms D minor concertos when he played them with the New York Philharmonic, conductor Leonard Bernstein felt compelled to

---

[12] "A fantastic description of a piece of music is possible only in so far as it is understood to be metaphorical." E. T. A. Hoffmann.

announce that it was Gould's idea, not his. His disclaimer amounted to an admission that the spark of life had gone out. That the beautiful butterfly on display was dead. It was all the more ironic that the visionary pianist should be portrayed as the strange one for trying to breathe life into a corpse. 'Respect them but don't disturb them.' This attitude toward the classic repertoire – is it not the very attitude appropriate to the dear departed?

SHELDRAKE, RUPERT. *A New Science of Life*. Los Angeles, J. P. Tarcher, Inc., 1981. Extremely interesting to find so many ideas applicable to the evolution of artistic thought in this, a book built on the life sciences. The legend of the hundredth monkey may well be apocryphal, but there are too many instances – Adams and Leverrier discovering Neptune, Newton and Leibnitz coming up with the calculus, virtually simultaneously – that would tend to indicate that there's *something* there.

WHITCOMB, IAN. *After the Ball*. New York: Simon & Schuster, 1972. A wonderful book. History, technology, sociology – all the root causes of why 'popular' music behaved the way it did are fleshed out in fascinating detail..

XENAKIS, IANNIS. *Formalized Music*. Bloomington: Indiana University Press, 1971. A translation of the book that appeared in France in 1963. Just because his music doesn't speak to me doesn't mean that I'm not enormously impressed with his contributions.

YOUNG, LA MONTE. *An Anthology*. New York: Heiner Friedrich, 1963. Fustest with the mostest, as General Sheridan put it, among the collections of aggressively inventive new scores. Later there came Cage's fine collection, *Notations*, and *Source* magazine, but it all started here.

## PERIODICALS

*Die Reihe*. Edited by Herbert Eimert and Karlheinz Stockhausen. Published by Universal Edition, Vienna (in German), and Theodore Presser, Philadelphia (in English).

*Incontri Musicali*. Edited by Luciano Berio. Published in Milan by Suvini Zerboni.

*Perspectives of New Music*. Princeton University Press.

All of these quasi periodicals appeared from the late fifties through the sixties. Many articles appeared in more than one of them in translation.

# 10/ PUMPING IVORY
## what to do until the piano teacher comes

> *"...take it from me:*
> *playing the piano is easy."*
> Heinrich Neuhaus

The best way to learn is by doing. Now, given a life span of several hundred years, a fine instrument, and the inclination to take the time to do it, most of us could get our level of playing up to Lisztian heights. The function of good instruction, then, is to save us time. A few decades here, a year saved there, and some timely advice here and there, and the task becomes more humanly manageable. You might discover something yourself, but it could take half your life. That time, effort, and more can be saved by an experienced player looking over your shoulder and making a suggestion or two.

"How many hours a day do you (what they really mean is 'should I') practice?" Stupid question. Even a well-intentioned answer can do more harm than good. You get kids paying more attention to some dumb egg timer on the piano than the business at hand. And even with the best of motivation, the petty mundanities that inundate our lives can leave scant room for anything else. Often every available scrap of time one can find to practice is scarcely enough. And those times when one *has* practiced 'enough,' it's not because a certain amount of time has elapsed.

The important consideration is how to *spend* that time, so as to use it to optimum advantage. 'Practice' and 'memorization' are such generalized terms, and as such are subject to misinterpretation. For example, the idea that one learns music by 'memorizing the notes,' is as absurd as the thought that one may grasp a language by learning its alphabet. The notion of each note as having its own solitary existence has no basis in reality. If you wait until after one note is played before you contemplate finding the next, you'll be limited to playing very, very slow pieces. Furthermore, the notes themselves are merely an abstraction. The true place where the music resides is not on the page or on the keys but in the hands.

There is no vehicular traffic up the mountain of musical knowledge. All who would make the climb do so by dint of zesty application of labor and lavish helpings of common sense. By the same token, it's unrealistic to expect that any progressive step will cover any more ground than the length of your metaphorical leg. It can be easy to lose sight of the fact that, until you *are* able to play a piece, you're *not!* You're gradually installing an associative network that cannot be expected to be fully functional until it's completed, or at least close to it. Before the tide is in, the boat is aground, and can't be moved. But that magic moment comes, when the water is deep enough, and the boat is suddenly a vehicle. Likewise, the ability to play a piece comes only after one's knowledge of it is deepened through practice.

On the way to achieving that ability, there are both sudden and gradual breakthroughs. Sometimes the only thing more frustrating than not knowing what you're doing wrong, is not knowing what you're doing right! Many of the most important lessons to be learned are subverbal – direct communication between the brain and networks of finger, hand, and/or arm muscles in their own primal autonomous language. Their discussion concerns the setting up of a certain situation or context, wherefrom the neural image may be deduced. Most études fit this model. You can't be told how to ride a bike, but you can work your way to a vantage point from which you can *apprehend* how it's done.

Apropos of exercises, the fine Austrian pianist Robert Majek expressed it best when he said, "How can you learn to play music by practicing something that is not music?" From my own experience, however, I can heartily recommend doing the Hanon exercises in all keys. Aside from their great value as digital calisthenics, practicing them this way will solidify one's feel for scale patterns far better than simply practicing the scales by themselves. Furthermore, it strengthens the 'footing' on those precarious black notes. The taxonomy of the various scales takes on tactile meaning – notice how D, A, and E major resemble one another, or how F#/Gb is a 'negative' of F and G major, with its two white notes at the points of the scale where the latters' black notes are. True, these exercises are not music – but scales and chords are the material out of which a lot of music has been fashioned.

Muscular development is important only at the most rudimentary stages. What well-written studies contribute is an arena wherein to examine the most relevant musical gestures in their every possible manifestation. Why wait until you've explored enough of the repertoire to give you a grasp of various technical problems when a thoughtful soul has taken the time and trouble to assemble a quick view of all of them? Why not take a well-hewn path through the woods to straightaway master and *surround* the material?

Even those who nominally reject exercises can't avoid them. Several have suggested that students derive their own 'exercises' from the specific works they're studying. That approach suffers from comparison with study of real exercises in that it is spotty and unrigorous. In my experience as student and teacher, I've noticed that such a regimen is so vague as to rarely get done. For a William Newman to write "the way to learn Beethoven is to practice Beethoven" sounds weighty and beyond dispute, but it's just plain wrong. Studies of his contemporaries (the 'three C's:' Clementi, Cramer, and Czerny are virtually alone in their generation in their having earned Beethoven's respect as pianists) add a dimension of understanding of Beethoven's music not possible otherwise.

A good exercise funtions like a trellis for your technique. In the absence of a caring teacher to chase you up the mountain like a tiger, exercises offer an opportunity to get some purchase in your steps toward musical progress. Getting out of that rut, making substantial improvement – almost by definition that means doing something that you're not doing now. And that's where practice comes in.

Practice, most simply defined, is the repetition of correct actions. The value of repetition on a cumulative basis is well known. That feeling of osmotically softening the hard edges – noticing how the next day things are 'inexplicably' easier – anyone who has studied music for more than a year has noticed it. What hasn't been as loudly heralded, however, is the value of immediate repetition – at the same sitting. Right away. Attempting to learn a piece of music without the reinforcement that repetitive practice gives is – to borrow from the incomparable Mullah Nazrudin – like trying to boil water with a candle. I have found that scant improvement is possible in practicing a piece fewer than three times at a single sitting. Five to ten times is yet better, although there is a point of diminishing returns, especially for beginners.

Individual passages (say, two to six measures in length) I have worked twenty-five times and more, but it must be said that the aim is not to play the piece well the fortieth time, but to be able to play it well the first time. On one occasion, having not solved a particularly sticky passage in a Debussy *Etude* to my satisfaction after twenty-five runs through, I decided to go for twenty-five more. Still dissatisfied with the results, I wound up deciding to try another brace of iterations, during which I discovered that I'd misconstrued the passage all along! I make it about the seventy-fifth run through. The definitions of genius of Carlyle: "The infinite capacity for taking pains," and Edison: "One percent inspiration and ninety-nine percent perspiration" come to mind. As a kid playing stickball in the streets, I remember deciding to catch the ball and hold on to it no matter how much it might hurt. Somehow it never seemed to hurt as much after that decision.

A famous virtuoso once said, "Don't take seriously the first thousand times you play a piece."

Generous applications of repetition on several levels result in an awareness of the doingness on a gestural plane. Practicing is thusly a process of gradually programming your neural circuitry for what is in effect digital choreography. The reiterative process consists of three phases. First, a simple run through of the piece. No intense concentration, strain or struggle – just to get the feel of it, and, even more, find out where the troublesome spots are. Aim at a tempo that is slow enough to be possible, yet fast enough to be alive.

Secondly, you can tackle those difficult areas, each in turn, until you feel more comfortable in approaching them. It's important to attack the problems at their source – the beginner's tendency is to play over and over those parts that they already know, neglecting the troublesome spots. I've even seen students try to get a running jump on a tough passage, as if they could leap over it like a pole vaulter! Naturally enough, students derive more pleasure from what they can do than what they haven't figured out yet.

The third phase is no less important, though: back up and practice the lead-in to every rough spot. These problems almost always translate into terms of either fingering or hand placement, and, just as in unraveling a knot, a solution in one area can often cause problems in another. Moreover, one can tend to stiffen unnaturally in anticipation of a once problematical passage, with the resultant hazards in the break in attention.

As one repeats the three phases, a clear, wire-to-wire image of the piece emerges and solidifies. My usual experience in such a practice regimen is that the first run through is a bit on the rough side. No matter – that's what practice is for, to make it better. Which is usually what the second attempt is, even if marginally. The third time I often don't feel like doing it again, but usually am glad that I went ahead and did, because it seems to clear things up for subsequently getting down to brass tacks and working out details.

The ultimate goal has to be a performance that you can be proud of. For that reason, I'll usually wind things up with a run through 'as if performing.' It's important not to ignore one's performance mode, since it's very different from practicing. While you perform you should feel as comfortable and natural as possible. One wants to make all the mistakes in practice instead of on stage! Let them happen, but notice where they occur and try to figure out why – relax into perfection.

Occasionally, giving your hand 'its head' can be useful in identifying and clarifying problems. Where does the hand seem to want to go, instead of the right place? Why? Is there a wrist or arm movement that's gone unnoticed, what with your attention concentrated elsewhere? Maybe the fingers are already where they should be, and for some reason you feel you have to move them somewhere else. It's easier to correct a movement after you've defined it. You might well discover that your hesitation is unwarranted, a chimera that needn't worry you any more. The overall aim is to liberate attention that was tied up in technical considerations, so you may concentrate more on the more 'musical' aspects of the work.

A lot of energy is needlessly wasted simply because the motion vectors of finger, wrist, arm, and shoulder are at odds with one another. Focus on how you shift your weight, how and when you pause, how you aim at the keys. As a rule of thumb, the center of gravity should be over the finger that is playing. That's how wrist movements arise, like in the Hanon Exercise #8, or the Chopin A$^b$ Etude, Op. 25, Nr. 1. It takes more than the fingers to make music, and examination of how wrist and arm movements come into play will ultimately reward the student with greater control for less effort.

Watch out for the tendency to hold back: "Maybe if I don't play as loud it won't be as noticeable if I make a mistake." Picture yourself running across a wide stream by stepping on stones that are close enough together for there always to be a way to 'get there from here,' even if you occasionally have to stretch. Depending on how seriously you want to practice, you can imagine piranhas or crocodiles in the water.

Fingering – now, there's a realm that teems with misunderstandings. Dynamics, phrasing, articulation – all these can be decided later. But not fingering. The idea is not to strain your brain to memorize numbers and notes and glue them together in your mind. It's simply the application of common sense to the problem of having a finger there when you need it to play a note. At least as important as the choice of finger is the position of the hand. We should be able to assume that a given piece of music wasn't written not to be able to be played (damn those defective verbs!), and that one can postulate a coherent and comprehensible set of gestures that will deliver up every note. The clarity and simplicity of those gestures can be masked by as little as their being out of phase with the beams or barlines. A piece of music can be thought of as a dynamic imaginary glove you want to fill with your fingers as fully as you can.

Once you've got a piece 'in your fingers,' moreover, it's not as immutable as learning a formula or mastering a paradigm. The knowingness, or noumenon, continues to behave organically, and is subject to all the vagaries thereof. Nuances that are there for the taking one performance will be tantalizingly unimaginable the next. "Pianists," to quote Mario Feninger, "are like the Moon." As the view of a landscape is altered by passing clouds, a work of music changes from time to time. Anton Rubinstein refused to hear a student play the same piece more than once, lest he confuse the student with conflicting ideas based on such changes.

Some gestures only occur when you play the piece at tempo. What a waste of time to wait till then to discover them! They often contain a hint to an easier way to perform the passage. I'll even make a game of it, first trying to find the tempo slow enough to play the entire piece confidently and continuously, and then seeing how fast the difficult spots can be negotiated. Ultimately the two tempi meet. I'll often, for another example, take a familiar piece and deliberately play it too fast – to shake out lingering rough spots – and then too slow – to see if any nuances might yet be revealed.

Much of the battle consists of getting the arm, hand and finger gestures as close as possible to those of the music. There are reasons for them to tend to diverge, and this is not an aspect of playing that improves without attention. Think of what it'll feel like when you're able to play the piece. Like a teenager playing 'air guitar,' you can imagine a causative relation between your movements and the sound.

Brahms once said that the best performance he ever heard of Beethoven's *Ninth Symphony* was what he imagined when he read the score. Reading through a piano piece without playing it can also have a liberating effect. You can explore the natural flow and momentum of the music, unencumbered by considerations of what it's possible for your hands to do. As you skim through a piece that you know, do you rush, even skip ahead here and there? Are these passages that you presume you know, or is there some lurking complication, the intricacy of which you've been putting off confronting?

With technical considerations factored out, conceptual uncertainties are highlighted. You can't get the music in your fingers if it isn't in your mind. Are there musical gestures and ideas you wouldn't dare try on a real keyboard? Ironically, removal of the imperative to find the notes can clear the air enough to reveal technical aspects, like fingering, hand placement, or movement – things you can apply when you get back to the keyboard.

Progress occurs in two distinct ways, each with its own appropriate response. There's the intensive, analytical process: working out the intricacies of strategy, the way one can negotiate a specific technicality, or more likely, a forest of them. Then there's the gradual advance of the level of ability that comes with deepening the imprint on the mind that repetition naturally causes. In practical terms, this means that there are times when it's important to see something through to a conclusion, and then there are times when it's prudent to leave the battle for another day.

It can be misleading sometimes to jump to conclusions about how well one is doing based on any given day's playing. An accomplishment might appear larger in prospect than in retrospect, or vice versa. Advances in understanding can raise your standards, making an achievement seem less impressive. There are plateaux, such as people encounter while earnestly trying to lose weight, when even sustained effort brings no apparent result. There are two times to make sure to continue practicing: when things are going so slowly you don't think you'll ever get anywhere, and when they're going so well you feel like saying, "Who, me practice?"

As you progress through the stages of a discipline, you get flashes of how it'll be on the next stage. Something to enjoy and learn from – but the return to the quotidian shouldn't signal any discouragement. You haven't 'lost' anything in the intervening twenty four hours. It's still there awaiting you, and you have all the better idea of where to find it, having had that delicious glimpse.

It is good to practice by memory – better still with eyes closed. Beginners will commonly bog down half way into a piece, because that's all they could find time for, and they always started at the beginning. I've tried learning pieces last measure first, then last two, last three, and so on. As a result, instead of getting ever more unsure of myself as the piece went on, I was feeling more and more confident.

Like knowing the way around one's home town, it's possible to know several ways to play the same piece equally well. Clementi and Hanon among others wrote studies with alternate fingerings. In his edition of the Chopin *Etudes*, Alfred Cortot often lists as many as ten different fingerings, for the same passage! To assert that one must learn one fingering and one fingering only reveals a low estimation of the student's abilities.

There is no substitute for knowing what you are doing, and nothing breeds confidence like practice. This growing feeling of certainty is very real, and can serve as an indicator of your progress. If your aim is certainty, speed will not be far behind. It's important to 'see' the notes, like a Ted Williams or Stan Musial would 'see' the ball. Nor are all mistakes overt and obvious. Hitting the right note either 'by accident' or with the wrong finger, can betoken insufficient certainty of one's material.

There are signs that are both good and bad – such as noticing that you've been daydreaming but the music continues to happen under your hands as if automatically. Like when you get to the bottom of the page in a book and you realize that you can't remember a single thing you've read. This is good news in that it means the digital programming is starting to 'take' – that motions once strained and contrived are getting to feel natural and unencumbered. A mind that's not operating makes no mistakes. You can even – tsk, tsk – get away with sloppy fingerings that you couldn't before.

The moment before one begins to play is of great importance. It's easy to lapse into the idea that you're 'as ready as you'll ever be,' and consequently get into the habit of beginning precipitously, like being shoved off a diving board into the cold water. 'Joining' the music in a relaxed manner, as if it were already in progress, not only calms jittery beginnings but makes continuing easier, as well. Artur Schnabel has suggested[1] imaginary beats before a work opens, so as not to upset the flow. This also counteracts the tendency to start at too rapid a tempo, out of nervousness or excitement.

[1] Wolff, Konrad. Op. Cit., Chapter 7: 'Rhythmic Articulation.' Page 71/Example 79. Referring, among many other examples, to the Schubert *Sonata* in B-flat, Op. Posth., Schnabel suggests fictional changes in meter to avoid undesired accents.

Find and learn to get comfortable within your level of ability. A beginner will look at all those sixteenth notes and assume that music is beyond that level. When the pyrotechnics start, it's easy to be caught up in the exhilaration of the moment and be drawn into skating beyond it – like driving beyond your headlights. I've noticed that music I've recorded sounds faster on playback than it felt while laying the track down. Slowing down thusly benefits me two ways: 1) it sounds less rushed to the listener and 2) it seems like I have more time while playing, and can relax more.

Time can even seemingly expand. You'll have more time to find your way through the piece, even as you're playing it faster than way back when it gave you such trouble. The border of ability extends farther – what was once unthinkable becomes easy. Yogi Berra said, "I can't think and hit at the same time." The time will come when you have to put all that behind you and *play*.

Music embraces an ocean of viewpoints to play in. At any given performance of a piece of music, there's the score, which is not necessarily the composer's only version, nor even necessarily close to the original imagined possibility. There's the performer's interpretation, drawn from sources ranging from subjective whims to scholarly research. The actual performance will most likely differ from this ideal to some degree. And then each listener has their own impressions and experiences for the piece to reflect through. So much to think about, if one is so inclined.

One may need to adjust to the acoustics or ambience of a performance space, or to an individual piano – like potential spouses, they are wondrously infinite in their variety. Similarly editions. Comparison of the Schnabel and Schenker editions of Beethoven, or the several Chopin editions adds a dimension to the understanding of the works themselves. There arise considerations of relating to other performers; of allowing for a balance of viewpoints, as from hearing differently from across the hall; or learning from comparing one's recollection with what comes out on the recorded playback. Ever more possibilities to consider, perceptions to evaluate, combinations to explore. But that's where the fun begins, don't you think?

## ANNOTATED BIBLIOGRAPHY

BACH, KARL PHILIPP EMMANUEL. *Essay on the True Method of Playing Keyboard Instruments.* New York: W. W. Norton & Co., 1949. That's 'Method,' not 'Art.' The German word is a cognate, not a synonym to its English eponym. It should be noted that the below cited Couperin work is rendered correctly in German: 'Kunst.' Anyhow, this work, dating back to 1753, by the most eminent of J. S. Bach's offspring, is of enormous significance. Beethoven used it as a text in his instruction, and it is the foundation upon which Czerny, Clementi, and Cramer developed their precepts. Its historic significance may be likened to the importance of the *Almagest* of Ptolemy to the science of astronomy. Like that ancient work, however, it was also the source of many ideas which have since been discredited.

For instance, the compulsive avoidance of use of the thumb on the 'black' keys may be traced to this work. Forgivable enough on the face of it, considering that use of the thumb at all was an eighteenth century innovation. The Chopin $E^b$ minor *Etude*, Op. 10, Nr. 6 is an effective antidote to that notion.

Also there is Bach's assertion that "very few passages permit alternative fingerings." I've found the exact opposite to be the case! In fact, the point can be attained where the consideration of what finger should play what note fades into irrelevance. Anton Rubinstein once answered a Josef Hofmann query about fingering with "Play it with your nose, but make it sound well!"

BACON, ERNST. *Notes on the Piano.* Syracuse: Syracuse University Press, 1963. I love this book! Delicious and nutritious, it's 'chock full' of Gee-I-wish-I'd-said-thats and But-of-courses!

BRÉE, MALWINE. *The Groundwork of the Leschetizsky Method.* (Translated by Dr. Theodore Baker) New York: G. Schirmer, 1902. Once you get past the Margaret Dumont style of delivery, there's a lot to this book – and 'method.' As revolutionary as some of these ideas might have seemed at the time, now they seem quite obvious.

BRENDEL, ALFRED. *Musical Thoughts and Afterthoughts.* Princeton: Princeton University Press, 1976. A collection of essays, as thoughtful and thought-provoking as the title would lead you to expect. I hope he'll be able to find the time to write more. His idea of a dictionary of prejudice in music fascinates me.

CLEMENTI, MUZIO. *Introduction to the Art of Playing the Piano Forte.* New York: Da Capo Press, 1974. Even more than Mozart, the history of piano playing begins with Clementi. And this work, appearing in 1801, signaled the growing awareness that the new *Hammerklaviere* posed different technical questions to the player than the older plucked string keyboard instruments. In later editions he included, for tutorial purposes, pieces by Handel, Couperin, Corelli, Domenico Scarlatti, and the elder Bach. This suggests that some of the concern evinced by recent 'early music' specialists over what piece might be appropriate for what instrument might well have been deemed moot by the protagonists themselves.

COUPERIN, FRANCOIS. *L'art de Toucher le Clavecin.* Leipzig: Breitkopf & Härtel, 1933. This treatise, which appeared in 1716, is regarded by many to be the first significant writing on the subject of keyboard playing. Aside from its historical value, however, it is full of insights into the mind of one of the most interesting Baroque composer/performers.

CRAMER, JOHN BAPTIST. *Sixty Studies for Piano.* (Edited by Hans von Bülow) Milan: Carisch S.p.A., 1934. Born in Germany but settled in England, and bearing a striking resemblance to the actor Patrick MacNee, this top professional displayed a deviously inventive mind in exploring strategies of hand and finger movement. Passing to the thumb on a black key (#22, into m.43, r.h.), inner finger crossings (#12I$^I$), how to get away with all those things that teachers tell you *not* to do – it's all here, as well as a host of insights that you can take and apply elsewhere. Talented amateurs should find him beguiling. His exercises have been widely praised as the high road to Clementi's monumental *Gradus ad Parnassum*, and thence to the Chopin *Etudes.*

CURCIO, LOUISE. *The Musician's Handbook.* New York: The Joseph Pattelson Music House, 1968. Interesting and useful exercises that don't require an instrument.

HANON, CHARLES-LOUIS. *The Virtuoso Pianist (Le Pianiste Virtuose).* New York: G. Schirmer, 1900. Interesting and useful exercises that do.

HOFMANN, JOSEF. *Piano Playing, a Little Book of Simple Suggestions.* New York: The McClure Co., 1908. Just the man to cut the problems of piano playing down to size! Readable and commonsensical from cover to cover. Unlike a pedant standing over you telling you to 'Do as I say!' This book conveys the distinct impression that every iota of informaton originated and was tested in the author's own experience at the keyboard.

HOROWITZ, JOSEPH. *Conversations with Arrau*. New York: Alfred A. Knopf, 1982. Frankly, my original impressions of Claudio Arrau's musicianship were negative. The first live experience I've had of his playing was back in the early sixties. It was essentially a wrestling match with Gerhard Samuel (who by then had already earned my musical respect) and the Oakland Symphony, over whose interpretation of Brahms' D minor Concerto should prevail. No one won. So I was surprised to find him so illuminating on so many aspects of concert performance. There is much to learn in this book, and the explosion of prejudice is all the more uplifting when it is one's own!

KULLAK, ADOLPH. *The Aesthetics of Pianoforte-playing*. New York: G. Schirmer, 1893. Translation by Dr. Theodore Baker of Third German edition (1889). German syntax translated into nineteenth century English: "double trouble," thought I during the first few chapters. With its incredibly verbose descriptions of simple movements, the book read like an encyclopedia from a bygone era. True enough, as far as it went, and valuable as a summation of the practice of the times, but suddenly after seven or eight chapters the haze cleared and the sense of what he was describing came into focus. From technicalities like fingerings of scale passages, to flights of subjective fancy, this expanded essay is like a crucibular arena wherein the spirit of Romanticism and the new questing mind of Science fight it out.

LEVANT, OSCAR. *A Smattering of Ignorance*. New York: Doubleday, Doran & Co., Inc., 1940.

_____. *Memoirs of an Amnesiac*. New York: G. P. Putnam's Sons, 1965. There's more to a life in music than the notes, and fewer more interesting raconteurs to tell you about it than whazisname.

LHEVINNE, JOSEF. *Basic Principles in Pianoforte Playing*. New York: Dover, 1972. A reprint of a classic that first appeared in the twenties.

MATTHAY, TOBIAS. *The Act of Touch in all of its Diversity*. London, New York, &c: Longmans, Green, & Co., 1903.

_____. *The Visible and Invisible in Piano Technique*. London: Oxford University Press, 1932. The pendulum swings both ways, and many a philosophy has been merely a reaction to past excesses. If Matthay, like his contemporary Rudolph Breithaupt, seems to err in the direction of weight transfer, it must be remembered that for much of the previous century emphasis had been too far in the other direction, that of finger technique. Moreover, much of the work to follow pursued pathways that he opened.

NEUHAUS, HEINRICH. *The Art of Piano Playing*. New York: Praeger Publishers, 1973. This book, by the teacher of Sviatoslav Richter, Emil Gilels, and Radu Lupu, is at once lucidly practical and transcendently spiritual. It's the kind of book I like to read and reread, inhaling its ideas like one repeatedly breathes in the aroma of a rose. Sometimes he frustrates me with an "I could go on, but..." making me wish I could be there to say "Caro mæstro, please do!" But this is merely shameless gluttony on my part – in truth he reveals a great deal.

ORTMANN, OTTO. *The Physical Basis of Piano Touch and Tone*. New York: E. P. Dutton & Co., 1925.

SCHULTZ, ARNOLD. *The Riddle of the Pianist's Finger*. Chicago: University of Chicago Press, 1936.

Rigorously exhaustive studies of the physiological aspects of piano playing, building on the work of, among others, Matthay and Leschetizky.

SCARLATTI, DOMENICO (Ralph Kirkpatrick, ed.) *Sixty Sonatas*. New York: G. Schirmer, 1953. Ralph Kirkpatrick's introductory comments go far beyond mere suggestions on how to make one's performance more historically 'correct.' They include several observations whose validity extends to other keyboard instruments in addition to the harpsichord. The section on fingering is particularly trenchant.

TAYLOR, HAROLD. *The Pianist's Talent*. New York: Taplinger Book Co., 1982. A marvelous compendium of compact, portable concepts that work wonders, this book at once encompasses and supersedes its predecessors in the study of the physiology of playing the piano.

WHITESIDE, ABBY. *Indispensables of Piano Playing*. New York: Coleman-Ross Co., 1955. A vacuous, pretentious book. Any dolt can hold up an established classic from a bygone century and say, "Now, here's greatness!" This self-deprecating deference to the monuments of yore makes them more distant, not less. Beyond that the book is a cornucopia of muddled, even misguided thinking. To cite just one example, she dismisses Hanon and Czerny out of hand, simply on the grounds that they are 'no fun.' This despite the fact that no less a figure than Beethoven regarded the latter as a great talent, and all her 'exercises' are to be found, in more comprehensive form, in Hanon. In almost the same breath she confesses that the Chopin octave étude (Op. 25, Nr. 10) took her twenty years to master. Do tell! The time could have doubtless been halved by (for instance) the Czerny octave étude, Op. 740, Nr. 33 – a piece that Josef Lhevinne thought enough of to record!

The perennial problem of the beginner is that music that is engaging is too difficult, while easy pieces are too dull. At the risk of coming off as pompous as she, I maintain that no one who is afraid of a little work can ever hope to achieve anything worthwhile in the study of music. Euclid's admonition to the king: "There is no Royal Road to Geometry," would apply here. She seems to advance the notion that work is like castor oil – good for you but unpleasant. A more savory comparison to me would be the delight in mastering a video game. At first I usually get eaten, or shot down, or whatever, but before long my skills sharpen, and the fun begins. *Arbeit macht das Leben süß!*

WOLFF, KONRAD. *The Teaching of Artur Schnabel: a Guide to Interpretation.* New York: Praeger, 1972. A marvelous compendium of Schnabel's thoughts on playing, this book focuses better on technical and interpretative questions than Schnabel's own atmospherically anecdotal *My Life in Music*, and his philosophically atmospheric *Reflections on Music*.

# PART 3/ THE ATTICS OF MY LIFE

Appendices, ancillæ, &c.

# T.C. Base 1 / PUBLICATIONS

In chronological order

## REVIEWS AND INTERVIEWS

'Music Program Featuring Composition by Student,'*Las Vegas Sun;* January 15, 1961, p.3.

Thompson, Jean. 'Vegas Serviceman Named Nellis Airman of the Month,'*Las Vegas Review-Journal:* Oct. 26, 1966, p.22.

Kapfer, Miriam B. 'Fugue in Fortran,' *Nevada Notes* (Official Publication of the Nevada Music Educators Association), 12 (April, 1968), 8-9.

Gromko, William. *Las Vegas Scene (Las Vegas Sun* Sunday magazine) 1962? Feature article on Las Vegas composers Bill Reddie, Barney Gray, & T.C.

Lydon, Michael. 'Good Old Grateful Dead,' *Rolling Stone,* # 40 (August 23, 1969).

Hudson, James A. *Fillmore East and West.* New York, London, *et al:* Scholastic Book Services. 1970.

Harris, David. 'Rock's First Family, the Grateful Dead,' *Circus,* 4 (March, 1970) 4.

Polesky, Alice. 'The Dead Head.' *Go Magazine,* 2 (March, 1970)1. Reprint from *Circus,* Vol. 1 No. 9.

Emerson, Ken. 'The Grateful Dead,' *Fusion,* No. 58, June 25, 71.

Putnam, Thomas. 'Constanten to Rock Sound of Dead to Life,' *Buffalo Courier-Express;* Sept. 29, 1974.

Anderson, Dale. 'Creative Associate with Modern Ideas,'*Buffalo Evening News;* December 7, 1974.

Harrison, Hank. 'T.C.,' *The Dead.* Millbrae, Calif.: Celestial Arts, 1980. pp. 68-74.

Reffkin, David. 'The Ragtime Machine.' Interview in *The Mississippi Rag;* Nov., 1981, p.7.

Jackson, Blair. 'Tom Constanten's Life After the Dead,' *BAM,* 157 (June 3, 1983), 25.

Kelp, Larry. 'Back from the Grateful Dead.' *Oakland Tribune/ Calendar;* June 12, 1983; p. 7.

Hunt, Ken. 'Conversation Pieces, Part I – The Keys to the Dead,' *Swing 51,* 8(1984), 30-35.

Hunt, Ken. 'Conversation Pieces, Part II – Fandango & Chaconne,' *Swing 51,* 9(1984), 31-37.

Jackson, Blair. 'Out in the Wild Blue Yonder with Tom Constanten,' *The Golden Road,* 3 (Summer, 1984), 20-24.

Edmonds, Elizabeth. 'Constanten Still Haunted by the Dead,' *Stars Magazine (Syracuse Herald American),* Oct. 14, 1984.

Stoddard, Kathy. 'Back from the Dead.' *Pioneer Valley Advocate* (also *Hartford Advocate*), October 17, 1984.

Daly, Sean. 'T.C. Returns from the Dead,' *Relix,* 12 (1985), 44.

Harrison, Hank. *The Dead Book.* San Francisco: The Archives Press, 1985. Especially pp. 88-92.

Gans, David and Simon, Peter. *Playin' in the Band.* New York: St. Martin's Press, 1985. Baron Wolman photo on p. 88.

Flaum, Eric. 'The Grateful Dead, Part 1: Sunshine Dream' *Goldmine.* July 17, 1987.

DiMartino, Dave. 'The Grateful Dead: In the Dark.' *Musician.* Number 107; Sept. 1987, p. 102. Nice delayed action record review.

Curry, Jack. *The Summer of Our Lives.* N.Y.: Weidenfeld and Nicholson, 1989. pp. 101-109, 190, 240.

Kelp, Larry. 'Grateful Dead's ex-keyboardist does a 'Star' turn' *Oakland Tribune / Weekend!* February 10, 1989, p. E-2

Brandelius, Jerilyn Lee. *Grateful Dead Family Album.* New York: Warner Books, 1989. Photos pp. 35, 53, 69.

Greene, Herb. *Book of the Dead.* New York: Dell Publishing (Delta), 1990. Photos pp. 105, 107, 112.

Scott, John; Stu Nixon; and Mike Dolgushkin. *Dead Base '89.* Hanover, NH: 1990.

Scott, John; Stu Nixon, & Mike Dolgushkin. *Dead Base III, IV, V.* Hanover, NH: 1990, 1991.

Harrison, Hank. *The Dead Book.,Volume I.* San Francisco: The Archives Press, 1990. Especially pp. 88-92.

Forkes, Tim. 'Bach in an Anthem of the Sun,' *Shepherd Express – Milwaukee's Weekly Newspaper.* Nov. 15-22, 1990, p. 1.

Doerschuk, Robert L. 'Tom Constanten,' *Keyboard Magazine.* March, 1990, p. 82 et seq.

Troy, Sandy. *One More Saturday Night.* New York: St. Martin's Press, 1991.

## ARTICLES BY T.C.

'Report on the Pan American College Summer Institute in the Astro-Sciences,' *The Strolling Astronomer* (Journal of the Association of Lunar and Planetary Observers), 9-10 (October, 1960), 140-146.

'Music, a Universal Language' with Michael King. (Sun Youth Forum topic), *Las Vegas Sun;* Nov. 14, 1960.

'The Portrait: a Fable,' *Matrix.* (Nevada Southern University Art and Literary Magazine); Spring, 1966; p.14.

'Computer Music Reflections: a Midstream Night's Summary,'*Computer Music Journal,* 8 (Fall, 1984), 6-7.

'Paul Dresher – a re:act:ion,' San Francisco Symphony Program Notes; December, 1984; p. 22, continued pp. 43-44.

'Dr. Z. Agonistes: An Appreciation' *The Dylan Companion.* Elizabeth Thomson and David Gutman, eds. New York: Delta (Dell Publishing), 1990.

## DISCOGRAPHY

1968   Grateful Dead: *Anthem of the Sun.* (Warner Brothers WS 1749). Keyboards, Electronic music realisation.

1969   Grateful Dead: *Aoxomoxoa* (Warner Brothers WS 1790). Keyboards, Electronic music realisation.

1970   Grateful Dead: *Live Dead* (Warner Brothers WS 1830).Organ.

1970   Incredible String Band: *U* (Elektra EKS 7E-2002). Arranger, Conductor, Pianist.

1972   Touchstone: *Tarot* (United Artists UAS 5563). Composer, Producer, Keyboards.

1981   Various performers: *The Waltz Project*, (Nonesuch Digital D-79011). Represented as Composer of *Dejavalse.* John Cobb, Pianist. Special Category Award. *Best Unclassifiable Album – 1981. Record World Magazine.

1983   The Electric Guitar Quartet: *The Electric Guitar Quartet* , (EGQ cassettes). Featured as Composer of *Alaric's Premonition, a Gothic Fugue en Rondeau on a theme* by J. Garcia.

1988   Rainer Maria Rilke, *Duino Elegies*, translated by Robert Hunter. (Hulogosi Publishers; book and casssette). Piano accompaniment to Hunter's reading.

1989   Henry Kaiser: *Alternate Versions* (SST Records CD-027). Piano and organ tracks on *Mason's Children.*

1989   Tom Constanten: *Fresh Tracks in Real Time.* (Self produced, self-released cassette).

1990   Henry Kaiser Band: *Heart's Desire.* (Reckless Records RECKD 19/ CD RECK 19). Keyboards, Vocal, Composer.

1990   *Stoned Again – A Tribute to the Stones*, (Imaginary Records ILL CD 600) with Henry Kaiser Band: *Tell Me* and *Play with Fire.*

1990   Tom Constanten: *OutSides* (Self produced, self-released cassette).

1991   Henry Kaiser: *Hope You Like our new Direction*, (Reckless Records RECKD 21/ CD RECK 121). Keyboards.

1991   Joe Miller: *West Coast Music for Guitar*, (Rising Sleeve CD 101) Represented as Composer of *Dejavalse*, and *The Green and Gold Take the Cakewalk*, arranged for guitar by Joe Miller.

1991   Robin Petrie: *A Victorian Christmas.* (Gourd Music CD and cassette GM125). Piano on several carols.

1991   Tom Constanten: *Sonatas by Beethoven ('Pastorale' Op. 28), Schubert ('Unfinished' D. 840), Haydn (Sonata in E, 1776).* CD (Mauroy Records, MR2001).

1992   Tom Constanten: *Nightfall of Diamonds.* (Relix CD RR-2046). Solo piano. Joined by Henry Kaiser, Guitar, on *Goin' Home* and *Dark Star.*

# T.C. Base 2/ COMPOSITIONS

In the absence of other indications, the composer is the soloist
R – Indicates recording session

## SERENADE IN THREE MOVEMENTS

for String Orchestra
Las Vegas: October – December, 1959

I. *Adagio Mysterioso con moto*
II. *Allegretto Giocoso*
III. *Quasi Pastorale.*

**1961**, January 16. Las Vegas, Nevada.
All School Orchestra, Frank E. Iddings, conductor. Fifth Street School – Music at Four Concert.
April 18. Las Vegas, Nevada. All School Orchestra, Frank E. Iddings, conductor. West Charleston School Auditorium.
April 18. Las Vegas, Nevada. All School Orchestra, Frank E. Iddings, conductor. Nellis Sc. Auditorium.

## IMPROMPTU FOR PIANO 'THE APOLOGY'

Las Vegas: March, 1960

**1960**, May 13. Las Vegas, Nevada
Rancho High Sch. Talent Assembly.

## TWO TWELVE-TONE TWO-PART INVENTIONS

Las Vegas: 1960.

## TEXT/PERFORMANCE PIECES

Canon for two pianos
Las Vegas: 1960-61

*Polyphony I*
*Canon for four voices*
*The Wayfarer*
*Prisms*
*Plurality*
*Inadvertency.*

**1961**, April. Las Vegas, Nevada
R*(Canon)* 1650 Michael Way.
August 3. Las Vegas, Nevada
R*(Polyphony I)* 1650 Michael Way.

August 20. Las Vegas, Nevada
R*(Wayfarer/Canon)* 1650 Michael Way.
With Bill Walker.
August 27. Las Vegas, Nevada
R*(Prisms)* 1650 Michael Way.
With Bill Walker.
August 29. Las Vegas, Nevada
R*(Plurality/Inadvertency)* 1650 Michael Way.

## CONVERSATION PIECE

for Piano and Orchestra
Las Vegas: March – May 5, 1961

**1961**, May 28. Las Vegas, Nevada.
T.C., pianist, with the Las Vegas 'Pops' Orchestra, Antonio Morelli, conductor. Las Vegas Convention Center Promenade.

## SKETCHES

for Piano (10)
Las Vegas (first two), Berkeley (last ten): March, 1961 – January, 1962.

**1962**, June 30. San Antonio, Texas
(#s 2, 5, 6, 7, & 9). Robert Sheff, pianist; San Antonio Music Company.

## SYNTHESIS III

for any number of Pianos
Berkeley: December 8, 1961.

**1962**, November 14. Oakland, California
R. Moran, S. Wong, pianists; Mills College.

## DURATIONS

for Organ
Las Vegas: December 23-24, 1961.

**1961**, December 24. North Las Vegas, Nevada. Immanuel Community Church.

## THREE PIECES

for Two Pianos
First two composed: Berkeley, January-

February, 1962, as *Variations for Piano* (set of five). Last three variations scrapped. First two arranged for two pianos: Berkeley, March-April, 1962. Third composed: Ojai, California: May 18, 1962.

**1962**, May 5. Los Angeles, California Shirley Wong, Robert Kuykendall. U.C.L.A. Composers' Symposium; SCHÖNBERG HALL (Second piece only).

May 19. Ojai, California. Laraine Youngsten, T.C. Ojai Festival (Second piece only).

May 27. Oakland, California. Shirley Wong, T.C. Mills College (First performance of all three pieces).

**1963**, March 26. Milan, Italy. Tape of May 27, 1962 performance; U.S.I.S.

April 21. København, Dk. Pierre and Francette Bartholomée.

April 22. Oslo, Norway. Pierre and Francette Bartholomée.

April 24. Stockholm, Sweden. Pierre and Francette Bartholomée.

July 25. Darmstadt, Germany. Pierre and Francette Bartholomée.

## SONATINA

for Piano
Berkeley: March 1-17, 1962. Dedicated to Phil Lesh on his 22nd birthday

Recorded: 1990: Tom Constanten. *OutSides* Self-released cassette.

**1962**, May 1. Oakland, California. Robert Moran, pianist. Mills College/COMPOSERS' FORUM CONCERT.

May 13. Berkeley, California. Robert Moran, pianist. University of California/ COMPOSERS' FORUM CONCERT.

May 21. Oakland, California. ᴿRobert Moran, pianist; Mills College.

**1963**, March 26. Milan, Italy. Pierangelo dal Seno, pianist; U.S.I.S.

**1981**, August 15. San Francisco, California. Community Music Center.

**1988**, July 9. San Francisco, California. Great American Music Hall. To accompany Robert Hunter's reading of his *Exploding Diamond Blues.*

November 9. San Francisco, Calif. First Unitarian Church/ New Release. AMERICAN MUSIC WEEK.

**1990**, May 7. New York, N.Y. The Knitting Factory.

December 3. Berkeley, California. KPFA-FM: *Mob Ecstasy*, with Ben Lindgren.

## QUINTOLET
## (SECTION 9 OF 'COLLAGE')

Berkeley: March – April 20, 1962.

**1962**, May 5. Los Angeles, California. U.C.L.A. Composers' Symposium. SCHÖNBERG HALL. Ensemble of 10 musicians, Luciano Berio, conductor.

## SONATINA II

for Piano
Las Vegas: June 9-10, 1962.

## THREE ELECTRONIC STUDIES

Bruxelles: Studio APELAC: #1, July 26; #2, August 28; #3, Sept. 1-4, 1962

Recorded: 1968, Grateful Dead, *Anthem of the Sun. (Study Number Three* used in montage: *We Leave the Castle.)*
1990, Tom Constanten, *OutSides*, Self-released cassette; *Study Number Three* only.

**1990**, December 14. Los Angeles, Calif. KPFK-FM: *Thursday Lunch, (Study #3 from OutSides).*

## EPISTLE

for Piano
Linguaglietta: completed Nov. 9, 1962.

## PHRASES

for Chamber Orchestra: 2 Flutes, 2 Oboes, 2 Clarinets, 2 Bassoons, 2 Percussionists, Xylophone, Vibraphone, Celesta, 2 Violins, 3 Violas, 3 'Celli, 2 Basses.
Berkeley, Darmstadt, Bruxelles, Linguaglietta, Milano:
October, 1961 – January, 1963.

## DIMENSIONI

for Piano(s)
Milano: March 13-15, 1963.

**1963**, March 26. Milan, Italy. Robert Moran, prepared piano (via tape made March 24, Louis Andriessen's apartment); U. S. I. S.

## PRELUDE

Milano: May 29, 1963

Recorded: 1990: Tom Constanten. *OutSides* Self-released cassette.

**1988**, November 9. San Francisco, Calif. First Unitarian Church/ New Release, AMERICAN MUSIC WEEK.

**1990**, January 12. Las Vegas, Nevada
R Paul Weitz/ Terry Ryan Studio.
December 3. Berkeley, California. KPFA-
FM: *Mob Ecstasy*, with Ben Lindgren.
**1991**, February 9. San Francisco, Calif.
WEST COAST WEEKEND/KQED-FM.
July 27. San Francisco, Calif. WEST COAST
WEEKEND/KQED-FM – rerun.

## PIANO PIECE #3

Milano: June, 1963.

**1964**, April 18. San Francisco, Calif.
R 453 Eureka Street.
May 21, 23. San Francisco, Calif.
MUSIC NOW KONCERTS.
MAY 29, 30. San Francisco Mime Troupe.

## STRING QUARTET

San Francisco, Las Vegas: October,
1963 – October, 1964
«Sinfonia»
Orchestrated in Las Vegas: 1966.

**1966**, June 12. Las Vegas, Nevada
University String Orchestra,
William Gromko, conductor.

## PROPAGATIONS

for String Orchestra
Composed with the aid of an IBM 1401
computer, Las Vegas: 1967.

**1967**, July 30. Las Vegas, Nevada
University String Orchestra,
William Gromko, conductor.
**1968**, April 6. Las Vegas, Nevada
University String Orchestra,
William Gromko, conductor.

## INVOCATION OF THE SUN

for Soprano Soloist, Chorus & Orchestra.
A Setting of the Prologue of Nikos
Kazantzakis's *The Odyssey: A Modern Sequel*
Las Vegas: 1968.

**1969**, May 25. Las Vegas, Nevada
University String Orchestra and Chorus,
William Gromko, conductor.

## TAROT

mime musical after the deck of cards
book by Joe McCord
Novato, New York: 1970

*The Turtle*
*The Old Fool's Reel*
*Greed*

*Harlequin (the Fool's Theme)*
*The Philosopher and the Tree of Life*
*The Maiden Waltz*
*The Lovers' Walk in the Magic Forest*
*The Mystic Carpenter*
*The Chariot/ Space Voyage*
*The Moon (Lunacy)*
*Return of the Philosopher*
*Death March*
*Sun Prelude*
*The Sun*

Recorded: 1972: Touchstone. *Tarot*, United
Artists Records UAS 5563.

**1970**, Summer. San Francisco, Calif.
R *(Harlequin/Maiden)* Pacific High
Recorders. Richard Greene, violin, T.C.,
piano (on *Maiden Waltz*). Autumn.
Albany, Calif. R *(Harlequin)* Studio.
December 11. Brooklyn, N.Y., Chelsea
Theatre Center; three week run. The
Rubber Band: Yolande Bavan, vocals;
Paul Dresher, guitar, flute, sitar;
'Chicken' Hirsch, drums; Wes Steele,
bass; Jim Byers, guitar; Art Fayer, violin;
and T.C., RMI Electra-piano.
December. New York, N.Y., WNET-TV –
*Free Time*. (*Lovers' Walk/The Moon*).
**1971**, March 4. New York, N.Y. Circle in
The Square; three week run. Touchstone:
Paul Dresher, guitar, flute, sitar;
'Chicken' Hirsch, drums; Wes Steele,
bass; Jim Byers, guitar; Art Fayer, violin;
and T.C., RMI Electra-piano.
April 21-24. New York, N.Y. R Electric Lady
Studios. Touchstone: Paul Dresher,
guitar, flute, sitar; 'Chicken' Hirsch,
drums; Wes Steele, bass; Jim Byers,
guitar; Art Fayer, violin; and T.C., RMI
Electra-piano.
**1972**, April 7. Hayward, California.
Tuckett Inn. (*Turtle/Greed/Lovers'/Moon/
Chariot*).
April 8. Hayward, California
(*Greed/Lovers'/Moon*) Tuckett Inn.
April 14, 15. Berkeley, California.
(*Lovers'/ Greed/Moon*) New Orleans
House.
April 20. Berkeley, California
(*Lovers'/Greed/Moon*) Long Branch.
April 21. Berkeley, California.
(*Lovers'/Greed/Moon*) Long Branch.
April 22. Cotati, California.
(*Lovers'/Greed/Moon*) Inn at the
Beginning.
May 5. Palo Alto, California.
(*Lovers'/Greed/Moon*) Homer's
Warehouse.

August 12. Berkeley, California.
(*Lovers'/Greed/Moon*) Provo Park.
August 16. Berkeley, California.
(*Lovers'/Greed/Moon*) Mandrake's.
August 27. Half Moon Bay, California.
(*Lovers'/Greed/Moon*). Bach's Dancing and
Dynamite Society.
August 31. Berkeley, California.
(*Lovers'/Greed/Moon*) Long Branch.
September 26. San Francisco, California.
(*The Moon*). KEMO-TV; *The Paisley
Teahouse*.
October. Point Richmond, California.
Community Center.
October. Boonville, California. McGovern
Campaign Benefit. Touchstone: Paul
Dresher, guitar; Bill Ruskin, guitar; Gene
Reffkin drums; Wes Steele, bass; & T.C.,
RMI Electra-piano.
**1974**, October 2. Buffalo, N.Y.
(*The Moon/Greed*). T.C., piano (Steinway)
with Art Levinowitz, sax; Joel Perry,
guitar; Murray Kohn, bass; and Albert
Furness, drums.
**1975**, January 20. Buffalo, N.Y. (*The Moon/
Greed*). T.C., Hammond B-3) with Art
Levinowitz, sax; Chuck Hammer, guitar;
Murray Kohn, bass; and Norm Skiba,
drums.
**1984**, Summer – to present. San Francisco,
Calif., St. Francis Hotel. St. Francis
Strings, David Reffkin, leader (*Harlequin/
Old Fool's Reel/Maiden Waltz*).
**1986**, November 15. San Francisco, Calif.
(*Harlequin/Return of the Philosopher*) Noe
Valley Ministry.
**1987**, January 3. San Francisco, Calif.
(*Harlequin/Return of the Philosopher*).
WEST COAST WEEKEND/KQED-FM.
January 30. Frankfurt a. M., Germany
(*Harlequin/Return of the Philosopher*),
Holle/Liebrecht Hauskonzert.
July 18. San Francisco, Calif.
(*Maiden Waltz*). WEST COAST
WEEKEND/KQED-FM.
July 31. Tiburon, California. THE DOCK
(*Harlequin/Return of Philosopher/Maiden
Waltz/Lovers' Walk*).
August 1. San Francisco, Calif.
(*Lovers' Walk*). WEST COAST
WEEKEND/KQED-FM.
August 22. San Francisco, Calif.
(*Maiden Waltz/Old Fool's Reel*).
WEST COAST WEEKEND/KQED-FM.
October 16. Tiburon, California. THE DOCK
(*Harlequin/Return of the Philosopher*).
November 21. San Francisco, Calif.

(*Greed*) WEST COAST WEEKEND/KQED-FM.
**1990**, February 1. San Francisco, Calif.
(*The Moon*) Last Day Saloon. Piano four
hands, with George Michalski.
April 5. San Rafael, California. (*The Moon*)
Fourth Street Tavern. Piano four hands,
with George Michalski.
April 7. Bolinas, California. (*The Moon*)
Bolinas Community Center. Piano four
hands, with George Michalski.
May 5. San Francisco, Calif. (*Harlequin/
Philosopher/Moon*). WEST COAST WEEKEND/
KQED-FM.
May 7. New York, N.Y. (*Harlequin/Return of
the Philosopher*). Knitting Factory.
May 26. San Francisco, Calif. (*The Moon*)
WEST COAST WEEKEND/KQED-FM.
June 2. San Francisco, Calif. (*The Moon*)
WEST COAST WEEKEND/KQED-FM.
August 18. San Francisco, Calif.(*Harlequin/
Philosopher/Moon*) WEST COAST WEEKEND/
KQED-FM (rerun of May 5, 90).
August 25. San Francisco, California.
(*The Moon*) WEST COAST WEEKEND/
KQED-FM (rerun of May 26, 1990).
September 28. San Francisco, California.
(*Harlequin/Return of the Philosopher*)
Psychedelic Shop.
September 28. San Francisco, California.
(*The Moon*) Psychedelic Shop. Piano four
hands, with George Michalski.
October 4, 12. San Francisco, California.
(*The Moon*) Last Day Saloon. Piano four
hands, with George Michalski.
October 18. San Francisco, Calif. (*Greed*)
Last Day Saloon, with Danny Kalb,
guitar; Ray Collins, saxophone, Mitchell
Holman, bass; and Ernest 'Boom' Carter,
drums.
October 31. San Francisco, California.
(*The Moon*) Last Day Saloon. Piano four
hands, with George Michalski.
**1991**, April 27. San Francisco, California.
(*The Moon*) with Henry Kaiser.
WEST COAST WEEKEND/KQED-FM.
May 18. San Francisco, Calif. (*The Moon*)
WEST COAST WEEKEND/KQED-FM.
August 11. Richmond, Virginia. (*The Moon*)
Kahootz.

## THE HUN

Rock fugue in 17/8
Novato, Brooklyn, Oakland: 1970

Touchstone: Paul Dresher, guitar; Bill
Ruskin, guitar; Gene Reffkin drums; Wes
Steele, bass; and T.C., RMI Electra-piano.

**1972**, April 7. Hayward, California
Tuckett Inn.
April 8. Hayward, California
Tuckett Inn.
April 14, 15. Berkeley, California
New Orleans House.
April 20. Berkeley, California
The Long Branch.
April 22. Cotati, California
Inn of the Beginning.
April 22. Half Moon Bay, California
Bach's Dancing and Dynamite Society.
July. Berkeley, California
Mandrake's.
August 16. Berkeley, California
Mandrake's.
August 31. Berkeley, California
The Long Branch.

## IDYLL OF SEA AND MOUNTAINS
for Orchestra
Novato, Brooklyn: 1970.

**1972**, March 5. Las Vegas, Nevada
University Chamber Orchestra,
G. Keith Moon, conductor.

## THE LOVE SONG OF CHARLES FABERMAN
Score for the Jeremy Paul Kagan film
Los Angeles: January, 1972

*Charles' Theme*
*Insalata Verde*
*Quartettschnitt*
*Waltz for a Peg Legged Octopus*
*Abel's Theme*
*Old Wine, New Bottles*
*R & R*
*Anne's Theme.*

**1972**, January 28. Beverly Hills, California.
ᴿAmerican Film Institute. (*Charles's,
Insalata, Quartettschnitt*). Yukiko Kamei,
Milton Thomas, + violin & 'cello; (*Waltz*)
string quartet with T.C., harpsichord
(Neupert).
January 29. Beverly Hills, California.
(*Abel's Theme*). T.C., harpsichord
(Neupert). (*Old Wine, R & R, Anne's
Theme*). Touchstone: Paul Dresher, guitar,
Art Fayer, violin, Wes Steele, bass,
George Suranovich, drums, and T.C.,
RMI electric piano.
April 8. Hayward, California. (*R & R*)
Tuckett Inn. Touchstone: Paul Dresher,
guitar, Art Fayer, violin, Wes Steele, bass,
Gene Reffkin, drums, and T.C., RMI
electric piano.

## RETRODISRESPECTIVE MARMALADE
Buffalo: October, 1974.

**1974**, October 17. Buffalo, N.Y. Baird Hall,
S.U.N.Y. Live performance with T.C.,
organ, Donald Knaack, percussion.
Broadcast live on WBFO-FM along with
two prerecorded collages.

## A GIRAFFE OF WYNE (AND THOU)
for any number of Percussionists
Buffalo: Autumn, 1974.

**1974**, December 8. Buffalo, New York.
Donald Knaack, percussionist. EVENINGS
FOR NEW MUSIC / ALBRIGHT-KNOX ART
GALLERY.
December 11. New York, N.Y.
Donald Knaack, percussionist. WBAI
Free Music Store.
**1977**, July 4. Lockport, N.Y.
Donald Knaack, percussionist
BLAZE OF GLORY FESTIVAL.
**1978**, March 25. Los Angeles, Calif.
Donald Knaack, percussionist
Theatre Vanguard.

## WHEN YOU GET TO THE *
an arcane theatrical ritual
with incidental music
Buffalo: Spring, 1975.

**1975**, April 16. Buffalo, New York.
BAIRD RECITAL HALL, S.U.N.Y. Broadcast
live on WBFO-FM. Joseph Kubera,
Donald Knaack, Eberhard Blum, & T.C.
May 4. Buffalo, New York. ALBRIGHT-KNOX
ART GALLERY, Evenings for New Music.
Joseph Kubera, Donald Knaack,
Benjamin Hudson, and T.C.
**1983**, December 15. San Francisco, Calif.
S. F. Art Institute. Greg Albright, Rachel
Wiessman, Ken Chu, and T.C.
**1990**, December 3. Berkeley, California
KPFA-FM: *Mob Ecstasy*, with Ben
Lindgren. Excerpt from air check of April
16, 1975 performance.

## CAUCASIAN CHALK CIRCLE
Score for excerpt from Berthold Brecht
play. San Francisco: 1976.

**1976**. Dec. 21, 22. San Francisco, Calif.
LEAVENWORTH STREET THEATRE. Dick Partee,
flute; Toad, 'cello; Jim McGarry, guitar.

## THE BALD SOPRANO
Prepared piano incidental music to Eugene
Ionesco play
San Francisco: 1978.

**1978**, Jan. 12-14. San Francisco, Calif.
LEAVENWORTH STREET THEATRE.

## THE COLLECTION
Electronic Soundscape for Harold Pinter
play, Lester Jones, director
San Francisco: Summer, 1979.

**1979**, Aug./Sept. San Francisco, Calif.
GUMPTION THEATRE.

## THE SYNTAX COLLECTOR
for Piano
Oakland: 1974 – 1976

   I.   *Praalude: The Haight Street Slither*
  II.  *That There Old West is Older Now*
       *than Ever*
 III.  *Lude: Licentious Bicentennial Rag*
 IV.  *The Green & Gold Take the*
       *Cakewalk*
  V.  *Postlude: The San Andreas Stomp*

Published: 1987: G. Schirmer, New York
[HL 50507860]

Recorded, 1989: *Fresh Tracks in Real Time* –
Self-released cassette. 1990: Henry Kaiser
Band, *Heart's Desire*, Reckless Records
RECKD 19 – LP only.*The San Andreas
Stomp* piano solo.

**1974**, October 2. Buffalo, New York
(#4) Baird Hall, S.U.N.Y.
**1975**, January 20. Buffalo, New York
(#2) WBFO Benefit, Fillmore Room,
S.U.N.Y. Chuck Hammer, guitar; Art
Levinowitz, sax; Murray Kohn, bass;
Norm Skiba, drums; T.C., organ
(Hammond B-3).
February 24. Buffalo, New York
(#4) Pianist Joseph Kubera's. Breakfast
Concert, broadcast live over WBFO-FM.
**1976**, May 21. San Francisco, Calif.
(#4) SPARC Benefit. A.P. Giannini JHS
Auditorium.
May 30. Claremont, California
(#s 1 thru 4) Holmes Hall, Pomona
College.
November 5. San Francisco, Calif.
CAPRICORN ASUNDER GALLERY
*First Performance of all Five Pieces.*
**1977**, January 12. Claremont, Calif.
Founders' Room, Pitzer College.

January 20. San Francisco, Calif.
LEAVENWORTH STREET THEATRE.
January 26. San Francisco, Calif.
(#s 4 and 5) Lone Mountain College.
January 28. San Francisco, Calif.
(#s 1 and 3) Lone Mountain College.
April 9. Portland, Oregon. Swann
Auditorium, Portland Museum of Art.
April 12. Portland, Oregon
Portland State University.
July 3. Lockport, New York. Kenan Center,
BLAZE OF GLORY FESTIVAL.
September 18. San Francisco, Calif.
AQUATIC PARK THEATRE.
November 4. San Francisco, Calif.
Dance Coalition Soirée.
**1978**, April 13. Worcester, Mass.
Joseph Kubera, pianist. Salon of the
Maison, Assumption College.
May 4. San Francisco, Calif.
LEAVENWORTH STREET THEATRE.
May 24. Zagreb, Yugoslavia
Student Center, Univ. of Zagreb.
May 27. Innsbruck, Austria
Conservatory of Music.
June 25. San Francisco, Calif.
Old Spaghetti Factory. CITY LIGHTS
BOOKSTORE 25TH ANNIVERSARY CELEBRATION.
November 1. New York, N.Y.
Joseph Kubera, pianist, St. Peter's
Lutheran Church (Citicorp Building).
**1979**, February 11. New York, N.Y.
(#3) Nurit Tilles, pianist. The New York
Historical Society (77th Street).
June 8. La Jolla, California
(#s 1 and 4) Mark Lockett, pianist
Mandeville Recital Hall, University of
California at San Diego.
**1980**, October. Woodstock, N.Y.
Mark Lockett, pianist. Creative Music
Studio.
December 6. San Francisco, Calif.
(#s 4 and 5) Community Music Center.
**1981**, January 2. San Francisco, Calif.
(#5) Old First Church.
January 23. Madrid, Spain
Joseph Kubera, pianist
Spanish National Radio.
March 26. San Francisco, Calif.
(#4) Giannini Auditorium
Bank of America Bldg.
March 27. London, England
(#s 1, 3, and 5) Mark Lockett, pianist
Center for Arts; The City University.
April 4. Staten Island, N.Y. Joseph Kubera,
pianist. Snug Harbor Cultural Center.
July 4. San Francisco, Calif.
(#5) Crissy Field.

July 16. London, England (#s 1, 3, and 5)
Mark Lockett, pianist British Music
Information Centre.
July 24. San Francisco, Calif. (#s 4 and 5)
Community Music Center.
August 15. San Francisco, Calif.
(#2) Community Music Center.
September 27. San Francisco, Calif.
(#3) Community Music Center.
October 4. San Francisco, Calif.
(#4) Old First Church.
December 15. San Francisco, Calif.
(#s 4 and 5) Calif. Historical Society.
**1982,** February 11. Newcastle, England.
(#3) Mark Lockett, pianist, King's Hall,
University of Newcastle-upon-Tyne.
June 9. Dartington, England. Mark Lockett,
pianist; Dartington Hall.
**1983,** June 19. San Francisco, Calif.
(#s 4 and 5) The Old Waldorf.
June 23. San Francisco, Calif.
(#5) Giannini Auditorium
Bank of America Bldg.
**1984,** September 19
Berkeley, California
(#s 4 and 5) Julia Morgan Theatre.
October 19. Roslyn, L. I., N.Y.
(#s 4 and 5) My Father's Place.
October 20. Syracuse, New York
(#s 4 and 5) Jabberwocky (Two Shows).
October 21. Ithaca, New York
(#s 4 and 5) Ramada Inn.
October 22. New Brunswick, N.J.
(#s 4 and 5) Rutgers University.
October 23. White Plains, N.Y.
(#s 4 and 5) Fore 'n Aft.
October 24. New York, N.Y.
(#s 4 and 5) The Bitter End.
October 25. Providence, R.I.
(#s 4 and 5) Lupo's.
October 26. Buffalo, New York
(#s 4 and 5) Slee Hall, S.U.N.Y.
October 27. Hartford, Conn.
(#s 4 and 5) Mad Murphy's Cafe.
October 28. Sunderland, Mass.
(#s 4 and 5) The Rusty Nail.
October 29. Cambridge, Mass.
(#s 4 and 5) Jack's.
October 30. Burlington, Vermont
(#s 4 and 5) Hunt's.
November 16. San Francisco, Calif.
(#5) San Francisco Art Institute.
**1985,** March 26. Kamuela, Hawaii
(#4) Hawaii Preparatory Academy.
May 23. New York, N.Y.
Joseph Kubera, pianist
Museum of the American Piano.

**1986,** February 9. St. Helena, Calif.
(#3) The White Barn.
April 10. Cambridge, Mass.
Harvard University
Music Dept. Lecture/Demonstration.
April 11. Cambridge, Mass.
(#s 4 and 5) Quincy House
Harvard University.
April 13. San Francisco, Calif. (#5)
WEST COAST WEEKEND/KQED-FM.
April 26. San Francisco, Calif. (#s 2 and 5)
WEST COAST WEEKEND/KQED-FM.
April 28. San Francisco, Calif.
(#s 2 and 5) Wolfgang's.
May 16. San Francisco, Calif.
(#s 4 and 5) Union Square. HANDS ACROSS
AMERICA/GODZILLA BIRTHDAY CELEBRATION.
June 11. San Francisco, Calif.
R(#5) Waters Upton Tea Room.
Sept. 18? Winfield, Kansas
(#4) Joe Miller, guitar. NATIONAL FINGER
PICKING CHAMPIONSHIP.
October 4. Staten Island, N.Y.
Joseph Kubera, pianist
Snug Harbor Cultural Center.
November 15. San Francisco, Calif.
Noe Valley Ministry.
**1987,** January 24. Frankfurt a. M.,
Germany. Elschenbroich/Schweitzer
Hauskonzert.
January 30. Frankfurt a. M., Germany
Holle/Liebrecht Hauskonzert.
May 2. San Francisco, Calif. (#4)
WEST COAST WEEKEND/KQED-FM.
May 16. San Francisco, Calif. (#1)
WEST COAST WEEKEND/KQED-FM.
June 12. San Francisco, Calif. (#4)
AMNESTY INTERNATIONAL BENEFIT
Noe Valley Ministry.
July 4. San Francisco, Calif. (#3)
WEST COAST WEEKEND/KQED-FM.
July 31. Tiburon, California
(#s 3 and 4) The Dock.
August 29. San Francisco, Calif. (#4)
WEST COAST WEEKEND/KQED-FM.
September 5. San Francisco, Calif. (#5)
WEST COAST WEEKEND/KQED-FM.
October 10. San Francisco, Calif. (#1)
WEST COAST WEEKEND/KQED-FM.
October 16. Tiburon, California
The Dock.
October 17. San Francisco, Calif. (#2)
WEST COAST WEEKEND/KQED-FM.
October 25. San Francisco, Calif.
(#s 1 and 2) Noe Valley Ministry.
November 21. Berkeley, Calif. (#4) Joe
Miller, guitar/Freight and Salvage.

**1988**, February 26. Tiburon, California
(#s 2, 4, and 5) The Dock.
February 27. Berkeley, California. (#4) Joe
Miller, guitar/Freight & Salvage.
July 9. San Francisco, Calif.
(#5) Great American Music Hall. To
accompany Robert Hunter's reading of
his *A Prophecy to the Year 1906.*
September 5. Las Vegas, Nevada. ᴿ(#s 1, 2,
and 5) Paul Weitz/ TR Studio.
September 6. Las Vegas, Nevada
ᴿ(#4) Paul Weitz/ Terry Ryan Studio.
September 7. Las Vegas, Nevada
ᴿ(#3) Paul Weitz/ Terry Ryan Studio.
**1989**, January 22. Santa Monica, Calif.
(#s 4 and 5) McCabe's Guitar Shop.
February 12. San Francisco, California.
(#5) Great American Music Hall.
April 15. San Francisco, California.
(#5) Fillmore Auditorium.
Sept. 23. San Francisco, Calif. (#2)
WEST COAST WEEKEND/KQED-FM.
October 14. San Francisco, Calif. (#4)
WEST COAST WEEKEND/KQED-FM.
October 21. Davis, California
(#5) The Palms.
October 22. Davis, California
(#5) The Palms.
November 2. Berkeley, California
ᴿ(#5) 1741 Alcatraz Studio.
December 1. San Francisco, California.
(#5) Noe Valley Ministry.
December 29. San Francisco, California.
(#5) Psychedelic Shop.
**1990**, February 2. San Francisco, Califor-
nia. (#2) Last Day Saloon
(February 3 – rerun). San Francisco, Calif.
(#2) WEST COAST WEEKEND/KQED-FM.
April 5. San Rafael, California
(#s 2 and 5) Fourth Street Tavern.
April 7. Bolinas, California
(#5) Bolinas Community Center.
May 7. New York, N.Y. (#s 2 and 5)
Knitting Factory.
May 20. Seattle, Washington
(#5) University of Washington. Theodore
Roethke Auditorium.
June 2. San Francisco, Calif. (#2)
WEST COAST WEEKEND/KQED-FM.
June 2. San Francisco, California.
(#5) Chi Chi Club.
June 6. San Francisco, Calif. (#s 2 and 5)
DeYoung Museum/ Hearst Court.
August onward. San Francisco, Calif.
(#2) St. Francis Strings/St. Francis Hotel.
Piano solo by Stephen Damonte.
September 10. San Francisco, California.
(#5) El Cerrito Cable TV/*On Stage.*

September 13. San Francisco, California.
(#5) Last Day Saloon.
September 19. Pacifica, Calif. (#5) Pacifica
Cable TV/*Bruce Latimer Show.*
October 31. San Francisco, California.
(#5) Last Day Saloon.
November 6. Philadelphia, Pennsylvania.
(#5) Chestnut Cabaret.
November 7. Washington, D.C.
(#5) Lisner Auditorium
George Washington University.
November 9. New York, N.Y.
(#5) The Ritz.
November 10. Somerville, Mass.
(#5) Somerville Theatre.
November 12. Charlottesville, Va. (#5)
Charlottesville Performing Arts Center.
November 13. Atlanta, Georgia
(#5) Center Stage.
November 15. Chicago, Illinois
(#5) Park West.
November 16. Milwaukee, Wisconsin
(#5) Avalon Theatre.
November 17. Boulder, Colorado
(#5) Boulder Theater.
November 26. San Francisco, Califkornia.
(#5) The Warfield.
**1991**, July 12, Berkeley, California
ᴿ(#s 1 and 2) Fantasy Studios.
September 20. Walnut Valley, Kansas. (#4)
Walnut Valley Festival. Joe Miller, guitar.
October 10. Laguna Beach, Calif. (#4)
Renaissance Cafe. Joe Miller, guitar.
October 12. Woodland Hills, Calif. (#4)
Cobalt Cafe. Joe Miller, guitar.
October 24. Plymouth, N. H. (#4)
Suzanne's Kitchen. Joe Miller, guitar.

## RECOMBINANT STRAINS

for any number of Pianos.
Oakland: 1977-86. *Land of the Hassled and
Free* (September – October 23, 1977). *Claude
Greenberg's Springtime Catch* (June –
October 7, 1977). *Dejavalse* (April 23, 1977.
Qtet arr.: July, 1982). *Dejavalise* (1985).
*Dejavalentino* (Early 1986). *Dejaboogie* (Early
1986)

Published: 1978: C.F. Peters, New York.
Waltzes by 25 Contemporary Composers
[66735]. *Dejavalse* only

Recorded, 1981: John Cobb. Nonesuch
Digital D-79011. *Dejavalse* only.
1989: Tom Constanten. *Fresh Tracks in Real
Time,* Self-released cassette, top three
pieces as rounds.
1990: Tom Constanten, *OutSides,*

Self-released cassette, *Dejavalse* piano solo.
1992: Tom Constanten, *Nightfall of
Diamonds*, (Relix CD RR-2046). *Dejavalse,
Dejavalentino*.

**1977,** July 3. Lockport, New York
*(Dejavalse)* – *co/première*. Kenan Centre,
BLAZE OF GLORY FESTIVAL.

July 6. Lockport, New York
*(Dejavalse)* – *co/première*. Joseph Kubera,
pianist. BLAZE OF GLORY FESTIVAL; Kenan
Centre.

**1978,** May 11. Chicago, Illinois. *(Dejavalse)*
Elizabeth Buccheri, pianist. Stock
Exchange Room; The Art Institute of
Chicago.

May 20. Köln, Germany
*(Dejavalse)* – *European première*. WDR;
John Cobb, pianist.

May 22. Beograd, Jugoslavia
*(Dejavalse)* – *First performance as a round*.
John Cobb and T.C., pianists. Student
Center, Univ. of Beograd.

May 23. Zagreb, Jugoslavia
*(Dejavalse)* John Cobb, pianist. Student
Center, Univ. of Zagreb.

May 24. Zagreb, Jugoslavia
*(LHFr/ClGbg/Deja)*. *First Performance of all
three*. Dejavalse as round with John Cobb,
pianist. Student Center, University of
Zagreb.

May 27. Innsbruck, Austria
*(Dejavalse)* Conservatory of Music. John
Cobb and T.C., pianists.

May 29. Graz, Austria. ᴿ*(Dejavalse)* ÖRF.
John Cobb and T.C., pianists.

**1979,** February 3. New York, N.Y.
*(Dejavalse)* Yvar Mikhashoff; The
Kitchen. Two performances – 8:30 and 11
P.M.

March 30. San Francisco, Calif.
*(Dejavalse)* San Francisco Art Institute.
8 P.M. – T.C. solo; 11 P.M. – John Cobb,
harpsichord, T.C., piano (round).

March 31. Buffalo, New York
*(Dejavalse)* Yvar Mikhashoff; S.U.N.Y.

April 2. Seattle, Washington
*(Dejavalse)* Don Gillespie, pianist.
And/Or Gallery.

April 3. Seattle, Washington
*(Dejavalse)* John Cobb, pianist.
MUSIC TEACHERS NATIONAL ASSOCIATION
Convention; Olympic Hotel.

June 15, 16. New York, N.Y.
*(Dejavalse)* John Cobb, pianist. Sculpture
Garden, Museum of Modern Art.

**1980,** Dec. 6. San Francisco, Calif.
*(Dejavalse)* Community Music Center.

**1981,** January 3. Amsterdam, Holland
*(Dejavalse)* Yvar Mikhashoff, pianist.
De Ijsbrekker.

April 10. San Francisco, California.
*(Claude Greenberg's Springtime Catch)*.
North American première – First perfor-
mance as a round. FACULTY BENEFIT RECITAL;
Cesar Cancino and T.C., pianists.

May 10. Berkeley, California.
*(Dejavalse)* Julia Morgan Theatre.

May 10. New York, N.Y.
*(Dejavalse)* John Cobb, pianist. Recorded
accompaniment to Phyllis Lamhut Dance
Company. RIVERSIDE DANCE FESTIVAL –
Riverside Church.

May 12, 13. Swindon, England
*(Dejavalse)* Mark Lockett, pianist.
Accompaniment to 'man-in-the-looking-
glass' by Extemporary Dance Company –
Wyvern Theatre.

May 20. Sheffield, England
*(Dejavalse)* Mark Lockett, pianist.
Accompaniment to 'man-in-the-looking-
glass' by Extemporary Dance Company –
Crucible Theatre.

June 18. San Francisco, Calif. *(Dejavalse)*
Golden Gate Park Bandshell.

July 24. San Francisco, Calif.
*(Dejavalse)* Community Music Center.

December 15. San Francisco, Calif.
*(Dejavalse)* California Historical Society.

**1982,** January 15. San Francisco, Calif.
*(Dejavalse)* World of Oil Theatre.

August 1. Burlingame, Calif. *(Dejavalse)*
Sisters of Mercy Quartet arrangement
commissioned for wedding of Scott
Hubbard & Susan Ruggeri perfkormed
by Kronos Quartet.

August 7. San Luis Obispo, Calif.
*(Dejavalse)*. California Polytechnic
University Mozart Festival; Lecture/
Demonstration – Piano version followed
immediately by quartet version; Kronos
Quartet.

December 11. Oberlin, Ohio
*(Dejavalse)*; Oberlin College.

**1983,** June 19. San Francisco, Calif.
*(Dejavalse/LHFr)*; The Old Waldorf. *Land
of the Hassled and Free* – U.S. première.

October 6. San Francisco, Calif.
*(Dejavalse)* Golden Gate Park Bandshell.

**1984,** April 7-8. Las Vegas, Nevada
ᴿ*(Dejavalse)* Evergreen/Terry Ryan
Studio.

March 4/12. Champaign, Ill.
*(Dejavalse)* Dance: Waltztime. Stephen
Whiting, pianist.

June 1. San Francisco, Calif. *(Dejavalse)*
Redwood Park, Transamerica Pyramid.
July 27. Berkeley, California
*(Dejavalse)* Freight and Salvage.
September 19. Berkeley, California
*(Dejavalse)* Julia Morgan Theatre.
October 19. Roslyn, L.I., N.Y.
*(Dejavalse)* My Father's Place.
October 20. Syracuse, New York
*(Dejavalse/LHFr)* Jabberwocky
(two shows).
October 21. Ithaca, New York
*(Dejavalse/LHFr)* Ramada Inn.
October 22. New Brunswick, N.J.
*(Dejavalse)* Rutgers University.
October 23. White Plains, N.Y.
*(Dejavalse/LHFr)* Fore 'n Aft.
October 24. New York, N.Y.
*(Dejavalse/LHFr)* The Bitter End (two
shows).
October 25. Providence, R.I.
*(Dejavalse)* Lupo's.
October 26. Buffalo, New York
*(Dejavalse/LHFr)* Slee Hall, S.U.N.Y.
October 27. Hartford, Conn.
*(Dejavalse/LHFr)* Mad Murphy's Cafe.
October 28. Sunderland, Mass.
*(Dejavalse/LHFr)* The Rusty Nail.
October 29. Cambridge, Mass.
*(Dejavalse/LHFr)* Jack's.
October 30. Burlington, Vermontt
*(Dejavalse/LHFr)* Hunt's.
November 16. San Francisco, Calif.
*(Dejavalse/LHFr)* San Francisco Art
Institute.
**1986**, February 9. St. Helena, Calif.
*(Dejavalse)* The White Barn.
April 10. Cambridge, Mass.
*(Dejavalse/valise)* Harvard University
Music Depart. Lecture/Demo.
April 11. Cambridge, Mass.
*(Dejavalse)* Quincy House,
Harvard University.
April 13. San Francisco, Calif.
*(Dejavalse/valise)*, WEST COAST WEEKEND/
KQED-FM.
April 26. San Francisco, Calif. *(Dejavalse)*
WEST COAST WEEKEND/KQED-FM.
April 28. San Francisco, Calif.
*(Dejavalse/valise)* Wolfgang's.
May 16. San Francisco, Calif.
*(Dejavalse)* Union Square. HANDS ACROSS
AMERICA RALLY/GODZILLA BIRTHDAY
CELEBRATION.
June 11. San Francisco, Calif.
ᴿ*(Dejavalse)* Waters Upton Tea Room.
November 2. San Francisco, Calif.

*(Dejavalse/valise)*. WEST COAST WEEKEND/
KQED-FM.
November 15. San Francisco, Calif.
*(Dejavalse/valise)* Noe Valley Ministry.
November. Hong Kong. *(Dejavalse)*. City
Hall Theatre; Betty Woo, pianist.
**1987**, January 3, San Francisco, Calif.
*(Dejavalse/valise/valentino)*
WEST COAST WEEKEND/KQED-FM.
January 10, 17. San Francisco, Calif.
*(Dejavalse/valise)* WEST COAST WEEKEND/
KQED-FM.
January 24. Frankfurt a. M., Germany
*(Dejavalse/valise)* Elschenbroich/
Schweitzer Hauskonzert.
January 30. Frankfurt a. M., Germany
*(Dejavalse/valise)* Holle/Liebrecht
Hauskonzert.
February 7, 14, 21, 28. San Francisco, Calif.
*(Dejavalse/valise)* WEST COAST WEEKEND/
KQED-FM.
March 14. San Francisco, Calif.
*(Dejavalse/valise/boogie)*
WEST COAST WEEKEND/KQED-FM.
March 21, 28; April 11, 18, 25. San
Francisco, Calif. *(Dejavalse/valise)*
WEST COAST WEEKEND/KQED-FM.
May 2. San Francisco, Calif.
*(Dejavalse/valise)* West Coast WEEKEND/
KQED-FM.
May 9. San Francisco, Calif.
*(Dejavalse/valise/boogie)*
WEST COAST WEEKEND/KQED-FM.
May 16, 23, 30; June 6. San Francisco, Calif.
*(Dejavalse/valise)* WEST COAST WEEKEND/
KQED-FM.
June 12. San Francisco, Calif.
*(Dejavalse/valise/LHFr)*
AMNESTY INTERNATIONAL BENEFIT;
Noe Valley Ministry.
June 13, 20. San Francisco, Calif.
*(Dejavalse/valise)* WEST COAST WEEKEND/
KQED-FM.
June 27. San Francisco, Calif.
*(Dejavalse/valise/LHFr)*
WEST COAST WEEKEND/KQED-FM.
July 4, 11, 18, 25. San Francisco, Calif.
*(Dejavalse/valise)* West Coast WEEKEND/
KQED-FM.
July 31. Tiburon, California
*(Dejavalse/valise/LHFr)* THE DOCK.
August 1, 8, 15, 22, 29. San Francisco, Calif.
*(Dejavalse/valise)* WEST COAST WEEKEND/
KQED-FM.
September 5. San Francisco, Calif.
*(Dejavalse/valise)*.
September 12. San Francisco, Calif.

*(Dejavalse / valise / boogie)*
WEST COAST WEEKEND / KQED-FM.
September 17. Winfield, Kansas
*(Dejavalse)* Joe Miller, guitar. NATIONAL
FINGER PICKING CHAMPIONSHIP.
September 19, 26. San Francisco, Calif.
*(Dejavalse / valise)* WEST COAST WEEKEND /
KQED-FM.
September 26. San Francisco, Calif.
*(Dejavalse)* Joe Miller, guitar.
WEST COAST WEEKEND / KQED-FM.
October 3, 10. San Francisco, Calif.
*(Dejavalse / valise)* WEST COAST WEEKEND /
KQED-FM.
October 16. Tiburon, California
*(Dejavalse / valise / LHFr)* THE DOCK.
October 17, 24. San Francisco, Calif.
*(Dejavalse / valise)* WEST COAST WEEKEND /
KQED-FM.
October 25. San Francisco, Calif.
*(Dejavalse)* Noe Valley Ministry.
October 31. San Francisco, Calif.
*(Dejavalse / valise)* WEST COAST WEEKEND /
KQED-FM.
November 7, 14. San Francisco, Calif.
*(Dejavalse / valise / boogie)*
WEST COAST WEEKEND / KQED-FM.
November 15. San Francisco, Calif.
*(Dejavalse)* Community Music CENTER.
FACULTY BENEFIT RECITAL – Five piano
version. T.C., with Shirley Wong, Grace
Huenemann, Robert Montes, and Peter
Maleitzke.
November 21. San Francisco, Calif.
*(Dejavalse / valise / boogie)*
WEST COAST WEEKEND / KQED-FM.
November 21. Berkeley, California
*(Dejavalse)* Joe Miller, guitar. Freight and
Salvage.
November 28. San Francisco, Calif.
*(Dejavalse / valise)* WEST COAST WEEKEND /
KQED-FM.
December 5. San Francisco, Calif.
*(Dejavalse / valise / boogie)*
WEST COAST WEEKEND / KQED-FM.
Dec. 12, 19. San Francisco, Calif.
*(Dejavalse / valise)* WEST COAST WEEKEND /
KQED-FM.
December 26. San Francisco, Calif.
*(Dejavalse / valise / boogie)*
WEST COAST WEEKEND / KQED-FM.
**1988**, 6, 13, 20, 27; March 5, 12, 19, 26;
April 2, 9, 16, 23, 30. San Francisco, Calif.
*(Deja* – evolved by this time)
WEST COAST WEEKEND / KQED-FM.
April 14, 15, 17. San Francisco, Calif.
*(Dejavalse)* New Performance Gallery
dance program.

May 5, 6, 8. New York, N.Y.
*(Dejavalse)* AMERICAN MUSIC FESTIVAL, New
York City Ballet, N.Y. State Theater,
Lincoln Center 'The Waltz Project,'
choreographed by Peter Martins, Jerry
Zimmerman, pianist.
May 7, (14, 21 – reruns), 28; June 4, 11, 18,
25. San Francisco, Calif. *(Deja)*
WEST COAST WEEKEND / KQED-FM.
July 2. San Jose, California *(Deja)*
WEST COAST WEEKEND / KQED-FM.
July 9, 16, 23, 30; Aug. (6, 13 – reruns), 20,
27. San Francisco, Calif. *(Deja)*
WEST COAST WEEKEND / KQED-FM.
September 7. Las Vegas, Nevada
R*(Dejavalse)* Paul Weitz / TR Studio.
September 8. Las Vegas, Nev. R*(LHFr)*
Paul Weitz / Terry Ryan Studio.
September 3, 10, 17; October 1, 8, 15, 22, 29;
November 5, 12, 19, 26. San Francisco,
Calif. *(Deja)* WEST COAST WEEKEND /
KQED-FM.
November 20. Berkeley, California
*(Dejavalse)* Finn Hall.
December 3, 10, 15, 24, 31. San Francisco,
Calif. *(Deja)* WEST COAST WEEKEND /
KQED-FM.
December 15. San Francisco, Calif.
*(Dejavalse)* Slim's.
**1989**, Jan. 1. Las Vegas, Nev. R*(CGbg)*
Paul Weitz / Terry Ryan Studio.
January 7, 14, (21 – rerun), 28. San
Francisco, Calif. *(Deja)*
WEST COAST WEEKEND / KQED-FM.
January 20. San Francisco, Calif.
*(Dejavalse, Dejavalentino)* Community
Music Center. Darius Milhaud Ensemble
concert; Shirley and Betty Wong, plus
T.C. on trio version of *Dejavalse.*
January 22. Santa Monica, Calif. *(Dejavalse)*
McCabe's Guitar Shop (two shows).
January 20, 28, 31, February 4, 5. New
York, N.Y. *(Dejavalse)* New York City
Ballet, N.Y. State Theater, Lincoln Center,
'The Waltz Project,' choreographed by
Peter Martins, Jerry Zimmerman, pianist.
February 4, 11, 18, 25. San Francisco, Calif.
*(Deja)* WEST COAST WEEKEND / KQED-FM.
February 12. San Francisco, Calif.
*(Dejavalse)* Great American Music Hall.
March 4, 11, 18, 25; April 1, 8, 15, 22, 29.
San Francisco, Calif. *(Deja)*
WEST COAST WEEKEND / KQED-FM.
April 15. San Francisco, Calif.
*(Dejavalse)* Fillmore Auditorium.
May 6, 13, 20, 27; June 3, 10, 17, 24. San
Francisco, Calif. *(Deja)*

WEST COAST WEEKEND/KQED-FM.
July 6. Berkeley, California
*(Dejavalse)* LaPeña; Joe Miller, guitar.
July 10. San Francisco, Calif. *(Dejavalse)*
Paradise Lounge; Joe Miller, guitar.
July 15. San Francisco, Calif.
*(Dejavalse)* Community Music Center;
Joe Miller, guitar.
July (1, 8, 15, 22, 29, August 5, 12, 19, 26 –
reruns); September 2, 9, 16, 23, 30;
October 7, 14, 21, 28; November 4, 11, 18,
25. San Francisco, Calif.
*(Deja)* WEST COAST WEEKEND/KQED-FM.
December 1. San Francisco, Calif.
*(Dejavalse)* Noe Valley Ministry.
December 2, 9, 16, 23, 30. San Francisco,
Calif. *(Deja)* WEST COAST WEEKEND/
KQED-FM.
December 9. San Francisco, Calif.
*(Dejavalse)* Chi Chi Club.
December 29. San Francisco, Calif.
*(Dejavalse)* Psychedelic Shop.
**1990**, Jan. 6. San Francisco, Calif.*(Deja)*
WEST COAST WEEKEND/KQED-FM.
January (13, 20, 27, February 3, 10, 17 –
reruns). San Francisco, Calif. *(Deja)*
WEST COAST WEEKEND/KQED-FM.
January 30. San Francisco, Calif. *(Deja)*
Great American Music Hall.
February 1. San Francisco, Calif.
*(Dejavalse)* Last Day Saloon.
February 12. Las Vegas, Nevada
R*(Dejavalse)* Paul Weitz/Terry Ryan
Studio.
February 24; March 3, 10, 17, 24, 31. San
Francisco, Calif. *(Deja)*
WEST COAST WEEKEND/KQED-FM.
April 5. San Rafael, California
*(Dejavalse)* Fourth Street Tavern.
April 7. Bolinas, Calif. *(Dejavalse)* Bolinas
Community Center.
April (7 – rerun) 14, 21, 28; May 5. San
Francisco, Calif. *(Deja)*
WEST COAST WEEKEND/KQED-FM.
May 7. New York, N.Y.
*(Dejavalse)* Knitting Factory.
May (12, 19 – reruns) 26; June 2. San
Francisco, Calif. *(Deja)*
WEST COAST WEEKEND/KQED-FM.
May 20. Seattle, Washington
*(Dejavalse)* University of Washington,
Theodore Roethke Auditorium.
June 2. San Francisco, Calif. *(Dejavalse)*
WEST COAST WEEKEND/KQED-FM.
June 2. San Francisco, Calif.
*(Dejavalse)* Chi Chi Club.
June 6. San Francisco, Calif. *(Dejavalse)*

De Young Museum/ Hearst Court.
June 9, 16, 23. San Francisco, Calif.
*(Deja)* WEST COAST WEEKEND/KQED-FM.
June 17. Pacifica, California
*(Dejavalse)* Cable Channel 8 – TV,
THE BRUCE LATIMER SHOW.
June 30. San Jose, California. *(Deja)*
WEST COAST WEEKEND/KQED-FM.
July 7, 14, 21, 28; August 4, 11, (18, 25 –
reruns); September 1, 8, 15, 22, 29. San
Francisco, Calif. *(Deja)*
WEST COAST WEEKEND/KQED-FM.
September 10. El Cerrito, Calif.
*(Dejavalse)* El Cerrito Cable TV/ON STAGE.
September 12. San Francisco, Calif.
*(Dejavalse)* La Bodega; Joe Miller, guitar.
September 13. San Francisco, Calif.
*(Dejavalse)* Last Day Saloon.
September 29. San Francisco, Calif.
*(Dejavalse)* Psychedelic Shop.
October 4. San Francisco, Calif.
*(Dejavalse* – twice) Last Day Saloon.
October (6 – rerun) 13, 20, 27. San
Francisco, Calif. *(Deja)*
WEST COAST WEEKEND/KQED-FM.
October 12. San Francisco, Calif.
*(Dejavalse* – twice) Last Day Saloon.
October 18. San Francisco, Calif.
*(Dejavalse* – twice) Last Day Saloon.
October 20. San Francisco, Calif.
*(Dejavalse)* The Boat House.
October 31. San Francisco, Calif.
*(Dejavalse)* Last Day Saloon.
Nov. 3. San Francisco, Calif. *(Deja)*
WEST COAST WEEKEND/KQED-FM.
November 6. Philadelphia, Penn.
*(Dejavalse* – twice) Chestnut Cabaret.
November 7. Washington, D.C.
*(Dejavalse* – twice) Lisner Auditorium,
George Washington University.
November 9. New York, N.Y.
*(Dejavalse* – twice) The Ritz.
November 10. San Francisco, Calif.
*(Deja)* WEST COAST WEEKEND/KQED-FM;
Diane Hidy, piano.
November 10, Somerville, Mass.
*(Dejavalse* – twice) Somerville Theatre.
November 12. Charlottesville, Va.
*(Dejavalse* – twice) Charlottesville
Performing Arts Center.
November 13. Atlanta, Georgia
*(Dejavalse* – twice) Center Stage.
November 15. Chicago, Illinois
*(Dejavalse* – twice) Park West.
November 16. Milwaukee, Wisconsin
*(Dejavalse* – twice) Avalon Theatre.
November 17. San Francisco, Calif.

*(Deja)* WEST COAST WEEKEND/KQED-FM;
Diane Hidy, piano.
November 17. Boulder, Colorado
*(Dejavalse* – twice) Boulder Theater.
Nov. 24. San Francisco, Calif. *(Deja)*
WEST COAST WEEKEND/KQED-FM.
November 26. San Francisco, Calif.
*(Dejavalse* – twice) The Warfield.
Dec. 1. San Francisco, Calif. *(Deja)*
WEST COAST WEEKEND/KQED-FM.
December 2. Berkeley, California
*(Deja/boogie)* The Ashkenaz.
December 8, 15, 22, 29. San Francisco, Calif.
*(Deja)* WEST COAST WEEKEND/KQED-FM.
December 14. Los Angeles, California
KPFK-FM: *Thursday Lunch,* (*Dejavalse*
from *OutSides*).
**1991**, January 5 (12, 19, 26 – reruns);
February 2, 9, 16, 23; March 2, 9, 16, 23
(30 -rerun). San Francisco, Calif.
*(Deja)* WEST COAST WEEKEND/KQED-FM.
March 22. Berkeley, California
*(Dejavalse)* Joe Miller, guitar; Freight and
Salvage.
April 6, 13. San Francisco, Calif. *(Deja)*
WEST COAST WEEKEND/KQED-FM.
April 20. San Francisco, Calif.
*(Deja)* WEST COAST WEEKEND/KQED-FM;
Diane Hidy, piano.
April 25. Kohala, Hawaii
*(Dejavalse)* Museum of the Pacific; Mauna
Lani Resort.
April 27. San Francisco, Calif. *(Deja)*
WEST COAST WEEKEND/KQED-FM.
May 4. San Francisco, Calif.
*(Deja/valentino)* WEST COAST WEEKEND/
KQED-FM.
May 11, 18, 25; June 1, 8, 15, 22, 29. San
Francisco, Calif. *(Deja)*
WEST COAST WEEKEND/KQED-FM.
July 5. Berkeley, California. ᴿ*(Dejavalse/
Dejavalentino)* Fantasy Studios.
July 6, 13 (20, 27; Aug. 3, 10, 17, 24, 31-
reruns). San Francisco, Calif. *(Deja)*
WEST COAST WEEKEND/KQED-FM.
July 12. Berkeley, California.
ᴿ*(Dejavalentino)* Fantasy Studios.
August 5. Arcata, California. *(Dejavalse)*
Joe Miller, guitar. 'Welcome Inn.'
Casa de Que Pasa. KHSU.
August 8. Eureka, California. *(Dejavalse)*
Lost Coast Brewery. Joe Miller, guitar.
August 10. Ashland, Oregon. *(Dejavalse)*
The Beanery. Joe Miller, guitar.
August 11. Ashland, Oregon. *(Dejavalse)*
Ashland's Marketplace.
Joe Miller, guitar.

August 11. Richmond, Virginia.
*(Dejavalse)* Kahootz.
August 12. Alexandria, Virginia.
*(Dejavalse)* The Birchmere (two shows).
August 13. Philadelphia, Penn.
*(Dejavalse)* Chestnut Cabaret.
August 14. Pittsburgh, Penn.
*(Dejavalse)* Graffitti's.
August 15. Harrisburg, Penn.
*(Dejavalse)* Club Met.
August 16. Eugene, Oregon
*(Dejavalse)* Allan Bros. Coffeehouse.
Joe Miller, guitar.
August 16. New Britain, Conn.
*(Dejavalse)* The Sting.
August 17. Ashland, Oregon
*(Dejavalse)* Rogue Brewery.
Joe Miller, guitar.
August 18. Portland, Maine
*(Dejavalse)* Raoul's Roadside Attraction.
August 20. Baltimore, Maryland
*(Dejavalse)* Steeltown.
August 22. Beaverton, Oregon
*(Dejavalse)* Shirley's Coffeehouse.
Joe Miller, guitar.
August 22. New York, N.Y.
*(Dejavalse)* The Bottom Line (two shows).
August 23. Sandy, Oregon
*(Dejavalse)* Elusive Trout.
Joe Miller, guitar.
August 23. Boston, Massachusetts
*(Dejavalse)* The Channel.
August 24. Olympia, Washington
*(Dejavalse)* Urban Onion.
Joe Miller, guitar.
August 25. Parksville, N.Y.
*(Dejavalse)* Arrowhead Ranch.
August 26. Buffalo, N.Y.
*(Dejavalse)* Melody Fair.
August 27. Toronto, Ontario
*(Dejavalse)* Rock 'n Roll Heaven.
August 31. Chicago, Illinois
*(Dejavalse)* Cubby Bear (two shows).
September 7, 14, 21, 28. San Francisco,
Calif. (Deja) WEST COAST WEEKEND/
KQED-FM.
September 20. Walnut Valley, Kansas.
*(Dejavalse)* Walnut Valley Festival.
Joe Miller, guitar.
September 22. Piedmont, California.
*(Dejavalse)* Earplay Benefit Gala.
Piedmont Piano Company: Eight Piano
Version. T.C. with Barbara Shearer,
Marvin Tartak, Naomi Sparrow, Karen
Rosenak, Louise Bidwell, George
Thomson, and Elizabeth Davidson.
October 5. San Francisco, Calif. *(Deja)*

WEST COAST WEEKEND/KQED-FM.
October 5. Pacific Grove, Calif. *(Dejavalse)*
Portofino. Joe Miller, guitar.
October 10. Solana Beach, Calif. *(Dejavalse)*
Belly Up Tavern.
October 10. Laguna Beach, Calif. *(Dejavalse)*
Renaissance Cafe. Joe Miller, guitar.
October 11. Los Angeles, Calif. *(Dejavalse)*
KPFK-FM: Thursday Lunch.
October 12. North Hollywood, Calif.
*(Dejavalse)* The Palomino.
October 12. Woodland Hills, Calif.
*(Dejavalse)* Cobalt Cafe. Joe Miller, guitar.
October 12, 19. San Francisco, Calif. *(Deja)*
WEST COAST WEEKEND/KQED-FM.
Diane Hidy, piano.
October 13. Isla Vista, California.
*(Dejavalse)* The Anaconda.
October 15. New York, N.Y. *(Dejavalse)*
Wetlands Preserve.
October 16. Springfield, Virginia.
*(Dejavalse)* Zaxx.
October 17. Lancaster, Pennsylvania.
*(Dejavalse)* The Village.
October 18. Philadelphia, Penn. *(Dejavalse)*
Chestnut Cabaret.
October 19. Virginia Beach, Virginia.
*(Dejavalse)* Peppermint Beach Club.
October 22. Knoxville, Tennessee.
*(Dejavalse)* Orpheus.
October 23. Nashville, Tennessee.
*(Dejavalse)* 328 Performance Hall.
October 24. Plymouth, N. H. *(Dejavalse)*
Suzanne's Kitchen. Joe Miller, guitar.
October 25. Tallahassee, Florida. *(Dejavalse)*
The Moon.
October 25. Harvard, Mass. *(Dejavalse)*
Warner Free Lectures. Joe Miller, guitar.
October 26. San Francisco, Calif. *(Deja)*
WEST COAST WEEKEND/KQED-FM.
J. R. Brody, piano.
November 2. Memphis, Tennessee.
*(Dejavalse)* 616 Club.
November 4. Solana Beach, Calif.
*(Dejavalse)* Belly Up Tavern.
November 8. Arcata, California. *(Dejavalse)*
Van Duzen Theatre, Humboldt State U.
November 9, 16, 23, 30. San Francisco,
Calif. *(Deja)* WEST COAST WEEKEND/
KQED-FM.
November 14. Palo Alto, California.
*(Dejavalse)* St. Michael's Alley.
Joe Miller, guitar.
November 21. Davis, California. *(Dejavalse)*
The Blue Mango. Joe Miller, guitar.
November 23. San Luis Obispo, Calif.
*(Dejavalse)* Linnaea's Cafe.

Joe Miller, guitar.
December 7, 14, 21, 28. San Francisco, Calif.
*(Deja)* WEST COAST WEEKEND/KQED-FM.
December 14. Costa Mesa, California.
*(Dejavalse)* Blue Marble Cafe.
Joe Miller, guitar.
December 15. Laguna Beach, Calif.
*(Dejavalse)* Renaissance Cafe.
Joe Miller, guitar.
December 16. Solana Beach, Calif.
*(Dejavalse)* Belly Up Tavern.

## SONATA DESAXIFICATA

for Harpsichord
Commissioned by Margaret Fabrizio

Oakland: 1978 – 1980.
*I. Encodex Punctilious* (Summer – Oct. 8,
1978). *II. Apocryphal Awry* (Nov., 1978 –
Jan., 1979). *III. Rondo Pazzo* (1979 – 1980)

Recorded: 1990, Tom Constanten. *OutSides*
– Self-released cassette. All three movements plus two extra *Rondo Pazzo*.

**1981**, September 6. Paris, France
Margaret Fabrizio, harpsichordist.
American Church in Paris, Quai d'Orsay
(First two movements only).
October 3. Munich, Germany
Margaret Fabrizio, harpsichordist.
Volkshochschule Unterpfaffenhofen-
Germering (First two movements only).
**1982**, April 4. Portland, Oregon
Margaret Fabrizio, harpsichordist. Evans
Auditorium; Lewis and Clark College.
(First two movements only).
April 19. San Francisco, Calif.
Margaret Fabrizio, harpsichordist.
San Francisco Art Institute.
(First two movements only).
**1983**, June 19. San Francisco, Calif.
OLD WALDORF. *(Fandango Maltallado* for
third movement).
**1984**, November 16. San Francisco, Calif.
San Francisco Art Institute.
(First two movements only).
**1987**, April 18-24. Las Vegas, Nevada
*R(Rondo Pazzo)* Paul Weitz/ TR Studio.
April 25. San Francisco, Calif. *(Encodex)*
WEST COAST WEEKEND/KQED-FM.
**1988**, March 26. San Francisco, Calif.
*(Apocryphal)* WEST COAST WEEKEND/
KQED-FM.
**1990**, February 1. San Francisco, Calif.
*(Apocryphal)* Last Day Saloon.
February 4. Las Vegas, Nevada
*R(Apocryphal)* Paul Weitz/ TR Studio.

February 5. Las Vegas, Nevada
R(Encodex/Rondo) Paul Weitz/ TR Studio.
February 10. Las Vegas, Nevada
R(Rondo) Paul Weitz/ TR Studio.
February 24. San Francisco, Calif.
(Apocryphal) WEST COAST WEEKEND/
KQED-FM.
November 7. Washington, D.C.
(Apocryphal) Lisner Auditorium,
George Washington University.
November 10. Somerville, Mass.
(Apocryphal) Somerville Theatre.
November 12. Charlottesville, Va.
(Apocryphal) Charlottesville Performing
Arts Center.
November 13. Atlanta, Georgia
(Apocryphal) Center Stage.
November 15. Chicago, Illinois
(Apocryphal) Park West.
November 17. Boulder, Colorado
(Apocryphal) Boulder Theater.
December 14. Los Angeles, California
KPFK-FM: Thursday Lunch, (Rondo Pazzo
from OutSides).

MAYA

Score for the Bertha Dominguez/
Alexander Salkind film
Flute, Guitar, Piano, Prepared Piano, and
Harp. London, Paris: March, 1980.

1980, March 20-21. Paris, France
RStudio Maya.

THE PEOPLE NEXT DOOR

Score for the Shire Films short subject
Oakland: 1980.

1980, September. El Cerrito, California
RTewksbury Sound Studios.

METASTROPHE

for Guitar
Oakland: 1980 – 1981.

1989, January 5. Las Vegas, Nevada
RPaul Weitz/ Terry Ryan Studio.

LIGNIFIED ROCK EPISODES

The Heretic Strut (Oakland: 1980 – 1981).
Alaric's Premonition: a Gothic Fugue en
rondeau on a theme by J. Garcia (Los
Angeles: 1971. Qtet arr. Oakland, 1980).
Fandango Maltallado (Oakland, 1982 – 1983).
Electric Red Water Getaway (Waimea: May,
1985). Montparnasse Memories (N.Y., Paris,

Waimea: 1971 – May, 1985). Disco Cynic
(Waimea: May, 1985). Kentucky Chaconne
(Oakland: 1982). Bugsy (Oakland: com-
pleted October 6, 1985).

Recorded:
Alaric's Premonition :1983: The Electric
Guitar Quartet – Self-released cassette.
1990: Tom Constanten. OutSides – Self-
released cassette. Fandango Maltallado,The
Disco Delius Banjo Bash (formerly Disco
Cynic), Bugsy: 1990 Tom Constanten.
OutSides – Self-released cassette.

1972, April 13. Berkeley, California
(Alaric) New Orleans House. Touchstone:
Paul Dresher, guitar; Bill Ruskin, guitar;
Gene Reffkin drums; Wes Steele, bass;
and T.C., RMI Electra-piano.
1974, October 2. Buffalo, New York
(Alaric) Baird Hall. Version with Rock
Band and Pipe Organ. Joel Perry, guitar;
Art Levinowitz, sax; Murray Kohn, bass;
Albert Furness, drums; T.C., organ.
1980, October 23. Oakland, California
(Alaric) Mills College. Kronos Quartet:
David Harrington, John Sherba, Hank
Dutt and Joan Jeanrenaud.
1981, July 20. Ashland, Oregon
(Hertc) Kronos Quartet, OREGON
SHAKESPEARE FESTIVAL.
August 7. San Francisco, Calif.
(Hertc) Kronos Quartet, GREAT AMERICAN
MUSIC HALL.
1982, August 2. Ashland, Oregon
(Hertc/Alaric/Deja/KChac). Kronos
Quartet; OREGON SHAKESPEARE FESTIVAL.
August 5. Arroyo Grande, Calif.
(Hertc/Alaric/Deja/KChac). Kronos
Quartet; SAN LUIS OBISPO MOZART FESTIVAL;
First United Methodist Church.
August 6. Paso Robles, California
(Hertc/Alaric/Deja/KChac). Kronos
Quartet; SAN LUIS OBISPO MOZART FESTIVAL.
August 6. Cambria, California
(Hertc/Alaric/Deja/KChac). Kronos
Quartet; SAN LUIS OBISPO MOZART FESTIVAL;
Veterans Memorial Building.
August 7. San Luis Obispo, Calif.
(Hertc/Alaric/Deja/KChac). Kronos
Quartet; SAN LUIS OBISPO MOZART FESTIVAL;
Cal Poly Auditorium.
November 6. Los Angeles, California
(Hertc/Alaric/Deja/KChac). Kronos
Quartet; Schönberg Institute; U. S. C.
November. Sacramento, California
(Hertc/Alaric/Deja/KChac). Kronos
Quartet; Cal Expo.

**1983**, May 1. San Francisco, Calif.
*(Alaric)*. Electric Guitar Quartet: Ken
Frankel, Kathy Greenstone, Warren
Sirota and Van Williamson. Community
Music Center.
September 18. Las Vegas, Nevada
*(Alaric/Deja/KChac)*. Charleston Heights
Library. Las Vegas Chamber Symphony
Orchestra, Masatoshi Miyamoto,
conductor.
**1984**, February 5. Las Vegas, Nevada
*(Hertc/Alaric/KChac)*. Cantor Quartet:
Russ Cantor, Carlene San Filippo,
Lyndl Miller and Tim Allcott. Charleston
Heights Library.
September 19. Berkeley, California
*(Hertc/Alaric)* Electric Guitar Quartet,
Julia Morgan Theatre
«Liquified Rock Explodes».
**1986**, October 25. San Francisco, Calif.
*(Hertc/Alaric/Mprnsse/Disco)*. Janine
Driscoll, Craig Fry, violins; Ken
Blacklock, viola; and John Dunlop, 'cello,
BAY AREA COMPOSERS' ALLIANCE/ NOE
VALLEY MINISTRY
«Parkinson's Ball».
December 16. Fremont, California
*(ElecRdWtr/Mprnsse/Alaric/KChac)*.
Ohlone Chamber Orchestra, Lawrence
Kohl, conductor.
**1989**, December 23. San Francisco, Calif.
*(ElecRdWtr)* WEST COAST WEEKEND/
KQED-FM. T.C. with Jeremy Cohen,
violin.
**1990**, January 13. Las Vegas, Nevada
*R(Disco/Fandango)* Paul Weitz/TR Studio.
January 14. Las Vegas, Nevada
*R(Alaric)* Paul Weitz/TR Studio.
February 6. Las Vegas, Nevada
*R(Alaric)* Paul Weitz/TR Studio.
December 3. Berkeley, California
KPFA-FM: *Mob Ecstasy*, with Ben
Lindgren. *(Disco Delius* from *OutSides)*.
December 14. Los Angeles, California
KPFK-FM: *Thursday Lunch, (Alaric's
Premonition* from *OutSides)*.

## CANTANKEROUS CONJURER
for Piano
For Stephen Goldstine
Oakland: 1982.

**1984**, November 16. San Francisco, Calif.
San Francisco Art Institute.

## ANY FACE CARD BEATS A '10'
for Piano
Oakland: 1984

Recorded: 1989, Tom Constanten. *Fresh
Tracks in Real Time*. Self-released cassette.

**1984**, November 16. San Francisco, Calif.
San Francisco Art Institute.
December 30. Las Vegas, Nevada
*R*Evergreen/Terry Ryan Studio.
**1986**, April 10. Cambridge, Mass.
Harvard Music Dept. Lecture/Demo.
April 11, Cambridge, Mass. Quincy House,
Harvard University.
April 13, San Francisco, Calif.
WEST COAST WEEKEND/KQED-FM.
April 28. San Francisco, Calif.
Wolfgang's.
November 15. San Francisco, Calif.
Noe Valley Ministry.
**1987**, January 3. San Francisco, Calif.
WEST COAST WEEKEND/KQED-FM.
January 24. Frankfurt a. M., Germany.
Elschenbroich/Schweitzer Hauskonzert.
January 30. Frankfurt a. M., Germany.
Holle/Liebrecht, Hauskonzert.
July 31. Tiburon, California. The Dock.
**1988**, September 4. Las Vegas, Nevada
*R*Paul Weitz/Terry Ryan Studio.
November 20. Berkeley, California
Finn Hall.
December 15. San Francisco, Calif.
Slim's.
**1989**, January 22. Santa Monica, Calif.
McCabe's Guitar Shop.
February 12. San Francisco, Calif.
Great American Music Hall.

## SONGS
Oakland: 1985

*Cometary Commentary*
*The Ballad of Shane Muscatell*
*Moonshine Superman*
*The Long and Wide*

Recorded:
*The Ballad of Shane Muscatell.*
1989: The Henry Kaiser Band: *Heart's
Desire*. Reckless Records RECKD 19.

**1985**, December. Berkeley, California
*R(Cometary)* Arch St./Josef Marc Studio.
T.C., vocal and piano bass, with Josef
Marc, drums and guitar.
December 5. Berkeley, Calif. *R(Halley's)*
Arch St./Josef Marc Studio.

**1986**, January 8. Berkeley, California
  *R(Shane)* Arch St./Josef Marc Studio. T.C.,
  vocal and piano, with Virginia Morgan,
  backup vocals, and Josef Marc, drums.
January 11, 15. Berkeley, California
  *R(Long/Wide)*. Arch St./ Josef Marc
  Studio. T.C., vocal and piano bass, with
  Josef Marc, drums.
January 15. Berkeley, California
  *R(Moonshine)*. Arch St./ Josef Marc
  Studio. T.C., vocal and Yamaha DX-7
  synthesizer, with Josef Marc, drums and
  guitar.
* *Public airings of these sessions:*
*February 10. San Francisco, Calif.
  *(Cometary)* DEADHEAD HOUR/KFOG-FM.
*Feb. 10. Nationwide. *(Cometary)* DR.
  DEMENTO SHOW #86-07.
*March 3. Nationwide. *(Cometary)* DR.
  DEMENTO SHOW #86-10.
*April 10. Cambridge, Mass.
  *(Cometary/Shane)*. Harvard University
  Music Department.
*April 13. San Francisco, Calif.
  *(Shane)* WEST COAST WEEKEND/KQED-FM.
*June 23. Nationwide *(Shane)* DR. DEMENTO
  SHOW #86-26.
*September. San Francisco, Calif.
  *(Shane)* WEST COAST WEEKEND/KQED-FM.
**1988**, July 2. San Jose, California
  *(Shane)* WEST COAST WEEKEND/KQED-FM
  with Bruce Walker Bellingham, guitar/
  at Mirassou Vineyards.
December 15. San Francisco, Calif.
  *(Shane)* Slim's.
**1989**, February 12. San Francisco, Calif.
  *(Shane)* Great American Music Hall with
  Henry Kaiser Band: Henry Kaiser and
  Bruce Anderson, guitars; Hilary Hanes,
  bass; and John Hanes, drums.
(July 1 – rerun). San Francisco, Calif.
  *(Shane)* WEST COAST WEEKEND/KQED-FM.
October 21. Davis, California *(Shane)* The
  Palms with Henry Kaiser Band.
October 22. Davis, California *(Shane)* The
  Palms with Henry Kaiser Band.
**1990**, May 8, 9. New York, N.Y.
  *(Shane)* Wetlands Preserve with Henry
  Kaiser Band.
May 18. Cotati, California *(Shane)*. The
  Commons; Sonoma State University with
  Henry Kaiser Band.
**1991**, October 12. No. Hollywood, Calif.
  The Palomino.

## LET IT RING

Mobile for Piano(s)
Oakland: November, 1987

Recorded: 1990: Tom Constanten. *OutSides*
– Self-released cassette.

**1987**, November 15. San Francisco, Calif.
  Community Music Center. FACULTY
  BENEFIT RECITAL – Five piano version. T.C.,
  with Shirley Wong, Grace Huenemann,
  Robert Montes, and Peter Maleitzke.
**1989**, January 20. San Francisco, Calif.
  Community Music Center, Darius
  Milhaud Ensemble concert. Shirley and
  Betty Wong.
**1990**, January 13. Las Vegas, Nevada
  *R*Paul Weitz/Terry Ryan Studio.
February 4. Las Vegas, Nevada
  *R*Paul Weitz/Terry Ryan Studio.
December 14. Los Angeles, California
  KPFK-FM: *Thursday Lunch*, from
  *OutSides.*

## DISPEPTICALLY SKEPTICALLY BLUE

Song
Oakland: December 25, 1987.

**1987**, Dec. 26. San Francisco, Calif.
  WEST COAST WEEKEND/KQED-FM.
**1988**, December 15. San Francisco, Calif.
  Slim's.

## THE AFFAIR OF RUE DE LOURCINE

Incidental music for the Labiche farce.
Translated and Directed by Carl Weber.
Oakland: March, 1989

*Overture*
1. *Let's eat*
2. *What's happened to us*
3. *We're brushing our fingers white*
4. *Reprise of #3*
5. *What kind of talk is that*
6. *Now it must be told*
7. *Progress reigns supreme today*
8. *Intermexxo inebriato*
9. *In the vineyards*
10. *When once we all arrive/*
    *Let's raise our voice*

Recorded: *Overture* : 1990. Tom
Constanten. *OutSides* – Self-released
cassette.

**1989,** April 12-15, 19-22. Palo Alto, California. Stanford University Drama Department. The Nitery; Old Union. Christopher Hart, Ian Cummings, Chris LaPuma, Shannon Jackson, and James Coulter, vocalists. Denise Boling: pianist, music director.

April 15. San Francisco, Calif. *(Overture)* WEST COAST WEEKEND/KQED-FM.

April 15. San Francisco, Calif. *(Overture)* FILLMORE AUDITORIUM.

April 22. San Francisco, Calif. *(Intermezzo Inebriato).* WEST COAST WEEKEND/KQED-FM.

December 1. San Francisco, Calif. *(Overture)* Noe Valley Ministry.

**1990,** January 12. Las Vegas, Nevada ^R*(Overture).* Paul Weitz/Terry Ryan Studio.

January 13. Las Vegas, Nevada ^R*(Intermezzo/Vineyards).* Paul Weitz/Terry Ryan Studio.

April 7. Bolinas, California *(Overture)* Bolinas Community Center.

May 7. New York, N.Y. *(Overture)* Knitting Factory.

June 6. San Francisco, Calif. *(Overture)* De Young Museum/ Hearst Court.

September 28. San Francisco, Calif. *(Overture)* Psychedelic Shop.

October 27. San Francisco, Calif. *(Overture)* WEST COAST WEEKEND/KQED-FM.

November 6. Philadelphia, Penn. *(Overture)* Chestnut Cabaret.

November 7. Washington, D.C. *(Overture)* Lisner Auditorium, George Washington University.

November 9. New York, N.Y. *(Overture)* The Ritz.

November 10. Somerville, Mass. *(Overture)* Somerville Theatre.

November 12. Charlottesville, Va. *(Overture)* Charlottesville Performing Arts Center.

November 13. Atlanta, Georgia *(Overture)* Center Stage.

November 15. Chicago, Illinois *(Overture)* Park West.

November 16. Milwaukee, Wisconsin *(Overture)* Avalon Theatre.

November 17. Boulder, Colorado *(Overture)* Boulder Theater.

December 3. Berkeley, California *(Overture)* KPFA-FM: *Mob Ecstasy,* with Ben Lindgren.

## MIDI SENDUPS
Las Vegas

*Post-expressionist Relief*
*The Unspeakable Pact of Mohair Bubba*
    *and Slim Salabim*
*V'loods*
*Another George for Terry*
*Baron von Wartzenall*
*Carnal Noncarol*
*Valse Burlesque*

Recorded: Uptown Boy (PostXprs), *Unspeakable Pact*: '90, Tom Constanten. *OutSides* – Self-released cassette.

**1990,** February 6. Las Vegas, Nevada ^R*(Post/Unspeak/V'loods)* Paul Weitz/Terry Ryan Studio.

December 3. Berkeley, Calif. KPFA-FM: *Mob Ecstasy,* with Ben Lindgren. *(Uptown Boy* from *OutSides).*

**1991,** January 7. Las Vegas, Nevada ^R*(Geo/Baron/Carn/Vals)* Paul Weitz/Terry Ryan Studio.

## FAKE FUR ELISE
San Pablo: February, 1991

Recorded, 1992: *Nightfall of Diamonds* (Relix CD RR-2046).

**1991,** February 2. San Francisco, Calif. WEST COAST WEEKEND/KQED-FM.

March 23. San Francisco, Calif. WEST COAST WEEKEND/KQED-FM.

July 5, Berkeley, Calif. ^RFantasy Studios.

August 14. Pittsburgh, Pennsylvania. Graffitti's.

August 22. New York, N.Y. The Bottom Line (2nd. Show).

# T.C. BASE 3/ PERFORMANCES

Many a novelist has written what amounts to a second book, never to be published, to ensure consistency in character development and other details in the main work. Here is the 'book behind the book' of this piece, assembled to the best of my friends' and my memory. A few gaps and questions remain. An occasional onstage accomplice has darted off after a show without leaving so much as a silver guitar pick to remember him by; some writers' credits still elude me; and I still can't nail down the date when, while still in the Air Force, I appeared with the Grateful Dead at the Las Vegas Convention Center. On the other hand, the chronicle extends through 1991, far beyond the preceding narrative. The accelerated level of activity should be evident, as seeds sown over the past decades began to germinate, evolving into an ever more intricate pattern of people, places, and music. Stages august and seamy, shared with musicians fine and otherwise, playing for brows of many and varied altitudes and plenitudes – here's one musician's view of the numerous threads of the multifarious musical worlds of the late twentieth century. (Compositions are by T.C. unless otherwise indicated. Parenthetical references to piano models are followed by attendance figures, when known.)

## 1960

May 13. Las Vegas, Nevada. Rancho High School. Talent Assembly. *Impromptu in A minor* – 'The Apology'.
December 6? Las Vegas, Nevada. Las Vegas High School Auditorium. First violinist, All School String Orchestra. Frank E. Iddings, conductor.

## 1961

January 16. Las Vegas, Nevada. Fifth Street School Auditorium. 'Music at Four' Concert. First violinist, All School String Orchestra. Frank E. Iddings, conductor.
April 18. Las Vegas, Nevada. West Charleston School Auditorium. First violinist, All School String Orchestra. Frank E. Iddings, conductor.
April 18. Las Vegas, Nevada. Nellis School Auditorium. First violinist, All School String Orchestra. Frank E. Iddings, conductor.
May 28. Las Vegas, Las Vegas Nevada. Convention Center (Baldwin). *Conversation Piece* for Piano & Orchestra, with Las Vegas Pops Orchestra, Antonio Morelli, conductor.
December 24. North Las Vegas, Nevada. Immanuel Community Church. (Hammond organ). *Kyrie* (from *Messa a 4 voci*) (Monteverdi). *Prelude and Aria* (Eberhardt). *Four Chorales: Erhalt uns, Herr, bei Deinem Wort. Allein zu Dir Herr Jesu Christ. Ach, Gott und Herr, wie groß und schwer. Ach, was soll ich Sünder machen?* (Sheff). *Durations.*

## 1962

May 1. Oakland, California. Mills College Concert Hall. *Winter Music* (Cage). T.C. with Luciano Berio, Robert Moran, Lillian T'seng, Patricia Caballero, Ann Uran, Robert Kuykendall, Irene Lathrop, Jane Hill, Philip Lesh, Nancy Thalhammer, Ronald Hotek, and Maxine Goldberg.
May 19. Ojai, California. *Ojai Festival.* Rodney Walker Residence. *Three Pieces for Two Pianos.* 2nd of 3, with Laraine Youngsten.
May 27. Oakland, California. Mills College Concert Hall. *Three Pieces for Two Pianos.* With Shirley Wong. First performance of all three.

## 1964

May 21, 23, 29, 30. San Francisco, California. San Francisco Mime Troupe. 'Music Now Koncerts'. *6 7/8 for Bernardo Moreno* (Lesh). T.C., prepared piano solo with Jon Gibson, clarinet; Gwen Watson, 'cello; Georges Rey, violin; & Paul Breslin, bass. *Piano Piece #3.* T.C., prepared piano solo with stereo tape. *Improvisation.* T.C., with Steve Reich, piano; Jon Gibson, clarinet; Gwen Watson, 'cello; Georges Rey, violin; and Paul Breslin, bass.

## 1967

Las Vegas, Nevada. U.N.L.V. *Deutsches Requiem* (Brahms). University of Nevada Orchestra and Chorus, G. Keith Moon, conductor. (Member of chorus).

Las Vegas, Nevada. U.N.L.V.: Student Union. Appearance (on electric bass and Farfisa organ) with *Daemon:* Bob Haney, Ron Gougé, John Farrar, and Don Farr.

*GRATEFUL DEAD APPEARANCES*

Grateful Dead: Ron 'Pigpen' McKernan, Organ and Harmonica; Jerry Garcia, guitar; Bob Weir, guitar; Phil Lesh, electric bass; Bill Kreutzmann, drums; Mickey Hart, drums; T.C., organ – Vox Super-Continental Electric and Hammond B3. (Specifics as to reportoire played can be found in *Dead Base* – see 'Scott, John' in T.C. Base 1.)

September ? Las Vegas, Nevada. Convention Center Rotunda.

## 1968

March 11. Sacramento, California. Memorial Auditorium.
November 23. Athens, Ohio. Memorial Auditorium; Ohio University.
November 24. Cincinnati, Ohio. Hyde Park Teen Center.
November 27, 28. Chicago, Illinois. Electric Theatre/Kinetic Playground.
December 1. Detroit, Michigan. Grande Ballroom.
December 6. Philadelphia, Pennsylvania. The Spectrum.
December 7. Louisville, Kentucky. Bellarmine College.
December 13, 14. Torrance, California. The Bank.
December 20, 21. Los Angeles, California. Shrine Auditorium.
December 28. Houston, Texas.
December 29. Hallandale, Florida. Miami Pop Festival; Gulfstream Park Racetrack.
December 31. San Francisco, California. Winterland.

## 1969

January 2-5. San Francisco, California. Fillmore West.
January 24-26. San Francisco, California. Avalon Ballroom.
January 31-February 1. Chicago, Illinois. Electric Theatre/Kinetic Playground.
February 3. Minneapolis, Minnesota. Guthrie Theater.
February 4. Omaha, Nebraska. The Music Box.
February 5. Kansas City, Kansas.
February 6. St. Louis, Missouri. Kiel Auditorium.

February 7. Pittsburgh, Pennsylvania. Stanley Theater.
February 11, 12. New York, N.Y. Fillmore East.
February 14, 15. Philadelphia, Pennsylvania. Electric Factory.
February 19. San Francisco, California. Fillmore West *(Celestial Synapse).*
February 21, 22. Napa/Vallejo, California. Dream Bowl.
February 27-3/2. San Francisco, California. Fillmore West.
March 12. San Francisco, California. Fillmore West.
March 15. San Francisco, California. S.F. Hilton; *Black and White Ball.*
March 21, 22. Pasadena, California. Rose Palace.
March 27. Merced, California.
March 28. Modesto, California.
March 29. Las Vegas, Nevada. Ice Palace.
April 4-6. San Francisco, California. Avalon Ballroom.
April 11. Tucson, Arizona. University of Arizona.
April 12. Salt Lake City, Utah. Student Union Ballroom; University of Utah.
April 13. Boulder, Colorado. Ballroom; University of Colorado.
April 15. Omaha, Nebraska. The Music Box.
April 17. St. Louis, Missouri. Washington University.
April 18. Lafayette, Indiana. Memorial Union Ballroom; Purdue University.
April 20. Worcester, Massachusetts. Clark University.
April 21-3. Boston, Massachusetts. The Ark.
April 25, 26. Chicago, Illinois. Electric Theatre/Kinetic Playground.
April 27. Minneapolis, Minnesota. Labor Temple.
May 2, 3. San Francisco, California. Winterland.
May 3. Rocklin, California. Sierra College.
May 7. San Francisco, California. Polo Field; Golden Gate Park.
May 9. San Mateo, California. Hall of Flowers; County Fairgrounds.
May 10. Pasadena, California. Rose Palace.
May 11. San Diego, California. San Diego Pop Festival; Aztec Bowl; S.D. State University.

May 16. Moraga, California.
Campolindo High School.
May 23, 24. Hollywood, Florida.
Big Rock Pow-wow.
May 28. San Francisco, Calif.
Winterland; *People's Park Benefit*.
May 29. Santa Barbara, Calif. UCSB;
Robertson Gymnasium.
May 30. Portland, Oregon.
Springer's Ballroom.
May 31. Eugene, Oregon.
University of Oregon.
June 5-8. San Francisco, California.
Fillmore West.
June 11. San Francisco, California.
California Hall. Scientology Benefit
Concert – Bobby Ace and the Cards off
the Bottom. T.C. with Bob Weir, Jerry
Garcia, Phil Lesh, Mickey Hart, Peter
Grant, and John Dawson.
June 13. Fresno, California.
Convention Center.
June 14. Monterey, California.
Monterey Performing Arts Center.
June 20, 21. New York, N.Y.
Fillmore East.
June 22. New York, N.Y.
Central Park.
June 27, 28. Santa Rosa, California.
Veterans' Auditorium.
July 3. Colorado Springs, Colorado.
July 4, 5. Chicago, Illinois.
Electric Theatre/Kinetic Playground.
July 7. Atlanta, Georgia.
Atlanta Pop Festival.
July 8. Toronto, Ontario.
Rock Pile.
July 10. Los Angeles, California.
Television City; *Playboy After Dark*.
July 11, 12. New York, N.Y. N.Y. State
Pavilion; Flushing Meadow Park.
July 16. San Francisco, California.
Longshoremens' Hall.
August 2, 3. San Francisco, California.
Family Dog on the Great Highway.
August 16. White Lake, N.Y.
*Woodstock Music and Arts Fair
– an Aquarian Exposition.*
August 20. Seattle, Washington.
Aqua Theatre.
August 23. St. Helens, Oregon.
Bullfrog Lake Festival.
August 28-30. San Francisco, Califkornia.
Family Dog at the Great Highway.
September 1. Prairieville, Louisiana.
New Orleans Pop Festival.
September 6, 7. San Francisco, California.
Family Dog on the Great Highway.

September 26, 27. New York, N.Y.
Fillmore East.
September 29 - October 1. New York, N.Y.
Cafe a GoGo.
October 2-4. Boston, Massachusetts.
Boston Tea Party.
October 6. San Francisco, California. Family
Dog at the Great Highway.
October 24-26. San Francisco, California.
Winterland.
October 31. San Jose, California.
San Jose State University.
November 1, 2. San Francisco, California.
Family Dog at the Great Highway.
November 7, 8. San Francisco, California.
Fillmore Auditorium.
November 15. Crockett, California.
Lanai Theatre *(Moratorium Day)*.
November 21. Sacramento, California.
Cal Expo.
December 4, 5, 7. San Francisco, California.
Fillmore West.
December 10-12. Los Angeles, California.
Thelma's.
December 13. San Bernardino, California.
Swing Auditorium.
December 14. Los Angeles, California.
Kaleidoscope.
December 19-21. San Francisco, California.
Fillmore Auditorium.
December 26. Dallas, Texas.
McFarlin Auditorium; S.M.U.
December 28. Hollywood, Florida. Interna-
tional Speedway; Hollywood Pop Festival.
December 29-31. Boston, Massachusetts.
Boston Tea Party.

## 1970

January 2, 3. New York, N.Y.
Fillmore East.
January 10. San Diego, California.
Community Concourse.
January 15. Seattle, Washington.
Aqua Theatre.
January 16,18. Portland, Oregon.
Springer's Ballroom.
January 17. Corvallis, Oregon.
Oregon State University.
January 22-6. Honolulu, Hawaii.
Civic Auditorium.
January 29. New Orleans, Louisiana.
The Warehouse.

*RUBBER DUCK COMPANY APPEARANCES*

Joe McCord (Rubber Duck), mime; Glen
Frendel, Jim Byers, guitar; Tom Glass, David
Garthwaite, or Wes Steele, bass; 'Chicken'
Hirsch, Ron Wilson, drums; Art Fayer,

Naomi Ruth Eisenberg, violin; and T.C.,
RMI electric piano.
Berkeley, California. Mandrake's. San Fran-
cisco, Calif. Fillmore West. San Francisco,
Calif. Pacific High Recorders/*Tarot* Demo
Session. *Harlequin. Maiden Waltz* with Rich-
ard Greene, violin.
July 14, 16. San Rafael, California. Euphoria.
First show with guitarist Paul Dresher.
August ? Albany, California. *Tarot* Demo
Session.
December? New York, N.Y. Village Gate.

*JIMMIE SPHEERIS APPEARANCES*

July. Berkeley, California. Pauley Ballroom;
U.C. Berkeley. (Hohner Clavinet courtesy
of Toni Brown.)
October? New York, N.Y. The Bitter End.

*TAROT*

Composer/Musical Director/Keyboardist
of the Off-Broadway musical. Two three
week runs, plus a week of previews: two
shows Sundays, dark Mondays.
December 1. New York, N.Y. Chelsea Theater
Cente, Brooklyn, New York. With The Rubber Band: Yolande Bavan, vocals; Paul
Dresher, guitar, flute, sitar; Wes Steele, bass;
'Chicken' Hirsch, drums; Jim Byers, guitar;
Art Fayer, violin; and T.C., RMI electric
piano.

November. New York, N.Y. WABC:
'Mike Cuscuna's Luncheonette.'
December. New York, N.Y. WNET-TV:
'Free Time.' Three musical numbers from
*Tarot: Lovers' Walk in the Magic Forest.
The Devil* (Steele). *The Moon.*

**1971**

March 4. Circle in the Square; Manhattan.
Two three week runs (*Tarot)*, plus a week of
previews: two shows Sundays, dark Mondays. With Touchstone: Paul Dresher, guitar, flute, sitar; Wes Steele, bass; 'Chicken'
Hirsch, drums; Jim Byers, guitar; Art Fayer,
violin; and T.C., RMI electric piano.

January 31. New York, N.Y.
Scientology Celebrity Center;
Lafayette Hotel.
March 10. New York, N.Y. WMCA:
'Alex Bennett Show.'
April 28. New York, N.Y. Fillmore East.
Sat in for a set with the Grateful Dead.
August. Pasadena, California.
KPPC: 'Dr. Sound.'

December 17. San Francisco, California.
KSAN-FM: 'Bob McClay Show.'
December. San Francisco, California.
KSAN-FM: 'Scientology Works.' Host of
series of radio shows produced by Paul
Boucher.

*TOUCHSTONE APPEARANCES*

Paul Dresher and Bill Ruskin, guitars; Wes
Steele, bass; Art Roach drums, and T.C.,
RMI electric piano.
November ? San Francisco, California.
Scientology Celebrity Center.

**1972**

*The Love Song of Charles Faberman.* Feature
length film directed by Jeremy Paul Kagan.
January 28. Beverly Hills, Calif. American
Film Institute. *Charles's Theme. Insalata Verde.
Quartetschnitt.* Yukiko Kamei, Milton Tho-
mas, plus violin & 'cello. *Waltz for a peg
legged Octopus.* String quartet, with T.C.,
harpsichord (Neupert).
January 29. *Abel's Theme.* T.C., harpsichord
(Neupert). *Old Wine, New Bottles.* R & R.
*Anne's Theme.* Touchstone: Paul Dresher,
guitar, Art Fayer, violin, Wes Steele, bass,
George Suranovich, drums, and T.C., RMI
electric piano.

Paul Dresher and Bill Ruskin, guitars; Wes
Steele, bass; Gene Reffkin drums, and T.C.,
RMI electric piano.
April 7. Hayward, California. Tuckett Inn.
*Invasion* (?). *Sly* (Dresher)/*The Turtle* (from
*Tarot). Lovers' Walk* (from *Tarot). Greed* (from
*Tarot)/Sneet* (Ryan). *6/8 Jazz. Hashish* (Lateef).
*The Moon* (from *Tarot). The Chariot* (from
*Tarot)/You Know, You Know* (Mahavishnu).
*The Hun. Disgraceful Litigation* (Dresher/
Ruskin). *Chicken Feed* (?). *Birth/Mandala*
(from *Tarot – Dresher). Mara* (Dresher). *Sly*
(Dresher)/*You Know, You Know* (Maha-
vishnu). *Invasion* (?).
April 8. Hayward, California. Tuckett Inn.
First set: *Invasion* (?). *Sly* (Dresher)/*You
Know, You Know* (Mahavishnu). *Lovers' Walk*
(from *Tarot). Greed* (from *Tarot)/Sneet* (Ryan).
Second Set: *Hashish* (Lateef). *6/8 Jazz. The
Hun. Birth/Mandala* (from *Tarot – Dresher).
Chicken Feed* (?). *Disgraceful Litigation*
(Dresher/Ruskin). *Diane's Song* (Dresher).
*The Moon* (from *Tarot). R & R. Mara*
(Dresher). *Invasion* (?).
April 14. Berkeley, California. Sproul Plaza;
U. C. Berkeley.
April 14. Berkeley, California. New Orleans

House. *Sly* (Dresher)/*Birth*/*Mandala* (from *Tarot* – Dresher). *Lovers' Walk* (from *Tarot*). *Greed* (from *Tarot*) / *Sneet* (Ryan). *6/8 Jazz*. *Chicken Feed* (?). *The Hun*. *Hashish* (Lateef). *The Moon* (from *Tarot*) / *You Know, You Know* (Mahavishnu). *Mara* (Dresher). *Disgraceful Litigation* (Dresher/Ruskin).

April 15. Berkeley, California. New Orleans House. *Sly* (Dresher)/*You Know, You Know* (Mahavishnu). *Lovers' Walk* (from *Tarot*). *Greed* (from *Tarot*/*Sneet* (Ryan). *6/8 Jazz*. *The Hun*. *Hashish* (Lateef). *Alaric's Premonition*. *The Moon* (from *Tarot*). *Birth*/*Mandala* (from *Tarot* – Dresher). *Disgraceful Litigation* (Dresher/Ruskin). *Mara* (Dresher).

April 20. Berkeley, California. Long Branch. *Invasion* (?). *Sly* (Dresher)/*You Know, You Know* (Mahavishnu). *Greed* (from *Tarot*)/*Sneet* (Ryan). *Lovers' Walk* (from *Tarot*). *Chicken Feed* (?). *The Hun*. *Disgraceful Litigation* (Dresher/Ruskin). *Hashish* (Lateef). *The Moon* (from *Tarot*) . *The Chariot* (from *Tarot*)/*Birth*/*Mandala* (from *Tarot* – Dresher). *6/8 Jazz*. *Mara* (Dresher).

April 21. Berkeley, California. Long Branch.

April 22. Cotati, California. Inn at the Beginning. First set: *Greed* (from *Tarot*)/*Sneet* (Ryan). *Lovers' Walk* (from *Tarot*). *6/8 Jazz*. *The Hun*. Second Set: *Hashish* (Lateef). *The Moon* (from *Tarot*). *Mara* (Dresher). *Disgraceful Litigation* (Dresher/Ruskin). *Invasion* (?).

May 5. Palo Alto, California. Homer's Warehouse.

July. Berkeley, California. Mandrake's. *Mara* (Dresher). *The Hun*.

August 12. Berkeley, California. Provo Park.

August 16. Berkeley, California. Mandrake's. First set: *Jam*. *Mara* (Dresher). *Invasion* (?). *Greed* (from *Tarot*) / *Sneet* (Ryan). *Lovers' Walk* (from *Tarot*). Second Set: *Hashish* (Lateef). *Sly* (Dresher)/*You Know, You Know* (Mahavishnu). *6/8 Jazz*. *Caligula's Mad Dash* (Dresher)/*The Hun*. *The Moon* (from *Tarot*). *Disgraceful Litigation* (Dresher/Ruskin).

August 27. Half Moon Bay, California. Bach's Dancing and Dynamite Society.

August 31. Berkeley, California. Long Branch. First set: *Lovers' Walk* (from *Tarot*). *Greed* (from *Tarot*) / *Sneet* (Ryan). *Hashish* (Lateef). *Mara* (Dresher)/*The Hun*. Second Set: *Sly* (Dresher)/*You Know, You Know* (Mahavishnu). *6/8 Jazz*. *Invasion* (?). *The Moon* (from *Tarot*) / *Disgraceful Litigation* (Dresher /Ruskin).

September 26. San Francisco, Calif. KEMO-TV: *The Paisley Teahouse*, with Jan Wooley.

*The Moon* (from *Tarot*). *Disgraceful Litigation* (Dresher/Ruskin). *The Devil* (from *Tarot*) (Steele).

October ? Pt. Richmond, California. Community Center.

October ? Boonville, California. McGovern Campaign Benefit.

## 1974

Spring–Summer. Mill Valley, California. Sweetwater Saloon. (Solo appearances). Sunday Afternoon Piano Solos. Gulliver's Pub. San Francisco, California.

May 1. Berkeley, California. Davidson Chiropractic Building. Grand Opening.

*CENTER FOR CREATIVE AND PERFORMING ARTS*

October 2. Buffalo, Baird Recital Hall;S.U.N.Y. New York. *Sly* (Dresher). *Greed* (from *Tarot*)/ '*Sneet* (Ryan). *The Moon* (from *Tarot*). Intermission. *The Devil* (from *Tarot*) (Steele). *Alaric's Premonition* (pipe organ w/ rock band). *You Know, You Know* (Mahavishnu). T.C. with Art Levinowitz, saxophone; Joel Perry, guitar; Murray Kohn, bass; and Albert Furness, drums. Encores (solo piano): *Magnetic Rag* (Joplin). *Green and Gold* (T.S.C. #4).

October 17. Buffalo, N.Y. Baird Recital Hall; S.U.N.Y. *Retrodisrespective Marmalade*. T.C., Hammond B-3 organ, with Donald Knaack, percussion plus two track prerecorded collage. Broadcast live over WBFO-FM.

October ? Buffalo, New York. Albright-Knox Art Gallery. *Evenings for New Music*. *Crow* (Oliveros). Ensemble participant.

November 5-6. Buffalo, New York. Baird Recital Hall; S.U.N.Y. *Vexations* (Satie). T.C. with Joseph Kubera, Robert Moog, David Cohen, Martin Kalve, James McKinnon, Claudia Hoca, Yvar Mikhashoff, Neal Hatch, Stephen Manes, Leila Melandinidas, Norma Sapp, Mark Brooks, Stephen Radecke, James Calabrese, and Richard Schulman, playing in half-hour shifts. (T.C. at 2:30 to 3:00 and 3:30 to 4:00 a.m.). Broadcast live over WBFO-FM.

November 20. Mt. Pleasant, Michigan. Central Michigan University. Warriner Auditorium. *From the Seven Days* (Stockhausen). T.C. with Eberhard Blum, Ralph Jones, and Jan Williams. *Crow* (Oliveros). T.C. with Julius Eastman, Elaine Jones, Eberhard Blum, Ralph Jones, Donald Knaack, Joseph Kubera, and Jan Williams.

December 11. New York, New York. WBAI;

Free Music Store. Introductory remarks to broadcast of. *A Giraffe of Wyne (and Thou)* performed by, percussionist Donald Knaack.

## 1975

January 20. Buffalo, New York. Fillmore Room; Student Union Bldg.; S.U.N.Y. Benefit for WBFO-FM (Hammond B-3 organ) with Art Levinowitz, saxophone; Chuck Hammer, guitar; Murray Kohn, bass, and Norm Skiba, drums. Broadcast live over WBFO-FM. *R & R, The Hun, The Lovers' Walk in the Magic Forest* (from *Tarot*), *The Devil* (from *Tarot*) (Steele), *Greed* (from *Tarot*)/*Sneet* (Ryan) *C Jam, Sly* (Dresher)/ *You Know, You Know* (Mahavishnu)/*The Moon* (from *Tarot*)/*E Jam, That There Old West...*, *The Moon* (from *Tarot*).

January–September. Buffalo, New York. WBFO-FM: *Ad Astra per Asparagus*. Host of weekly hour-long musical radio program. Produced by Wally Gajewski. Sundays 11 a. m. – January through April. Wednesdays 10 p. m. – May through September.

February 15. Buffalo, New York. Albright-Knox Art Gallery. Evenings for New Music. *L'apres-midi du Dracoula* (Moran). With Judith Martin, Eberhard Blum, Ben Hudson, Donald Knaack, and Jan Williams. Joseph Kubera, director.

April 13. Amherst, N.Y. Amherst Cable Television: *Art Beat*. Interviewed on the air re/ upcoming concerts.

April 16. Buffalo, New York. Baird Recital Hall; S.U.N.Y. *When you get to the \**. T.C. with Eberhard Blum, Joseph Kubera, and Donald Knaack. Broadcast live over WBFO-FM, with Walter Gajewski and Terry Gross doing play by play commentary.

April 22. Buffalo, New York. Baird Recital Hall; S.U.N.Y. *From the Seven Days* (Stockhausen). T.C. with Eberhard Blum, Ralph Jones, Judith Martin, and Jan Williams. Broadcast live over WBFO-FM.

May 4. Buffalo, New York. Albright-Knox Art Gallery. Evenings for New Music. *Edition* (Werner Heider). T.C. with Eberhard

Blum, Donald Knaack, Ben Hudson, and Jan Williams. *Chorale/Touch* (Martin). T.C. with Alan Pearce, Judith Martin, Julius Eastman, Gerald Eastman, and Jan Williams. *When you get to the \**. T.C. with Eberhard Blum, Ben Hudson, and Donald Knaack.

June 2. Buffalo, New York. Baird Recital Hall; S.U.N.Y. *Music for Amplified Toy Pianos* (Cage). With Joseph Kubera, Martin Kalve, Donald Knaack, and James Calabrese.

June 11. Buffalo, New York. Baird Recital Hall; S.U.N.Y. *Winter Music* (Cage). T.C. with Mark Brooks, James Calabrese, Peter Gena, Neal Hatch, Ben Hudson, Margaret Knaack, Joseph Kubera, Steve Radecke, Casey Sokol, and Yong Suk-Won.

## 1976

*BACK WEST AGAIN*

May 21. San Francisco, California. Giannini J.H.S. Auditorium. SPARC Benefit. *Green and Gold* (T.S.C. #4).

May 30. Claremont, California. Holmes Hall; Pomona College. *Fig Leaf* (Joplin). *THE SYNTAX COLLECTOR: I. Haight St. Slither. II. That There Old West... III. Lude/Licentious. IV. Green and Gold.*

November 5. San Francisco, California. Capricorn Asunder Gallery. *Fig Leaf Rag* (Joplin). *THE SYNTAX COLLECTOR: I. Haight St. Slither. II. That There Old West... III. Lude/ Licentious. IV. Green and Gold. V. San Andreas Stomp*. First performance of entire suite.

## 1977

January 12. Claremont, California. Founders' Room; Pitzer College. *THE SYNTAX COLLECTOR: I. Haight St. Slither. II. That There Old West... III. Lude/Licentious. IV. Green and Gold. V. San Andreas Stomp.*

January 20. San Francisco, California. Leavenworth Street Theatre. *THE SYNTAX COLLECTOR: I. Haight St. Slither. II. That There Old West... III. Lude/Licentious. IV. Green and Gold. V. San Andreas Stomp.*

January 26. San Francisco, California. Lone Mountain College. *Dance Film Festival*. Intermission Feature. *The Banjo* (Gottschalk). *Green and Gold* (T.S.C. #4). *San Andreas Stomp* (T.S.C. #5).

January 28. San Francisco, California. Lone Mountain College. *Dance Film Festival*. Intermission Feature. *Haight St. Slither* (T.S.C. #1). *Lude: Licentious Bicentennial Rag* (T.S.C. #3).

April 9. Portland, Oregon. Swann Auditorium; Portland Art Museum. Through Cloud and Eclipse Festival. *American Beauty* (Lamb). *Pastime #4* (Mathews). *Pastime #5* (Mathews). *THE SYNTAX COLLECTOR: I. Haight St. Slither. II. That There Old West... III. Lude/Licentious. IV. Green and Gold. V. San Andreas Stomp.*

April 12. Portland, Oregon. Portland State University. *Toccata and Fugue in D Minor* (Bach-Busoni). *American Beauty* (Lamb). *Pastime #4* (Mathews). *Pastime #5* (Mathews). *THE SYNTAX COLLECTOR: I. Haight St. Slither. II. That There Old West... III. Lude/Licentious. IV. Green and Gold. V. San Andreas Stomp.*

July 3. Lockport, New York. Kenan Center. Blaze of Glory Festival. *The Banjo* (Gottschalk). *Manchega* (Gottschalk). *Souvenir de Porto Rico* (Gottschalk). *Weeping Willow* (Joplin). *Augustan Club Waltz* (Joplin). *Elite Syncopations* (Joplin). Intermission. *Through Eden's Gates* (Bolcom). *THE SYNTAX COLLECTOR: I. Haight St. Slither. II. That There Old West... III. Lude/Licentious. IV. Green and Gold. V. San Andreas Stomp. Dejavalse (Co-première).*

September 18. San Francisco, California. Aquatic Park Theatre. *Elite Syncopations* (Joplin). *THE SYNTAX COLLECTOR: I. Haight St. Slither. II. That There Old West... III. Lude/Licentious. IV. Green and Gold. V. San Andreas Stomp.*

November 4. San Francisco, California. Dance Coalition Soirée. *The Banjo* (Gottschalk). *Manchega* (Gottschalk). *Souvenir de Porto Rico* (Gottschalk). *THE SYNTAX COLLECTOR: I. Haight St. Slither. II. That There Old West... III. Lude/Licentious. IV. Green and Gold. V. San Andreas Stomp.*

Fall. San Francisco, California. *L. O. Sloan's, Three Black and Three White. Refined Jubilee Minstrels, an American Documentary.* Anthony Cabello, Stephen Chroninger, Robbi Coverton, Lester Jones (later Fini Ferguson), Nat Williams, and Paul von Rotz, singers and dancers. Robert Power, chorus master and banjo. T.C., pianist. Performances including: Intersection Theatre in San Francisco's North Beach, Thu-Sun (November 24-27, December 1-4, 8-11, 15-18, 22-3, and 29-30). National League of Cities under the rotunda at. San Francisco City Hall. Larkin St. Showcase – San Francisco. Leavenworth Street Theater – San Francisco.

## 1978

January 12, San Francisco, California. Leavenworth Street Theatre. 14. *The Bald Soprano.* Prepared piano music for the Ionesco play.

May 4. San Francisco, California. Leavenworth Street Theatre. *Impecunious Davis* (Mills). *The Entertainer* (Joplin). *Augustan Club Waltz* (Joplin). *Magnetic Rag* (Joplin). *Buffalo Rag* (Turpin). *American Beauty* (Lamb). *Efficiency Rag* (Scott). Intermission. *Pastime #4* (Mathews). *Pastime #5* (Mathews). *THE SYNTAX COLLECTOR: I. Haight St. Slither. II. That There Old West... III. Lude/Licentious. IV. Green and Gold. V. San Andreas Stomp.*

May 22. Beograd, Yugoslavia. Student Center; University of Beograd. *The Entertainer* (Joplin). *Augustan Club Waltz* (Joplin). *Magnetic Rag* (Joplin). *Pastime #4* (Mathews). *Pastime #5* (Mathews). *American Beauty* (Lamb). *Dejavalse.* Duo with John Cobb. *Impromptu* (Savic). With John Cobb, Robert Moran and Misa Savic.

May 24. Zagreb, Yugoslavia. Student Center; University of Zagreb. Taped for television broadcast on the upright piano: *Impecunious Davis* (Mills). *The Entertainer* (Joplin). *Efficiency Rag* (Scott). *Buffalo Rag* (Turpin). *American Beauty* (Lamb). *Augustan Club Waltz* (Joplin). *Magnetic Rag* (Joplin). *Pastime #4* (Mathews). *Pastime #5* (Mathews): Intermission. On the grand piano (Steinway). *Fields of Flowers* (Bolcom) *(première).* THE SYNTAX COLLECTOR: *(European première). I. Haight St. Slither. II. That There Old West... III. Lude/Licentious. IV. Green and Gold. V. San Andreas Stomp.* RECOMBINANT STRAINS: *(first performance of entire set). Dejavalse.* Duo with John Cobb. *Claude Greenberg's Springtime Catch. Land of the Hassled and Free.*

May 27. Innsbruck, Austria. Conservatory of Music (Bösendorfer). *The Entertainer* (Joplin). *Augustan Club Waltz* (Joplin). *Dejavalse.* – Duo with John Cobb. *THE SYNTAX COLLECTOR: I. Haight St. Slither. II. That There Old West... III. Lude/Licentious. IV. Green and Gold. V. San Andreas Stomp. Pastime #4* (Mathews). *Pastime #5* (Mathews).

May 29. Graz, Austria. ÖRF (Bösendorfer). Taped for Radio broadcast. *Dejavalse. Modern Love Waltz* (Glass) – Duo w/ John Cobb.

June 25. San Francisco, California. The Old Spaghetti Factory. City Lights Bookstore.

25th Anniversary Celebration. *Fig Leaf* (Joplin). *THE SYNTAX COLLECTOR: I. Haight St. Slither. II. That There Old West... III. Lude/Licentious. IV. Green and Gold. V. San Andreas Stomp.*

November 8. San Francisco, California. Leavenworth Street Theatre. *The Reflections of Our Lives.* Pianist for theatrical revue.

## 1979

March 30. San Francisco, California. San Francisco Art Institute (Steinway). *Dejavalse.* Two performances: Piano Solo and as a round with John Cobb, harpsichord (Herbert Wm. Burton – Lincoln, Nebraska).

## 1980

December 6. San Francisco, California. Community Music Center: The Asbestos Players. (Steinway). 'It's Heavy on the Levee in Apple Blossom Time.' Piano solos: *The Banjo* (Gottschalk). *O ma charmante, épargnez-mois!* (Gottschalk). *Fuga Giocosa* (Paine). With Lester Jones. *Champagne Charlie* (Leybourne/Lee). *Waiting for the Robert E. Lee* (Gilbert/Muir). *Memories* (Kahn/van Alstyne). Piano solo: *Eli Green's Cakewalk* (Koninsky). *Pastime #4* (Mathews). *Pastime #5* (Mathews). *Reindeer Rag* (Lamb). Intermission. With Lester Jones. *(I'm Forever) Blowing Bubbles* (Kenbrovin/Kellette). *Does your Spearmint lose its Flavor (on the Bedpost Overnight)* (Rose/Bloom/Breuer). Piano solo: *Green and Gold* (T.S.C. #4). *Dejavalse. San Andreas Stomp* (T.S.C. #5). With Lester Jones. *Nobody* (Rogers/Williams). *Ain't we got Fun* (Kahn/Egan/Whiting). *Good Bye!* (Whyte/Melville/Tosti).

## 1981

January 2. San Francisco, California. Old First Church (Baldwin). Take One Ragtime Ensemble: David Reffkin, violin/leader; Diana Dorman, clarinet; Diane Foster, 'cello; Allen Ingersoll, bass; Ward Spangler, percussion; and T.C., piano. *Maple Leaf Rag* (Joplin). *The Dark Town Swell* (O. E. Sutton). *Going Some (March)* (Loveland). *Beautiful Ohio* (Mary Earl). *King Porter Stomp* (Morton). *(I'll be in my) Dixie Home again Tomorrow* (Turk/Robinson). *Frisco Jazz Band Blues* (Rich). *Non-Profit Rag* (Reffkin). *San Andreas Stomp* (T.S.C. #5) – Piano solo. *Peacherine Rag* (Joplin). *Sugar Cane* (Joplin). *Ophelia Rag* (Scott). *General Mixup, U.S.A.* (Cobb).

February 13, 14, 15. San Francisco, California.

Performance Gallery. *Quintet – Influence of India* (S. Dickman). T.C. with Douglas Johnson, violin; Janet Maestre, flute; Katherine Johnk, viola; and Diane Foster, 'cello.

March 26. San Francisco, California. Giannini Auditorium; Bank of America Bldg. Take One Ragtime Ensemble: David Reffkin, violin/leader; Diana Dorman, clarinet; Chuck Metzger, trumpet; Hall Goff, trombone; Nancy Bien, 'cello; Allen Ingersoll, bass; Ward Spangler, percussion; and T.C., piano. *Maple Leaf Rag* (Joplin). *Original Rags* (Joplin). *Green and Gold* (T.S.C. #4) – Piano solo. *Frisco Jazz Band Blues* (Rich). *Non-Profit Rag* (Reffkin). *Sobre las Olas* (Rosas). *Top Liner Rag* (Lamb). *The Dark Town Swell* (O. E. Sutton). *Rose Leaf Rag* (Joplin). *Gladiolus Rag* (Joplin).

April 10. San Francisco, California. Community Music Center (Steinway). Faculty Benefit Recital. *Claude Greenberg's Springtime Catch.* First performance as a round, with Cesar Cancino at the other piano (Duo-Art).

May 10. Berkeley, California. Julia Morgan Theatre. Take One Ragtime Ensemble: David Reffkin, violin/leader; Diana Dorman, clarinet; Chuck Metzger, trumpet; Hall Goff, trombone; Nancy Ewing, viola; Diane Foster, 'cello; Ward Spangler, percussion; Allen Ingersoll, bass; and T.C., piano. *Maple Leaf Rag* (Joplin). *Climax Rag* (Scott). *Top Liner Rag* (Lamb). *Entry of the Gladiators* (Fucik). *Dejavalse* – Piano solo. *Yellow Rose Rag* (Terry Waldo). *Swipesy* (Arthur Marshall). *Dill Pickles* (Charles Johnson). *Dead Man Blues* (Morton). *Gladiolus Rag* (Joplin). *Black and White* (Botsford). *Black Smoke* (Charles Johnson). *Cheops* (Cobb). *Ragtime Escape* (Reffkin).

June 18. San Francisco, California. Golden Gate Park Bandshell. Take One Ragtime Ensemble: David Reffkin, violin/leader; Diana Dorman, clarinet; and T.C., piano. *Alexander's Ragtime Band* (Berlin). *Non-profit Rag* (Reffkin). *Over the Waves* (Rosas). *Pine Apple Rag* (Joplin). *Dejavalse* – Piano solo. *Pastime Rag #5* (Mathews) – Piano solo. *Magnetic Rag* (Joplin) – Piano solo. *Last Night on the Back Porch* (Brown/Schraubstader) – piano & vocal.

July 4. San Francisco, California. Crissy Field. Take One Ragtime Ensemble: David Reffkin, violin/leader; Chuck Metzger, trumpet; Barry Boland, trombone; Allen Ingersoll, bass; Jim Zimmerman, percussion; and T.C., piano. *The Dark Town Swell* (Sutton) – here-

tofore announced as *Theme. Maple Leaf Rag* (Joplin). *Ophelia Rag* (Scott). *Cheops* (Cobb). *Non-profit Rag* (Reffkin). *San Andreas Stomp* (T.S.C. #5) – Piano solo. *Over the Waves* (Rosas). *Pine Apple Rag* (Joplin). *The Entertainer* (Joplin). *Gen. Mixup, U. S. A.* (Allen).
July 24. San Francisco, California. Community Music Center: The Asbestos Players. (Steinway). 'Bubbly Avalon Memories.' Piano solo: *Souvenir de Porto Rico* (Gottschalk). *Manchega* (Gottschalk). With Lester Jones. *Champagne Charlie* (Leybourne/Lee). *Waiting for the Robert E. Lee* (Gilbert/Muir). *Does your Spearmint lose its Flavor (on the Bedpost Overnight)* (Rose/Bloom/Breuer). Piano solo: *Magnetic Rag* (Joplin). *Dixie Dimples* (Scott). *Blue Goose Rag* (Birch). Intermission. With Lester Jones. *Memories* (Kahn/van Alstyne). *Avalon* (Jolson/Rose). *Deep River* (Traditional). Piano solo: *Green and Gold* (T.S.C. #4). *Dejavalse. San Andreas Stomp* (T.S.C. #5). With Lester Jones. *Ice Cream* (Johnson/Moll/King). *(I'm Forever) Blowing Bubbles* (Kenbrovin/Kellette). *Pretty Baby* (Kahn/Jackson/van Alstyne).
August 1. San Francisco, California. KUSF-FM: *The Ragtime Machine.* With David Reffkin. via tape. Interview with recorded musical examples.
August 15. San Francisco, California. Community Music Center. on the harpsichord (Herbert Wm. Burton–Lincoln, Nebraska). *Sonata in D* (F. W. Herschel – 1759). on the piano (Steinway). *Sonatina.* on prepared piano (Duo-Art). *Cedar Tavern* (Landy) *(première).* on the piano (Steinway). *Valse Marion* (E. Blake). *Eccentricity* (J. P. Johnson). *That There Old West...* (T.S.C. #2). *Waltz for Debby* (Evans). Intermission. *Nr. 2 Klavierstück III* (Stockhausen). *(Parallax)I and II* (Ryan). *American Beauty* (Lamb). *Buffalo Rag* (Turpin). *Pastime #4* (Mathews). *Pastime #5* (Mathews). *Broadway Rag* (Scott). *Rose Leaf Rag* (Joplin).
August 23. Belmont, California. Twin Pines Park. Take One Ragtime Ensemble: David Reffkin, violin/leader; David Promesti, trombone; David Schoenbrunn, bass; Kent Reed, percussion; and T.C., piano. *The Dark Town Swell* (Sutton). *Maple Leaf Rag* (Joplin). *Pride of the Army* (M. H. Andrews). *Black Smoke* (Charles Johnson). *Augustan Club Waltz* (Joplin) – Piano solo. *Alcoholic Blues* (Albert von Tilzer). *Circus Maximus* (C. C. Samuels). *Take me out to the Ball Game* (Albert von Tilzer). *Magnetic Rag* (Joplin) – Piano solo. *Cheops* (Cobb). *The Rag Time Dance*

(Joplin). *Going Some* (Carl Loveland). *Ragtime Escape* (Reffkin). *Pine Apple Rag* (Joplin) – Piano solo. *Frisco Jazz Band Blues* (Freddie Rich). *Dill Pickles* (Johnson). *Des Negers Geburtstag* (Lincke). *Swipesy* (Marshall).
September 27. San Francisco, California. Community Music Center (Steinway). *Fig Leaf Rag* (Joplin). *Ragtime Nightmare* (Turpin). *Razzazza Mazzazza* (Pryor). *Queen of Love* (Hunter). *Efficiency Rag* (Scott). *Lude: Licentious Bicentennial Rag* (T.S.C. #3). *Boogie Woogie Man* (Ammons/Johnson). *12th St. Rag* (Bowman). *Dizzy Fingers* (Confrey).
October 4. San Francisco, California. Old First Church (Baldwin). Take One Ragtime Ensemble: David Reffkin, violin/leader; Diana Dorman, clarinet; Kurt Patzner, trombone; Rick Clark, tuba; Mark Cepeda, percussion; and T.C., piano. *Maple Leaf Rag* (Joplin). *Pride of the Army* (M. H. Andrews). *Original Jelly Roll Blues* (Morton). *St. Louis Rag* (Turpin). *O ma charmante, épargnez-mois!* (Gottschalk) – Piano solo. *Mephistopheles Two Step* (Wilkes). *Powder Rag* (Charles Johnson). *The Dark Town Swell* (O. E. Sutton). *That There Old West...* (T.S.C. #2) – Piano solo. *Part Time Rag* (Reffkin). *Rose Leaf Rag* (Joplin). *In a Tea Garden* (Frank Grey). *Des Negers Geburtstag* (Lincke). *Alexander's Rag Time Band* (Berlin). *Cheops* (Cobb). *Maple Leaf Rag* (Joplin).
December 15. San Francisco, California. California Historical Society. *The Entertainer* (Joplin). *Rose Leaf Rag* (Joplin). *Pine Apple Rag* (Joplin). *Solace* (Joplin). *Green and Gold* (T.S.C. #4). *Dejavalse. San Andreas Stomp* (T.S.C. #5).

## 1982

January 15. San Francisco, California. World of Oil Theatre; Standard Oil Bldg. Take One Ragtime Ensemble: David Reffkin, violin/leader; Kelly Boyer, 'cello; Ward Spangler, percussion; and T.C., piano. *The Dark Town Swell* (O. E. Sutton). *Maple Leaf Rag* (Joplin). *Alexander's Rag Time Band* (Berlin). *Top Liner Rag* (Lamb). *Cheops* (Cobb). *Non-Profit Rag* (Reffkin). *Going Some* (Carl Loveland). *Dejavalse* – Piano solo. *Powder Rag* (Johnson). *Peacherine Rag* (Joplin). *Des Negers Geburtstag* (Lincke).
May 12. San Francisco, California. Cathedral Hill School Benefit (Knabe). *The Entertainer* (Joplin). *Solace* (Joplin). *Rose Leaf Rag* (Joplin). *Pastime #5* (Mathews). *Reindeer Rag* (Lamb). *Razzazza Mazzazza* (Pryor).
July 5. San Francisco, California. KUSF-FM:

*The Ragtime Machine.* With David Reffkin. Via tape. Excerpt of August 1, 1981 interview.

August 5. San Luis Obispo, California. KCBX-FM. via tape. Interview re/Mozart Festival.

August 7. San Luis Obispo, California. Cal Poly – Lecture demonstration with Kronos Quartet. Mozart Festival. *Dejavalse.*

September 10. San Francisco, California. Nancy Walker Fundraiser. *The Entertainer* (Joplin). *Augustan Club Waltz* (Joplin). *Rose Leaf Rag* (Joplin). *Pine Apple Rag* (Joplin). *American Beauty* (Lamb). *Pastime #5* (Mathews).

September 23. San Francisco, California. Hall of Flowers; Golden Gate Park. American Ragtime Ensemble: David Reffkin, violin/leader; Pat Klobas, bass; and T.C., piano. *The Dark Town Swell* (Sutton). *Smokey Mokes* (Abe Holzmann). *Tres Moutarde* (Macklin). *Serenade Romantique* (Gomer Bath). *16ᵗʰ Regiment March* (F. H. Losey). *I Wonder who's Kissing her now* (Joseph E. Howard). *Castle Walk* (Europe).

## 1983

May 14. Oakland, California. Oakland-Piedmont Jewish Community Center. Benefit. American Ragtime Ensemble: David Reffkin, violin/leader; Lucy Schoening, flute; Diana Dorman, clarinet; Kurt Patzner, trombone; Ward Spangler, percussion; and T.C., piano. *The Dark Town Swell* (Sutton). *Ophelia Rag* (Scott). *Grace and Beauty* (Scott). *Going Some (March)* (Loveland). *Top Liner Rag* (Lamb). *Alexander's Rag Time Band* (Berlin). *Dill Pickles* (Johnson). *(I'll be in my) Dixie Home again Tomorrow* (Turk/Robinson). *Peacherine Rag* (Joplin). *Gen. Mixup, U. S. A.* (Cobb). *Maple Leaf Rag* (Joplin). *Pine Apple Rag* (Joplin). *Circus Maximus* (C. C. Samuels). *Solace* (Joplin) – Piano solo. *Contentment Rag* (Lamb). *Non-Profit Rag* (Reffkin). *Des Negers Geburtstag* (Lincke). *Beale St. Blues* (Handy). *Cheops* (Cobb). *Entry of the Gladiators* (Fucik).

June 19. San Francisco, California. The Old Waldorf (Yamaha/250). From Ragtime to Dark Star. *Cold Rain and Snow* (Obray Ramsey *via* McGannahan Skjellyfetti). *Ragtime Dance* (Joplin). *Solace* (Joplin). *That Hand Played Rag* (Silverman/Ward). *Green and Gold* (T.S.C. #4). *San Andreas Stomp* (T.S.C. #5). *Fields of Flowers Rag* (Bolcom). *Boogie Woogie Blues* (Ammons). *Speaking* (Forrester). *Parallax* (Ryan). *Land of the Hassled and Free (first U.S. performance).*

*Dejavalse. Dark Star* (Hunter/Grateful Dead). *The Banjo* (Gottschalk). *Sonata Desaxificata (Fandango Maltallado* for III mvt). *The Entertainer* (Joplin). Encores: *Rialto Ripples* (Gershwin/Donaldson *via* Kovacs). *Prelude: Le Tombeau de Couperin* (Ravel). *Finale: Symphonic Etudes, Op. 13* (Schumann).

June 23. San Francisco, California. Giannini Auditorium; Bank of America Bldg. American Ragtime Ensemble: David Reffkin, violin/leader; Becky Sebring, viola; Janet Witharm, 'cello; and T.C., piano. *The Dark Town Swell* (Sutton). *Mississippi Rag* (Krell). *Maple Leaf Rag* (Joplin). *Grace and Beauty* (Scott). *San Andreas Stomp* (T.S.C. #5) – Piano solo. *Andalusian Serenade* (Bonnet). *In a Tea Garden* (Frank Grey). *Beale St. Blues* (Handy). *Des Negers Geburtstag* (Lincke). *Liberty Bell* (Sousa).

October 6. San Francisco, California. Golden Gate Park Bandshell. American Ragtime Ensemble: David Reffkin, violin/leader; Becky Sebring, viola; Janet Witharm, 'cello; and T.C., piano. *The Dark Town Swell* (Sutton). *Contentment Rag* (Lamb). *Elite Syncopations* (Joplin). *Dusty* (May Aufderheide). *Dejavalse* – Piano solo. *Beale St. Blues* (Handy). *The Dying Poet* (Gottschalk). *Mississippi Rag* (Krell). *King Cotton* (Sousa). *Gladiolus Rag* (Joplin).

December 15. San Francisco, California. San Francisco Art Institute; M. A. T. *When you get to the* * with Greg Albright, Rachel Wiessman, and Ken Chu.

## 1984

April 7-8. Las Vegas, Nevada. Terry Ryan Studio. (Chickering). Terry Ryan, D. Gause, and Donnie Whitbeck, engineers. *Cold Rain and Snow* (Obray Ramsey *via* McGannahan Skjellyfetti). *Dejavalse.*

June 1. San Francisco, California. Redwood Park; Transamerica Pyramid. American Ragtime Ensemble: David Reffkin, violin/leader; Diana Dorman, clarinet; Pat Klobas, bass; Ward Spangler, percussion; and T.C., piano. *The Dark Town Swell* (Sutton). *Mississippi Rag* (Krell). *Big Ben* (Allen). *Beale St. Blues* (Handy). *San Francisco* (Meyer). *Dejavalse* – Piano solo. *Maple Leaf Rag* (Joplin). *Turkish Towel Rag* (Allen). *Gladiolus Rag* (Joplin).

July 27. Berkeley, California. Freight and Salvage. American Ragtime Ensemble: David Reffkin, violin/leader; Jane Grimaldi, viola; Janet Witharm, 'cello; Ward Spangler, percussion; and T.C., piano. *Dejavalse* – Piano solo.

August 23. San Francisco, California. Golden Gate Park Bandshell. American Ragtime Ensemble: David Reffkin, violin/leader; Janet Witharm, 'cello; Pat Klobas, bass; Trisha Gooch, vocal; Ward Spangler, percussion; and T.C., piano. *The Dark Town Swell* (Sutton). *Ophelia Rag* (Scott). *You've got to See* (Rose/Conrad). *Pine Apple Rag* (Joplin). *Maple Leaf Rag* (Joplin). *Last Night on the Back Porch* (Brown/Schraubstader). *Des Negers Geburtstag* (Lincke). *Take me to the Land of Jazz* (Wendling). *Silver Heels* (Neil Moret). *San Francisco* (Meyer). *Wall Street Rag* (Joplin). *Cheops* (Cobb).

September 17. Berkeley, California. KPFA-FM: Russ Jennings Show. Interviewed with Electric Guitar Quartet regarding upcoming concert.

September 19. Berkeley, California. Julia Morgan Theatre (60). *Sinfonia Concertante, K. 279b – 1st mvt.* (Mozart). On Roland/Juno Synthesizer. With Electric Guitar Quartet: Ken Frankel, Kathy Greenstone, Warren Sirota, and Van Williamson. Intermission. *Cold Rain and Snow* (Obray Ramsey via McGannahan Skjellyfetti). *American Beauty* (Lamb). *Pastime #4* (Mathews). *Pastime #5* (Mathews). *Dead Man Blues* (Morton). *Dejavalse. Green and Gold* (T.S.C. #4). *San Andreas Stomp* (T.S.C. #5).

*FROM RAGTIME TO DARK STAR: THE TOUR*

October 19. Roslyn, New York. My Father's Place. Long Island, *Cold Rain and Snow* (Obray Ramsey via McGannahan Skjellyfetti)/*American Beauty* (Lamb). *Magnetic Rag* (Joplin). *Pastime #4* (Mathews). *Pastime 5* (Mathews). *Dead Man Blues* (Morton)/*Hesitation Blues* (Davis). *Tabby Cat Walk* (Bolcom). *Boogie Woogie Blues* (Ammons). *Parallax* (Ryan). *Dejavalse. Dark Star* (Hunter/Grateful Dead). Encore: *Bagatelle, Op. 126 #4* (Beethoven).

October 20. Syracuse, New York. Jabberwocky (Yamaha/250/247). First Show. *Cold Rain and Snow* (Obray Ramsey via McGannahan Skjellyfetti)/*American Beauty* (Lamb). *Magnetic Rag* (Joplin). *Pastime 4* (Mathews). *Pastime #5* (Mathews). *Green and Gold* (T.S.C. #4). *Tabby Cat Walk* (Bolcom). *Dead Man Blues* (Morton)/*Hesitation Blues* (Davis). *Boogie Woogie Blues* (Ammons). *Parallax* (Ryan). *Dark Star* (Hunter/Grateful Dead). *The Banjo* (Gottschalk). *Dejavalse. San Andreas Stomp* (T.S.C. #5). *Rose Leaf Rag* (Joplin). *The Entertainer* (Joplin). Encores:

*Bagatelle, Op. 126 #4* (Beethoven). *'New' Rag* (Joplin). Second Show. *Cold Rain and Snow* (Obray Ramsey via McGannahan Skjellyfetti). *American Beauty* (Lamb). *Rose Leaf Rag* (Joplin). *Dead Man Blues* (Morton)/*Hesitation Blues* (Davis). *Boogie Woogie Blues* (Ammons). *Dark Star* (Hunter/Grateful Dead). *Dejavalse. Land of the Hassled and Free. San Andreas Stomp* (T.S.C. #5). *Parallax* (Ryan). *Tabby Cat Walk* (Bolcom). *The Banjo* (Gottschalk). *Magnetic Rag* (Joplin). *Ragtime Nightmare* (Turpin). *Green and Gold* (T.S.C. #4). *The Entertainer* (Joplin). Encores: *'New' Rag* (Joplin). *Etude, Op. 42. #3* (Scriabin). *Pine Apple Rag* (Joplin).

October 21. Ithaca, New York. Ramada Inn; Gazebo Room. *Cold Rain and Snow* (Obray Ramsey via McGannahan Skjellyfetti). *American Beauty* (Lamb). *Rose Leaf Rag* (Joplin). *Ragtime Nightmare* (Turpin). *Pastime #4* (Mathews). *Pastime #5* (Mathews). *Green and Gold* (T.S.C. #4). *Land of the Hassled and Free. Dead Man Blues* (Morton)/*Hesitation Blues* (Davis). *Boogie Woogie Blues* (Ammons). *Dark Star* (Hunter/Grateful Dead). *Tabby Cat Walk* (Bolcom). *Dejavalse. Parallax* (Ryan). *San Andreas Stomp* (T.S.C. #5). *Pine Apple Rag* (Joplin). *The Banjo* (Gottschalk). *The Entertainer* (Joplin). Encores: *Bagatelle, Op. 126 #4* (Beethoven). *'New' Rag* (Joplin).

October 22. New Brunswick, New Jersey. Rutgers University (Yamaha CP 70). *Hesitation Blues* (Davis). *Rose Leaf Rag* (Joplin). *Pine Apple Rag* (Joplin). *Pastime #4* (Mathews). *Pastime #5* (Mathews). *Cold Rain and Snow* (Obray Ramsey via McGannahan Skjellyfetti). *American Beauty* (Lamb). *Boogie Woogie Blues* (Ammons). *Tabby Cat Walk* (Bolcom). *Parallax* (Ryan). *Dead Man Blues* (Morton). *Green and Gold* (T.S.C. #4). *San Andreas Stomp* (T.S.C. #5). *Dark Star* (Hunter/Grateful Dead). *Dejavalse. The Banjo* (Gottschalk). *The Entertainer* (Joplin). Encores: *Bagatelle, Op. 126 #4* (Beethoven). *'New' Rag* (Joplin).

October 23. White Plains, New York. Fore 'n Aft. One set, similar to others on the tour, including: *Cold Rain and Snow* (Obray Ramsey via McGannahan Skjellyfetti). *Boogie Woogie Blues* (Ammons). *Hesitation Blues* (Davis). *Dark Star* (Hunter/Grateful Dead). *Parallax* (Ryan). *Green and Gold* (T.S.C. #4). *San Andreas Stomp* (T.S.C. #5). *Dejavalse. Land of the Hassled and Free.*

October 24. New York, New York. The Bitter End (Yamaha). First of two shows. *Hesita-*

tion Blues (Davis). Rose Leaf Rag (Joplin).
Pine Apple Rag (Joplin). Pastime #4
(Mathews). Pastime #5 (Mathews). Tabby
Cat Walk (Bolcom). Cold Rain and Snow
(Obray Ramsey via McGannahan Skjel-
lyfetti). American Beauty (Lamb). Parallax
(Ryan). The Answer (Forrester). Boogie Woogie
Blues (Ammons). Dark Star (Hunter/Grate-
ful Dead). Dejavalse. Green and Gold (T.S.C.
#4). San Andreas Stomp (T.S.C. #5). The Banjo
(Gottschalk). Ragtime Nightmare (Turpin).
The Entertainer (Joplin). Encore: Land of the
Hassled and Free.
October 25. Providence, Rhode Island. Lupo's
(Yamaha CP 70). Hesitation Blues (Davis).
Rose Leaf Rag (Joplin). American Beauty
(Lamb). Pastime #4 (Mathews). Pastime #5
(Mathews). Cold Rain and Snow (Obray
Ramsey via McGannahan Skjellyfetti).
Boogie Woogie Blues (Ammons). Parallax
(Ryan). Tabby Cat Walk (Bolcom). Dead Man
Blues (Morton). Dark Star (Hunter/Grate-
ful Dead). Dejavalse. Green and Gold (T.S.C.
#4). 'New' Rag (Joplin). The Entertainer
(Joplin). Etude, Op. 42 #3 (Scriabin).
October 26. Buffalo, New York. Slee Hall; S.
U. N.Y. (Steinway). Cold Rain and Snow
(Obray Ramsey via McGannahan Skjel-
lyfetti). American Beauty (Lamb). Rose Leaf
Rag (Joplin). Pastime #4 (Mathews). Pastime
#5 (Mathews). Buffalo Rag (Turpin). Tabby
Cat Walk (Bolcom). Dead Man Blues (Morton).
Hesitation Blues (Davis). Boogie Woogie Blues
(Ammons). Parallax (Ryan). The Answer
(Forrester). Dark Star (Hunter/Grateful
Dead). The Banjo (Gottschalk). Dejavalse.
Land of the Hassled and Free. Green and Gold
(T.S.C. #4). San Andreas Stomp (T.S.C. #5).
The Entertainer (Joplin). Encores: Bagatelle,
Op. 126 #4 (Beethoven). 'New' Rag (Joplin).
October 27. Hartford, Connecticut. Mad
Murphy's Cafe (Knabe). First set: Rose Leaf
Rag (Joplin). Magnetic Rag (Joplin). Ameri-
can Beauty (Lamb). Dead Man Blues (Morton).
Hesitation Blues (Davis). Pine Apple Rag
(Joplin). Pastime #4 (Mathews). Pastime #5
(Mathews). Ragtime Nightmare (Turpin).
Bohemia (Lamb). 'New' Rag (Joplin). Tabby
Cat Walk (Bolcom). Second Set: Cold Rain
and Snow. Boogie Woogie Blues (Ammons).
Parallax (Ryan). The Answer (Forrester). Dark
Star (Hunter/Grateful Dead). The Banjo
(Gottschalk). Dejavalse. Green and Gold
(T.S.C. #4). San Andreas Stomp (T.S.C. #5).
The Entertainer (Joplin). Land of the Hassled
and Free. Bagatelle, Op. 126 #4 (Beethoven).
October 28. Sunderland, Massachusetts. The

Rusty Nail. Rose Leaf Rag (Joplin). American
Beau(ty (Lamb). Dead Man Blues (Morton).
Hesitation Blues (Davis). Pastime #4
(Mathews). Pastime #5 (Mathews). Mag-
netic Rag (Joplin). Ragtime Nightmare
(Turpin). Tabby Cat Walk (Bolcom). Cold
Rain and Snow. Parallax (Ryan). The Answer
(Forrester). Boogie Woogie Blues (Ammons).
Dark Star (Hunter/Grateful Dead).
Dejavalse. Land of the Hassled and Free. Green
and Gold (T.S.C. #4). San Andreas Stomp
(T.S.C. #5). The Entertainer (Joplin). Encores:
Bagatelle, Op. 126 #4 (Beethoven). 'New' Rag
(Joplin). Prelude in C minor (W.T.C. Vol. II) (J.
S. Bach). The Banjo (Gottschalk).
October 29. Cambridge, Massachusetts. Jack's.
Second of two sets. Cold Rain and Snow. Pine
Apple Rag (Joplin). Pastime #4 (Mathews).
Tabby Cat Walk (Bolcom). The Answer
(Forrester). Parallax (Ryan). Dark Star
(Hunter/Grateful Dead). Boogie Woogie
Blues (Ammons). Dejavalse. Land of the
Hassled and Free. The Banjo (Gottschalk). San
Andreas Stomp (T.S.C. #5). Encores: Etude,
Op. 42 #3 (Scriabin). Bagatelle, Op. 126 #4
(Beethoven).
October 30. Burlington, Vermont. Hunt's. Cold
Rain and Snow. Rose Leaf Rag (Joplin). Mag-
netic Rag (Joplin). Pastime #4 (Mathews).
Pastime #5 (Mathews). Ragtime Nightmare
(Turpin). American Beauty (Lamb). Dead Man
Blues (Morton)/Hesitation Blues (Davis).
Tabby Cat Walk (Bolcom). Parallax (Ryan).
The Answer (Forrester). Boogie Woogie Blues
(Ammons). Dark Star (Hunter/Grateful
Dead). Dejavalse. Land of the Hassled and
Free. Green and Gold (T.S.C. #4). San Andreas
Stomp (T.S.C. #5). The Banjo (Gottschalk).
The Entertainer (Joplin). Encores: Etude, Op.
42 #3 (Scriabin). 'New' Rag (Joplin). Buffalo
Rag (Turpin). Pine Apple Rag (Joplin).
November 16. San Francisco, California. San
Francisco Art Institute. Entre-Genre: Key-
board Gems from between the Cracks. Les
Baricades Misterieuses (Couperin). Bagatelle,
Op. 126 #4 (Beethoven). Sonata Desaxificata
(I and II mvts). Fuga Giocosa (Paine). Au-
gustan Club Waltz (Joplin). The Banjo
(Gottschalk). Minstrels (Debussy). That Hand
Played Rag (Silverman/Ward). Pastime #4
(Mathews). Parallax (Ryan). Dejavalse. Land
of the Hassled and Free. Any Face Card Beats a
'10' (première). Cantankerous Conjurer
(première). Funeral March of a Marionette
(Gounod). Encores: Cold Rain and Snow. San
Andreas Stomp (T.S.C. #5).
December 30. Las Vegas, Nevada. Terry Ryan

Studio. (Chickering). Terry Ryan, D. Gause, and Donnie Whitbeck, engineers. *Any Face Card Beats a '10'. Parallax* (Ryan). *Tabby Cat Walk* (Bolcom).

## 1985

February 22. San Francisco, California. Old First Church (Baldwin). American Ragtime Ensemble: David Reffkin, violin/leader; Diana Dorman, clarinet; Karen Baccaro, trumpet; Kurt Patzner, trombone; Becky Sebring, viola; Jennifer Culp, 'cello; Pat Klobas, bass; Kent Reed, percussion; and T.C., piano. *The Dark Town Swell* (Sutton). *Original Rags* (Joplin). *Efficiency Rag* (Scott). *Dance of the Lunatics* (Allen). *Wild Cherries* (Snyder). *Tabby Cat Walk* (Bolcom) – Piano solo. *Gladiolus Rag* (Joplin). *Milenberg Joys* (Morton). *Part Time Rag* (Reffkin). *Pilgrim's Song of Hope* (Batiste). *Lude: Licentious Bicentennial Rag* (T.S.C. #3) – Piano solo. *Des Neger's Geburtstag* (Lincke). *The Pachelbel Rag* (Reffkin).

March 26. Kamuela, Hawaii. Hawaii Preparatory Academy. *Dejavalse. Green and Gold* (T.S.C. #4). *Praeambulum: Partita. #5* (J. S. Bach). *Pine Apple Rag* (Joplin). *Etude (after Czerny)* (Debussy).

August 19. San Francisco, California. Fort Mason Center. Wang Computers. American Ragtime Ensemble: David Reffkin, violin/leader; Will Sudmeier, trombone; Pat Klobas, bass; Kent Reed, percussion; and T.C., piano. *The Dark Town Swell* (Sutton). *Pine Apple Rag* (Joplin). *Cheops* (Cobb). *Silver Heels* (Neil Moret). *Milenberg Joys* (Morton). *The Last Kiss* (Blake). *Buena Vista* (Hirsch). *Cabaret Capers* (Allen). *Darktown Strutters Ball* (Brooks). *Ethiopia Rag* (Lamb). *Swipesy* (Marshall). *Dill Pickles* (Johnson). *Wall Street Rag* (Joplin). *Liberty Bell* (Sousa). *Beale St. Blues* (Handy). *Symphia Waltzes* (Holzmann). *Fiorentiner March* (Fucik). *Circus Maximus* (C. C. Samuels). *Grace and Beauty* (Scott). *Efficiency Rag* (Scott). *Alexander's Rag Time Band* (Berlin). *Des Neger's Geburtstag* (Lincke). *Artist's Life* (Strauss). *Apple Jack* (Johnson). *Twelfth Street Rag* (Bowman). *Ophelia Rag* (Scott). *San Francisco* (Meyer). *Clear Track* (Eduard Strauss). *Maple Leaf Rag* (Joplin). Piano solos: *Rose Leaf Rag* (Joplin). *Ragtime Nightmare* (Turpin). *Magnetic Rag* (Joplin). *Pastime #5* (Mathews).

September 9. San Francisco, California. De Young Museum. Hearst Court. American Ragtime Ensemble: David Reffkin, violin/

leader; Diana Dorman, clarinet; Will Sudmeier, trombone; Pat Klobas, bass; Kent Reed, percussion; and T.C., piano. Same program as August 19,1985.

*RECORDING SESSIONS*

December. Berkeley, California. Arch St. (A. B. Chase). Josef Marc, engineer. *Cometary Commentary* – T.C., vocal and piano bass; Josef Marc, drums, guitar.

December 5. *Halley's Comet Rag* (Lincoln) – T.C., solo piano.

## 1986

January 8. *The Ballad of Shane Muscatell* – T.C., vocal and piano; Josef Marc, drums; Virginia Morgan, backup vocals.

January 11, 15. *Moonshine Superman* – T.C., vocal and Yamaha DX-7 synthesizer; Josef Marc, drums, guitar.

January 15. *The Long and Wide* – T.C., vocals and piano bass; Josef Marc, drums.

January ?. *The Nine Planets* (J. Marc): *III: Astronomy* – T.C., solo piano. *III: Astronomy* – T.C., DX-7 synthesizer. *VIII: Venus* – T.C., piano with Virginia Morgan, viola; Josef Marc, DX-7. *XI: Uranus* – T.C., piano with Josef Marc, DX-7 and steel string guitar. *XIII: Earth* – T.C., piano with Virginia Morgan, voice; Josef Marc, guitar, bass, drums, voice, and DX-7.

February 9. St. Helena, California. The White Barn (Estey [S.T.] Welte). American Ragtime Ensemble: David Reffkin, violin/leader; Janet Witharm, 'cello; Ida Borin, bass; Kent Reed, percussion; and T.C., piano. *The Dark Town Swell* (Sutton). *Peacherine Rag* (Joplin). *Grace and Beauty* (Scott). *Alexander's Rag Time Band* (Berlin). *Beautiful Ohio* (Mary Earl). *Perigee! Halley's Comet Rag* (H. Lincoln) – Piano solo. *Beale Street Blues* (Handy). *Cheops* (Cobb). *Ethiopia Rag* (Lamb). *Apple Jack* (Johnson). *Lude: Licentious Bicentennial Rag* (T.S.C. #3) – Piano solo. *Kinklets* (Marshall). *San Francisco* (Meyer). *Whay d'ye mean you lost yer Dog?* (Daly/Allen). *American Beauty Rag* (Lamb) – Piano solo. *Love will find a way* (Blake). *Pine Apple Rag* (Joplin).

February 10. Nationwide. The Doctor Demento Show. 86-07. via tape made December, *Cometary Commentary*.

February 10. San Francisco, California. KFOG-FM: 'The Deadhead Hour', with David Gans. via tape. Interview with recorded musical examples.

March 3. Nationwide. The Doctor Demento Show. 86-10. via tape made December, *Cometary Commentary*. *Halley's Comet Rag* (H. Lincoln).

April 10. Cambridge, Massachusetts. Harvard University Music Department. (Steinway). *(Claude Greenberg –* with Eric Kramer). *Perihelion!*. *Halley's Comet Rag* (H. Lincoln). *THE SYNTAX COLLECTOR: I. Haight St. Slither. II. That There Old West... III. Lude/ Licentious. IV. Green and Gold. V. San Andreas Stomp. Dejavalse/Dejavalise*. *Dejavalse* (tape of round). *Any Face Card Beats a '10'*. *The Ballad of Shane Muscatell* (tape).

April 11. Cambridge, Massachusetts. Harvard University; Quincy House. (Steinway). *Any Face Card Beats a '10'*. *Dejavalse. Green and Gold* (T.S.C. #4). *San Andreas Stomp* (T.S.C. #5). *Sonata Desaxificata*. Margaret Fabrizio tape.

April 13. San Francisco, California. KQED-FM: 'West Coast Weekend', With Sedge Thomson (Studio B/Steinway). taped Feb. 15. *Halley's Comet Rag* (H. Lincoln). *San Andreas Stomp* (T.S.C. #5). *Dejavalse/ Dejuvalise*. *Astronomy* (J. Marc – tape of syn:h). *Tabby Cat Walk* (Bolcom). *The Ballad of Shane Muscatell* (tape). *Any Face Card Beats a '10'*.

April 26. San Francisco, California. KQED-FM: 'West Coast Weekend', With Sedge Thomson (Studio B/Steinway). *San Andreas Stomp* (T.S.C. #5). *That There Old West...* (T.S.C. #2). *Hesitation Blues* (Davis).

April 28. San Francisco, California. Wolfgang's (Yamaha). Dunn Benefit. *That There Old West...* (T.S.C. #2). *Halley's Comet Rag* (H. Lincoln). *Dejavalse/Dejavalise/Hesitation Blues. Any Face Card Beats a '10'*. *San Andreas Stomp* (T.S.C. #5). *Dark Star* (Hunter/Grateful Dead). Encore: *Praeambulum: Partita. 5* (J. S. Bach).

May 16. San Francisco, California. Union Square. Hands across America Rally. Godzilla Birthday Celebration. *Cold Rain and Snow* (Traditional). *Halley's Comet Rag* (H. Lincoln). *Dejavalse. Green and Gold* (T.S.C. #4). *San Andreas Stomp* (T.S.C. #5). Encore: *Hesitation Blues* (Davis).

May 30. San Francisco, California. Transamerica Pyramid Park. American Ragtime Ensemble: David Reffkin, violin/ leader; David Moebs, clarinet; Pat Klobas, bass; Kent Reed, percussion; and T.C., piano. *The Dark Town Swell* (Sutton). *Dill Pickles* (Johnson). *Grace and Beauty* (Scott). *Swipesy* (Marshall). *Dixie Dimples* (James Scott) - Piano solo. *Fiorentiner March* (Fucik). *Ethiopia Rag* (Lamb). *Circus Maximus* (C. C. Samuels). *Wall Street Rag* (Joplin). *Cabaret Capers* (Allen).

June 11. San Francisco, California. Waters Upton Tea Room. Stuart Rosenthal, engineer. *Dejavalse. San Andreas Stomp* (T.S.C. #5).

June 12. San Francisco, California. Golden Gate Park Bandshell. American Ragtime Ensemble: David Reffkin, violin/leader; David Moebs, clarinet; Kurt Patzmer, trombone; Pat Klobas, bass; Kent Reed, percussion; and T.C., piano. *The Dark Town Swell* (Sutton). *Dill Pickles* (Johnson). *Grace and Beauty* (Scott). *Swipesy* (Marshall). *Dixie Dimples* (James Scott) - Piano solo. *Fiorentiner March* (Fucik). *Ethiopia Rag* (Lamb). *Elite Syncopations* (Joplin) – Piano solo. *Circus Maximus* (C. C. Samuels). *Wall Street Rag* (Joplin). *Pastime #5* (A. Mathews) – Piano solo. *Pine Apple Rag* (Joplin). *Cabaret Capers* (Allen). *Cheops* (Cobb).

June 20. San Francisco, California. Plant Bros. Building Opening. American Ragtime Ensemble: David Reffkin, violin/leader; David Moebs, clarinet; Pat Klobas, bass; Tyler Mac, percussion; and T.C., piano. *The Dark Town Swell* (Sutton). *Dill Pickles* (Johnson). *Grace and Beauty* (Scott). *Swipesy* (Marshall). *Dixie Dimples* (James Scott) - Piano solo: *Fiorentiner March* (Fucik). *Ethiopia Rag* (Lamb). *Circus Maximus* (C. C. Samuels). *Wall Street Rag* (Joplin). *Cabaret Capers* (Allen). *Cheops* (Cobb). *Slippery Elm Rag* (Woods). *Symphia Waltzes* (Holzmann). *Alexander's Rag Time Band* (Berlin). *Ragtime Nightingale* (Lamb). *Pine Apple Rag* (Joplin). *Peacherine Rag* (Joplin). *Big Ben* (Allen). *Maple Leaf Rag* (Joplin).

June 23. Nationwide. 'The Doctor Demento Show.' 86-26. via tape made January 8, *The Ballad of Shane Muscatell*.

July 18. San Francisco, California. Old First Church (Baldwin). American Ragtime Ensemble: David Reffkin, violin/leader; Clark Fobes, clarinet; Karen Baccaro, trumpet; Don Couch, trombone; Vicky Gunn, viola; Mark Summer, 'cello; Pat Klobas, bass; Allen Biggs, percussion; and T.C., piano. *The Dark Town Swell* (Sutton). *Turkish Towel Rag* (Allen). *Cheops* (Cobb). *Palm Leaf Rag* (Joplin). *Non-Profit Rag* (Reffkin). *Dixie Dimples* (James Scott) – Piano solo. *Mannering Waltzes* (Devereux). *Ragtime Nightingale* (Lamb). *Entrance of the Gladiators* (Fucik). *Fields of Flowers Rag* (Bolcom) –

Piano solo. *Yellow Rose Rag* (Terry Waldo).
*Kansas City Blues* (Bowman). *Slippery Elm Rag* (Woods). *Fiorentiner March* (Fucik). *Maple Leaf Rag* (Joplin).

August 23. Sacramento,California. Cal Expo. American Ragtime Ensemble: David Reffkin, violin/leader; David Moebs, clarinet; Karen Baccaro, trumpet; Don Couch, trombone; Joe Hebert, 'cello; Brian Marcus, bass; Ray Bachand, drums; and T.C., piano. *The Dark Town Swell* (Sutton). *Palm Leaf Rag* (Joplin). *Yellow Rose Rag* (Waldo). *Entrance of the Gladiators* (Fucik). *Mannering Waltzes* (Devereux). *Cheops* (Cobb). *Pastime #5* (A. Mathews) – Piano solo. *Turkish Towel Rag* (Allen). *Maple Leaf Rag* (Joplin). *Fiorentiner March* (Fucik). *Pine Apple Rag* (Joplin). *Peacherine Rag* (Joplin). *Powder Rag* (Johnson). *Symphia Waltzes* (Holz-mann). *San Francisco* (Meyer). *Wall Street Rag* (Joplin). *Ophelia Rag* (Scott). *Gen. Mixup, U. S. A.* (Cobb). *Dill Pickles* (Johnson). *Circus Maximus* (C. C. Samuels). *Apple Jack* (Johnson). *Alexander's Rag Time Band* (Berlin). *California* (Friend/Conrad). *I Love You, California* (Frankenstein/Silverwood). *I'm Going back to California* (Brennan/Ball).

November 2. San Francisco, California. KQED-FM: 'West Coast Weekend', with Sedge Thomson (Studio B/Steinway). *Sound Celebration. Dejavalse/valise. Through Eden's Gates* (Bolcom).

November 15. San Francisco, California. Noe Valley Ministry (George Steck/31). *Manchega* (Gottschalk). *Augustan Club Waltz* (Joplin). *That Hand Played Rag* (Silverman/Ward). *Magnetic Rag* (Joplin). *Through Eden's Gates* (Bolcom. *THE SYNTAX COLLECTOR: I. Haight St. Slither. II. That There Old West... III. Lude/Licentious. IV. Green and Gold. V. San Andreas Stomp. Intermission. Cold Rain and Snow. Hesitation Blues. Harlequin and the Philosopher* (from *Tarot*). *Any Face Card Beats a '10'. The Answer* (Forrester). *Parallax* (Ryan). *Dark Star* (Hunter/Grateful Dead). *Dejavalse/valise. Etude (after Czerny)* (Debussy). Encores: *Praeambulum: Partita #5* (J. S. Bach). *Etude, Op. 25. #6* (Chopin). *Prelude, Op. 28. #10 (Night Moth)* (Chopin).

December 6. San Francisco, California. Idris Ackamoor: Cultural Odyssey. Noe Valley Ministry (George Steck). *Minstrels* (Debussy). With Lester Jones. *Deep River* (Traditional). *Come Sunday* (Ellington).

December 9. San Francisco, California. Louise M. Davies Hall (Yamaha DX7). Broadcast live over KQED-FM. *Sing-it-Yourself Mes-*

*siah.* Intermission Features: *Harmonious Blacksmith* (Handel). '*Overture' (Titles to The Saragossa Manuscript)* (Penderecki). *Wigs/Royal Navy* Sketch (Thomson/Bellingham) – background music. *Crown and Anchor* Segment. *Wooden Teeth* Sketch (Thomson). With Sedge Thomson.

## 1987

January 3. San Francisco, California. KQED-FM: 'West Coast Weekend', with Sedge Thomson (Studio A/Steinway). *Dejavalse/valise. Harlequin* (from *Tarot*). *Dejavalentino. Any Face Card Beats a '10'.*

January 10. San Francisco, California. KQED-FM: 'West Coast Weekend', with Sedge Thomson (Studio A/Steinway). *Dejavalse/valise. Magnetic Rag* (Joplin).

January 17. San Francisco, California. KQED-FM: 'West Coast Weekend', with Sedge Thomson (Studio A/Steinway). *Dejavalse/valise. American Beauty* (Lamb). *Wooden Teeth* Sketch (Thomson). With Sedge Thomson.

January 24. Frankfurt am Main, Germany. Elsch-enbroich/Schweitzer Hauskonzert. (Blüthner/44). *Pine Apple Rag* (Joplin). *Eli Green's Cakewalk* (Koninsky). *Minstels* (Debussy). *Solace* (Joplin). *That Hand Played Rag* (Silverman/Ward). *Magnetic Rag* (Joplin). *Through Eden's Gates* (Bolcom). *THE SYNTAX COLLECTOR: I. Haight St. Slither. II. That There Old West... III. Lude/Licentious. IV. Green and Gold. V. San Andreas Stomp.* Intermission. *Cold Rain and Snow. Fields of Flowers Rag* (Bolcom). *The Answer* (Forrester). *Any Face Card Beats a '10'. Hesitation Blues* (Davis). *Parallax* (Ryan). *Dejavalse/valise. Dark Star* (Hunter/Grateful Dead). *Tabby Cat Walk* (Bolcom). Encores: *Pastime #5* (Mathews). *Praeambulum: Partita. #5* (J. S. Bach). *Pastime #4* (Mathews).

January 30. Frankfurt am Main, Germany. Holle/Liebrecht Hauskonzert. (August Förster {Löbau – Sachsen}/40). *American Beauty* (Lamb). *O ma charmante, épargnez-mois!* (Gottschalk). *That Hand Played Rag* (Silverman/Ward). *Rose Leaf Rag* (Joplin). *Horseshoe Rag* (Niebergall). *Magnetic Rag* (Joplin). *Pastime #4* (Mathews). *Pastime #5* (Mathews). *Tabby Cat Walk* (Bolcom). Intermission. *Cold Rain and Snow. Fields of Flowers Rag* (Bolcom). *Harlequin and the Philosopher* (from *Tarot*). *Hesitation Blues* (Davis). *Dejavalse/valise. Parallax* (Ryan). *The Answer* (Forrester). *THE SYNTAX COLLECTOR: I. Haight St. Slither. II. That There Old West... III. Lude/Licentious. IV. Green and Gold. V.*

*San Andreas Stomp. Manchega* (Gottschalk). Encores: *Any Face Card Beats a '10'. Pine Apple Rag* (Joplin). *Praeambulum: Partita. #5* (J. S. Bach). *Prelude, Op. 28. #10 (Night Moth)* (Chopin). *Prelude, Op. 28. #22 (Impatience)* (Chopin). *Etude, Op. 25. #6* (Chopin).

February 7. San Francisco, California. KQED-FM: 'West Coast Weekend', with Sedge Thomson (C.M.C./Steinway). *Dejavalse/valise. Tabby Cat Walk* (Bolcom).

February 14. San Francisco, California. KQED-FM: 'West Coast Weekend', with Sedge Thomson (C.M.C./Steinway). (Starting with this show, a brief introduction proceeds the opening theme; often alluding to something topical. It is indicated here, and henceforth, by an open-ended bracket). *{Rhapsody in Blue* opening/*Dejavalse/valise. Horseshoe Rag* (Niebergall).

February 21. San Francisco, California. KQED-FM: 'West Coast Weekend', with Sedge Thomson (C.M.C./Steinway). *{Beethoven 'Pastorale'* opening/*Dejavalse/valise.*

February 28. San Francisco, California. KQED-FM: 'West Coast Weekend', with Sedge Thomson (C.M.C./Steinway). *Dejavalse/valise. Elite Syncopations* (Joplin).

March 14. San Francisco, California. KQED-FM: 'West Coast Weekend', with Sedge Thomson (Studio A/Steinway). *{Jaws* (?)/ *Dejavalse/valise/boogie.*

March 21. San Francisco, California. KQED-FM: 'West Coast Weekend', with Sedge Thomson (Studio A/Steinway). *{Spring* (Vivaldi)/*Dejavalse/valise. Modern Love Waltz* (Philip Glass). *A Waltz for Evelyn Hinrichsen* (Lou Harrison).

March 28. San Francisco, California. KQED-FM: 'West Coast Weekend', with Sedge Thomson (Studio A/Steinway). *{Last Rose of Summer* (?)/*Dejavalse/valise. Russian Rag* (Cobb).

April 4. San Francisco, California. KQED-FM: 'West Coast Weekend', with Sedge Thomson (Studio A/Steinway). *{When April Showers* (?)/*Dejavalse/valise. Speaking* (Forrester). *O ma charmante, épargnez-mois!* (Gottschalk). *Pastime #5* (Mathews).

April 11. San Francisco, California. KQED-FM: 'West Coast Weekend', with Sedge Thomson (Studio A/Steinway). *Dejavalse/valise.*

April 18. San Francisco, California. KQED-FM: 'West Coast Weekend', with Sedge Thomson (Studio A/Steinway). *{I Left my Heart in San Francisco* (?)/*Dejavalse/valise.*

April 18-24. Las Vegas, Nevada. Terry Ryan

Studio. Terry Ryan, producer/engineer. *Hungarian Rock (Chaconne)* (Ligeti). *Rondo Pazzo. Dejavalse.*

April 25. San Francisco, California. KQED-FM: 'West Coast Weekend', with Sedge Thomson (Studio A/Steinway). *{Captain Spaulding (Groucho Theme) – 'Sledge Thomson'* Sketch (?)/*Dejavalse/valise. Encodex Punctilious* (SonDex I) – on harpsichord. *Pine Apple Rag* (Joplin).

May 2. San Francisco, California. KQED-FM: 'West Coast Weekend', with Sedge Thomson (Studio A/Steinway). *{Internationale* (De Geyter)/*Let it be.* (Beatles). *Dejavalse/valise. Green and Gold* (T.S.C. #4). *Come Swing with me on the Golden Gate* (Cy Owens). With Bruce Bellingham. *Post-Pone.*

May 9. San Francisco, California. KQED-FM: 'West Coast Weekend', with Sedge Thomson (Studio B/Steinway). *{Cheers* (?)/ *Dejavalse/valise. Mother was a Lady* (Marks/ Stern). With Bruce Bellingham and Sedge Thomson. *TV Ministers' Hymn.* With Bruce Bellingham.

May 16. San Francisco, California. KQED-FM: 'West Coast Weekend', with Sedge Thomson (Studio A/Steinway). *{Police radio Sketch* – Gershwin ninths/*Dejavalse/ valise. Haight St. Slither* (T.S.C. #1). *Shalimar* excerpts (Hovhaness). *Parallax* (Ryan).

May 23. San Francisco, California. KQED-FM: 'West Coast Weekend', with Sedge Thomson (Studio B/Steinway). *{C maj. 2 part invention* (J. S. Bach)/*Dejavalse/valise. Garôto* (Nazareth). *Khrushchev in Disneyland.* With Sedge Thomson, Tim Fox, and Bruce Bellingham. *The only Pal I ever had came from Good Old' Frisco Town.* (Earle Jones/Charles Daniels). With Sedge Thomson and Bruce Bellingham.

May 30. San Francisco, California. KQED-FM: 'West Coast Weekend', with Sedge Thomson (Studio A/Steinway). *{Rustles of Spring* (Sinding)/*Dejavalse/valise. Sway Dance* (Cowell). *Black and Blue* (Waller).

June 6. San Francisco, California. KQED-FM: 'West Coast Weekend', with Sedge Thomson (Studio B/Steinway). *{Morning Edition* (Liederman)/*Dejavalse/valise. Gnossienne #2* (Satie). *Rose Leaf Rag* (Joplin). *Bay Bridge Drags.* With Sedge Thomson and Bruce Bellingham. *Bedbug Blues/Blame it on the Blues.* With Eric and Suzy Thompson. *Romanian Dance #4* (Bartók).

June 12. San Francisco, California. Noe Valley Ministry (George Steck/13). Amnesty International Benefit. *Eya* (Traditional)/*St.*

*Stephen* (Hunter/Lesh/Garcia)/*Hesitation Blues* (Davis). *Russian Rag* (Cobb). *Land of the Hassled and Free. Garôto* (Nazareth). *Green and Gold* (T.S.C. #4). *Danse de Travers #1* (Satie). *Dejavalse/valise.* Encores: *Gnossienne #2* (Satie). *Etude #25* (Chopin).
June 13. San Francisco, California. KQED-FM: 'West Coast Weekend', with Sedge Thomson (Studio A/Steinway). *[Prairie Home intro* (?)/*Dejavalse/valise. Gnossienne #4* (Satie). *Black and Blue* (Waller).
June 20. San Francisco, California. KQED-FM: 'West Coast Weekend', with Sedge Thomson (Studio B/Steinway). *[It's Summertime* (Jamies)/*Dejavalse/valise. Rumanian Folk Dance #1* (Bartók). *Danses de Travers #1* (Satie). *Gnossienne #2* (Satie). *Nachklangstudie, Op. 16 #4* (Hauer).
June 27. San Francisco, California. KQED-FM: 'West Coast Weekend', with Sedge Thomson (Studio B/Steinway). *[Summertime* (Gershwin)/*Dejavalse/valise. Land of the Hassled and Free. Klavierstück, Op. 19 #2* (Schönberg).
July 4. San Francisco, California. KQED-FM: 'West Coast Weekend', with Sedge Thomson (Studio B/Steinway). Taped June 27. *[Sousa Fanfare* (?)/*Dejavalse/valise. Lude: Licentious Bicentennial Rag* (T.S.C. 3).
July 11. San Francisco, California. KQED-FM: 'West Coast Weekend', with Sedge Thomson (Studio B/Steinway). *[Sumer is Icumen* (?)/*Dejavalse/valise. Dixie Dimples* (Scott). *Hesitation Blues* (Davis).
July 18. San Francisco, California. KQED-FM: 'West Coast Weekend', with Sedge Thomson (Studio B/Steinway). *[In my Life* (Beatles)/*Dejavalse/valise. Maiden Waltz* (from *Tarot*). *Gnossienne #2* (Satie). *Eintritt (Waldszenen, Op. 82 #1)* (Schumann). *Klavierstück, Op. 19 #4* (Schönberg).
July 25. San Francisco, California. KQED-FM: 'West Coast Weekend', with Sedge Thomson (Studio B/Steinway). *[Waltzing Matilda* (?)/*Dejavalse/valise. That's a Plenty* (Gilbert/Pollack). *Brain Fade* Sketch.
July 31. Tiburon, California. The Dock (Story and Clark/32). First Set: *Efficiency Rag* (Scott). *Pine Apple Rag* (Joplin). *Garôto* (Nazareth). *Hesitation Blues* (Davis). *Any Face Card Beats a '10'. Through Eden's Gates* (Bolcom). *Dejavalse/valise. The Banjo* (Gottschalk). Second Set: *That's a Plenty* (Gilbert/Pollack). *Blues.* With Bruce Bellingham. *Reindeer Rag* (Lamb). *Escorregando* (Nazareth). *Green and Gold* (T.S.C. #4). *Tabby Cat Walk* (Bolcom). *Minstrels*

(Debussy). *Lude: Licentious Bicentennial Rag* (T.S.C. #3). *Harlequin and the Philosopher* (from *Tarot*). Third Set: *Rose Leaf Rag* (Joplin). *Maiden Waltz* (from *Tarot*). *Lovers' Walk.* (from *Tarot*)/*Dark Star* Digression. *Gnossienne #2* (Satie). *Land of the Hassled and Free. Etude #25* (Chopin). *Etude, Op. 25 #6* (Chopin). *Russian Rag* (Cobb). *Danses de Travers #1* (Satie). *Praeambulum: Partita #5* (J. S. Bach). *Etude, Op. 10 #1* (Chopin).
August 1. San Francisco, California. KQED-FM: 'West Coast Weekend', with Sedge Thomson (Studio B/Steinway). *[Day Tripper* (Beatles)/*Dejavalse/valise. Praeambulum: Partita #5* (J. S. Bach). *Reindeer Rag* (Lamb). *Lovers' Walk in the Magic Forest* (from *Tarot*).
August 8. San Francisco, California. KQED-FM: 'West Coast Weekend', with Sedge Thomson (Studio A/Steinway). *[Morning (Peer Gynt)* (Grieg)/*Dejavalse/valise. Audience Adventure Boogie. All I Have to Do in Dream* (Bryant). Improvisation with Bruce Bellingham, guitar.
August 15. San Francisco, California. KQED-FM: 'West Coast Weekend', with Sedge Thomson (Studio A/Steinway). *[Close Encounters* (?)/*Dejavalse/valise. Audience Adventure Boogie. Prelude, Op. 11 #13* (Scriabin). *Living on Tokyo Time* (Danny Flowers/Bruce Bellingham). With Bruce Bellingham, Mark Stech-Novak, and Van Williamsson. *Escorregando* (Nazareth). *Don't be Cruel* (for Elvis, with Bruce Bellingham). *Im-personnel Placement Service.*
August 22. San Francisco, California. KQED-FM: 'West Coast Weekend', with Sedge Thomson (Studio A/Steinway). *[Lucy in the Sky* (Beatles)/*Dejavalse/valise. Audience Adventure Boogie. Prelude, Op. 28 #11 (Dragon Fly)* (Chopin). *Maiden Waltz* (from *Tarot*). *Old Fool's Reel* (from *Tarot*). *Cantina Theme (Star Wars)* (Williams).
August 29. San Francisco, California. KQED-FM: 'West Coast Weekend', with Sedge Thomson (Studio A/Steinway). *[You Can't Always Get What You Want* (Jagger/Richards)/*Dejavalse/valise. Audience Adventure Boogie. Prelude, Op. 32 #11* (Rachmaninoff). *Green and Gold* (T.S.C. #4). *Cantina Theme (Star Wars)* (Williams).
September 5. San Francisco, California. KQED-FM: 'West Coast Weekend', with Sedge Thomson (Studio B/Steinway). *[Try to Remember* (?)/*Dejavalse/valise. Audience Adventure Boogie. San Andreas Stomp* (T.S.C. #5). *Dr. Science* Bridge.
September 12. San Francisco, California.

KQED-FM: 'West Coast Weekend', with Sedge Thomson (Studio B/Steinway). *{My Way* (Anka)/*Dejavalse/valise/boogie. Audience Adventure Boogie. Not so Quiet week in Vegas.* With Bruce Bellingham. *Je t'aime, moi non plus* (Gainsbourg/Birkin). *Rialto Ripples* (Gershwin/Donaldson *via* Kovacs). *Beauty and the Cowboy* (Bellingham). With Bruce Bellingham and Tim Fox. *Caprice, Op. 44 #12* (Sinding). *Dr. Science* Bridge.

September 19. San Francisco, California. KQED-FM: 'West Coast Weekend', with Sedge Thomson (Life on the Water/Steinway). First show from Life on the Water. Building B/Fort Mason. *{Walking with my baby down beside the San Francisco Bay* (?)/*Dejavalse/valise. Beauty and the Cowboy* (Bellingham). With Bruce Bellingham and Tim Fox. *Escorregando* (Nazareth).

September 26. San Francisco, California. KQED-FM: 'West Coast Weekend', with Sedge Thomson (Life on the Water/Steinway). *{Prokofiev 'Classical'/Dejavalse/valise. Audience Adventure Boogie. Rialto Ripples* (Gershwin/Donaldson *via* Kovacs). *Je t'aime, moi non plus* (Gainsbourg/Birkin).

October 3. San Francisco, California. KQED-FM: 'West Coast Weekend', with Sedge Thomson (Life on the Water/Steinway). *{Vodvil Fanfare* (?)/*Dejavalse/valise. Je t'aime, moi non plus* (Gainsbourg/Birkin). *Reggae Promenade.*

October 10. San Francisco, California. KQED-FM: 'West Coast Weekend', with Sedge Thomson (Life on the Water/Steinway). *{Bye bye Baby (Giants baseball)* (Harwell)/*Dejavalse/valise. Audience Adventure Boogie. Je t'aime, moi non plus* (Gainsbourg/Birkin). *Beauty and the Cowboy* (Bellingham). With Bruce Bellingham and Tim Fox. *Haight St. Slither* (T.S.C. #1). *Through Eden's Gates* – excerpt (Bolcom). *Blue Angels Blues.* With Bruce Bellingham and Tim Fox. *Reggae Promenade.*

October 16. Tiburon, California. The Dock (Story and Clark/60). First Set: *Elite Syncopations* (Joplin). *Razzazza Mazzazza* (Pryor). *O ma charmante, épargnez-mois!* (Gottschalk). *Escorregando* (Nazareth). *Black and Blue* (Waller). *Tabby Cat Walk* (Bolcom). *Harlequin and the Philosopher* (from *Tarot*). *Parallax* (Ryan). *Dejavalse.* THE SYNTAX COLLECTOR: *I. Haight St. Slither. II. That There Old West... III. Lude/Licentious. IV. Green and Gold. V. San Andreas Stomp. Prelude, Op. 32 #1* (Rachmaninoff). Second Set: *American Beauty Rag* (Lamb). *Land of the Hassled and Free. Hesitation Blues* (Davis). With Jody

Salino and David Ray. *Boogie Woogie Blues* (Ammons). *Green and Gold* (T.S.C. #4). *Prelude, Op. 11 #14* (Scriabine). *Escorregando* (Nazareth). *Etude #25* (Chopin). *Fantasia in C minor* (J. S. Bach).

October 17. San Francisco, California. KQED-FM: 'West Coast Weekend', with Sedge Thomson (Life on the Water/Steinway). *{Movie Fanfare* (?)/*Dejavalse/valise. That There Old West...* (T.S.C. #2). *Je t'aime, moi non plus* (Gainsbourg/Birkin). *Black and Blue* (Waller). *Reggae Promenade.*

October 24. San Francisco, California. KQED-FM: 'West Coast Weekend', with Sedge Thomson (Life on the Water/Steinway). *{Something (Abbey Road)* (Beatles)/*Dejavalse/valise. Je t'aime, moi non plus* (Gainsbourg/Birkin). *Fog Repellent* (Thomson) Sting. *O ma charmante, épargnez-mois!* (Gottschalk). *Audience Adventure Boogie. Reggae Promenade. Carioca* Bridge (Nazareth). *Urban Geographer* Intro/Outro.

October 25. San Francisco, California. Noe Valley Ministry. Josh Duberman Benefit (George Steck/75). *Pine Apple Rag* (Joplin). *Eintritt (Waldszenen, Op. 82 #1)* (Schumann). *O ma charmante, épargnez-mois!* (Gottschalk). *Garôto* (Nazareth). *Tabby Cat Walk* (Bolcom). *Hesitation Blues* (Davis). *Waltz for Debby* (Evans). *Haight St. Slither* (T.S.C. #1). *That There Old West...* (T.S.C. #2). *Parallax* (Ryan). *Dejavalse. Prelude, Op. 32 #11* (Rachmaninoff). *Prelude, Op. 32 #1* (Rachmaninoff). *Boogie Woogie Blues* (Ammons).

October 31. San Francisco, California. KQED-FM: 'West Coast Weekend', with Sedge Thomson (Life on the Water/Steinway). *{Witches' Sabbath* (Berlioz)/*Dejavalse/valise. Je t'aime, moi non plus* (Gainsbourg/Birkin). *Beauty and the Cowboy* (Bellingham). With Bruce Bellingham and Tim Fox. *Audience Adventure Boogie. Carioca* Bridge (Nazareth). *Reggae Promenade. Urban Geographer* Intro/Outro.

November 7. San Francisco, California. KQED-FM: 'West Coast Weekend', with Sedge Thomson (Life on the Water/Steinway). *{Magnificat* (Bach)/*Dejavalse/valise/boogie. Urban Geographer* Intro/Outro. *Les Baricades Misterieuses* (Couperin). *Beauty and the Cowboy* (Bellingham). With Bruce Bellingham and Tim Fox. *Courante in A* (Bach). *Waltz for Debby* (Evans). *Reggae Promenade.*

November 14. San Francisco, California. KQED-FM: 'West Coast Weekend', with Sedge Thomson (Life on the Water/

Steinway). Investment in Ideas '87. {Brother Can You Spare a Dime (?)/Dejavalse/valise/boogie. That Hand Played Rag (Silverman/Ward). That's a Plenty (Gilbert/Pollack). City Ice Sketch (Thomson) In/Out/During. Urban Geographer Intro/Outro. Nostalgic Commercials (with Sedge Thomson). Reggae Promenade. Rialto Ripples (Gershwin/Donaldson via Kovacs).

November 15. San Francisco, California. Community Music Center. Faculty Benefit Recital. Let it Ring (première). Dejavalse. With Shirley Wong, Grace Huenemann, Robert Montes, and Peter Maleitzke. (Steinway, Duo-art, Steinway, Wurlitzer, and Steinway).

November 21. San Francisco, California. KQED-FM: 'West Coast Weekend', with Sedge Thomson (Life on the Water/Steinway). {Pilgrims' Chorus (Tannhäuser) (Wagner)/Dejavalse/valise/boogie (in E). Sentimental Waltz (Ashforth). Urban Geographer Intro/Outro. Greed (from Tarot). Beauty and the Cowboy (Bellingham). With Bruce Bellingham and Tim Fox. City Ice Sketch (Thomson) In/Out/During. Reggae Promenade.

November 28. San Francisco, California. KQED-FM: 'West Coast Weekend', with Sedge Thomson (Life on the Water/Steinway). {It's Beginning to Look a Lot Like Xmas (?)/Dejavalse/valise/Boar's Head Carol. Urban Geographer Intro/Outro. A Waltz for Evelyn Hinrichsen (Lou Harrison). Beauty and the Cowboy (Bellingham). With Bruce Bellingham and Tim Fox. Banana (Bellingham). With Bruce Bellingham. Pine Apple Rag (Joplin).

December 5. San Francisco, California. KQED-FM: 'West Coast Weekend', with Sedge Thomson (Life on the Water/Steinway). {I am a Rock (Simon)/Dejavalse/valise/boogie. Dear Averill (Bellingham) March. The Answer (Forrester). Urban Geographer Intro/Outro. Beauty and the Cowboy (Bellingham). With Bruce Bellingham and Tim Fox. Reggae Promenade.

December 12. San Francisco, California. KQED-FM: 'West Coast Weekend', with Sedge Thomson (Life on the Water/Steinway). {Coventry Carol (Traditional)/Dejavalse/valise. Xmas medley – Un Flambeau, Jeannette, Isabelle (17th century Provençal carol). Les Anges des nos Campagnes (19th century French carol). The Holly and the Ivy (17th century English carol). Puccini/Toscanini Anecdote. Reindeer Rag (Lamb).

Urban Geographer Intro/Outro. Beauty and the Cowboy (Bellingham). With Bruce Bellingham and Tim Fox. Good, Bad, and Irradiated Sketch (Thomson). Xmas song: God Rest ye Merry, Gentlemen (18th century English carol). Reggae Promenade. Xmas song: As with Kindness men of Old (Dix/Kocher).

December 19. San Francisco, California. KQED-FM: 'West Coast Weekend', with Sedge Thomson (Life on the Water/Steinway). {Kinderszenen (Op. 15 #1 – Schumann)/Xmas Song/Dejavalse/valise (in G). Xmas songs: O Tannenbaum (German carol). Jeg er så glad hver Julekveld (Knudsen). Deck the Halls with Boughs of Holly (Welsh carol). Urban Geographer Intro/Outro. Beauty and the Cowboy (Bellingham). With Bruce Bellingham. Good, Bad, and Irradiated Sketch (Thomson). Reggae Promenade.

December 26. San Francisco, California. KQED-FM: 'West Coast Weekend', with Sedge Thomson (Life on the Water/Steinway). {St. Stephen (Garcia/Lesh/Hunter)/Dejavalse/valise. Fog Repellent Sketch (Thomson). Good King Wenceslas (Piae Cantiones, 1502). Dispeptically Skeptically Blue. Moonshadow (Stevens). Beauty and the Cowboy (Bellingham). With Bruce Bellingham. Urban Geographer Intro/Outro. Magnetic Rag (Joplin)

## 1988

January 2. San Francisco, California. KQED-FM: 'West Coast Weekend', with Sedge Thomson (Life on the Water/Steinway). Rebroadcast of September 26, 1987 show.

January 9. San Francisco, California. KQED-FM: 'West Coast Weekend', with Sedge Thomson (Life on the Water/Steinway). {We've only just Begun (Carpenters)/Dejas (Abbreviated from here on because evolved considerably from score). Modern Love Waltz (Glass). Urban Geographer Intro/Outro. Good, Bad, and Irradiated Sketch (Thomson). Beauty and the Cowboy (Bellingham). With Bruce Bellingham. Audience Adventure Boogie.

January 16. San Francisco, California. KQED-FM: 'West Coast Weekend', with Sedge Thomson (Life on the Water/Steinway). {Don't let me be Misunderstood (Animals)/Dejas. Audience Adventure Boogie. Music Box Waltz (Zygmunt Krauze). Blue Goose Interlude (Birch). Beauty and the Cowboy (Bellingham). With Bruce Bellingham and Tim Fox. Good, Bad, and Irradiated Sketch (Thomson). Rockabilly Promenade.

January 23. San Francisco, California. KQED-FM: 'West Coast Weekend', with Sedge Thomson (Life on the Water/Steinway). {Pac-man (?)/Dejas. Waltz in memoriam Maurice Ravel (Moran). Beauty and the Cowboy (Bellingham). With Bruce Bellingham. Audience Adventure Boogie. Rockabilly Promenade.

January 31. San Francisco, California. KQED-FM: 'West Coast Weekend', with Sedge Thomson (Life on the Water/Steinway). {Did You Ever Have to Make up Your Mind (?)/ Dejas. Fig Leaf Rag (Joplin). Three-in-one Two-step. With Eric and Suzy Thompson. Untitled Boogie Break. Rialto Ripples Break (Gershwin/Donaldson via Kovacs). Audience Adventure Boogie. Boogie Lullaby.

February 2. San Francisco, California. Emerald City Studio (Steinway). Robert Hunter Duino Elegy Sessions. Stuart Rosenthal, recording engineer. Sonata #1, Op. 1: II mvt. (Brahms). Intermezzo in A, Op. 118 #2 (Brahms). Intermezzo in E, Op. 116 #6 (Brahms). Intermezzo in A♭, Op. 76 #3 (Brahms). Romance in F, Op. 118 #5 (Brahms).

February 3. Etude #25 in F minor (Chopin). Nocturne in B♭ minor, Op. 9 #1 (Chopin). Nocturne in F# minor, Op. 48 #2 (Chopin). Prelude in A minor, Op. 28 #2 (Chopin). Sonata in C (Unfinished) II mvt. (Schubert). Prelude in E minor, Op. 11 #4 (Scriabin).

February 6. San Francisco, California. KQED-FM: 'West Coast Weekend', with Sedge Thomson (Life on the Water/Steinway). {Melon Sketch/Dejas. Fog Repellent Sting. Sugar Cane (Joplin). Audience Adventure Boogie. Urban Geographer Intro/Outro. Good, Bad, and Irradiated Sketch (Thomson). Beauty and the Cowboy (Bellingham). With Bruce Bellingham. Rockabilly Promenade.

February 13. San Francisco, California. KQED-FM: 'West Coast Weekend', with Sedge Thomson (Life on the Water/Steinway). {Jack Benny Sketch (Thomson)/Love in Bloom/ Dejas. Mild Olympics Sketch (Thomson). Romance, Op. 118 #5 (Brahms). Beauty and the Cowboy (Bellingham). With Bruce Bellingham. Devoted to You (Bryant) Break. All I Have to do is Dream (Bryant). With Virginia Morgan and Bruce Bellingham. Rockabilly Promenade. Audience Adventure Boogie. Good, Bad, and Irradiated Sketch (Thomson). Ennui.

February 20. San Francisco, California. KQED-FM: 'West Coast Weekend', with Sedge Thomson (Life on the Water/Steinway). {I hear a Symphony (Supremes)/Dejas. Favorito

(Nazareth). 'Sneet (Ryan). Urban Geographer Intro/Outro. Good, Bad, and Irradiated Sketch (Thomson). Beauty and the Cowboy (Bellingham). With Bruce Bellingham and David Garelic. Rockabilly Promenade.

February 26. Tiburon, California. The Dock (Story and Clark/60). From Riches to Rags. First Set: San Andreas Stomp (T.S.C. #5). Modern Love Waltz (Glass). Favorito (Nazareth). Fig Leaf Rag (Joplin). Through Eden's Gates (Bolcom). Magnetic Rag (Joplin). Green and Gold (T.S.C. #4). Prelude, Op. 32 #11 (Rachmaninoff). Sugar Cane (Joplin). Romance, Op. 118 #5 (Brahms). Dejavalse. Second Set: Moonshadow (Stevens). Halley's Comet Rag (Lincoln). Dark Star (Hunter/ Garcia/Hart/Kreutzmann/Lesh/ McKernan/Weir). Etude #25 (Chopin). Speaking (Forrester). Chopped Liver (Ryan). Hesitation Blues (Davis). Harlequin and the Philosopher (from Tarot). That There Old West... (T.S.C. #2). Fantasy in C minor (J. S. Bach). Dejavalse. Encores: Prelude, Op. 32 #1 (Rachmaninoff). Intermezzo, Op. 118 #2 (Brahms). Etude, Op. 25 #6 (Chopin).

February 27. San Francisco, California. KQED-FM: 'West Coast Weekend', with Sedge Thomson (Life on the Water/Steinway). {Satisfaction (Jagger/Richards)/Dejas. Audience Adventure Boogie. Rialto Ripples (Gershwin/Donaldson via Kovacs). With Tim Fox. Je t'aime, moi non plus (Gainsbourg/ Birkin). Rockabilly Promenade. Good, Bad, and Irradiated Sketch (Thomson).

March 5. San Francisco, California. KQED-FM: 'West Coast Weekend', with Sedge Thomson (Life on the Water/Steinway). {Listen to the Rhythm of the Falling Rain (?)/ Dejas. Audience Adventure Boogie. Je t'aime, moi non plus (Gainsbourg/Birkin). Chopped Liver (Ryan). Etude #25 (Chopin). Prelude, Op. 28 #10 (Night Moth) (Chopin).

March 12. San Francisco, California. KQED-FM: 'West Coast Weekend', with Sedge Thomson (Life on the Water/Steinway). {Al Entrada de Temps Clar (?)/Dejas. Audience Adventure Boogie. Holiday for Strings (Rose). Blue Goose (Birch). Urban Geographer Intro/Outro. Blues in E. With Bruce Bellingham and Tim Fox. Je t'aime, moi non plus (Gainsbourg/Birkin). Break. Etude, Op. 42 #3 (Scriabin). Kukla, Fran, and Ollie Break. Good, Bad, and Irradiated Sketch (Thomson). Rockabilly Promenade.

March 19. San Francisco, California. KQED-FM: 'West Coast Weekend', with Sedge Thomson (Life on the Water/Steinway).

*{Spring Song* (Mendelssohn)/*Birthday* (Lennon/McCartney)/*Dejas. Gilligan's Island* Vamp. *Goldberg Variation #4* (J.S. Bach). *Goldberg Variation #19* (J. S. Bach). *Beauty and the Cowboy* (Bellingham). With Bruce Bellingham. *Audience Adventure Boogie. Diabelli Theme* (Beethoven). *Goldberg Variation #18* (J. S. Bach). *Good, Bad, and Irradiated* Sketch (Thomson). *Ennui.*

March 26. San Francisco, California. KQED-FM: 'West Coast Weekend', with Sedge Thomson (Life on the Water/Steinway). *{Sheherazade* (Rimsky-Korsakoff)/*Dejas. Apocryphal Awry. Audience Adventure Boogie. Urban Geographer* Intro/Outro. *Beauty and the Cowboy* (Bellingham). With Bruce Bellingham. *Rockabilly Promenade. Good, Bad, and Irradiated* Sketch (Thomson).

April 2. San Francisco, California. KQED-FM: 'West Coast Weekend', with Sedge Thomson (Life on the Water/Steinway). *{Return to Sender* (Elvis)/*Dejas. Weeping Willow* (Joplin). *Bagatelle, Op. 126 #4* (Beethoven). *Urban Geographer* Intro/Outro. *'Sneet* (Ryan). *Rockabilly Promenade. Good, Bad, and Irradiated* Sketch (Thomson).

April 9. San Francisco, California. KQED-FM: 'West Coast Weekend', with Sedge Thomson (Life on the Water/Steinway). *{Cool Water* (?)/*Dejas. Goin' Home* (Jagger/Richard). *Quanto sia liet' il giorno* (Verdelot). *Urban Geographer* Intro/Outro. *Beauty and the Cowboy* (Bellingham). With Bruce Bellingham, Tim Fox, and Darol Anger. *Rockabilly Promenade. Lady Jane* (Jagger/Richard). With Bruce Bellingham. *Good, Bad, and Irradiated* Sketch (Thomson).

April 16. San Francisco, California. KQED-FM: 'West Coast Weekend', with Sedge Thomson (Life on the Water/Steinway). *Investment in Ideas '88. {Money Makes the World go Around* (?)/*Dejas. John Muir* Sketch (Thomson) – spoken. *Wildflowers* (Kallick). *Up against the Wall Street Travel* Sketch (Thomson). *Urban Geographer* Intro/Outro. *You've Got to Hide Your Love Away* (Lennon/McCartney). With Bruce Bellingham and Tim Fox. *Hesitation Blues* (Davis). *Audience Adventure Boogie. Je t'aime, moi non plus* (Gainsbourg/Birkin). With Robert Hunter: *Duino Elegy #7* (Rilke/Hunter translation). *Romance, Op. 118 #5* (Brahms). *Nocturne, Op. 9 #1* (Chopin). Robert Petersen Poems. *Don't Think Twice, it's Alright* (Dylan). *Rialto Ripples* (Gershwin/Donaldson *via* Kovacs). *Good, Bad, and Irradiated* Sketch (Thomson).

April 23. San Francisco, California. KQED-

FM: 'West Coast Weekend', with Sedge Thomson (Life on the Water/Steinway). *{Ennui* Sketch (Bellingham)/*Dejas. Wooden Teeth* Sketch (Thomson). With Sedge Thomson. *Gnossienne #2* (Satie). *Vexations* (Satie – excerpt). *Danse de travers #1* (Satie). *Beauty and the Cowboy* (Bellingham). With Bruce Bellingham and Tim Fox. *Je t'aime, moi non plus* (Gainsbourg/Birkin). *Audience Adventure Boogie. Good, Bad, and Irradiated* Sketch (Thomson). *Rialto Ripples* (Gershwin/Donaldson *via* Kovacs). *Urban Geographer* Intro/Outro.

April 30. San Francisco, California. KQED-FM: 'West Coast Weekend', with Sedge Thomson (Life on the Water/Steinway). *{Dueling Banjos* (?)/*Dejas. Internationale* (Degeyter). *Je t'aime, moi non plus* (Gainsbourg/Birkin). *When it's Sleepy Time down South* (René, René, and Muse *via* Waller). *Beauty and the Cowboy* (Bellingham). With Bruce Bellingham and Steve Seskin. *Rockabilly Promenade. Good, Bad, and Irradiated* Sketch (Thomson).

May 7. San Francisco, California. KQED-FM: 'West Coast Weekend', with Sedge Thomson (Life on the Water/Steinway). *{Raindrops keep Fallin'* (?)/*Racetrack Fanfare* (?)/*Dejas. Banana* (Bellingham). With Bruce Bellingham, Tim Fox, and Becky McCahon. *A Waltz for Evelyn Hinrichsen* (Lou Harrison). *Beauty and the Cowboy* (Bellingham). With Bruce Bellingham. *Audience Adventure Boogie. Rockabilly Promenade. Good, Bad, and Irradiated* Sketch (Thomson).

May 14. San Francisco, California. KQED-FM: 'West Coast Weekend', with Sedge Thomson (Life on the Water/Steinway). Rebroadcast of January 23, 1988 show.

May 21. San Francisco, California. KQED-FM: 'West Coast Weekend', with Sedge Thomson (Life on the Water/Steinway). Rebroadcast of January 9, 1988 show.

May 28. San Francisco, California. KQED-FM: 'West Coast Weekend', with Sedge Thomson (Life on the Water/Steinway). *{Werewolves of London* (Zevon)/*Blue Moon* (?)/*Dejas. Fog Repellent* Tags. *Odeon* (Nazareth). *Rockabilly Promenade. Beauty and the Cowboy* (Bellingham). With Bruce Bellingham and Tim Fox. *Je t'aime, moi non plus* (Gainsbourg/Birkin). *Ennui. Good, Bad, and Irradiated* Sketch (Thomson).

June 4. San Francisco, California. KQED-FM: 'West Coast Weekend', with Sedge Thomson (Life on the Water/Steinway). *{Ode to Billy Joe* (Gentry)/*Dejas. Fog Repellent*

Sting. *Prelude: Le Tombeau de Couperin* (Ravel). *Kitty Boot Camp* Intro. *Powder Milk* Outro. *Beauty and the Cowboy* (Bellingham). With Bruce Bellingham and Tim Fox. *Audience Adventure Boogie. Rockabilly Promenade. Caprice, Op. 44 #12* (Sinding). *Good, Bad, and Irradiated* Sketch (Thomson). *Banana* (Bellingham). With Bruce Bellingham.
June 11. San Francisco, California. KQED-FM: 'West Coast Weekend', with Sedge Thomson (Life on the Water/Steinway). *{Camelot (?)/Dejas. Fog Repellent* (Thomson) Sting. *Dixie Dimples* (Scott). *Gaudeamus Igitur* Intro for Charlie Varon Sketch. *Beauty and the Cowboy* (Bellingham). With Bruce Bellingham and Tim Fox. *Je t'aime, moi non plus* (Gainsbourg/Birkin). *Urban Geographer* Intro/Outro. *Rockabilly Promenade. Wild about my Lover* (Sebastian). With Bruce Bellingham. *Sleepin' with the Light on* (from *Slow Fire*) (Dresher). With Bruce Bellingham. *Good, Bad, and Irradiated* Sketch (Thomson).
June 18. San Francisco, California. KQED-FM: 'West Coast Weekend', with Sedge Thomson (Life on the Water/Steinway). *{O my Papa* (?)/*Dejas. Fog Repellent* Sketch (Thomson) – 'Mayor' part and Sting. *Two Boogie Breaks. Oriental (Spanish Dance #2)* (Granados). *Urban Geographer* Intro/Outro. *Je t'aime, moi non plus* (Gainsbourg/Birkin). *Rockabilly Promenade.*
June 25. San Francisco, California. KQED-FM: 'West Coast Weekend', with Sedge Thomson (Life on the Water/Steinway). *{It Don't Come Easy/Dejas. Fog Repellent* Sketch (Thomson) – 'Bob' part and Sting. *Rockabilly Promenade. Good, Bad, and Irradiated* Sketch (Thomson).
July 2. San Jose, California. KQED-FM: 'West Coast Weekend', with Sedge Thomson. (Mirassou Vineyards/Sherman Clay). *{The Piano has been Drinking/Dejas. Fog Repellent* (Thomson) Sting. *Wildflowers* (Kallick). *Urban Geographer* (Waits) Intro/Outro. *Once in a While* (Green/Edwards *via* Shearing). *Declaration of Independence* Reading. *Lift Every Voice* (Johnson/Johnson) Bed. *Rockabilly Promenade. The Ballad of Shane Muscatell. First live performance*, with Bruce Bellingham, guitar. *Good, Bad, and Irradiated* Sketch (Thomson). *Ennui* Sketch (Bellingham).
July 9. San Francisco, California. KQED-FM: 'West Coast Weekend', with Sedge Thomson (Life on the Water/Steinway). *{Magnificent Seven* (Bernstein)/*Dejas. Fog Repellent* Sketch (Thomson) – 'Mayor' part and Sting. *Rumanian Folk Dance #1* (Bartók).

*Urban Geographer* Intro/Outro. *Beauty and the Cowboy* (Bellingham). With Bruce Bellingham. *Rockabilly Promenade. Good, Bad, and Irradiated* Sketch (Thomson).
July 9. San Francisco. California. Great American Music Hall (Yamaha). Accompaniment to readings by Robert Hunter. *Answer to the Question Why* (Hunter): *Klavierstück, Op. 19 #1* (Schönberg). *Red Dog's Decoration Day* (Hunter): *Klavierstücke, Op. 19 #s 2, 4*, and *6* (Schönberg). *Tarbean* (Hunter): *Oriental (Spanish Dance #2)* (Granados). *Prelude: Le Tombeau de Couperin* (Ravel) – Piano solo. *The Brass Axis* (Hunter): *Prelude, Op. 32 #12* (Rachmaninoff); *Prelude, Op. 28 #6 (Tolling Bells);* (Chopin); *Prelude, Op. 28 #15 (Raindrops);* (Chopin). *Duino Elegy #1* (Rilke – Hunter translation): *Sonata #1: Second Movement* (Brahms). *Duino Elegy #7* (Rilke – Hunter translation): *Romance, Op. 118 #5* (Brahms). *Nocturne, Op. 9 #2* (Chopin); *Gnossienne #2* (Satie) – Piano solo. *Exploding Diamond Blues* (Hunter): *Sonatina* (Constanten). *The Boxes of Doctor Spasmodeus* (Hunter): *Rumanian Folk Dances #s 3 & 4* (Bartók). *Rodney Albin's Farewell Lecture* (Hunter): *Hello, Hello* (Sopwith Camel). *One for Bobby Petersen* (Hunter): *Caprice, Op. 44 #12* (Sinding). *A Prophecy for the Year 1906* (Hunter): *The San Andreas Stomp* (T.S.C. #5). Intermission. *Odeon* (Nazareth) – Piano solo. *Portia* (Hunter): *Preludes; Op. 11 #s 13 and 15* (Scriabin). *Sonnets to Orpheus* (Rilke – Hunter translation): *Eintritt (Waldszenen, Op. 82 #1)* (Schumann); *Fremder Mann (bis), Op. 68 #30* (Schumann). *The Flight of the Marie Helena* (Hunter). Encore: *Holigomena* (Hunter): *Sonata #9* (opening) (Scriabin).
July 16. San Francisco, California. KQED-FM: 'West Coast Weekend', with Sedge Thomson (Life on the Water/Steinway). *{I Remember You* (Ifield)/*Dejas. Fog Repellent* (Thomson) Sting. *There's no Answer* (Thomson) Sting. *Klavierstück, Op. 19 #1* (Schönberg). *Beauty and the Cowboy* (Bellingham). With Bruce Bellingham, Peppino d'Agostino, and Tim Fox. *Jazz/Boogie Breaks. Rockabilly Promenade. Good, Bad, and Irradiated* Sketch (Thomson). *Menuet: Le Tombeau de Couperin* (Ravel).
July 23. San Francisco, California. KQED-FM: 'West Coast Weekend', with Sedge Thomson (Life on the Water/Steinway). *{It's De-lovely* (?)/*Dejas. Fog Repellent* (Thomson) Sting. *Funeral March of a Marionette* (Gounod). *Urban Geographer* Intro/Outro. *Audience Adventure Boogie. Rockabilly*

*Promenade. Peter Gunn* Vamp. *Good, Bad, and Irradiated* Sketch (Thomson). *Raymond Chandler Tribute* (T. Fox) *(Town without Pity* Theme).

July 30. San Francisco, California. KQED-FM: 'West Coast Weekend', with Sedge Thomson (Life on the Water/Steinway). *(Fresh Air* (Byard)/*Dejas. Fog Repellent* (Thomson) Sting. *Je t'aime, moi non plus* (Gainsbourg/Birkin). *Intermezzo, Op. #6* (Brahms). *Rockabilly Promenade. Audience Adventure Boogie. Good, Bad, and Irradiated* Sketch (Thomson).

August 3. San Francisco, California. Möbius Studios (Yamaha grand/DX-7 Synthesizer). Henry Kaiser Sessions. Oliver DiCicco, engineer. *Mason's Children* (Hunter/Garcia).

August 6. San Francisco, California. KQED-FM: 'West Coast Weekend', With Sedge Thomson (Life on the Water/Steinway). Rebroadcast of November 7, 1987 show.

August 13. San Francisco, California. KQED-FM: 'West Coast Weekend', with Sedge Thomson (Life on the Water/Steinway). Rebroadcast of April 9, 1988 show.

August 20. San Francisco, California. KQED-FM: 'West Coast Weekend', with Sedge Thomson (Life on the Water/Steinway). *(Weekend Edition* (Liederman)/*Dejas. Fog Repellent* (Thomson) Sting. *Ennui* (Bellingham). *Beauty and the Cowboy* (Bellingham). With Bruce Bellingham, Bob Franke, and David Garelic. *Audience Adventure Boogie. What Love Can Do* (Will Williams). With Will Williams, vocal; Terry Dowling, slide guitar, Avi Bortnik, guitar, and Alex Schnitzler, harmonica. *Rockabilly Promenade. Good, Bad, and Irradiated* Sketch (Thomson).

August 27. San Francisco, California. KQED-FM: 'West Coast Weekend', with Sedge Thomson (Life on the Water/Steinway). *(Fanfare for the Common Man* (Copland)/*Dejas. Fog Repellent* (Thomson) Sting. *Chiclets* (Ryan). *Skeeter Feeder* (Thomson) Tag. *'To Look Sharp'* Vamp. *Beauty and the Cowboy* (Bellingham). With Bruce Bellingham and Gene Parsons. *Audience Adventure Boogie. Rockabilly Promenade. Moonshadow* (Stevens). *Good, Bad, and Irradiated* Sketch (Thomson). *Dear Averill* (Bellingham) March.

August 31. San Francisco, California. 345 Hyde Street Studios. C.M.C. Promotion Sessions. Don Richards, producer. *San Andreas Stomp* (T.S.C. #5). *Dejavalse. Forlane: Le Tombeau de Couperin* (Ravel). *Fantasy in C minor* (J. S. Bach).

September 3. San Francisco, California. KQED-FM: 'West Coast Weekend', with Sedge Thomson (Life on the Water/Steinway). *(September in the Rain* (?)/*Dejas. Fog Repellent* (Sting). *Forlane: Le Tombeau de Couperin* (Ravel). *Sway Dance* (Cowell). *Audience Adventure Boogie. Rockabilly Promenade. Urban Geographer* Intro/Outro. *Good, Bad, and Irradiated* Sketch (Thomson). *Bruckner Birthday Tribute.* With Sedge Thomson. *Who Do You Love* (Bo Diddley). With Bruce Bellingham, Mike Henderson, and John Packer.

*RECORDING SESSIONS*

September 4. Las Vegas, Nevada. Terry Ryan Studio. (Yamaha pf-85). 'Fresh Tracks in Real Time.' Terry Ryan, producer/engineer. *Moonshadow* (Stevens). *Hesitation Blues* (Davis). *Any Face Card Beats a '10'. Chiclets* (Ryan). September 5. THE SYNTAX COLLECTOR: I. The Haight St. Slither. II. That There Old West is Older Now than Ever. V. The San Andreas Stomp.

September 6. THE SYNTAX COLLECTOR: IV. The Green and Gold Take the Cakewalk.

September 7. THE SYNTAX COLLECTOR: III. Lude: Licentious Bicentennial Rag. Cold Rain and Snow (Obray Ramsey via McGannahan Skjellyfetti). Dejavalse. Speaking (Forrester).

September 8. *Tabby Cat Walk* (Bolcom). *Land of the Hassled and Free.*

September 9. *Dark Star* (Hunter/Garcia et al). The one that got away.

September 10. San Francisco, California. KQED-FM: 'West Coast Weekend', with Sedge Thomson (Life on the Water/Steinway). *(Daydream Believer* (Monkees)/*Dejas. Fog Repellent* (Thomson) Sting. *Pastime #4* (Mathews). *'Mein!'* (Die Schöne Müllerin) (Schubert). With Bruce Bellingham, Tenor. *Rockabilly Promenade. Beauty and the Cowboy* (Bellingham). With Bruce Bellingham and Tim Fox, guitars. *Audience Adventure Boogie. Good, Bad, and Irradiated* Sketch (Thomson). *Urban Geographer* Intro/Outro.

September 17. San Francisco, California. KQED-FM: 'West Coast Weekend', with Sedge Thomson (Life on the Water/Steinway). *(Olympic Fanfare* (?)/*Dejas. Fog Repellent* (Thomson) Sting. *Gaillarda 3a (2a Libro di Toccate)* (Frescobaldi). *Villanesca (Spanish Dance #4)* (Granados). *I Need You* (Harrison) Bed. *Urban Geographer* Intro/

Outro. *Rockabilly Promenade. Audience Adventure Boogie. Ebb Tide* (Ian Shoales Intro). *Good, Bad, and Irradiated* Sketch (Thomson).
September 24. San Francisco, California. KQED-FM: 'West Coast Weekend', with Sedge Thomson (Life on the Water/Steinway). *{Chariots of Fire* (?)/*Dejas. Fog Repellent* (Thomson) Sting. *{Mrs. Robinson (Candidates' debate)/Dejas. Dear Averill* (Bellingham) March. *Urban Geographer* Intro/Outro. *Beauty and the Cowboy* (Bellingham). With Bruce Bellingham and Tim Fox. *Audience Adventure Boogie. Olympic Themes. Rockabilly Promenade. Good, Bad, and Irradiated* Sketch (Thomson).
October. Nationwide. *Dead Head Television.* Show #7. Interview.
October 1. San Francisco, California. KQED-FM: 'West Coast Weekend', with Sedge Thomson (Life on the Water/Steinway). Third Anniversary Party and Benefit. *{It Was a Very Good Year* (?)/*Dejas. Love is Blue* (Popp). *Nachtstück, Op. 23* #4 (Schumann). *Olympic Fanfare/How sweet it is (to be loved by you). Urban Geographer* Intro/Outro. *Beauty and the Cowboy* (Bellingham). With Bruce Bellingham and Tim Fox. *Audience Adventure Boogie. Dear Averill* (Bellingham) March. *Rockabilly Promenade. Good, Bad, and Irradiated* Sketch (Thomson). *Ennui* (Bellingham).
October 8. San Francisco, California. KQED-FM: 'West Coast Weekend', with Sedge Thomson (Life on the Water/Steinway). *{O Sole mio* (?)/*Dejas. Compendium of Human Knowledge* (T. Fox) (*Dr. Science*) Intro/Outro. *Sonata #24* (Cimarosa). *Dear Averill* (Bellingham) March. *Rockabilly Promenade. Beauty and the Cowboy* (Bellingham). With Bruce Bellingham and Paul Mehling, guitars; Brian Godchaux, violin; and Joe Preussner, bass. *Audience Adventure Boogie. Good, Bad, and Irradiated* Sketch (Thomson). *City Ice* Sketch (Thomson) In/Out/During.
October 15. San Francisco, California. KQED-FM: 'West Coast Weekend', with Sedge Thomson (Life on the Water/Steinway). *{Earth Angel* (?)/*Dejas. Fog Repellent* (Thomson) TC Yoshi and Sting. *A's for the A's. Day Care Segment* (Thomson) Outro. *Audience Adventure Boogie. Beauty and the Cowboy* (Bellingham). With Bruce Bellingham and Tim Fox. *Rockabilly Promenade.*
October 22. San Francisco, California. KQED-FM: 'West Coast Weekend', with Sedge Thomson (Life on the Water/Steinway). *{La Fille aux Cheveux du Lin* (Debussy)/*Dejas. Fog Repellent* (Thomson) Sting. *Long, Long*

*Time* (?). *Beauty and the Cowboy* (Bellingham). With Bruce Bellingham and Tim Fox. *Audience Adventure Boogie. Ad Hawk* Intro/Outro. *Rockabilly Promenade. Dear Averill* (Bellingham) March. *Ball Game* Intro/Outro. *City Ice* Sketch (Thomson) In/Out/During.
October 29. San Francisco, California. KQED-FM: 'West Coast Weekend', with Sedge Thomson (Life on the Water/Steinway). Campaign 88.5. *{Witchcraft* (?)/*Dejas. Meditation Parking Garage* (Thomson) Tag. *Fog Repellent* (Thomson) Tag. *Cantina Theme (Star Wars)* (Williams). Jazz Break. *Dejavalentino. Dead Language Institute* (Thomson) Tag. *Good, Bad, and Irradiated* Sketch (Thomson). *Rialto Ripples* (Gershwin/Donaldson via Kovacs). *Rockabilly Promenade. Urban Geographer* Intro/Outro.
November 5. San Francisco, California. KQED-FM: 'West Coast Weekend', with Sedge Thomson (Life on the Water/Steinway). *{Think for Yourself* (Harrison)/*Dejas. Voters' Quick Pick* (Thomson) Tags. *Rockabilly Promenade. Xerox* Tag. *Beauty and the Cowboy* (Bellingham). With Bruce Bellingham, Tim Fox, and Suzy Thompson.
November 9. San Francisco, California. First Unitarian Church (Steinway {Hamburg}/70). *American Music Week/New Release.* Piano solo: *Prelude* (1963). *Sonatina* (1962).
November 12. San Francisco, California. KQED-FM: 'West Coast Weekend', with Sedge Thomson (Life on the Water/Steinway). *{Don't Worry, Be Happy* (McFerrin)/*C'mon Get Happy* (?)/*Dejas. Je t'aime, moi non plus* (Gainsbourg/Birkin). *Minstrels* (Debussy). *Beauty and the Cowboy* (Bellingham). With Bruce Bellingham, Tim Fox, and Ilya Tsarfin Domra. *Audience Adventures Boogie. Rockabilly Promenade.*
November 19. San Francisco, California. KQED-FM: 'West Coast Weekend', with Sedge Thomson (Life on the Water/Steinway). *{My Cup Runneth Over* (?)/*Dejas. Gnossienne #3* (Satie). *Fog Repellent* (Thomson) Tag. *Word Aversion* (Thomson/Bellingham) Tag. *Dear Averill* (Bellingham) March. *Audience Adventure Blues.* With Bruce Bellingham, guitar. *Rockabilly Promenade.*
November 20. Berkeley, California. Finn Hall. Josh Duberman Benefit (Steinway). *Prelude in C minor (W.T.C. Vol II)* (J. S. Bach). *I Need You* (Harrison). *Favorito* (Nazareth). *That's a Plenty* (Gilbert/Pollack). *American Beauty* (Lamb). *Odeon* (Nazareth). *Magnetic Rag* (Joplin). *Minstrels* (Debussy). *Chopped Liver* (Ryan). *Any Face Card Beats a '10'. Chiclets*

(Ryan). *Etude #25* (Chopin). *Nachtstück, Op. 23 #4* (Schumann). *Prelude, Op. 32 #1* (Rachmaninoff). *Dejavalse. Etude, Op. 25 #6* (Chopin).

November 26. San Francisco, California. KQED-FM: 'West Coast Weekend', with Sedge Thomson (Life on the Water/Steinway). *{Anticipation (These are the good old days)/Dejas. Fog Repellent* (Thomson) Sting. *Love is Blue* (Popp) Bed. *City Ice* Sketch (Thomson) In/Out/During. *Urban Geographer* Intro/Outro. *I am Waiting* (Richard). With Bruce Bellingham, guitar. *Audience Adventure Boogie. Rondo alla Turc* (Mozart). *Good, Bad, and Irradiated* Sketch (Thomson). *That's a Plenty* (Gilbert/Pollack).

December 3. San Francisco, California. KQED-FM: 'West Coast Weekend', with Sedge Thomson (Life on the Water/Steinway). *{Lo, How a Rose e'er Blooming* (Praetorius)/*Dejas. Fog Repellent* (Thomson) Sting. *That's a Plenty* (Gilbert/Pollack). *M Y'Malel/My Dreidl* (Hanukah Songs). *Rockabilly Promenade. My Dreidl/C Blues.* With Bruce Bellingham and Dix Bruce, guitars; Jim Kerwin, bass; and Jeremy Cohen, violin. *Audience Adventure Boogie. Xmas Finds (Stealth Car Wax)* (Thomson) Intro/Outro. *Dear Averill* (Bellingham) March. *Good, Bad, and Irradiated* Sketch (Thomson).

December 10. San Francisco, California. KQED-FM: 'West Coast Weekend', with Sedge Thomson (Life on the Water/Steinway). *{Pretty Woman* (Orbison Tribute)/*Dejas. Fog Repellent* (Thomson) Sting. *Cuisine Doc* (Thomson) Bed. *A Virgin Unspotted* (18th century English carol). *Dr. Science* Intro/Outro. *Beauty and the Cowboy* (Bellingham). With Bruce Bellingham, guitar; and Florie Brown (of Golden Bough), violin. *Audience Adventure Boogie. Dear Averill* (Bellingham) March. *Fishin' Hole* (Hagen/Spencer)/*Dark Star* (Hunter/Grateful Dead). With Henry Kaiser and Bruce Anderson, guitars; Hilary Hanes, bass; John Hanes, drums; and Cary Sheldon, vocals. *Good, Bad, and Irradiated* Sketch (Thomson). *Deck us All with Boston Charley* Singalong.

December 15. San Francisco, California. Slim's (Yamaha/439 plus 50 comps). First Set – Piano solo. *Long, Long Time (?)/Hesitation Blues* (Davis). *Magnetic Rag* (Joplin). *Chiclets* (Ryan). *Bagatelle, Op. 126 #4* (Beethoven). *Dejavalse. Moonshadow* (Stevens). *Etude #25* (Chopin). *Chopped Liver* (Ryan). *The Ballad of Shane Muscatell. Dispeptically Skeptically Blue. Any Face Card Beats a '10'. I am Waiting*

(Richard)/*I Need You* (Harrison). *Fantasy in C minor* (J. S. Bach). Second Set with the Henry Kaiser Band: Henry Kaiser and Bruce Anderson, guitars; Hilary Hanes, bass; John Hanes, drums; Cary Sheldon, vocals, and T.C., keyboards. (Hammond B-3 organ courtesy of Merl Saunders). *Dark Star* (Hunter/Grateful Dead).

December 17. San Francisco, California. KQED-FM: 'West Coast Weekend', with Sedge Thomson (Life on the Water/Steinway). *{The Weight* (The Band)/*Dejas. Fog Repellent* Sketch (Thomson). *Rewritten Carols - O Little Town of Bethlehem. Joy to the World. Wassail Song.* With Oakland Symphony Chorus, Joseph Liebling, director. *All This Night my Heart Rejoices* (Horatio Parker). *Urban Geographer* Intro/Outro. *Beauty and the Cowboy* (Bellingham). With Bruce Bellingham, Tim Eschliman, Frankie Lane, Paul Rogers, Dave Hurley, Jim Rothamel, Blake Richardson, Gregory Leroy Dewey, and Nancy Rumbel. *Audience Adventure Boogie.* With Jim Rothamel. *What Child is This?* (Carol). *Rockabilly Promenade. Gift Ideas for Musicians.*

December 17. San Francisco, California. Eureka Theatre. 'Pulp Playhouse': (Kohler and Campbell). Holiday Magick. Pianist for evening of Improv with actors: Brian Lohmann, Micheal McShane, Barbara Scott, Regina Saisi, Reed Kirk Rahlmann, O-lan Jones, and Rafe Chase.

December 24. San Francisco, California. KQED-FM: 'West Coast Weekend', with Sedge Thomson (Life on the Water/Steinway). *{Chipmunks' Xmas (?)/Dejas/Angels We Have Heard on High. Fog Repellent* Sketch (Thomson) – *Three Kings* allusion. *Etude in E♭ Minor* (J. B. Cramer). *Dear Averill* (Bellingham) March. *Ennui* (Bellingham). *Auld Land Syne* Bed. *Beauty and the Cowboy* (Bellingham). With Bruce Bellingham, Tim Fox, and Jim Rothamel. *Audience Adventure Boogie.* With Jim Rothamel. *Wind in the Willows* – reading by Sedge Thomson: *O Kinderlein Kommet* (Schultz)/*The Friendly Beasts* (Medieval French carol). *Rise up Shepherd* (Traditional spiritual). *Good, Bad, and Irradiated* Sketch (Thomson).

December 31. San Francisco, California. KQED-FM: 'West Coast Weekend', with Sedge Thomson (Life on the Water/Steinway). *{Auld Lang Syne* (Traditional)/*Dejavalse/Dejas. Fog Repellent* (Thomson) Sting. *Urban Geographer* Intro/Outro. *Audience Adventure Boogie. Fax Machine* Spot

218                                      BETWEEN ROCK AND HARD PLACES

(Varon). With Charlie Varon and Sedge
Thomson. *Rockabilly Promenade. Good, Bad,
and Irradiated* Sketch (Thomson)

## 1989

January 1. Las Vegas, Nevada. Terry Ryan
Studio. (Yamaha pf-85). 'Fresh Tracks in
Real Time.' Terry Ryan, producer/engi-
neer. *Claude Greenberg's Springtime Catch.*
January 2. *Dark Star* (Hunter/Grateful
Dead). January 4. *Quanto sia liet' il giorno*
(Verdelot). January 5. *Metastrophe.*
January 7. San Francisco, California. KQED-
FM: 'West Coast Weekend', with Sedge
Thomson (Life on the Water/Steinway).
*{What's New* (?)/*Dejas. Fog Repellent*
(Thomson) Sting. *Day Care* (Thomson) Tag.
*Dear Averill* (Bellingham) March. *Rockabilly
Promenade. Danse de Travers #2* (Satie). *A
Quiet Week in New York* (Varon) Tag. With
Charlie Varon and Sedge Thomson. *Audi-
ence Adventure Boogie.* With Bruce
Bellingham. *Je t'aime, moi non plus* (Gains-
bourg/Birkin). *Good, Bad, and Irradiated*
Sketch (Thomson). *Rialto Ripples*
(Gershwin/Donaldson *via* Kovacs). *Sonata
in G minor, L. 390* (Scarlatti).
January 14. San Francisco, California. KQED-
FM: 'West Coast Weekend', with Sedge
Thomson (Life on the Water/Steinway).
*{Never on Sunday* (?)/*Dejas. Fog Repellent*
(Thomson) Sting. *American Beauty* (Lamb).
*Rockabilly Promenade. Audience Adventure
Boogie.* With Bruce Bellingham. *Good, Bad,
and Irradiated* Sketch (Thomson).
January 20. San Francisco, California. Com-
munity Music Center (Duo-Art). Encore:
*Dejavalse.* With Shirley Wong, harpsichord
(Herbert Wm. Burton), and Betty Wong,
piano (Steinway).
January 21. San Francisco, California. KQED-
FM: 'West Coast Weekend', with Sedge
Thomson (Life on the Water/Steinway).
Rebroadcast of October 8, 1988 show.
January 22. Santa Monica, California.
McCabe's Guitar Shop (Kawai upright/
165/36-50). Piano solo: *That Hand Played
Rag* (Silverman/Ward)/*Hesitation Blues*
(Davis). *Tabby Cat Walk* (Bolcom). *Minstrels*
(Debussy). *Quanto sia liet' il giorno*
(Verdelot). *Chiclets* (Ryan). *Dejavalse. Pine
Apple Rag* (Joplin). *Etude #25* (Chopin). *Any
Face Card Beats a '10'. American Beauty*
(Lamb). *Oriental (Spanish Dance #2)*
(Granados). *San Andreas Stomp* (T.S.C. #5).
With the Henry Kaiser Band: Henry Kaiser
and Scott Colby, guitars; Rick Crawford,

bass; Mark McQuade-Crawford, drums;
and T.C., keyboards: *Mystery Train* (Junior
Parker). *Dark Star* (Hunter/Grateful Dead).
*Goodbye to Love* (Carpenter). Second solo
piano set: *Long, Long Time* (?). *Rose Leaf Rag*
(Joplin). *Chiclets* (Ryan). *Dejavalse.
Nachtstück, Op. 23 #4* (Schumann). *Green
and Gold Take the Cakewalk* (T.S.C. #4). With
the Henry Kaiser Band: *What's Become of the
Baby* (Hunter/Garcia). *Dark Star* (Hunter/
Grateful Dead).
January 28. San Francisco, California. KQED-
FM: 'West Coast Weekend', with Sedge
Thomson (Life on the Water/Steinway).
*{When you wish upon a star* (?)/*Bush Sketch*
(Thomson). *{Hail to the Chief/Mickey Mouse
Club/Dejas. Fog Repellent* (Thomson) Sting.
*Oriental (Spanish Dance #2)* (Granados).
*Existential News Gatherers* (Thomson/
Bellingham) Outro. *Urban Geographer* Intro/
Outro. *Beauty and the Cowboy* (Bellingham).
With Bruce Bellingham and Tim Fox. *Audi-
ence Adventure Boogie.* With Bruce Bel-
lingham. *Rockabilly Promenade. Good, Bad,
and Irradiated* Sketch (Thomson).
February 4. San Francisco, California. KQED-
FM: 'West Coast Weekend', with Sedge
Thomson (Life on the Water/Steinway).
*{Let it Snow* (?)/*Dejas. Desserts that are chores
to eat* (Thomson) Tag. *Chiclets* (Ryan). *Secre-
tary of Kindness and Gentility* (Varon) Intro/
Outro. With Charlie Varon and Sedge
Thomson. *Dear Averill* (Bellingham) March.
*Beauty and the Cowboy* (Bellingham). With
Tony Marcus, Piper Heisig, Bruce Bel-
lingham, and Tim Fox. *Audience Adventure
Boogie. Ennui* (Bellingham). *City Ice* Sketch
(Thomson) In/Out/During.
February 11. San Francisco, California. KQED-
FM: 'West Coast Weekend', With Sedge
Thomson (Life on the Water/Steinway).
*Investment in Ideas. {Turn on your Lovelight/
Dejas. Fog Repellent* (Thomson) Sting. *Avalon*
(Jolson/Rose). *Rockabilly Promenade. Je
t'aime, moi non plus* (Gainsbourg/Birkin).
*City Ice* Sketch (Thomson) In/Out/During.
*Air in the Cherokee* (Clementi).
February 12. San Francisco, California. Great
American Music Hall (Baldwin/174 plus
20). Piano solo: *St. Stephen* (Hunter/Garcia)/
*A Day in the Life* (Lennon/McCartney).
*Corrente in A* (J. S. Bach). *Chiclets* (Ryan).
*Pine Apple Rag* (Joplin). *A Waltz for Evelyn
Hinrichsen* (Lou Harrison). *Dejavalse. Any
Face Card Beats a '10'. Etude #25* (Chopin).
*American Beauty Rag* (Lamb). *San Andreas
Stomp* (T.S.C. #5). With the Henry Kaiser

Band: Henry Kaiser and Bruce Anderson, guitars; Hilary Hanes, bass; John Hanes, drums; Cary Sheldon, vocals, and T.C., keyboards: *Mountains of the Moon* (Hunter / Garcia). *The Ballad of Shane Muscatell*. T.C., vocal. *Kind and Gentle Life* (?). *Dark Star* (Hunter / Grateful Dead). *Ode to Billy Joe* (Gentry). *Madness of Love* (Thompson). *That's it for the Other One* (Weir / Kreutzmann). *Liberty Valance* (Bacharach / David).

February 18. San Francisco, California. KQED-FM: 'West Coast Weekend', with Sedge Thomson (Life on the Water / Steinway). *(Dock of the Bay* (Redding) / *Dejas. Veep Sketch* (Thomson) Tag *(Second Hand Rose). 27 Grain Bread* (Thomson) Flourishes. *Courante in A* (J. S. Bach). *Bookstore Sketch* (Thomson) Tag *(My Romance). Urban Geographer* Intro / Outro. *Audience Adventure Boogie*. With Bruce Bellingham. *Dear Averill* (Bellingham) March. *Rockabilly Promenade. City Ice* Sketch (Thomson) In / Out / During.

February 25. San Francisco, California. KQED-FM: 'West Coast Weekend', with Sedge Thomson (Life on the Water / Steinway). *(Rain* (Lennon / McCartney) / *Dejas. Rain/Fog* Sketch (Thomson) Tags. *Romanian Dance #1* (Bartók). *Fog Repellent* (Thomson) Sting. *Romanian Dances # s 2 and 3* (Bartók). *City Ice* Sketch (Thomson) In / Out / During. *Urban Geographer* Intro / Outro. *Audience Adventure Boogie*. With Bruce Bellingham and the. Turtle Island String Quartet: David Balakrishnan and Darol Anger, violins; Irene Sazar, viola; and Mark Sommer, 'cello. *Dear Averill* (Bellingham) March. *Good, Bad, and Irradiated* Sketch (Thomson).

March. Nationwide. *Dead Head Television*. Show #10. Video of Henry Kaiser Band at Slim's December 15, 1988.

March 4. San Francisco, California. KQED-FM: 'West Coast Weekend', with Sedge Thomson (Life on the Water / Steinway). *(Springtime for Hitler* (?) / *Dejas. Russian Rag* (Cobb). With Jeremy Cohen, violin. *Cellular Therapy* (Thomson) Tag. *Rockabilly Promenade. Urban Geographer* Intro / Outro. *Dear Averill* (Bellingham) March. *Beauty and the Cowboy* (Bellingham). With Bruce Bellingham and Jeremy Cohen. *Audience Adventure Boogie*. With Bruce Bellingham. *Good, Bad, and Irradiated* Sketch (Thomson). *Liebesfreud* (Kreisler). With Jeremy Cohen, violin.

March 11. San Francisco, California. KQED-FM: 'West Coast Weekend', with Sedge Thomson (Life on the Water / Steinway).

*(It's my Party* (?) / *Dejas. 27 Grain Bread* (Thomson) Tag. *Fog Repellent* (Thomson) Sting. *Wildflowers* (Kallick). *Urban Geographer* Intro / Outro. *Beauty and the Cowboy* (Bellingham). With Bruce Bellingham and Tim Fox. *Audience Adventure Boogie*. With Bruce Bellingham. *City Ice* Sketch (Thomson) In / Out / During. *Rockabilly Promenade. Dear Averill* (Bellingham) March.

March 18. San Francisco, California. KQED-FM: 'West Coast Weekend', with Sedge Thomson (Life on the Water / Steinway). *(The Patriot Game* (?) / *Dejas. 27 Grain Bread* (Thomson) Tag. *Je t'aime, moi non plus* (Gainsbourg / Birkin). *Dr. Tinkleberry's Safe Fruit Experiment* (Varon) Tag *(Apple Tree)*. With Charlie Varon and Sedge Thomson. *Rusty Bells* (?). With Queen Esther Morrow, vocalist. *Urban Geographer* Intro / Outro. *City Ice* Sketch (Thomson) In / Out / During. *Beauty and the Cowboy*. With Bruce Bellingham and the Modern Mandolin Quartet. *Audience Adventure Boogie*. With Bruce Bellingham. *Good, Bad, and Irradiated* Sketch (Thomson). *Fantasy in C minor* (J. S. Bach). *Rockabilly Promenade*.

March 25. San Francisco, California. KQED-FM: 'West Coast Weekend', with Sedge Thomson (Life on the Water / Steinway). *(Early Morning Rain* (?) / *Dejas. Baldwin's Easter Egg* (Thomson) Tag. *Sugar Cane* (Joplin). *Rockabilly Promenade. Urban Geographer* Intro / Outro. *Beauty and the Cowboy*. With Bruce Bellingham, Peppino d'Agostino, and Tim Fox. *Audience Adventure Boogie*. With Bruce Bellingham and Peppino d'Agostino. *Good, Bad, and Irradiated* Sketch (Thomson).

March 30. Davis, California. The Palms (Hamilton / 126). Piano solo: *Modern Love Waltz* (Glass). *Hesitation Blues* (Davis). *Chiclets* (Ryan). *Quanto sia liet' il giorno* (Verdelot). *Minstrels* (Debussy). *Chopped Liver* (Ryan). *Dejavalse. Sugar Cane* (Joplin). *Etude, Op. 25 #9* (Chopin). *Etude, Op. 25 #9* (Chopin), ragged. First Set with the Henry Kaiser Band: Henry Kaiser and Bruce Anderson, guitars; Hilary Hanes, bass; John Hanes, drums; Cary Sheldon, vocals, and T.C., keyboards. *Play with Fire* (Jagger / Richard). *Fishin' Hole* (Sloane / Hagen / Spencer). *Don't let a Thief Steal into your Heart* (Thompson). *The Ballad of Shane Muscatell*. T.C., vocal. *Ode to Billy Joe* (Gentry). *Dark Star* (Hunter / Grateful Dead). *People Don't Change* (Anderson) / *River's Edge* (Anderson). Second Set with the Henry Kaiser Band. *Mountains of the Moon* (Hunter / Garcia).

*Madness of Love* (Thompson)/*The Other One* (Hunter/Weir/Garcia). *Liberty Valance* (Bacharach/David). *Mr. McGuffin* (?). *I'm so Glad* (?).

April 1. San Francisco, California. KQED-FM: 'West Coast Weekend', with Sedge Thomson (Life on the Water/Steinway). *Dejaboogie. Taxman* (Beatles) Tag. *Dear Averill* (Bellingham) March. *Brindisi Rag. BBC Baseball* (Varon) Intro/Outro. With Charlie Varon and Sedge Thomson. *Audience Adventure Boogie*. With Bruce Bellingham and Henry Kaiser. *Devil in the Drain* (Pinkwater/Kaiser). With Henry Kaiser. *Play with Fire* (Jagger/Richard). With Henry Kaiser. *Rockabilly Promenade. Good, Bad, and Irradiated* Sketch (Thomson).

April 8. San Francisco, California. KQED-FM: 'West Coast Weekend', with Sedge Thomson (Life on the Water/Steinway). *{Havin' a Heat Wave* (?)/*Dejas. On we Go* (Thomson) Tag. *Etude, Op. 25 #9* (Chopin). *Urban Geographer Intro/Outro. Dear Averill* (Bellingham) March. *Guantanamera* Bridge. *Beauty and the Cowboy* (Bellingham). With Bruce Bellingham and Alasdair Fraser, violin. *Audience Adventure Boogie*. With Bruce Bellingham and Alasdair Fraser, violin. *Rockabilly Promenade. Focaccia Man* Sketch (Thomson).

April 10. San Francisco, California. Möbius Studio (Yamaha). Oliver DiCicco, engineer. With the Henry Kaiser Band: Henry Kaiser and Bruce Anderson, guitars; Hilary Hanes, bass; John Hanes, drums; Cary Sheldon, vocals; and T.C., keyboards. *Play with Fire* (Jagger/Richard). Bruce Anderson, vocal. *Tell Me* (Jagger/Richard). Cary Sheldon, vocal.

April 14. Berkeley, California. Berkeley Square. (DX7-Roland courtesy of Henry Kaiser/150 plus 46). With the Henry Kaiser Band: Henry Kaiser and Bruce Anderson, guitars; Hilary Hanes, bass; John Hanes, drums; T.C., keyboards; and Cary Sheldon, vocals. *Fishin' Hole* (Sloane/Hagen/Spencer). *Play with Fire* (Jagger/Richard). *Don't let a Thief Steal into your Heart* (Thompson). *Ode to Billy Joe* (Gentry)/*The Other One* (Hunter/Weir/Garcia)./*Liberty Valance* (Bacharach/David)/*River's Edge* (Anderson). *Tell Me* (Jagger/Richard). *Dark Star* (Hunter/Grateful Dead)/*Madness of Love* (Thompson)./*Cryin' in your Beer* (Anderson). *The Ballad of Shane Muscatell*. T.C., vocal. *Loner* (Young). Encore: *People Don't Change* (Anderson).

April 15. San Francisco, California. KQED-FM: 'West Coast Weekend', with Sedge Thomson (Life on the Water/Steinway). *{Come Saturday Morning* (Previn)/*Dejas. Fog Repellent* (Thomson) Tags. *Overture, The Affair of Rue de Lourcine. E Blues.* With Bruce Bellingham and Wayne Doba. *Off the Wall Street Travel* (Thomson) Tags. *Je t'aime, moi non plus* (Gainsbourg/Birkin). *City Ice* Sketch (Thomson) In/Out/During. *Dear Averill* (Bellingham) March. *Beauty and the Cowboy* (Bellingham). With Bruce Bellingham, Jeremy Cohen, and Don Burnham. *Audience Adventure Boogie*. With Bruce Bellingham, Jeremy Cohen, and Don Burnham. *Pine Apple Rag* (Joplin) – first half. *Good, Bad and Irradiated* Sketch (Thomson).

April 15. San Francisco, California. Fillmore Auditorium (Sherman Clay/c. 1300). Piano solo: *Cold Rain and Snow* (Obray Ramsey *via* McGanahan Skjellyfetti). *Sugar Cane* (Joplin). *Modern Love Waltz* (Glass). *Dejavalse. Chiclets* (Ryan). *Nr. 2 Klavierstück III* (Stockhausen). *Overture, The Affair of Rue de Lourcine. Holiday for Strings* (Rose). *Chopped Liver* (Ryan). *San Andreas Stomp* (T.S.C. #5). With the Henry Kaiser Band: Henry Kaiser and Bruce Anderson, guitars; Hilary Hanes, bass; John Hanes, drums; Cary Sheldon, vocals, and T.C., keyboards: *Fishin' Hole* (Sloane/Hagen/Spencer). *Don't let a Thief Steal into your Heart* (Thompson). *Dark Star* (Hunter/Grateful Dead)/*Play With Fire* (Jagger/Richard)./*Liberty Valance* (Bacharach/David). *Tell Me* (Jagger/Richard). *Loner* (Young). Encore: *Ode to Billy Joe* (Gentry).

April 22. San Francisco, California. KQED-FM: 'West Coast Weekend', with Sedge Thomson (Life on the Water/Steinway). *{I never promised you a rose garden* (?)/*Dejas. Intermezzo inebriato, The Affair of Rue de Lourcine. Focaccia Man* (Thomson) Intro/Outro. *Beauty and the Cowboy* (Bellingham). With Bruce Bellingham, and Will Volker, harpsichord. *Audience Adventure Boogie*. With Bruce Bellingham. *Rockabilly Promenade*.

April 29. San Francisco, California. KQED-FM: 'West Coast Weekend', with Sedge Thomson (Life on the Water/Steinway). *{Voices of Spring* (Strauss)/*Dejas. Reality Adjustment* Sketch (Thomson)(*Farewell to Stromness* -Davies). *Modern Love Waltz* (Glass). *Rockabilly Promenade. Audience Adventure Boogie*. With Bruce Bellingham.

Nachklangstudie, Op. 16 #4 (Hauer). Lost Penny Boogie (after Beethoven).
May 6. San Francisco, California. KQED-FM: 'West Coast Weekend', with Sedge Thomson (Life on the Water/Steinway). {Cielito Lindo (?)/Dejas. There's no answer (Thomson) Tag (All alone by the telephone). Diabelli theme. Urban Geographer Intro/Outro(Green Door). Audience Adventure Boogie. With Bruce Bellingham. Je t'aime, moi non plus (Gainsbourg/Birkin). Dear Averill (Bellingham) March. Ennui (Bellingham).
May 13. San Francisco, California. KQED-FM: 'West Coast Weekend', with Sedge Thomson (Life on the Water/Steinway). {Motherly Love (Zappa)/Dejas. Desktop Mother's Day (Thomson): 1ᵉʳ Arabesque – (Debussy)/Fog Repellent (Thomson) Sting. Urban Geographer Intro/Outro. Audience Adventure Boogie. With Bruce Bellingham. Notes From the Coast (Thomson) Tag (Allemande – Bach). Dear Averill (Bellingham) March. Good, Bad, and Irradiated (Thomson).
May 20. San Francisco, California. KQED-FM: 'West Coast Weekend', with Sedge Thomson (Life on the Water/Steinway). {The Entertainer (Joplin)/Dejas. Health and Safety Tips Sketch (Thomson/Fox). (Farewell to Stromness-Davies). Urban Geographer Intro/Outro. Andante con Variazioni, Op. 3 #4 (Weber). Piano four hands, with Elisabeth Ingham. Beauty and the Cowboy (Bellingham). With Bruce Bellingham and the. Turtle Island String Quartet: David Balakrishnan and Darol Anger, violins; Irene Sazar, viola; and Mark Sommer, 'cello. Audience Adventure Boogie. With Bruce Bellingham and Irene Sazer. Sedge Thomson/Terry Gross Interview. Fresh Air Intro/Outro. Rockabilly Promenade. Waltz in memoriam Maurice Ravel (Moran).
May 27. San Francisco, California. KQED-FM: 'West Coast Weekend', with Sedge Thomson (Life on the Water/Steinway). {Minstrel Boy (?)/Dejas. Health Tips Sketch (Thomson). Fog Repellent (Thomson) Sting. Urban Geographer Intro/Outro. City Ice Sketch (Thomson) In/Out/During. Audience Adventure Boogie. With Bruce Bellingham and Irene Sazer. Eintritt (Waldszenen, Op. 82 #1) (Schumann).
June 3. San Francisco, California. KQED-FM: 'West Coast Weekend', with Sedge Thomson (Life on the Water/Steinway). {One-two-three (?)/Dejas. Richard Brautigan Poems read by Sedge Thomson: Promenade/

The Old Castle (Musorgski). Fog Repellent (Thomson) Volga Sting. Opening Titles Theme, Saragossa Manuscript (Penderecki). Urban Geographer Intro/Outro. Rockabilly Promenade. City Ice Sketch (Thomson) In/Out/During. Audience Adventure Boogie. With Bruce Bellingham. Wildflowers (Kallick). Dear Averill (Bellingham) March. Je t'aime, moi non plus (Gainsbourg/Birkin). FoccacciaMan (Thomson).
June 10. San Francisco, California. KQED-FM: 'West Coast Weekend', with Sedge Thomson (Life on the Water/Steinway). {Windy (Association/Dejas. Fresno Water Tower (Saroyan) read by Sedge Thomson: June Barcarolle, Op. 37 #6 (Tchaikovsky). Unknown Facts (T. Fox) Country Gardens Bed. Urban Geographer Intro/Outro. Do Lord Bridge. City Ice Sketch (Thomson) In/Out/During. Beauty and the Cowboy (Bellingham). With Bruce Bellingham, Jeremy Cohen, and John Imholtz. Audience Adventure Boogie. With Bruce Bellingham, Jeremy Cohen, and John Imholtz. Caprice, Op. 44 #12 (Sinding) into: Rockabilly Promenade. Dear Averill (Bellingham) March. Rialto Ripples (Gershwin/Donaldson via Kovacs).
June 17. San Francisco, California. KQED-FM: 'West Coast Weekend', with Sedge Thomson (Life on the Water/Steinway). {Summer in the City (?)/Dejas. Fog Repellent (Thomson) Sting. Urban Geographer Intro/Outro. Lingual Clarity League (Varon) – Forum Intro/Outro (Vad) into: I Wanna Hold Your Hand (Lennon/McCartney) into: Rockabilly Promenade. Song for my Father (Horace Silver). City Ice Sketch (Thomson) In/Out/During. Beauty and the Cowboy (Bellingham). With Bruce Bellingham. Audience Adventure Boogie. With Bruce Bellingham. Dear Averill (Bellingham) March. 'Butterfly' Rag (Chopin à la Joplin).
June 24. San Francisco, California. KQED-FM: 'West Coast Weekend', with Sedge Thomson (Life on the Water/Steinway). {Summertime Blues (?)/Dejas. Sedge Thomson announcements. Weeping Willow (Joplin) Bed. Batfax Bed. Bambouzla (Schubert via Gottschalk). Urban Geographer Intro/Outro. City Ice Sketch (Thomson) In/Out/During. Beauty and the Cowboy (Bellingham). With Bruce Bellingham, Tim Fox, and Joe Miller. Audience Adventure Boogie. With Bruce Bellingham, Tim Fox, and Joe Miller. Molson Canadian (?) Theme. Dear Averill (Bellingham) March. Rockabilly Promenade. Good, Bad, and Irradiated (Thomson) Sketch. D

*Blues.* With Bruce Bellingham, Tim Fox, and Joe Miller.
July 1. San Jose, California. KQED-FM: 'West Coast Weekend', with Sedge Thomson. (Mirassou Vineyards/Sherman Clay). Rebroadcast of July 2, 1988 show.
July 6. Berkeley, The Ashkenaz (150 plus 46). California. (DX7-Roland courtesy of Henry Kaiser). With the Henry Kaiser Band: Henry Kaiser and Bruce Anderson, guitars; Hilary Hanes, bass; John Hanes, drums; Cary Sheldon, vocals, and T.C., keyboards. First Set: *Loner* (Young). *Fishin' Hole* (Sloane/Hagen/Spencer). *Cryin' in your Beer* (Anderson). *Dancin' in the Streets* (Stevenson/Gaye/Hunter). *River's Edge* (Anderson). *Don't let a Thief Steal into Your Heart* (Thompson). *Leopard Skin Pillbox Hat* (Dylan). With Gary Lambert, bass and vocal. *Liberty Valance* (Bacharach/David). Second Set: *Folsom Prison Blues* (Cash). With Gary Lambert, bass and vocal. *Dark Star* (Hunter/Grateful Dead)/*The Other One* (Hunter/Weir/Garcia). *Puff the Magic Dragon* (Lenny Lipton)/*Tell me* (Jagger/Richard). *People Don't Change* (Anderson).
July 8. San Francisco, California. KQED-FM: 'West Coast Weekend', with Sedge Thomson (Life on the Water/Steinway). Rebroadcast of June 25, 1988 show.
July 8. San Francisco, California. KUSF-FM: 'Whole Earth Miscellaneous Music Show.' via tape. Interview with recorded music examples with David Reffkin.
July 15. San Francisco, California. KQED-FM: 'West Coast Weekend', with Sedge Thomson (Life on the Water/Steinway). Rebroadcast of June 18, 1988 show.
July 22. San Francisco, California. KQED-FM: 'West Coast Weekend', with Sedge Thomson (Life on the Water/Steinway). Rebroadcast of July 23, 1988 show.
July 24. Berkeley, California. KPFA-FM: *The Morning Concert.* Guest Host/Programmer with Russ Jennings.
July 29. San Francisco, California. KQED-FM: 'West Coast Weekend', With Sedge Thomson (Life on the Water/Steinway). Rebroadcast of March 11, 1989 show.
August 5. San Francisco, California. KQED-FM: 'West Coast Weekend', With Sedge Thomson (Life on the Water/Steinway). Rebroadcast of August 20, 1988 show.
August 12. San Francisco, California. KQED-FM: 'West Coast Weekend', with Sedge Thomson (Life on the Water/Steinway). Rebroadcast of September 3, 1988 show.

August 19. San Francisco, California. KQED-FM: 'West Coast Weekend', with Sedge Thomson (Life on the Water/Steinway). Rebroadcast of October 8, 1988 show.
August 26. San Francisco, California. KQED-FM: 'West Coast Weekend', with Sedge Thomson (Life on the Water/Steinway). Rebroadcast of May 20, 1989 show.
September 2. San Francisco, California. KQED-FM: 'West Coast Weekend', with Sedge Thomson (Life on the Water/Steinway). *{Hello, Stranger (Seems like a mighty long time)* (?)/*Dejas. Rum and Coca Cola* (?) Waltz/Vamp. *Nice Work in you can get it* (Gershwin/Gershwin) Tag. *Rockin' Promenade. City Ice* Sketch (Thomson) In/Out/During. *Space Medley: Science Fiction Theatre* Theme (?)/*Hey, Mr. Spaceman* (Byrds)/*Rocket Man* (Elton John)/*2000 Light Years from Home* (Jagger/Richard). *Audience Adventure Boogie.* With Bruce Bellingham, Tim Fox, and Joe Miller. *Popeye the Sailor* Tag. *Je t'aime, moi non plus* (Gainsbourg/Birkin). *Summer Tabloid Gulch* Tag. *Dear Averill* (Bellingham) March. *Green Piece* Intro/Outro.
September 9. San Francisco, California. KQED-FM: 'West Coast Weekend', with Sedge Thomson (Life on the Water/Steinway). *{The Times, they are a-changin'/Dejas. Italic Speaking Sketch* Sting. *City Ice Promo* Intro/Outro. *Dear Averill* (Bellingham) March. *Beauty and the Cowboy* (Bellingham). With Bruce Bellingham, Dan Hicks, Brian Godchaux, Paul Mehling, and Joe Preussner. *Audience Adventure Boogie.* With Bruce Bellingham. *Bruce's Aging Spot (Silver Threads/Grandfather's Clock). Kodine* (Ste.-Marie).
September 16. San Francisco, California. KQED-FM: 'West Coast Weekend', with Sedge Thomson (Life on the Water/Steinway). *{What'll I do* (?)/*Dejas. Prelude, Op. 32 #1* (Rachmaninoff). *City Ice Promo* Intro/Outro. *Klavierstück, Op. 19 #5* (Schönberg). Tim Ferris – *Star Trek* Outro. *Rockin' Promenade. City Ice* Sketch (Thomson) In/Out/During. *Beauty and the Cowboy* (Bellingham). With Bruce Bellingham; Eric and Suzy Thompson. *Audience Adventure Boogie.* With Bruce Bellingham. *Boris the Spider* (Entwistle). *Green Piece* Intro/Outro. *Dear Averill* (Bellingham) March.
September 23. San Francisco, California. KQED-FM: 'West Coast Weekend', with Sedge Thomson (Life on the Water/Steinway). *{She's a Rainbow* (Jagger/

Richards)/*Dejas. Saragossa Manuscript –
Opening Titles* (Penderecki). *White Noise*
(Don Delillo) – read by Sedge Thomson:
*Prelude, Op. 28 #15 (Raindrops)* (Chopin).
*That There Old West...* (T.S.C. #2). *Flying*
(Lennon/McCartney). *Urban Geographer*
Intro/Outro. *City Ice* Sketch (Thomson) In/
Out/During. *Beauty and the Cowboy*
(Bellingham). With Bruce Bellingham; Mitzi
Johnson, lute; and John Loose, percussion
(from Blue Rubies). *Audience Adventure
Boogie.* With Bruce Bellingham. *Rockin'
Promenade. Dear Averill* (Bellingham) March.
*Personal Ads* Tag. *Mother Teresa Incident*
(Bellingham) Tag.
September 30. San Francisco, California.
KQED-FM: 'West Coast Weekend', with
Sedge Thomson (Life on the Water/
Steinway). National Public Radio Pilot.
Margaret Moos Pick, Consulting Producer.
{*This Land is Your Land* (Guthrie)/*Dejas*. With
the Klezmorim. *Gianetics* (Varon) Bed. *Fly-
ing* (Lennon/McCartney). *Urban Geographer*
Intro/Outro. *BBC World News* (Varon).
*Beauty and the Cowboy* (Bellingham). With
Bruce Bellingham and Paul Hanson, clari-
net. *Audience Adventure Boogie.* With Bruce
Bellingham. *Rockin' Promenade. Whiter Shade
of Pale* (Procol Harum). *Dear Averill*
(Bellingham) March. *City Ice* Sketch
(Thomson) In/Out/During. *Goin' Home*
(Jagger/Richards).
October 7. San Francisco, California. KQED-
FM: 'West Coast Weekend', with Sedge
Thomson (Life on the Water/Steinway).
National Public Radio Pilot. Margaret Moos
Pick, Consulting Producer. {*Charley Brown/
Dejas*. With Turtle Island String Quartet:
David Balakrishnan and Darol Anger, vio-
lins; Katrina Wreede, viola; and Mark Sum-
mer, 'cello. *Dear Averill* (Bellingham) March.
*Urban Geographer* Intro/Outro. *BBC World
News* (Varon). *Beauty and the Cowboy*
(Bellingham). With Bruce Bellingham and
the Turtle Island String Quartet. *Audience
Adventure Boogie.* With Bruce Bellingham.
*Rockin' Promenade. Bad Moon Rising*
(Fogerty). *City Ice* Sketch (Thomson) In/
Out/During. *Quant je parti de m'amie* (Mont-
pelier Codex) Bed. *Dr. Upshaw* Sketch
(Varon) Intro/Outro. *Green Piece* Intro/
Outro. *Happy Together* (Turtles). *Warm San
Francisco Night* (Burdon).
October 14. San Francisco, California. KQED-
FM: 'West Coast Weekend', with Sedge
Thomson (Life on the Water/Steinway).
{*Around the World* (Young)/*Dejas*. With Joan

Baez Band: Jamie Fox, guitar; Bob Babbitt,
bass; Steve McCray, keyboard; and Rick
Slosser, drums. *Dear Averill* (Bellingham)
March. *Rialto Ripples* (Gershwin/
Donaldson) Bridge. *Bullwinkle Tribute*
(Steiner). *Pine Apple Rag* (Joplin) Bridge.
*A's/Giants Piece* – Spoken. *Green and Gold*
(T.S.C. #4). *Quant je parti de m'amie* (Mont-
pelier Codex). *Chaucer Sportscast* (Varon)
Intro/Outro. *BBC World News* (Varon).
*Beauty and the Cowboy* (Bellingham). With
Bruce Bellingham and Joan Baez Band. *Au-
dience Adventure Boogie.* With Bruce
Bellingham. *Rockin' Promenade.*
October 21. San Francisco, California. KQED-
FM: 'West Coast Weekend', with Sedge
Thomson (KQED Master Control/Accord).
{*Help* (Beatles)/*Dejas. Rockin' Promenade. Half
a Minute Not a Waltz. Dead Language Insti-
tute* Sketch (Thomson) Intro/Outro. *Too
Much Razzberry* (Sydney Russell). *Art Talk*
Sketch (Thomson) Intro/Outro. *Urban Ge-
ographer* Intro/Outro. *Tim Fox Essay* Outro.
*City Ice* Sketch (Thomson) In/Out/During.
*Klavierstück, Op. 19 #3* (Schönberg).
October 21. Davis, California. The Palms
(Roland Digital Piano RD-300s. Korg quasi
B-3 courtesy of Henry Kaiser/134). *Heart's
Desire.* Live Album Recording. Robert
Shumaker and Oliver DiCicco, engineers.
With the Henry Kaiser Band: Henry Kaiser
and Bruce Anderson, guitars; Hilary Hanes,
bass; John Hanes, drums; Cary Sheldon,
vocals, and T.C., keyboards. First Set: *Lib-
erty Valance* (Bacharach/David). *Play with
Fire* (Jagger/Richard). *Fishin' Hole* (Sloane/
Hagen/Spencer). *King Harvest* (J. R.
Robertson). *Losin' Hand* (Calhoun). *Nr. 2
Klavierstück III* (Stockhausen) – Piano solo.
*The Ballad of Shane Muscatell. Cryin' in your
Beer* (Anderson). *Don't let a Thief Steal into
your Heart* (Thompson). Second Set: *Loner*
(Young). *San Andreas Stomp* (T.S.C. #5) –
Piano solo. *Anyone who had a heart*
(Bacharach/David). *Are You Experienced?*
(Hendrix). *Buried Treasure* (Hanes). *Dark
Star* (Hunter/Grateful Dead)/*River's Edge*
(Anderson). Encores: *Never Again* (Ander-
son). *Fishin' Hole* (Sloane/Hagen/Spencer).
October 22. Davis, California. The Palms (134/
Roland Digital Piano RD-300s. Korg quasi
B-3 courtesy of Henry Kaiser). *Heart's De-
sire.* Live Album Recording. Robert
Shumaker and Oliver DiCicco, engineers.
With the Henry Kaiser Band: Henry Kaiser
and Bruce Anderson, guitars; Hilary Hanes,
bass; John Hanes, drums; Cary Sheldon,

vocals, and T.C., keyboards. First Set: *Loner* (Young). *Ode to Billy Joe* (Gentry). *Cryin' in your Beer* (Anderson). *Anyone who had a Heart* (Bacharach/David). *Flavor Bud Living* (Van Vliet) – HK guitar solo. *Fishin' Hole* (Sloane/Hagen/Spencer). *Nr. 2 Klavierstück III* (Stockhausen) – Piano solo. *Dark Star* (Hunter/Grateful Dead) *River's Edge* (Anderson). Second Set: *King Harvest* (J. R. Robertson). *Buried Treasure* (Hanes). *Never Again* (Anderson). *The Ballad of Shane Muscatell. Don't let a Thief Steal into your Heart* (Thompson). *Losin' Hand* (Calhoun). *Are You Experienced?* (Hendrix). *San Andreas Stomp* (T.S.C. #5) – Piano solo. *Play with Fire* (Jagger/Richard). *Liberty Valance* (Bacharach/David).

October 28. San Francisco, California. KQED-FM: 'West Coast Weekend', with Sedge Thomson (Life on the Water/Steinway). *{San Francisco* (?)]/Dejas*. With Bruce Bellingham and Ian Whitcomb. *Need You* (Harrison). *Season of the Witch* (Leitch). With Bruce Bellingham. *Urban Geographer* Intro/Outro. *Dear Averill* (Bellingham) March. *Beauty and the Cowboy* (Bellingham). With Bruce Bellingham and Ian Whitcomb. *Audience Adventure Boogie*. With Bruce Bellingham and Ian Whitcomb. *Rockin' Promenade. City Ice* Sketch (Thomson) In/Out/During. *Klavierstück, Op. 19 #6* (Schönberg).

November 2. Berkeley, California. Bay Records (Yamaha). *Heart's Desire*. Touchups. Robert Shumaker, Engineer. *San Andreas Stomp* (T.S.C. #5). *Loner* (Young).

November 4. San Francisco, California. KQED-FM: 'West Coast Weekend', with Sedge Thomson (Life on the Water/Steinway). *{Bridge over Troubled Water* (Simon)/*Dejas*. With the Banana Slug String Band and Bruce Bellingham. Sedge Thomson Reading: *Weeping Willow* (Joplin). *Decomposition Breakdown Blues*. With the Banana Slug String Band and Bruce Bellingham. *I am Waiting* (Jagger/Richard). With Bruce Bellingham. *Nr. 2 Klavierstück III* (Stockhausen). *Quake Prevention* (Varon) Outro. *Rockin' Promenade. Beauty and the Cowboy* (Bellingham). With Bruce Bellingham and BSSB. *Audience Adventure Boogie*. With Bruce Bellingham. *Urban Geographer* Intro/Outro. *Rialto Ripples* (Gershwin/Donaldson *via* Kovacs). *City Ice* Sketch (Thomson) In/Out/During.

November 11. San Francisco, California. KQED-FM: 'West Coast Weekend', with

Sedge Thomson (Life on the Water/Steinway). Fall Membership Drive. *{Uncle John's Band (Are you Kind?)* (Hunter/Garcia)/*Dejas*.– with Union Station. *'Tis the Last Rose of Summer* (Moore arr. Mendelssohn). *Dear Averill* (Bellingham) March. *Rockin' Promenade. City Ice* Sketch (Thomson) In/Out/During. *That's a Plenty* (Gilbert/Pollack) – with Union Station. *Beauty and the Cowboy* (Bellingham) – with Bruce Bellingham and Union Station. *Audience Adventure Boogie*. With Bruce Bellingham and Union Station. *Urban Geographer* Intro/Outro. *Ode to Joy* (Beethoven arr. Liszt).

November 13. Nationwide. *The Grateful Dead Hour*, with David Gans. #60. via tape. Interview (taped July 14) with recorded music examples.

November 18. San Francisco, California. KQED-FM: 'West Coast Weekend', with Sedge Thomson (Life on the Water/Steinway). *{Bridge over the River Kwai* (?)/*Dejas*. With the I'll be Right Home, Honey Band: Joan Bassett, guitar; Rex Higginbotham, guitar; Bob Peterson, bass; Marty Reutiger, guitar; David Rice, mandolin, plus Bruce Bellingham, harmonica. *Ferry 'Cross the Mersey*. With Bruce Bellingham, guitar. *Green Piece* Intro/Outro. *To a Wild Rose, Op. 51 #1* (MacDowell). House Pianist Segment, with Sedge Thomson. *City Ice* Sketch (Thomson) In/Out/During. *Beauty and the Cowboy* (Bellingham). With Bruce Bellingham, Bob Peterson, and Marty Reutiger. *Audience Adventure Boogie*. With Bruce Bellingham. *Love is Blue* (Popp). *Urban Geographer* Intro/Outro.

November 25. San Francisco, California. KQED-FM: 'West Coast Weekend', with Sedge Thomson (Life on the Water/Steinway). *{Stealin'* (Traditional)/*Dejas*. *Lisbon Antigua* (?) Break. *Open Air Message* (Varon) Intro/Outro. *Bad, Bad, Leroy Brown* (Croce). With Bruce Bellingham. *Dear Averill* (Bellingham) March. *City Ice* Sketch (Thomson) In/Out/During. *BBC World News* (Varon). *Beauty and the Cowboy* (Bellingham). With Bruce Bellingham and Duck Baker. *Audience Adventure Boogie*. With Bruce Bellingham and Duck Baker. *Mellow Yellow* (Leitch). With Bruce Bellingham. *Urban Geographer* Intro/Outro. *Rialto Ripples* (Gershwin/Donaldson) Bridge.

December 1. San Francisco, California. Noe Valley Ministry (George Steck/65). 'Josh Duberman Celebration.' *Etude #25 in F mi-*

*nor* (Chopin). *Chiclets* (Ryan). *Pine Apple Rag* (Joplin). *La Cathédrale Engloutie* (Debussy). *Saragossa Manuscript Overture* (Penderecki). *San Andreas Stomp* (T.S.C. #5). *Weeping Willow* (Joplin). *Overture, the Affair of Rue de Lourcine. Sonata in E* (1776) (Haydn). *Dejavalse.* Encore: *Prelude, Op. 32 #1* (Rachmaninoff).

December 2. San Francisco, California. KQED-FM: 'West Coast Weekend', with Sedge Thomson (Life on the Water/Steinway). *{We didn't start the fire* (Joel)/*Dejas. All in the Game* (?). *Rockin' Promenade. Glory of Love* (?). With Claudia Schmidt. *Upshaw* Sketch (Varon) Intro/Outro. *City Ice* Sketch (Thomson) In/Out/During. *Beauty and the Cowboy* (Bellingham). With Bruce Bellingham. *Audience Adventure Boogie.* With Bruce Bellingham. *Urban Geographer* Intro/Outro.

December 9. San Francisco, California. KQED-FM: 'West Coast Weekend', with Sedge Thomson (Life on the Water/Steinway). *{Morning – Wm. Tell* (Rossini)/*Dejas. Runaway* (Shannon) Tango. *Concerto #4* (Beethoven) Opening. *Rialto Ripples* (Gershwin/Donaldson *via* Kovacs) Bridge. Anne Lamott Intro/Outro: *Can't get Indiana off my Mind* (Carmichael). *Dear Averill* (Bellingham) March. *City Ice* Sketch (Thomson) In/Out/During. *BBC World News* (Varon). *Beauty and the Cowboy* (Bellingham). With Bruce Bellingham and David Maloney. *Audience Adventure Boogie.* With Bruce Bellingham and David Maloney. *Singles in Crisis* (Fox). *Ferry 'Cross the Mersey* Bridge. *Rockin' Promenade. Warm San Francisco Night* Bridge.

December 9. San Francisco, California. Chi-Chi Club. (Roland Digital piano RD-300s. courtesy of George Michalski). Jessica Blue Sky's Benefit Bash. *Pine Apple Rag* (Joplin). *San Andreas Stomp* (T.S.C. #5). *Chiclets* (Ryan). *Need You* (Harrison). *Dejavalse. Prelude, Op. 32 #1* (Rachmaninoff). Encore: *Dark Star* (Hunter/Grateful Dead).

December 16. San Francisco, California. KQED-FM: 'West Coast Weekend', with Sedge Thomson (Life on the Water/Steinway). *{Winter Wonderland* (?)/*Dejas. O Tannenbaum* Sketch (Thomson) Intro/Outro. *Marche des Rois* (13th century Provençal carol). *City Ice* Sketch (Thomson) In/Out/During. *Beauty and the Cowboy* (Bellingham). With Bruce Bellingham, Eric Tingstad, and Nancy Rumbel. *Audience Adventure Boogie.* With Bruce Bellingham, Eric

Tingstad, and Nancy Rumbel. *Urban Geographer* Intro/Outro. *Singles in Crisis* (Fox) Intro/Outro. *Bus Stop* (Hollies).

December 23. San Francisco, California. KQED-FM: 'West Coast Weekend', with Sedge Thomson (Life on the Water/Steinway). *{Baby, It's Cold Outside* (?)/*Dejas.* With Bruce Bellingham and Xmas Jug Band. *Klez Frosty. The Devil's Trick* (Isaac Bashevis Singer) read by Sedge Thomson: *Birhos Hanuka. O Hanuka. Mi Y'malel.* With Jeremy Cohen, violin. *A Foggy Xmas* (Thomson). *Beauty and the Cowboy* (Bellingham). With Bruce Bellingham and Xmas Jug Band. *Audience Adventure Boogie.* With Bruce Bellingham and Xmas Jug Band. *Urban Geographer* Intro/Outro. *Electric Red Water Getaway.* With Jeremy Cohen, violin. Anne Lamott Intro/Outro. *Can't get Indiana off my Mind* (Carmichael). *Romanza Andaluz* (Sarasate). With Jeremy Cohen, violin. *Dear Averill* (Bellingham) March. *Friend of the Devil* (Garcia/Dawson/Hunter).

December 29. San Francisco, California. Psychedelic Shop. (Roland Digital piano RD-300s. courtesy of George Michalski). First Set: *American Beauty* (Lamb). *Pastime #4* (Mathews). *Eli Green's Cake Walk* (Koninsky). *Weeping Willow* (Joplin). *Pine Apple Rag* (Joplin). *Pastime #5* (Mathews). *Magnetic Rag* (Joplin). *San Andreas Stomp* (T.S.C. #5). Second Set: *Chiclets* (Ryan). *Sister Kate* (Piron). *Etude #25 in F minor* (Chopin). *Rose Leaf Rag* (Joplin). *Dejavalse. Friend of the Devil* (Hunter/Dawson/Garcia). *Nachtstück, Op. 23 #4* (Schumann). *Eintritt (Waldszenen, Op. 82 #1)* (Schumann) excerpt. *Dark Star* (Hunter/Grateful Dead). *Etude in G# minor, Op. 25 #6* (Chopin). *Rondo (Sonata in E) - (1776)* (Haydn). Encore: *Dark Star* (Hunter/Grateful Dead).

December 30. San Francisco, California. KQED-FM: 'West Coast Weekend', with Sedge Thomson (Life on the Water/Steinway). *{There'll be some changes made* (?)/*Dejas.* segue to *On the Air,* performed by the Jesters. *Flintstones* (?). *Green Piece* Intro/Outro. *Rockin' Promenade. Singles in Crisis* (Fox). *All in the Game* (?). *Beauty and the Cowboy* (Bellingham). With Bruce Walker Bel- 1989lingham. *Audience Adventure Boogie.* With Bruce Bellingham. Leonard Pitt: *Stan Laurel Story* Outro. *Urban Geographer* Intro/Outro. *Dear Averill* (Bellingham) March.

# 1990

January 6. San Francisco, California. KQED-FM: 'West Coast Weekend', with Sedge Thomson (Life on the Water/Steinway). *{Für Elise* (Beethoven)/*Dejas* (in F). With Bruce Bellingham and Roy Rogers. *Nachklangstudie, Op. 16 #4* (Hauer) Bed. *Rockin' Promenade. C'est si bon* (?). *Urban Geographer* Intro/Outro. *BBC Update* (Varon) Outro. *Beauty and the Cowboy* (Bellingham). With Bruce Bellingham and Roy Rogers. *Audience Adventure Boogie.* With Bruce Bellingham. Anne Lamott Intro/Outro. *Dear Averill* (Bellingham) March.

January 12. Las Vegas, Nevada. Terry Ryan Studio. (Yamaha pf-85). *'OutSides.'* Terry Ryan, producer/engineer. *Prelude* (1963). *Overture, The Affair of Rue de Lourcine.* January 13. *Disco Cynic. Intermezzo Inebriato. In the Vineyards of Claudine. Let it Ring.*

January 13. San Francisco, California. KQED-FM: 'West Coast Weekend', With Sedge Thomson (Life on the Water/Steinway). Rebroadcast of September 2, 1989 show.

January 14. Las Vegas, Nevada. Terry Ryan Studio. (Yamaha pf-85). *'OutSides.'* Terry Ryan, producer/engineer. *Alaric's Premonition.*

January 20. San Francisco, California. KQED-FM: 'West Coast Weekend', with Sedge Thomson (Life on the Water/Steinway). Rebroadcast of September 9, 1989 show.

January 27. San Francisco, California. KQED-FM: 'West Coast Weekend', with Sedge Thomson (Life on the Water/Steinway). Rebroadcast of September 16, 1989 show.

January 30. San Francisco, California. Great American Music Hall (Baldwin/174 plus 20). Spoken Word. *Prelude, Op. 32 #1* (Rachmaninoff). *Boris the Spider* (Entwistle). *Dejavalse. All in the Game* (?). Accompaniment to readings by Robert Hunter. *Three Poems* (Hunter): *Herb. Judith* (Hunter): *Aria, Goldberg Variations* (J. S. Bach). *Portia* (Hunter): *Prelude in D♭, Op. 11 #15* (Scriabin). *Jazz* (Hunter): *Naugahide Schönberg. Tango Hit Palace* (Hunter): *Sympathy for the Tango. Full Moon Cafe* (Hunter): *Herb. Rain Water Sea* (Hunter): *Celtic Improvisation. Mountains of the Moon* (Hunter/Garcia). *Holigomena* (Hunter): *Sonata #9* opening (Scriabin). Encore: *Brass Axis* (Hunter): *Prelude in D♭, Op. 28 #15* (Chopin).

February 1. San Francisco, California. Last Day Saloon. (Roland digital piano RD-300s. courtesy of George Michalski). Night of the Living Piano. Solo set by George Michalski.

Solo set by T.C.: *Friend of the Devil* (Hunter/Dawson/Garcia). *Les Baricades Misterieuses* (Couperin). *Boris the Spider* (Entwistle). *All in the Game* (?). *Dejavalse. Apocryphal Awry. That There Old West...* (T.S.C. #2). *Whiter Shade of Pale* (Reid/Brooker). *Chiclets* (Ryan). *Dark Star* (Hunter/Grateful Dead). With George Michalski, piano four hands: *Dear Prudence* (Lennon/McCartney). *The Moon* (from *Tarot*)/*C Boogie. We Bid You Goodnight* (Traditional). Encore: With George Michalski. *C Boogie.*

February 3. San Francisco, California. KQED-FM: 'West Coast Weekend', with Sedge Thomson (Life on the Water/Steinway). Rebroadcast of September 23, 1989 show.

February 4. Las Vegas, Nevada. Terry Ryan Studio. (Yamaha pf-85). *'OutSides.'* Terry Ryan, producer/engineer. *Apocryphal Awry. Let it Ring.* February 5. *Encodex Punctilious. Rondo Pazzo.* February 6. *Alaric's Premonition. Ma Fin est mon Commencement* (Machaut). *Friend of the Devil* (Hunter/Dawson/Garcia). *Dark Star* (Hunter/Grateful Dead). *The Unspeakable Pact of Mohair Bubba and Slim Salabim. Post-expressionist Relief. V'loods.* February 10. *Rondo Pazzo.*

February 10. San Francisco, California. KQED-FM: 'West Coast Weekend', with Sedge Thomson (Life on the Water/Steinway). Rebroadcast of October 7, 1989 show.

February 11. Las Vegas, Nevada. Terry Ryan Studio. (Yamaha pf-85). *'OutSides.'* Terry Ryan, producer/engineer. *Dejavalse.*

February 17. San Francisco, California. KQED-FM: 'West Coast Weekend', with Sedge Thomson (Life on the Water/Steinway). Rebroadcast of October 14, 1989 show.

February 17. Berkeley, California. 'Grateful Dead Hour Marathon.' With David Gans and Gary Lambert. Interview with recorded examples.

February 24. San Francisco, California. KQED-FM: 'West Coast Weekend', with Sedge Thomson (Life on the Water/Steinway). *{Age of Aquarius* (Rado/Ragni/McDermott)/*Dejas. Can't Get Used to Losing You* (?). *I Am Waiting* (Jagger/Richard). *Feel the Earth* (King) *Bridge. Rockin' Promenade. BBC Update* (Varon) Outro. *Wet Dream* (Addotta). With Jeremy Cohen, violin; Dix Bruce, guitar; and Jim Kerwin, bass. *Audience Adventure Boogie. Singles in Crisis* (Fox) Intro/Outro. *Urban Geographer* Intro/Outro. *Apocryphal Awry.*

February 24. San Francisco, California. Private party. (Roland Digital piano RD-300s.

courtesy of George Michalski). *Friend of the Devil* (Garcia/Dawson/Hunter). *Can't Get Used to Losing You* (?). *Rialto Ripples* (Gershwin/Donaldson *via* Kovacs). *Dark Star* (Hunter/Grateful Dead). *Praeambulum, Partita #5* (J. S. Bach). *Dear Prudence* (Lennon/McCartney)/*C Boogie*. With George Michalski. *Alabama Bound* (Charlatans)/Two more Rock tunes. With Mike Wilhelm, Chris Berry, guitars; Don Graham, drums; and Mitchell Holman, bass.
March 3. San Francisco, California. KQED-FM: 'West Coast Weekend', with Sedge Thomson (Life on the Water/Steinway). *{There's no Business like Show Business* (?)/ *Dejas*. With Big Lou and Caroline Dahl. *Urban Geographer* Intro/Outro. *Urban Spaceman* (Bonzo Dog Band). *Audience Adventure Boogie. Green Piece* Intro/Outro. *Rockin' Promenade. Singles in Crisis* (Fox) Intro/ Outro. *Song of the Nairobi Trio* (Kovacs?).
March 10. San Francisco, California. KQED-FM: 'West Coast Weekend', with Sedge Thomson (Life on the Water/Steinway). *{It Might as well be Spring* (?)/*Dejas. Wildflowers* (Kallick). *White Room* (Cream). Alice Kahn reading Bed. *Urban Geographer* Intro/Outro. *City Ice* Sketch (Thomson) In/Out/During. *BBC Update* (Varon) Outro. *Euphoria.* With Eric and Suzy Thompson. *Audience Adventure Boogie.* Anne Lamott Intro/Outro. *Rockin' Promenade.*
March 17. San Francisco, California. KQED-FM: 'West Coast Weekend', with Sedge Thomson (Life on the Water/Steinway). *{When Irish Eyes are Smiling* (?)/*Dejas*. With Chaskinakuy: Edmond Badoux and Francy Vidal. *Audience Adventure Boogie. Sheebeg & Sheemore* (Carolan) Bridge. *Urban Geographer* Intro/Outro. *Sway Dance* (Cowell). *The Consolation of Philosophy* (Fox) Intro/Outro. *Audience Adventure Boogie.* Lane Nishikawa *Intermezzi. Rockin' Promenade. Etude, Op. 25 #6* (Chopin).
March 24. San Francisco, California. KQED-FM: 'West Coast Weekend', with Sedge Thomson (Life on the Water/Steinway). *{Here Comes the Sun* (Beatles)/*Dejas*. With Richard Savino and Sara Freiberg. Historic Tuning Comment. *Anything that you want* (Lennon/McCartney). *Don't Fence me in* Bridge. *Urban Geographer* Intro/Outro. *Whiter Shade of Pale* (Reid/Brooker). *Audience Adventure Boogie.* Anne Lamott Intro/ Outro. *Green Piece* Intro/Outro.
March 31. San Francisco, California. KQED-FM: 'West Coast Weekend', with Sedge

Thomson (Life on the Water/Steinway). *{Laugh, Laugh* (?)/*Dejas*. With Mitzi Johnson, lute. Cleanliness next to... Comment. *I Know I'll never Find Another You* (Seekers). *Dear Prudence* (Lennon/McCartney). With George Michalski. *City Ice* Sketch (Thomson) In/Out/During. *Mention my Name in Sheboygan* Tag. *BBC Update* (Varon) Outro. *Audience Adventure Boogie.* New Age/Space Bridge.
April 5. San Rafael, California. Fourth Street Tavern. (Roland digital piano RD-300s courtesy of George Michalski). Night of the Living Piano. Solo set by George Michalski. Solo set by T.C.: *Friend of the Devil* (Hunter/ Dawson/Garcia). *That Hand Played Rag* (Silverman/Ward). *Boris the Spider* (Entwistle). *Prelude in E♭, Op. 23 #6* (Rachmaninoff). *San Andreas Stomp* (T.S.C. #5). *Chiclets* (Ryan). *Dejavalse. Oriental (Spanish Dance #2)* (Granados). *Escorregando* (Nazareth). *That There Old West...*(T.S.C. #2). *Whiter Shade of Pale* (Reid/Brooker). *Etude, Op. 10 #11* (Chopin). Encore: *Dark Star* (Hunter/Grateful Dead). With George Michalski, piano four hands: *Dear Prudence* (Lennon/McCartney). *The Moon* (from *Tarot)/Me and My Uncle* (Phillips)/*G Boogie* – joined by Vince Wallace, saxophone. *We Bid You Goodnight* (Traditional). Encore: With George Michalski and Vince Wallace. *Nobody Wants You when You're Down and Out* (?).
April 7. San Francisco, California. KQED-FM: 'West Coast Weekend', with Sedge Thomson (Life on the Water/Steinway). Rebroadcast of December 30, 1989 show.
April 7. Bolinas, California. Bolinas Community Center. (Roland digital piano RD-300s. courtesy of George Michalski). Night of the Living Piano. Solo set by George Michalski. Solo set by T.C.: *Friend of the Devil* (Hunter/ Dawson/Garcia). *San Andreas Stomp* (T.S.C. #5). *La Cathédrale Engloutie* (Debussy). *Whiter Shade of Pale* (Reid/Brooker). *Overture, The Affair of Rue de Lourcine. Etude, Op. 10 #6* (Chopin). *Chiclets* (Ryan). *Dejavalse. Dark Star* (Hunter/Grateful Dead). *Oriental (Spanish Dance #2)* (Granados). *Prelude in E♭, Op. 23 #6* (Rachmaninoff). Encore: *That Hand Played Rag* (Silverman/Ward). With George Michalski, piano four hands: *Dear Prudence* (Lennon/McCartney). *Me and My Uncle* (Phillips). *The Moon* (from *Tarot)/G Boogie. We Bid You Goodnight* (Traditional). Encores: With George Michalski and Terry Dolan: *In-laws and Outlaws* (Dolan). With

George Michalski. *When the Power Goes* (Michalski).
April 8. San Francisco,California. Slim's. (Yamaha piano/Korg B-3 courtesy of Henry Kaiser). Henry Kaiser Band. Henry Kaiser and Bruce Anderson, guitars; Hilary Hanes, bass; John Hanes, drums; Cary Sheldon, vocals, and T.C., keyboards. First Set: *Tell Me* (Jagger/Richard). *California Dreamin'* (Phillips). *Play With Fire* (Jagger/Richard). *Anyone who had a Heart* (Bacharach/David). *Mr. Music* Sketch. *Four Systems* (Earle Brown). *Go Go Pogo* (Kelly). *It's a Lie* (Anderson). *Fishin' Hole* (Sloane/Hagen/Spencer). *Love's Made a Fool of You* (Holly). Second Set: *Cryin' in Your Beer* (Anderson). *Are You Experienced* (Hendrix). *Tijuana* (Cale). *Do What You Like* (Winwood). *The Other One* (Garcia/Hunter/Weir). *Liberty Valance* (Bacharach/David). *Loner* (Young). Encore: *Losin' Hand* (Calhoun).
April 14. San Francisco, California. KQED-FM: 'West Coast Weekend', with Sedge Thomson (Life on the Water/Steinway). *{Another Opening of Another Show* (?)*]/Dejas*. With Danny Kalb. *My Gal's a Corker* (Traditional). *Quake Prevention* Tag. *Urban Geographer* Intro/Outro. *Gorbachev (Leroy Brown)* (Croce) – with Bill Strauss of the Capitol Steps. *Rockin' Promenade*. *E Blues* – with Danny Kalb. *Audience Adventure Boogie. Just Like Tom Thumb's Blues* (Dylan).
April 21. San Francisco, California. KQED-FM: 'West Coast Weekend', with Sedge Thomson (Life on the Water/Steinway). Spring Pledge Festival. *{I'd Like to Teach the World to Sing* (?)*]/Dejas*. With Eric Tingstad, Nancy Rumbel, and Alex DeGrassi. *Mantra* Tag. *Rejected Fund Raising Concept #106 – Minimalist MacNeil-Lehrer*. *My Gal's a Corker* (Traditional). *Rejected Fund Raising Concept #17 – Oral Roberts* – spoken. *Rejected Fund Raising Concept #56* Bed. Anne Lamott Intro/Outro. *City Ice* Sketch (Thomson) In/Out/During. *Rejected Fund Raising Concept #67* Bed. *Rockin' Promenade. BBC News* (Varon) Outro. *Audience Adventure Boogie. Micheal McShane* Bed.
April 28. San Francisco, California. KQED-FM: 'West Coast Weekend', with Sedge Thomson (Life on the Water/Steinway). *{Swanee River à la Ed Norton/Dejas*. With California Klezmer Band. *New Wave Wimoweh*. Wayne Wang interview Intro/Outro. *Prelude in E♭, Op. 23 #6* (Rachmaninoff). *Rockin' Promenade. Census* Sketch (Fox) Intro/Outro. *Audience Adventure*

*Boogie*. Victoria Nelson Interview Intro/Outro. *Singles in Crisis – Jack, the Date from Hell* (Fox) Intro/Outro.
May 3. Berkeley, California. The Ashkenaz (DX-7 courtesy of Henry Kaiser). Henry Kaiser Band. Henry Kaiser and Bruce Anderson, guitars; Hilary Hanes, bass; John Hanes, drums; Cary Sheldon, vocals, and T.C., keyboards. *Play With Fire* (Jagger/Richard)*/Ode to Billy Joe* (Gentry). *Tell Me* (Jagger/Richard). *It's a Lie* (Anderson). *Liberty Valance* (Bacharach/David). *Don't Let a Thief Steal Into Your Heart* (Richard Thompson). *Tijuana* (Cale)*/California Dreamin'* (Phillips). *Never Again* (Anderson). *The Old Man of the Shells* (Kaiser) *Do What You Like* (Winwood). *The Other One* (Garcia/Hunter/Weir) *Love's Made a Fool of You* (Holly). *Loner* (Young). *Fishin' Hole* (Sloane/Hagen/Spencer) *Are You Experienced* (Hendrix). Encore: *Dark Star* (Hunter/Grateful Dead) *River's Edge* (Anderson).
May 5. San Francisco, California. KQED-FM: 'West Coast Weekend', with Sedge Thomson (Life on the Water/Steinway). *{Warm California Sun* (Beach Boys)*/Dejas*. With Turtle Island String Quartet: David Balakrishnan and Darol Anger, violins, Katrina Wreede, viola; and Mark Summer, 'cello. *Harlequin* Bridge. *Prelude* Bridge. *Green Piece* Intro/Outro. *Moon* Bridge. *Cielito Lindo* in 5. *City Ice* Sketch (Thomson) In/Out/During. *BBC News* (Varon) Outro. *Sunny Moon for Two*. With Turtle Island String Quartet. *Audience Adventure Boogie*. Anne Lamott Intro/Outro. *Urban Geographer* Intro/Outro. *Harlequin and the Philosopher*. *Upshaw* (Varon) Intro/Outro.
May 7. New York, New York. Knitting Factory (Roland digital piano RD-300s/52). First Set: *Friend of the Devil* (Hunter/Garcia). *Boris the Spider* (Entwistle). *San Andreas Stomp* (T.S.C. #5). *La Cathédrale Engloutie* (Debussy). *Harlequin and the Philosopher*. *Dark Star* (Hunter/Grateful Dead). *Dejavalse*. *Sonatina*. *Romance, Op. 118 #5* (Brahms). *Goin' Home* (Jagger/Richard). Second Set: *Oriental (Spanish Dance #2)* (Granados). *That Hand Played Rag* (Silverman/Ward). *All in the Game* (?). *Rialto Ripples* (Gershwin/Donaldson *via* Kovacs). *Overture, The Affair of Rue de Lourcine. Chiclets* (Ryan). *That There Old West...* (T.S.C. #2). Encore: *Prelude in E♭, Op. 23 #6* (Rachmaninoff). *American Beauty* (Lamb).
May 8. New York, New York. Wetlands Preserve (Roland digital piano RD-300s). Henry

Kaiser Band. Henry Kaiser and Bruce Anderson, guitars; Hilary Hanes, bass; John Hanes, drums; Cary Sheldon, vocals, and T.C., keyboards. First Set: *Fishin' Hole* (Sloane/Hagen/Spencer). *Tell Me* (Jagger/Richard). *Play With Fire* (Jagger/Richard). *California Dreamin'* (Phillips). *Go Go Pogo* (Kelly). *Cryin' in Your Beer* (Anderson). *Anyone who had a Heart* (Bacharach/David). *Dark Star* (Hunter/Grateful Dead)/*Tijuana* (Cale). *Do What You Like* (Winwood)/*Liberty Valance* (Bacharach/David). Second Set: *Don't Let a Thief Steal into Your Heart* (Richard Thompson). *Loner* (Young). *The Ballad of Shane Muscatell*. *Are You Experienced* (Hendrix)/*Love Supreme* (Coltrane). *Ode to Billy Joe* (Gentry)/*I'm so Glad* (Cream). Encore: *Friend of the Devil* (Hunter/Dawson/Garcia)/*Boris the Spider* (Entwistle) – Piano solo. *People Don't Change* (Anderson).
May 9. New York, New York. Wetlands Preserve (Roland digital piano RD-300s). Henry Kaiser Band. Henry Kaiser and Bruce Anderson, guitars; Hilary Hanes, bass; John Hanes, drums; Cary Sheldon, vocals, and T.C., keyboards. First Set: *Don't Let a Thief Steal into Your Heart* (Richard Thompson). *Fishin' Hole* (Sloane/Hagen/Spencer). *Love's Made a Fool of You* (Holly). *Losin' Hand* (Calhoun). *Ode to Billy Joe* (Gentry)/*Dark Star* (Hunter/Grateful Dead). *Tijuana* (Cale)/*Are You Experienced* (Hendrix). *Dark Star* (Hunter/Grateful Dead)/*River's Edge* (Anderson). *Tell Me* (Jagger/Richard). *Loner* (Young). Second Set: *Play With Fire* (Jagger/Richard)/*Do What You Like* (Winwood). *The Other One* (Garcia/Hunter/Weir). *Liberty Valance* (Bacharach/David). *California Dreamin'* (Phillips). *Never Again* (Anderson). *Mr. McGuffin* (Kaiser). *The Ballad of Shane Muscatell*. *It's a Lie* (Anderson). *Four Systems* (Earle Brown). *I'm so Glad* (Cream). Encore: *The Old Man of the Shells* (Kaiser).
May 11. New York, New York. R.A.P.P. Center (Steinway). Bang on a Can Festival. *In C* (Riley). Terry Riley, La Monte Young, Marian Zazeela, Shabda Owens, Molly Holm, and Mihr'un'issa Douglass, vocals; George Brooks, Bill Douglass, Jon Gibson, Jaron Lanier, Jim Newman, Bruce Williamson, and Lisa ?, winds; Simma Williamson, DX-7 (pulse); Kronos String Quartet; Barbara Higbie, violin; Henry Kaiser, guitar; George Marsh, percussion; and T.C., piano.
May 12. San Francisco, California. KQED-FM: 'West Coast Weekend', with Sedge

Thomson (Life on the Water/Steinway). Rebroadcast of September 2, 1989 show.
May 18. Santa Rosa,California. KAFE Cable Radio. *Bill Bowker Show*. Interview with Henry Kaiser and recorded musical examples.
May 18. Cotati, California. The Commons; Sonoma State University. (Korg B-3 and Roland digital piano RD-300s. courtesy of Henry Kaiser). Henry Kaiser Band. Henry Kaiser and Bruce Anderson, guitars; Hilary Hanes, bass; John Hanes, drums; Cary Sheldon, vocals, and T.C., keyboards. First Set: *The Old Man of the Shells* (Kaiser). *Tell Me* (Jagger/Richard). *Fishin' Hole* (Sloane/Hagen/Spencer)/*Love's Made a Fool of You* (Holly). *Play With Fire* (Jagger/Richard)/*Do What You Like* (Winwood). *The Other One* (Garcia/Hunter/Weir)/*Liberty Valance* (Bacharach/David). *It's a Lie* (Anderson). *Anyone who had a Heart* (Bacharach/David). *The Ballad of Shane Muscatell*. *California Dreamin'* (Phillips). Second Set: *Don't Let a Thief Steal into Your Heart* (Richard Thompson). *Are You Experienced* (Hendrix)/*Dark Star* (Hunter/Grateful Dead). *Tijuana* (Cale)/*Dark Star* (Hunter/Grateful Dead)/*Never Again* (Anderson). *Loner* (Young). *Losin' Hand* (Calhoun). Encores: *Friend of the Devil* (Hunter/Dawson/Garcia) – Piano solo. *Ode to Billy Joe* (Gentry).
May 19. San Francisco, California. KQED-FM: 'West Coast Weekend', with Sedge Thomson (Life on the Water/Steinway). Rebroadcast of June 3, 1989 show.
May 19. Seattle, Washington. University of Washington. Theodore Roethke Auditorium (ca.400/Yamaha). *Dejavalse*. *Romance, Op. 118 #5* (Brahms). Katie Johntz reading her poems. *The San Andreas Stomp* (T.S.C. #5). *Friend of the Devil* (Hunter/Dawson/Garcia). *Prelude in E♭, Op. 23 #6* (Rachmaninoff). *Goin' Home* (Jagger/Richard). Michael McClure reading his poems. Intermission. *Dark Star* (Hunter/Grateful Dead)/*Herb*. Robert Hunter enters and reads his poems: *Like a Basket*. *Exploding Diamond Blues* (Hunter): *Herb. Portia* (Hunter): *Prelude in D♭, Op.11 #15* (Scriabin). *Aladdin's Nite Lite* (Hunter): *Copland Fifths*. *Value for Cold Cash* (formerly *Answer to the Question Why); As Though as if* (formerly *Full Moon Cafe*) (Hunter): *Herb. Judith* (Hunter): *Aria, Goldberg Variations* (J. S. Bach). *Tango Hit Palace* (Hunter): *Sympathy for the Tango. Jazz* (Hunter): *Naugahide Schönberg. Rainwater Sea. idem* (Hunter). *Mountains of the Moon*

(Hunter/Garcia). *Tarbean* (Hunter): *Oriental (Spanish Dance #2)* (Granados). *Holigomena* (Hunter): *Sonata #9* opening (Scriabin). Encore: *Lia Lepsis. La Cathédrale Engloutie* (Debussy).

May 26. San Francisco, California. KQED-FM: 'West Coast Weekend', with Sedge Thomson (Life on the Water/Steinway). *{Sequidilla (Carmen)* (Bizet)/*Dejas.* With Yomo Toro and his band. *Prelude in D♭, Op. 11 #15* (Scriabin). *Fat Genes* Sketch (Fox) Intro/Outro. *City Ice* Sketch (Thomson) In/Out/During. *Audience Adventure Boogie. Louis B. Jones* Outro (*We're in the Money*). *The Moon* Bridge.

June 2. San Francisco, California. KQED-FM: 'West Coast Weekend', with Sedge Thomson (Life on the Water/Steinway). *{Rocky* (?)/*Dejas.* With the Good Old Persons: Kathy Kallick, guitar; Bethany Raine, bass; John Reischman, mandolin; Sally van Meter, dobro; and Kevin Wimmer, violin. *Simple Gifts* (Traditional). *Green Piece* Intro/Outro. *San Jose Fanfare. Sympathy for the Devil* (Jagger/Richard). *Singles in Crisis* Sketch (Fox) Intro/Outro. *Audience Adventure Boogie. Dejavalse. That There Old West...* (T.S.C. #2). *Sara Overton* Bed (*Rialto Ripples*).

June 2. San Francisco, California. Chi Chi Club. (Roland digital piano RD-300s. courtesy of George Michalski). Jessica Blue Sky's Benefit Bash II. Two Pieces with: Jerry Miller, Dan Arbuthnot, and Danny Kalb, guitars; Mitchell Holman, bass; and Chris, drums. *E Blues. Who do you Love* (Bo Diddley). With Danny Kalb, guitar; Mitchell Holman, bass; and Chris, drums. Solo Piano set: *Friend of the Devil* (Hunter/Dawson/Garcia). *Sympathy for the Devil* (Jagger/Richard). *San Andreas Stomp* (T.S.C. #5). *Goin' Home* (Jagger/Richard). *Boris the Spider* (Entwistle). *Dejavalse. Dark Star* (Hunter/Grateful Dead). Encore: *Prelude, Op. 23 #6* (Rachmaninoff).

June 6. San Francisco, California. De Young Museum (Steinway). Hearst Court. Night of the Living Piano. Solo set by George Michalski. Solo set by T.C.: *American Beauty* (Lamb). *Minstrels* (Debussy). *That Hand Played Rag* (Silverman and Ward). *Nachtstück, Op. 23 #4* (Schumann). *Goin' Home* (Jagger/Richard). *San Andreas Stomp* (T.S.C. #5). *Romance, Op. 118 #5* (Brahms). *Overture, The Affair of Rue de Lourcine. Friend of the Devil* (Hunter/Dawson/Garcia). *Oriental (Spanish Dance #2)* (Granados). *Dejavalse. Chiclets* (Ryan). *Dark Star*

(Hunter/Grateful Dead). *That There Old West...* (T.S.C. #2). With George Michalski, piano four hands: *Dear Prudence* (Lennon/McCartney). *Me and My Uncle* (Phillips)/*G Boogie. Sympathy for the Devil* (Jagger/Richard). *Stars and Stripes Forever* (Sousa). Encore: *We Bid You Goodnight* (Traditional).

June 9. San Francisco, California. KQED-FM: 'West Coast Weekend', with Sedge Thomson (Life on the Water/Steinway). *{Are you ready* (?)/*Dejas.* With Peppino d'Agostino and Michael Manring. *Ferry 'Cross the Mersey* (?). *Twin Peaks* Bridge. *Comedy Survey* (Fox) Tag (*As It Happens* Theme). *Pulp Playhouse I: The Wine Salesman.* With Brian Lohmann, Barbara Scott, and Rafe Chase. *Oriental (Spanish Dance #2)* (Granados). *Graduate* Sketch (Fox) In/Out. *Mercy, Mercy, Mercy* (Zawinul). With Peppino d'Agostino and Michael Manring. *Audience Adventure Boogie. French in Action* Bridge. *Pulp Playhouse II: Carolyn's Diary.* With Brian Lohmann, Barbara Scott, and Rafe Chase. *Rockin' Promenade.*

June 11. Berkeley, California. KPFA-FM: 'The Morning Concert.' With Russ Jennings. History and the Composer's Dilemma. Reading with musical examples.

June 16. San Francisco, California. KQED-FM: 'West Coast Weekend', with Sedge Thomson (Life on the Water/Steinway). *{Das Rheingold* opening (Wagner)/*Dejas.* With Those Darned Accordions. *Shalimar: First Interlude* (Hovhaness). *Friend of the Devil* (Hunter/Dawson/Garcia). *Shalimar: Rain Jhala* (Hovhaness). *Shalimar: Jhala of the Fountains* (Hovhaness). *San Jose Fanfare. City Ice* Sketch (Thomson) In/Out/During. *Audience Adventure Boogie. Singles in Crisis* Sketch (Fox) Intro/Outro. *Rockin' Promenade. Pulp Playhouse: Karen's Diary.* With Brian Lohmann, Barbara Scott, and Rafe Chase.

June 23. San Francisco, California. KQED-FM: 'West Coast Weekend', with Sedge Thomson (Life on the Water/Steinway). *{Heat* Theme/*Dejas.* With Dale Miller. *San Jose Fanfares. Rockin' Promenade – The Stripper. Pulp Playhouse: The Wood Sculptor.* With Brian Lohmann, Barbara Scott, and Rafe Chase. *Free Speech* Sketch (Fox) Outro. *Audience Adventure Boogie. Thirty Something* (?) Bridge. *Pulp Playhouse: Miriam's Diary.* With Brian Lohmann, Barbara Scott, and Rafe Chase.

June 27. Pacifica, California. Pacifica Cable Channel 8. 'The Bruce Latimer Show' (Baldwin upright). *Dejavalse. Dear Prudence*

(Lennon/McCartney). With George Michalski.

June 30. San Jose, California. KQED-FM: 'West Coast Weekend', with Sedge Thomson (Mirassou/Sherman Clay). *{Saturday in the Park* (?)/*Dejas. Dark Star* (Hunter/Grateful Dead). T.C. and the Band that won the West: Tim Fox, guitar; Hilary Hanes, bass; John Hanes, drums; and T.C., piano. *Summer Wine* (?). *Carl Stallings* Bridge. *Balloon* Outro. *Simpsons* Tag. *Urban Geographer* Intro/Outro. *City Ice* Sketch (Thomson) In/Out/During. *BBC News* (Outro). *E Blues*. TC and the Band that won the West plus Big Bones, harmonica. *Audience Adventure Boogie. Bill of Rights* Bed (Bill – Wodehouse/Kern). *Rockin' Promenade. Friend of the Devil* (Hunter/Dawson/Garcia).

July 3. San Francisco, California. Last Day Saloon. (Roland digital piano RD-300s. courtesy of George Michalski). *Dear Prudence* (Lennon/McCartney). With George Michalski. *Friend of the Devil* (Hunter/Dawson/Garcia). *Boris the Spider* (Entwistle).

July 7. San Francisco, California. KQED-FM: 'West Coast Weekend', with Sedge Thomson (Life on the Water/Steinway). *{007* Theme (?)/*Dejas*. With Laurie Lewis, violin; Tony Furtado, banjo; Scott Nygaard, guitar; Tom Rozum, mandolin; and Tammy Fassaert, bass. *Ich Fuhr mich über Rhein* (Sweelinck). *Moon Harp* (from *Komachi*) (Hovhaness). *Meandering Marauding Motion Picture Maven* (Fox) In/Out. *City Ice* (Thomson) In/Out/During. *BBC News* (Varon) Outro. *Audience Adventure Boogie. Valley Lady* (Fox) In *(Young at Heart)*/Out (*When I'm 64*).

July 14. San Francisco, California. KQED-FM: 'West Coast Weekend', with Sedge Thomson (Life on the Water/Steinway). *{La Marsaillaise* Theme (DeLisle)/*Dejas. If There's Anything that You Want* (Lennon/McCartney). *Simple Gifts* (Traditional). *Rockin' Promenade. House Pianist* Sketch (Fox) In/Out/During. *Audience Adventure Boogie. Green Piece* Intro/Outro. *French Movie* Sketch (Fox) Intro/Outro. *Urban Geographer* Intro/Outro/*Dejas*. With Big Lou and Caroline Dahl.

July 14. San Francisco, California. Chi-Chi Club. (Yamaha DX-7 courtesy of Barry Flast). Jessica Blue Sky's Benefit Bash III. About a half dozen blues numbers with: Danny Kalb, guitar and vocals; John Murphy, pedal steel guitar; Eric van Dorn, bass; and Bob Ulius, drums.

July 21. San Francisco, California. KQED-FM: 'West Coast Weekend', with Sedge Thomson (Life on the Water/Steinway). *{Letterman* Theme (Schaffer)/*Dejas*. T.C. and the Band that Won the West: Tim Fox, guitar, Hilary Hanes, bass, and John Hanes, drums. *Thirty Something* (?) Bridge. *Sheebeg & Sheemore* (Carolan) Bridge. *My Gal's a Corker* (?) Bridge. *San Francisco (Flowers in Your Hair)* (Phillips) Bridge. *Incomprehensible Playhouse* (Fox) Music Cues. *BBC News* (Varon) Outro. *Equinox* (Coltrane). T.C. and the Band that Won the West: Tim Fox, guitar, Hilary Hanes, bass, and John Hanes, drums. *Barnacle Bill the Sailor* (?) with Tim Fox, guitar. *Summer Movies* Sketch (Fox) Music Cues.

July 21. San Francisco, California. Private Party. (Roland digital piano RD-300s. courtesy of George Michalski). *Dark Star* (Hunter/Grateful Dead). *Friend of the Devil* (Hunter/Dawson/Garcia). *I'm in Love Again* (Domino)/*Season of the Witch* (Leach). With David Gans, guitar; Alan Chamberlain, bass; and Bob Euless, drums. *E Blues*. Joined by Danny Kalb, guitar. *A Blues*. Joined by Mitchell Holman, bass.

July 28. San Francisco, California. KQED-FM: 'West Coast Weekend', with Sedge Thomson (Life on the Water/Steinway). *{The Other One* (Garcia)/*Dejas*. With Ginny Reilly, guitar. *The Eternal Summer of Sacramento* (Mark Twain), read by Sedge Thomson: *Ferry 'Cross the Mersey* (?) Bed. *Urban Geographer* Intro/Outro(*Call Me* Tag). *Play the Game* (McShee/Portman-Smith). *Sex, Life, and Junk Food* Sketch (Fox) In/Out. *Bus Stop* (Hollies). With Ginny Reilly, guitar. *Audience Adventure Boogie. Heatface* (Talen) Outro(*You Gotta Have Heart*). *Rockin' Promenade* (Took the T-Bird Away).

August 4. San Francisco, California. KQED-FM: 'West Coast Weekend', With Sedge Thomson (Life on the Water/Steinway). *{Seasons in the Sun* (?)/*Dejas*. With Bob Brozman, steel guitar. Kite Story. *Fractured Fairytale* (Steiner) Bridge. *Rialto Ripples* (Gershwin/Donaldson *via* Kovacs). *Calypso Break*. With Bob Brozman, steel guitar. *Audience Adventure Boogie. Crime and Punishment* Sketch (Fox) Intro/Outro. *Urban Geographer* Intro/Outro(*Games People Play* Tag). *Hilo Hula/Maikai no Kauai* (Pahinui). With Bob Brozman, steel guitar.

August 11. San Francisco, California. KQED-FM: 'West Coast Weekend', with Sedge Thomson (Life on the Water/Steinway). *{See You in September* (?)/*Dejas*. With Brian

Godchaux, violin; Paul Mehling, guitar; and Joe Preussner, bass. *Summer in the City* (Lovin' Spoonful) Tag. *The Windmills of Golden Gate Park* (Frank Levin). *Rockin' Promenade*. With Tim Fox, guitar. *Braindead* Sketch (Fox) Intro. *Green Door* (?) Bridge. *A River of Highway* (Angelis). With Kim Angelis, violin. *Audience Adventure Boogie*. *Green Piece* Intro/Outro. *Simple Gifts* (Traditional) Bridge. *Urban Geographer* Intro/Outro. With Tim Fox, guitar.

August 18. San Francisco, California. KQED-FM: 'West Coast Weekend', with Sedge Thomson (Life on the Water/Steinway). Rebroadcast of May 5, 1990 show.

August 19. San Francisco, California. Möbius Studios (Yamaha). Oliver DiCicco, engineer. *Love's Made a Fool of You* (Holly). *California Dreaming* (Phillips). *Rock on* (Essex). With The Henry Kaiser Band: Henry Kaiser and Bruce Anderson, guitars, Hilary Hanes, bass; John Hanes, drums, Cary Sheldon and Greg Gumbel, vocals.

August 21. San Francisco, California. Last Day Saloon. (Roland Juno Synthesizer). Sat in with George Michalski Band. Bobby Scott and Alex Guinness, guitars, Carl Sealove, bass, and Ernest 'Boom' Carter, drums.

August 25. San Francisco, California. KQED-FM: 'West Coast Weekend', with Sedge Thomson (Life on the Water/Steinway). Rebroadcast of May 26, 1990 show.

September 1. San Francisco, California. KQED-FM: 'West Coast Weekend', with Sedge Thomson (Life on the Water/Steinway). Rebroadcast of June 9, 1990 show.

September 8. San Francisco, California. KQED-FM: 'West Coast Weekend', with Sedge Thomson (Life on the Water/Steinway). *{Sheik of Araby* (?) over *Jaws* (?)/*Dejas*. With Tim Fox, and Eric and Suzy Thompson. *Quasi De Falla* Tag. *Rockin' Promenade*. With Tim Fox, electric guitar. *Desert Chic* Sketch (Thomson) Bed. *Footprints* (Shorter). With Tim Fox, electric guitar. *BBC News* (Varon) Outro. *C Jam*. With Joe Miller, Duck Baker, and Eric and Suzy Thompson. *Audience Adventure Boogie*. *Geography Patrol* Sketch (Thomson) In/Out/During. Anne Lamott In/Out. *Goodbye Pork Pie Hat* (Mingus), with Tim Fox, electric guitar.

September 10. El Cerrito, California. Bay Cable Channel 28. *On Stage* (Winter). Night of the Living Piano. Solo set by George Michalski. Solo set by T.C.: *Friend of the Devil* (Hunter/Dawson/Garcia). *Boris the Spider*

(Entwistle). *The San Andreas Stomp* (T.S.C. #5). *Dejavalse*. With George Michalski, piano four hands: *Dear Prudence* (Lennon/McCartney). *City Boy* (Michalski). *C Boogie*. *We Bid You Goodnight* (Traditional).

September 13. San Francisco, California. Last Day Saloon. (Roland digital piano RD-300s. courtesy of George Michalski). With Crazy Fingers: David Gans, guitar and vocals, Bob Nakamine, guitar; Tom Yacoe, bass; and Mike Shaw, drums. *Season of the Witch* (Leitch)/*Dark Star* (Hunter/Grateful Dead). *China Cat Sunflower* (Hunter/Garcia)/*Season of the Witch* (Leitch). Night of the Living Piano. Solo set by George Michalski. Solo set by T.C.: *Boris the Spider* (Entwistle). *Play the Game* (McShee/Portman-Smith). *I've Just Seen a Face* (Lennon/McCartney). *The San Andreas Stomp* (T.S.C. #5). *Dejavalse*. With George Michalski, piano four hands: *Dear Prudence* (Lennon/McCartney). *City Boy* (Michalski). *C Boogie*. *And We Bid You Goodnight* (Traditional).

September 15. San Francisco, California. KQED-FM: 'West Coast Weekend', with Sedge Thomson (Life on the Water/Steinway). *{A Little Help from my Friends*. (Beatles *via* Joe Cocker)/*Dejas*. With Valerio Longoria y su Conjunto. Valerio Longoria Sr., accordion; Valerio Longoria, Jr., bass; Valerio Longoria IV, drums; Flavio Longoria, saxophone; and Juan Garcia, bajo sexto. *These Boots Were Made for Walkin'* (*via* Nancy Sinatra). *Rockin' Promenade*. *City Ice* Sketch (Thomson) In/Out/During. *Audience Adventure Boogie*. Socks segment.

September 19. Pacifica, California. Pacifica Cable Channel 8. 'The Bruce Latimer Show' (Baldwin upright). *I've Just Seen a Face* (Lennon/McCartney). *The San Andreas Stomp* (T.S.C. #5). *Dark Star* (Hunter/Grateful Dead).

September 22. San Francisco, California. KQED-FM: 'West Coast Weekend', With Sedge Thomson (Life on the Water/Steinway). *{I'll Follow the Sun* (Beatles)/*Dejas*. With The Modern Mandolin Quartet. Mike Marshall, Dana Rath, Paul Binkley, and John Imholz. *I've Just Seen a Face* (Lennon/McCartney). *Tooth Fairy* Sketch (Varon) Outro. *Rockin' Promenade*. *Pritikin Playhouse* (Fox) In/Out/During. *Deja Waltz*. With Mike Marshall, Dana Rath, and Paul Binkley. *Audience Adventure Boogie*. *Paranoid/Schizophrenic Playhouse* (Fox) Intro/Outro. *Phobia Phollies* Sketch (Fox) Intro/Outro.

September 28. San Francisco, California. Psychedelic Shop. (Roland Digital piano RD-300s. courtesy of George Michalski). Night of the Living Piano. Solo set by George Michalski. Solo set by T.C.: *I've Just Seen a Face* (Lennon/McCartney). *Overture, The Affair of Rue de Lourcine. All in the Game* (?)/ *Play the Game* (McShee/Portman-Smith). *Harlequin/Return of the Philosopher* (from *Tarot*). *Fantasy in C minor* (J. S. Bach). *Dejavalse. Prelude, Op. 23 #6* (Rachmaninoff). *Etude, Op. 10 #6* (Chopin). *Boris the Spider* (Entwistle). With George Michalski, piano four hands: *Dear Prudence* (Lennon/ McCartney). *City Boy* (Michalski). *The Moon* (from *Tarot*). *G Boogie/Chopsticks* ending. *We Bid You Goodnight* (Traditional). Encore: With George Michalski. *Layla* (Clapton).

September 29. San Francisco, California. KQED-FM: 'West Coast Weekend', with Sedge Thomson (Life on the Water/ Steinway). First show Carried on WHYY-FM – Philadelphia. One week delay. *{California Here I Come* (?)/*Dejas.* With Henry Kaiser Quartet. Henry Kaiser, Gary Lambert, John McCain, and Mark McQuade-Crawford. *Civil War Music* segment. *Twin Peaks* Theme (?). *Green Piece* Intro/Outro. *Carioca* (Nazareth) Outro. *The Consolation of Philosophy* Sketch (Fox) Intro/Outro. *Dark Star* (Hunter/Grateful Dead). With Henry Kaiser Quartet. Henry Kaiser, Gary Lambert, John McCain, and Mark McQuade-Crawford. *Audience Adventure Boogie. Rockin' Promenade.*

October 4. San Francisco, California. Last Day Saloon. (Roland Digital piano RD-300s. courtesy of George Michalski). Solo set by Danny Kalb. Night of the Living Piano. Solo set by George Michalski. Solo set by T.C.: *Dejavalse. I've Just Seen a Face* (Lennon/ McCartney). *Boris the Spider* (Entwistle). *Play the Game* (McShee/Portman-Smith). *Prelude in C# minor, Op. 28 #10* (Chopin). *Dark Star* (Hunter/Grateful Dead) *Friend of the Devil* (Hunter/Dawson/Garcia). *Dark Star* (Hunter/Grateful Dead). *Sonata in E – 3rd Movement* (1776) (Haydn). *Dejavalse.* With George Michalski, piano four hands: *Dear Prudence* (Lennon/McCartney). *City Boy* (Michalski). *The Moon* (from *Tarot*) . *Sympathy for the Devil* (Jagger/Richard). *The Moon* (from *Tarot*). *G Boogie We Bid You Goodnight* (Traditional). Encores: With George Michalski. *Somewhere Over the Rainbow* (Arlen). With Danny Kalb, George Michalski, and Bruce Bellingham. *E Blues.*

October 6. San Francisco, California. KQED-FM: 'West Coast Weekend', with Sedge Thomson (Life on the Water/Steinway). Rebroadcast of July 21, 1990 show.

October 12. San Francisco, California. Last Day Saloon. (Roland digital piano RD-300s. courtesy of George Michalski). Set by Crazy Fingers. Night of the Living Piano. Solo set by George Michalski. Solo set by T.C.: *Dejavalse. Boris the Spider* (Entwistle). *Dark Star* (Hunter/Grateful Dead). *Friend of the Devil* (Hunter/Dawson/Garcia). *Dejavalse.* With George Michalski, piano four hands: *Dear Prudence* (Lennon/McCartney). *City Boy* (Michalski). *The Moon* (from *Tarot*). *And We Bid You Goodnight* (Traditional).

October 13. San Francisco, California. KQED-FM: 'West Coast Weekend', with Sedge Thomson (Life on the Water/Steinway). *{East is East, and West is West/Dejas.– with John Handy with Class. John Handy, saxophone; Julie Carter, Yehudit, and Sandi Poindexter, violins; and Tim Hauf, bass. *Bach/Chopin C minor prelude/etude. E Blues* Tag. *Kamennoi/St. Elmo* Break. *Pet Shop* Sketch (Fox) Intro/Outro. *BBC News* (Varon) Outro. *Audience Adventure Boogie. Pulp Playhouse: Wendy's Week* – with Brian Lohmann, Barbara Scott, and Rafe Chase/ *Dejas.* With Will Scarlett, harmonica; 'Daddy Squeeze' Newton, accordion; Greg Anton, drums; and Marty Holland, bass.

October 18. San Francisco, California. Last Day Saloon. (Roland digital piano RD-300s courtesy of George Michalski). Night of the Living Piano. Solo set by George Michalski. Solo set by T.C.: *Dejavalse. I've Just Seen a Face* (Lennon/McCartney). *Boris the Spider* (Entwistle). *Friend of the Devil* (Hunter/ Garcia). *Eintritt, Waldszenen, Op. 82 #1* (Schumann). *Dark Star* (Hunter/Grateful Dead). *Etude, Op. 25 #6* (Chopin). *Dejavalse.* With George Michalski, piano four hands: *Dear Prudence* (Lennon/McCartney). *City Boy* (Michalski). Danny Kalb Blues Band. With Danny Kalb, guitar and vocals, Ray Collins, saxophone and flute; Mitchell Holman, bass; Ernest 'Boom' Carter, drums; and T.C., piano. *Mean Old Southern* (?). *Black Night is Falling* (Charles Brown). *Greed* (from *Tarot*). *Dance with Me* (Mitchell Holman). *Don't go to Strangers* (J. J. Cale). *Magnolia* (Ray Collins). *Danville Dame* (Tim Hardin). Encore: *Jelly Jelly* (?).

October 20. San Francisco, California. KQED-FM: 'West Coast Weekend', with Sedge Thomson (Life on the Water/Steinway).

*{Somewhere* (Bernstein)/*Dejas.* With Dale Miller, guitar; and Dean Reilly, bass. *Top Ten List* Outro. *Lorena* (Webster/Webster) Bridge. *The Letter* (Box Tops) Break. *Rockin' Promenade. Audience Adventure Boogie. Pulp Playhouse.* With Brian Lohmann, Barbara Scott, and Reed Kirk Rahlmann.

October 20. San Francisco, California. The BoatHouse. (Roland Digital piano RD-300s. courtesy of George Michalski). Solo set by Danny Kalb. *Night of the Living Piano.* Solo set by George Michalski. Solo set by T.C.: *Dejavalse. Boris the Spider* (Entwistle). *Rialto Ripples* (Gershwin/Donaldson *via* Kovacs). *I've Just Seen a Face* (Lennon/ McCartney). With George Michalski, piano four hands: *Dear Prudence* (Lennon/ McCartney). *City Boy* (Michalski). With Crazy Fingers: David Gans, guitar and vocals, Bob Nakamine, guitar; Tom Yacoe, bass; and Mike Shaw, drums. *Mason's Children* (Hunter/Garcia)/*New Speedway Boogie* (Hunter/Garcia)/*?. Season of the Witch* (Leitch)/*Dark Star* (Hunter/Grateful Dead). *Friend of the Devil* (Hunter/Dawson/ Garcia). *Hard to Handle* (Redding).

October 26. San Francisco, California. Townsend Street Studios. 'Won't Get Fooled Again'. Presented by Vietnam Veterans of America. in memory of Jane Dornacker. *Night of the Living Piano.* With George Michalski, piano four hands: *Dear Prudence* (Lennon/McCartney). *City Boy* (Michalski). *The Moon* (from *Tarot*). *Sympathy for the Devil* (Jagger/Richard). *The Moon* (from *Tarot*).

October 27. San Francisco, California. KQED-FM: 'West Coast Weekend', with Sedge Thomson (Life on the Water/Steinway). *{You Only Live Twice* (?)/*Dejas.* With Dale Wolford, saxophone; Danny Carnahan, guitar; and Robin Petrie, hammer dulcimer. *Overture, The Affair of Rue de Lourcine.* Anne Lamott Intro/Outro. *All in the Family* (Kellaway) Outro. *Rockin' Promenade. Red Haired Boy* (Scottish Traditional). With Danny Carnahan, guitar; and Robin Petrie, hammer dulcimer. *Audience Adventure Boogie. Green Piece* Intro/Outro. *O Haupt voll Blut und Wunden* (J. S. Bach). *Pulp Playhouse.* With Rafe Chase, Barbara Scott, and Reed Kirk Rahlmann.

October 31. San Francisco, California. Last Day Saloon. (Roland digital piano RD-300s. courtesy of George Michalski). With Crazy Fingers: David Gans, guitar and vocals, Bob Nakamine, guitar; Tom Yacoe, bass;

and Mike Shaw, drums. *Mason's Children* (Hunter/Garcia)/*?/New Speedway Boogie* (Hunter/Garcia)/*?*. Joined by Danny Kalb, guitar. Three pieces. *Night of the Living Piano.* Solo set by George Michalski. Solo set by T.C.: *Boris the Spider* (Entwistle). *The San Andreas Stomp* (T.S.C. #5). *Whiter Shade of Pale* (Reid/Brooker). *Dejavalse/Dark Star.* Joined in progress by David Gans, guitar; Tom Yacoe, bass; and Mike Shaw, drums. *Dejavalse.* With George Michalski, piano four hands: *Dear Prudence* (Lennon/ McCartney). *The Moon* (from *Tarot*). *City Boy* (Michalski).

November 3. San Francisco, California. KQED-FM: 'West Coast Weekend', With Sedge Thomson (Life on the Water/Steinway). *{I'll be Seeing You* (?)/*They can't Take that Away from me* (?)/*Dejas. Heat* Theme. *Rockin' Promenade. Whiter Shade of Pale* (Reid/Brooker). *I've Just Seen a Face* (Lennon/McCartney). *Audience Adventure Boogie. Warm San Francisco Night* (Burdon). *Simple Gifts* (Traditional).

November 6. Philadelphia, Pennsylvania. Chestnut Cabaret (Korg SFG-1D Sampling Piano/c.1200). Solo Set by T.C.: *I've Just Seen a Face* (Lennon/McCartney). *Dejavalse. Overture, The Affair of Rue de Lourcine. Boris the Spider* (Entwistle). *The San Andreas Stomp* (T.S.C. #5). *Chopped Liver* (Ryan). *Friend of the Devil* (Hunter/Dawson/Garcia). *Play the Game* (McShee/Portman-Smith). *All in the Game* (?). *Whiter Shade of Pale* (Reid/ Brooker). *Dark Star* (Hunter/Grateful Dead). *Dejavalse.* Encore: *Etude, Op. 10 #11* (Chopin). Two solo sets plus encores by Robert Hunter.

November 7. Washington, D. C. Lisner Auditorium; George Washington University. (Baldwin/c. 1200). Solo Set by T.C.: *Dejavalse. Overture, The Affair of Rue de Lourcine. Butterfly Rag. Boris the Spider* (Entwistle). *The San Andreas Stomp* (T.S.C. #5). *Chopped Liver* (Ryan). *Friend of the Devil* (Hunter/dawson/Garcia). *All in the Game* (?). *Apocryphal Awry. Fantasy in C minor* (J. S. Bach). *Dark Star* (Hunter/Grateful Dead). *Dejavalse.* Encore: *Etude, Op. 10 #11* (Chopin). Two solo sets plus encores by Robert Hunter.

November 9. New York, New York. The Rita (Yamaha/c. 1500). Solo Set by T.C.: *Dejavalse. I've Just Seen a Face* (Lennon/ McCartney). *Overture, The Affair of Rue de Lourcine. Butterfly Rag. Boris the Spider* (Entwistle). *The San Andreas Stomp* (T.S.C.

#5). *Chopped Liver* (Ryan). *Friend of the Devil* (Hunter/Dawson/Garcia). *All in the Game* (?). *Apocryphal Awry. Fantasy in C minor* (J. S. Bach). *Dark Star* (Hunter/Grateful Dead). *Dejavalse.* Encores: *Etude, Op. 10 #11* (Chopin). *Whiter Shade of Pale* (Reid/Brooker). Two solo sets plus encores by Robert Hunter.

November 10. Somerville,Massachusetts. Somerville Theatre (Yamaha CP-80/1500). Solo Set by T.C.: *Dejavalse. I've Just Seen a Face* (Lennon/McCartney). *Overture, The Affair of Rue de Lourcine. Boris the Spider* (Entwistle). *The San Andreas Stomp* (T.S.C. #5). *Chopped Liver* (Ryan). *Friend of the Devil* (Hunter/Dawson/Garcia). *Play the Game* (McShee/Portman-Smith). *Apocryphal Awry. Dark Star* (Hunter/Grateful Dead). *Whiter Shade of Pale* (Reid/Brooker). *Dejavalse.* Encore: *Sonata in E – 3rd Movement* (1776) (Haydn). *Etude, Op. 10 #11* (Chopin). Two solo sets plus encores by Robert Hunter.

November 12. Charlottesville, Virginia. Charlottesville Performing Arts Center (Steinway). Solo Set by T.C.: *Dejavalse. I've Just Seen a Face* (Lennon/McCartney). *Overture, The Affair of Rue de Lourcine. Butterfly Rag. Boris the Spider* (Entwistle). *The San Andreas Stomp* (T.S.C. #5). *Chopped Liver* (Ryan). *Friend of the Devil* (Hunter/Garcia). *Rialto Ripples* (Gershwin/Donaldson *via* Kovacs). *Apocryphal Awry. Fantasy in C minor* (J. S. Bach). *Dark Star* (Hunter/Grateful Dead). *Whiter Shade of Pale* (Reid/Brooker). *Dejavalse.* Two solo sets plus encores by Robert Hunter.

November 13. Atlanta, Georgia. Center Stage (Yamaha CP-80/700). Solo Set by T.C.: *Dejavalse. I've Just Seen a Face* (Lennon/McCartney). *Overture, The Affair of Rue de Lourcine. Play the Game* (McShee/Portman-Smith). *The San Andreas Stomp* (T.S.C. #5). *Chopped Liver* (Ryan). *Friend of the Devil* (Hunter/Garcia). *Apocryphal Awry. Fantasy in C minor* (J. S. Bach). *Dark Star* (Hunter/Grateful Dead). *Dejavalse.* Encores: *Boris the Spider* (Entwistle). *Sonata in E – 3rd Movement* (1776) (Haydn). Two solo sets plus encores by Robert Hunter.

November 15. Chicago, Illinois. Park West (Yamaha/1000). Solo Set by T.C.: *Dejavalse. I've Just Seen a Face* (Lennon/McCartney). *Overture, The Affair of Rue de Lourcine. Butterfly Rag. The San Andreas Stomp* (T.S.C. #5). *Chopped Liver* (Ryan). *Friend of the Devil* (Hunter/Dawson/Garcia). *Play the Game*

(McShee/Portman-Smith). *Apocryphal Awry. Fantasy in C minor* (J. S. Bach). *Dark Star* (Hunter/Grateful Dead). *Dejavalse.* Encore: *Boris the Spider* (Entwistle). Two solo sets plus encores by Robert Hunter.

November 16. Milwaukee,Wisconsin. Avalon Theatre (Yamaha CP-70/800). Solo Set by T.C.: *Dejavalse. Friend of the Devil* (Hunter/Dawson/Garcia). *Overture, The Affair of Rue de Lourcine. I've Just Seen a Face* (Lennon/McCartney). *The San Andreas Stomp* (T.S.C. #5). *Chopped Liver* (Ryan). *Whiter Shade of Pale* (Reid/Brooker). *Eintritt, Waldszenen, Op. 82* (Schumann). *Dark Star* (Hunter/Grateful Dead). *Dejavalse.* Encores: *Boris the Spider* (Entwistle). *Play the Game* (McShee/Portman-Smith). *Sonata in G minor, K. 4/L. 390* (Scarlatti). Two solo sets plus encores by Robert Hunter.

November 17. Boulder, Colorado. Boulder Theatre (Steinway/c. 1200). Solo Set by T.C.: *Dejavalse. Friend of the Devil* (Hunter/Dawson/Garcia). *Overture, The Affair of Rue de Lourcine. The San Andreas Stomp* (T.S.C. #5). *Chopped Liver* (Ryan). *I've Just Seen a Face* (Lennon/McCartney). *Apocryphal Awry. Fantasy in C minor* (J. S. Bach). *Dark Star* (Hunter/Grateful Dead). *Dejavalse.* Encores: *Boris the Spider* (Entwistle). *Etude, Op. 10 #11* (Chopin). Two solo sets plus encores by Robert Hunter.

November 24. San Francisco, California. KQED-FM: 'West Coast Weekend', with Sedge Thomson (Life on the Water/Steinway). *{The Long and Winding Road* (Beatles)/*Dejas.* With Odile LaVault, accordion. Tour Update – talk with ST. *Twin Peaks* Tag. *Paperback Writer* (Lennon/McCartney). BBC News (Varon) Outro. *Barnum's Circus March* (King). With Odile LaVault, accordion. *Audience Adventure Boogie.* Anne Lamott Theme. *Tomorrow Never Knows* (Lennon). *Urban Geographer* Intro/Outro.

November 26. San Francisco,California. The Warfield (Yamaha CP-80/c. 1200). Solo Set by T.C.: *Dejavalse. Friend of the Devil* (Hunter/Garcia). *Overture, The Affair of Rue de Lourcine. Whiter Shade of Pale* (Reid/Brooker). *I've Just Seen a Face* (Lennon/McCartney). *The San Andreas Stomp* (T.S.C. #5). *Fantasy in C minor* (J. S. Bach). *Dark Star/St. Stephen* (Hunter/Garcia)/*A Day in the Life* (Lennon). *Dejavalse.* Encore: *Boris the Spider* (Entwistle). Two solo sets plus encores by Robert Hunter. *Mountains of the Moon* (Hunter/Garcia), with Robert Hunter.

December 1. San Francisco, California. KQED-FM: 'West Coast Weekend', with Sedge Thomson (Life on the Water/Steinway). *(I Feel the Earth Move Under my Feet* (King). *Meet me in St. Louis, Louis/Dejas.* With Dennis James, glass harmonica. Ad Hoc Country Bridge. *Ashokan Farewell* (Ungar) Bridge. *The Beat Goes on Raga.* Fiddle Tune with Sierra String Quartet: Kati Kyme, Joseph Edelberg, Phyllis Kamrin, and Sarah Freiberg. *Audience Adventure Boogie. Webern Variations* Excerpt. *De Falla* Bridge. *Green Piece.*

December 2. Berkeley, California. The Ashkenaz. (Hohner electric keyboard courtesy f Danny Kalb). Solo set by David Gans. Solo set by T.C.: *Friend of the Devil* (Hunter/Garcia). *I've Just Seen a Face* (Lennon/McCartney). *Audience Adventure Boogie. Dejaboogie. Friend of the Devil* (Hunter/Dawson/Garcia). With Crazy Fingers: David Gans, guitar and vocals, Bob Nakamine, guitar; Tom Yacoe, bass; and Mike Shaw, drums. *Jam/Dark Star* (Hunter/Grateful Dead). *Mason's Children* (Hunter/Garcia)/*New Speedway Boogie* (Hunter/Garcia). *Bertha* (Hunter/Garcia).

December 3. Berkeley, California. KPFA-FM: *Mob Ecstasy*, with Ben Lindgren. Studio B (Bösendorfer). *Designer Chaos* (Anderson/Constanten/Kaiser) from Henry Kaiser Band Album: *Heart's Desire. Nr. 2 Klavierstück III* (Stockhausen). *Chopped Liver* (Ryan). *Overture, The Affair of Rue de Lourcine. Sonatina. Prelude* (1963). *When you get to the* \* (Excerpt of concert recording from April 16, 1975). *Vexations* (Satie) with Joseph Kubera. *Dark Star* (Hunter/Grateful Dead).

December 8. San Francisco, California. KQED-FM: 'West Coast Weekend', With Sedge Thomson (Life on the Water/Steinway). *(Eve of Destruction* (McGuire)/*Dejas.* With The Klezmer Maniax: Kaila Flexer, Mike Marshall, Joe Preussner, and Joe Craven. *Simple Gifts* (Traditional). Anne Lamott Intro/Outro. *BBC News* (Varon) Outro. *Klezarabia* (Flexer). With The Klezmer Maniax: Kaila Flexer, Mike Marshall, Joe Preussner, and Joe Craven. *Audience Adventure Boogie. Rockin' Promenade. Spend the Night Together* Bridge. *Dreidl* Tag.

December 14. Los Angeles, California. KPFK-FM: 'Thursday Lunch.' With Tom Norton and Bob Young. Interview with recorded examples from *OutSides: Dejavalse. Rondo Pazzo. Electronic Study #3. Let it Ring. Alaric's Premonition.*

December 15. San Francisco, California. KQED-FM: 'West Coast Weekend', with Sedge Thomson (Life on the Water/Steinway). *(Copenhagen* (?)/*Dejas.* With The Golden Bough: *Annual O Tannenbaum* Segment (ST) Intro/Outro. *Flute Thing* (Kuhlberg) Bridge. *Mom Rap* with Diane Conway, Carol Christiansen, and Marilyn M. Kentz. *Ashokan Farewell* (Ungar). *Carol of the Bells* (Traditional) Bed. With The Golden Bough: *Audience Adventure Boogie. Christmas Decorations* Sketch (Fox) Intro/Outro. *Rockin' Promenade. Jingle Bell Rock* (?). With The Golden Bough: Margie Butler, Florie Brown, and Paul Espinoza.

December 22. San Francisco, California. KQED-FM: 'West Coast Weekend', with Sedge Thomson (Life on the Water/Steinway). *(Beethoven Fourth Concerto* Opening/*Dejas. Carol of the Bells* (Traditional)/*Godfather Theme* (Rota) Bridge. Anne Lamott Intro/Outro. *Audience Adventure Boogie. Green Piece* Intro/Outro.

December 22. Hayward, California. Cal State Hayward Recital Hall (Bösendorfer). *Sonata in E* (1776) (Haydn). *I. Moderato. II. Allegretto. III. Finale: Presto. Sonata #15 in D, Op. 28 (Pastorale)* (Beethoven). *I. Allegro. II. Andante.*

December 23. Hayward, California. Cal State Hayward Recital Hall (Bösendorfer). *Sonata in E* (1776) (Haydn). *I. Moderato. II. Allegretto. III. Finale: Presto. Sonata #15 in D, Op. 28 (Pastorale)* (Beethoven). *I. Allegro. II. Andante. III. Allegro Vivace. IV. Allegro ma non Troppo.*

December 24. Hayward, California. Cal State Hayward Recital Hall (Bösendorfer). *Sonata in C, D. 840 (Unfinished)* (Schubert). *I. Moderato. II. Andante. III. Menuetto: Allegro. IV. Rondo: Allegro.* Third and Fourth Movements completed by William Bolcom.

December 29. San Francisco, California. KQED-FM: 'West Coast Weekend', with Sedge Thomson (Life on the Water/Steinway). *(Turn, Turn, Turn* (Seeger)/*Dejas. Un Flambeau, Jeannette, Isabella* (17th century Provençal Carol). *Quasi Moon* (from *Tarot)* Bridge. *St. James Infirmary* (?) Bridge. *I've Just Seen a Face* (Lennon/McCartney). *Audience Adventure Boogie. Rockin' Promenade.*

## 1991

January 5. San Francisco, California. KQED-FM: 'West Coast Weekend', with Sedge Thomson (Life on the Water/Steinway).

{Universal Soldier (Ste. Marie)/Dejas. This Little Piggy Theme. Entertainment Tonite Bridge. National Theatre of the Deranged Intro/Outro. Rockin' Promenade. BBC News (Varon) Outro. Audience Adventure Boogie. Need You (Lennon/McCartney). National Theatre of the Deranged Intro/Outro.

January 6. Las Vegas, Nevada. Terry Ryan Studio. (Yamaha pf-85). Terry Ryan, producer/engineer. Madonna, per voi ardo (Verdelot). Afflitti spirti miei (Verdelot). Madonna, qual certezza (Verdelot).

January 7. Las Vegas, Nevada. Terry Ryan Studio. (Yamaha pf-85). Terry Ryan, producer/engineer. Another George for Terry. Baron von Wartzenall. Carnal Noncarol. Valse Burlesque.

January 12. San Francisco, California. KQED-FM: 'West Coast Weekend', with Sedge Thomson (Life on the Water/Steinway). Rebroadcast of August 4, 1990 show.

January 19. San Francisco, California. KQED-FM: 'West Coast Weekend', with Sedge Thomson (Life on the Water/Steinway). Rebroadcast of August 11, 1990 show.

January 26. San Francisco, California. KQED-FM: 'West Coast Weekend', with Sedge Thomson (Life on the Water/Steinway). Rebroadcast of September 22, 1990 show.

February 2. San Francisco, California. KQED-FM: 'West Coast Weekend', with Sedge Thomson (Life on the Water/Steinway). {Me and my Shadow (?)/Dejas with Will Scarlett. Fake Fur Elise. Rockin' Promenade. I am Waiting (Jagger/Richard). C Shuffle with Will Scarlett. Audience Adventure Boogie. Need You (Harrison).

February 9. San Francisco, California. KQED-FM: 'West Coast Weekend', with Sedge Thomson (Life on the Water/Steinway). {What the World Needs Now (?)/Dejas. Prelude (1963). Folksong Army (Lehrer) Bridge. Possible Piggy Bridge. I'm Gonna Sit Right Down and Write Myself a Letter (Lert/Young). With Ralph Litwin. Audience Adventure Boogie. Rockin' Promenade. Positively Fourth Street over Twin Peaks Bridge.

February 16. San Francisco, California. KQED-FM: 'West Coast Weekend', with Sedge Thomson (Life on the Water/Steinway). {Lara's Theme (?)/Dejas. With Dale Miller and Sam Page. Speaking (Forrester). Boris the Spider (Entwistle). Farcical Bridge. D Blues with Sam Page. Audience Adventure Boogie.

February 23. San Francisco, California. KQED-FM: 'West Coast Weekend', with Sedge

Thomson (Life on the Water/Steinway). One Hour Show due to War Coverage. {Always (?)/Dejas. Audience Adventure Boogie. BBC News (Varon) Outro.

February 26. San Francisco, California. Wellhausen Studios. Robin Petrie: A Victorian Christmas. Wexford Carol. Sussex Carol. Cherry Tree Carol. Furry Day Carol.

March 2. San Francisco, California. KQED-FM: 'West Coast Weekend', with Sedge Thomson (Life on the Water/Steinway). {Start off each Day with a Song (Durante)/Dejas. Ashokan Farewell (Ungar). Graceful Ghost (Bolcom). McNeil/Lehrer Ramble. Audience Adventure Boogie. The Mountains High (Dick & DeeDee). Rockin' Promenade.

March 9. San Francisco, California. KQED-FM: 'West Coast Weekend', with Sedge Thomson (Life on the Water/Steinway). {Prelude Op. 32 #5.(Rachmaninoff)/Dejas. I Am Waiting (Jagger/Richard). Italian Symphony (Mendelssohn) Excerpt. Rockin' Promenade. Flying (Lennon/McCartney). Audience Adventure Boogie. Ashokan Farewell (Ungar) Bridge. NPR Tabloid Sketch Outro. Rain Outro.

March 16. San Francisco, California. KQED-FM: 'West Coast Weekend', with Sedge Thomson (Life on the Water/Steinway). {Small Circle of Friends.(Ochs)/Dejas. Concerto, Op. 3 #7 (Vivaldi) Excerpt. If There's Anything That You Want (Lennon/McCartney). Rockin' Promenade. Flying (Lennon/McCartney). With Pastiche Band. Audience Adventure Boogie. Friend of the Devil (Hunter/Dawson/Garcia) Tag.

March 23. San Francisco, California. KQED-FM: 'West Coast Weekend', with Sedge Thomson (Life on the Water/Steinway). {One Tin Soldier (?)/Dejas. Green Piece. Wildflowers (Kallick). Fake Fur Elise. Rockin' Promenade (People are Strange Outro). BBC News (Varon) Outro. J. D.'s Boogie (J.D.). With Kim Angelis and John Gault. Audience Adventure Boogie. Spirit of the Dove (Angelis). With Kim Angelis and John Gault.

March 23. San Francisco, California. The I Beam. (Roland digital piano RD-300s. courtesy of George Michalski). Oracle Be-in. Piano solo: Friend of the Devil (Hunter/Dawson/Garcia)/Boris the Spider (Entwistle). With George Michalski, piano four hands: Dear Prudence (Lennon/McCartney).

March 30. San Francisco, California. KQED-FM: 'West Coast Weekend', with Sedge Thomson (Life on the Water/Steinway). Rebroadcast of August 4, 1990 show.

April 13. San Francisco, California. KQED-FM: 'West Coast Weekend', with Sedge Thomson (Life on the Water/Steinway). *{Goin' Home* (Dvořák)/*Dejas*. With the San Francisco Saxophone Quartet: David Schrader, Bill Aron, David Henderson, and Kevin J. Stewart. *Giulietta degli Spiriti* (Nino Rota). *Rockin' Promenade. Audience Adventure Boogie. Possessed Washing Machine* Sketch (Fox) Intro/Outro.

April 14. San Mateo, California. B Street Music Studios (Korg TK-1 Digital keyboard). Grape Session. George Rivas, engineer. *Grape Escape Boogie* (Mark Lashley). *Castro Street Blues* (Mark Lashley). *Bitter Wind* (Bob Moseley). *I am a Dreamer* (Bob Moseley). *Everybody Knows* (Mark Lashley).

April 25. Kohala, Hawaii. Museum of the Pacific (Steinway). *Dejavalse. Romance, Op. 118 #5* (Brahms). *Etude, Op. 25 #6* (Chopin). *Prelude, Op. 28 #10 (Night Moth)* (Chopin). *Eintritt, Op. 82 #1* (Schumann). *Friend of the Devil* (Hunter/Dawson/Garcia)/*Boris the Spider* (Entwistle).

April 27. San Francisco, California. KQED-FM: 'West Coast Weekend', with Sedge Thomson (Life on the Water/Steinway). *{Hi'ilawe* (Pahinui)/*Dejas. Italian Symphony* (Mendelssohn) Excerpt. *Prelude, Op. 28 #10 (Night Moth)* (Chopin). Improv w/fourths. *The Moon* (from *Tarot*), with Henry Kaiser, guitar. *Audience Adventure Boogie. Mondegreens* (Carroll, ed.), with Jon Carroll.

May 4. San Francisco, California. KQED-FM: 'West Coast Weekend', with Sedge Thomson (Life on the Water/Steinway). *{Neil Diamond intro/Dejas. Cielito Lindo* in five (Traditional *via* Brubeck). *Dejavalentino. BBC News* (Varon) Outro. *Audience Adventure Boogie. Rockin' Promenade. Andante Amoroso* from *Sonata, K. 282* (Mozart).

May 11. San Francisco, California. KQED-FM: 'West Coast Weekend', with Sedge Thomson (Life on the Water/Steinway). *{I'd Walk a Million Miles for One of your Smiles/Dejas*. With Irene Sazer, violin; Elizabeth Meade, vocals; Ho Young Kim, guitar; and Eric Heilman, bass. *I Know You Rider* (Traditional). *Dinosaurs* Sketch (Fox) Bed. *D Blues*. With Irene Sazer, violin. *Audience Adventure Boogie*.

May 13. El Cerrito, California. Bay Cable Channel 28. *On Stage*. Danny Kalb Band: Danny Kalb, guitar and vocals; Ray Collins, saxophones; Arnon Palty, bass; Clay Lilleston, drums; and T.C., piano (Winter). *Mean Old Southern* (Traditional). *Black Night*

*is Falling* (Traditional). *Magnolia* (Collins). *Ball Game on a Rainy Day* (Kalb). *Danville Dame* (Hardin).

May 18. San Francisco, California. KQED-FM: 'West Coast Weekend', with Sedge Thomson (Life on the Water/Steinway). *{Relax your Mind* (?)/*Dejas. Simple Gifts* (Traditional). *If There's Anything that you Want* (Lennon/McCartney). *Rockin' Promenade (Lavender Blue* Outro). *Audience Adventure Boogie. The Moon* (from *Tarot*). *A Green Piece* –piano accompaniment to Pulp Playhouse: Rafe Chase, Diane Barry, and Paul Kilham. *Four Systems* (Earle Brown). *Green Piece. Modern Primitives* Sketch (Fox) Intro.

May 25. San Francisco, California. KQED-FM: 'West Coast Weekend', with Sedge Thomson (Life on the Water/Steinway). *{Just Like a Woman* (Dylan)/*Dejas. Chopped Liver* (Ryan). *Klavierstück, Op. 19 #4* (Schönberg). *Rockin' Promenade. Wooly Bully* (Sam the Sham). *Audience Adventure Boogie*.

May 27. San Mateo, California. B Street Music Studios (Korg TK-1 Digital keyboard). Grape Session. George Rivas, engineer. *Pollution Kills the World* (Mark Lashley/Pat Mahoney/Craig Juan). *Can You Feel it in Your Heart* (Craig Juan).

June 1. San Francisco, California. KQED-FM: 'West Coast Weekend', with Sedge Thomson (Life on the Water/Steinway). *{June is Bustin' out all over* (?)/*Dejas*. With Al Rapone, accordion. Household Nerd Anecdote (Spoken). *Elizabethan Farewell* (Fa-la-la-la-la Good-thee-bye). Lisa Besayns Intro/Outro. Josh Kornbluth Intro/Outro. *Audience Adventure Boogie. Jambalaya* (Hank Williams). With Al Rapone and the Zydeco Express: Al Rapone, accordion; Leonard Gill, guitar; Mark Metoyer, bass; and Mark Keen, drums. *Rockin' Promenade*.

June 7. San Francisco, California. Hank Smith Productions. (Roland A-50). Milk Advisory Board Spot Music Bed.

June 8. San Francisco, California. KQED-FM: 'West Coast Weekend', with Sedge Thomson (Life on the Water/Steinway). Sound Reasons '91. *{Call Me* (?)/*Dejas. Mozart Tango* Bridge. *Rejected Pledge Ideas* Bed. *Rockin' Promenade. BBC News* (Varon) Outro. *Audience Adventure Boogie. Treasure Hunt* Intro/Outro. *Warm San Francisco Night* (Burdon).

June 15. San Francisco, California. KQED-FM: 'West Coast Weekend', with Sedge Thomson (Life on the Water/Steinway). *{Midsummer Night's Dream* (Mendelssohn)/

*Dejas. De Falla* Bridge. *Audience Adventure Boogie. Urban Geographer* Intro/Outro.
June 17. San Mateo, California. B Street Music Studios (Digital keyboard). Grape Session. George Rivas, engineer. *Paint the White House Blue* (Mark Lashley). *Blowin'* (Mark Lashley).
June 22. San Francisco, California. KQED-FM: 'West Coast Weekend', with Sedge Thomson (Life on the Water/Steinway). *{I Don't Want to Set the World on Fire* (?)/*Dejas. Elvis Debussy* Bridge. *Rockin' Promenade. Elizabethan Farewell (Fa-la-la-la-la Good-thee-bye). Green Piece. BBC News* (Varon) Outro. *Audience Adventure Boogie. Prelude, Op. 28 #10* (Chopin) Excerpt. *Urban Geographer* Intro/Outro.
June 29. San Francisco, California. KQED-FM: 'West Coast Weekend', with Sedge Thomson (Life on the Water/Steinway). *{You've Got a Friend* (Taylor)/*Dejas,* with Dan Seamans, bass and Bob Lurie, drums. *Urban Geographer* Intro/Outro. *Sedge's Birthday* (Lennon/McCartney), with Ed Herrmann. *Rockin' Promenade. BBC News* (Varon) Intro *(Lillibulero* {Purcell})/Outro. *Poor People of Paris* (?). With Big Lou, accordion. *Audience Adventure Boogie.* Josh Kornbluth Intro/Outro.
July 3. Pacifica, California. Pacifica Cable Channel 8. 'The Bruce Latimer Show' (Baldwin upright). First segment. *Flight if the Bumble Bee* (Rimsky-Korsakoff arr. Rachmaninoff). *Boris the Spider* (Entwistle). *Graceful Ghost* (Bolcom). *Friend of the Devil* (Hunter/Dawson/Garcia). Second Segment: *Prelude, Op. 23 #6* (Rachmaninoff). *Wildflowers* (Kallick). Closing Segment: *Rialto Ripples* (Gershwin/Donaldson *via* Kovacs).
July 5. Berkeley, California. Fantasy Studios (Studio D/Steinway). Stephen Hart, Engineer. *Dejavalse. Dejavalentino. Graceful Ghost* (Bolcom). *Butterfly Rag* (Chopin arr. T.C.). *Chopped Liver* (Ryan). *Fake Fur Elise. That Hand Played Rag* (Silverman and Ward). *Oriental* (Granados). *Prelude, Op. 23 #6* (Rachmaninoff). *Flight if the Bumble Bee* (Rimsky-Korsakoff arr. Rachmaninoff). *Speaking* (Forrester). *Wildflowers* (Kallick). *Friend of the Devil* (Hunter/Dawson/Garcia).
July 6. San Francisco, California. KQED-FM: 'West Coast Weekend', with Sedge Thomson (Life on the Water/Steinway). *{Also Sprach Zarathustra* (Strauß)/*Dejas. Urban Geographer* Intro/Outro. *Flight if the Bumble*

*Bee* (Rimsky-Korsakoff arr. Rachmaninoff). *BBC News* (Varon) Intro *(Lillibulero* {Purcell})/Outro. *Audience Adventure Boogie. Rockin' Promenade.*
July 12. Berkeley, California. Fantasy Studios (Studio C/Yamaha). Stephen Hart, Engineer. *Haight Street Slither* (T.S.C. #1). *That There Old West...* (T.S.C. #2). *Parallax* (Ryan). With Henry Kaiser: *Dark Star* (Hunter/Grateful Dead). *Goin' Home* (Jagger/Richard). Piano solo: *Boris the Spider* (Entwistle). *Play the Game* (McShee/Portman-Smith). *Dejavalentino. Whiter Shade of Pale* (Reid/Brooker).
July 13. San Francisco, California. KQED-FM: 'West Coast Weekend', with Sedge Thomson (Life on the Water/Steinway). Rebroadcast of March 11, 1989 show.
July 20. San Francisco, California. KQED-FM: 'West Coast Weekend', with Sedge Thomson (Life on the Water/Steinway). Rebroadcast of December 1, 1990 show.
July 27. San Francisco, California. KQED-FM: 'West Coast Weekend', with Sedge Thomson (Life on the Water/Steinway). Rebroadcast of February 9, 1991 show.
August 3. San Francisco, California. KQED-FM: 'West Coast Weekend', with Sedge Thomson (Life on the Water/Steinway). Rebroadcast of February 16, 1991 show.
August 3. Berkeley, California. Winheld Party (Zuckerman Spinet). Danny Kalb Farewell. Several solo keyboard pieces. Several Blues Numbers with Danny Kalb, guitar; Bruce Barthol, bass guitar; and friends.
August 10. San Francisco, California. KQED-FM: 'West Coast Weekend', with Sedge Thomson (Life on the Water/Steinway). Rebroadcast of March 2, 1991 show.

## GRATEFULLY YOURS: THE TOUR

August 11. Richmond, Virginia. Kahootz (KORG Digital Keyboard/600). Kingfish set. T.C. solo set: *Friend of the Devil* (Hunter/Dawson/Garcia)/*Boris the Spider* (Entwistle). *Presto* from *Sonata in E* (Haydn). *Dejavalse. Wildflowers* (Kallick)/*Ashokan Farewell* (Ungar). *Eintritt* from *Waldszenen, Op. 82 #1* (Schumann). *The Moon* (from *Tarot). Mountains of the Moon* (Hunter/Garcia). *Dark Star* (Hunter/Grateful Dead). Joined by Merl Saunders and the Rainforest Band: Merl Saunders, D-60 digital keyboard; Steve Kimock, guitar; Fred Campbell, bass; and Peewee Johnson, drums. Rejoining the Rainforest Band: *Save the Earth* (Saunders/Garcia).

August 12. Alexandria, Virginia. The Birchmere (Yamaha/350/350). First Show. Kingfish set. T.C. solo set: *Mountains of the Moon* (Hunter/Garcia). *Play the Game* (McShee/Portman-Smith). *Ashokan Farewell* (Ungar). *Dejavalse*. *Presto* from *Sonata in E* (Haydn). *Dark Star* (Hunter/Grateful Dead). Joined by Merl Saunders and the Rainforest Band: Merl Saunders, D-60 digital keyboard; Steve Kimock, guitar; Fred Campbell, bass; and Peewee Johnson, drums. Rejoining the Rainforest Band: *Sugaree* (Hunter/Garcia) plus Papa John Creach, violin. Second Show. Kingfish set. T.C. solo set: *Friend of the Devil* (Hunter/Dawson/Garcia). *Dejavalse*. *Rialto Ripples* (Gershwin/Donaldson *via* Kovacs). *Prelude, Op. 28 #10* (Chopin). *Dark Star* (Hunter/Grateful Dead). Joined by Merl Saunders and the Rainforest Band: Merl Saunders, D-60 digital keyboard; Steve Kimock, guitar; Fred Campbell, bass; and Peewee Johnson, drums. Rejoining the Rainforest Band: *Sugaree* (Hunter/Garcia) plus Papa John Creach, violin.

August 13. Philadelphia, Pennsylvania. Chestnut Cabaret (Roland A80/700). Kingfish set. T.C. solo set: *Mountains of the Moon* (Hunter/Garcia). *Dejavalse*. *Friend of the Devil* (Hunter/Dawson/Garcia)/*Boris the Spider* (Entwistle). *Presto* from *Sonata in E* (Haydn). *Dark Star* (Hunter/Grateful Dead). Joined by Merl Saunders and the Rainforest Band: Merl Saunders, D-60 digital keyboard; Steve Kimock, guitar; Fred Campbell, bass; and Peewee Johnson, drums. Rejoining the Rainforest Band: *Sugaree* (Hunter/Garcia) plus Papa John Creach, violin. Encores: *Save the Earth* (Saunders/Garcia).

August 14. Pittsburgh, Pennsylvania. Graffitti's (Kurtzmann/550). Kingfish set. T.C. solo set: *Friend of the Devil* (Hunter/Dawson/Garcia)/*Boris the Spider* (Entwistle). *Dejavalse*. *Graceful Ghost* (Bolcom). *Fake Fur Elise*. *Mountains of the Moon* (Hunter/Garcia). *Prelude, Op. 23 # 6* (Rachmaninoff). *Dark Star* (Hunter/Grateful Dead). Joined by Merl Saunders and the Rainforest Band: Merl Saunders, D-60 digital keyboard; Steve Kimock, guitar; Fred Campbell, bass; and Peewee Johnson, drums. Rejoining the Rainforest Band: *Sugaree* (Hunter/Garcia) plus Papa John Creach, violin.

August 15. Harrisburg, Pennsylvania. Club Met (K. Kawai 7'/1000). Kingfish set. T.C. solo set: *Mountains of the Moon* (Hunter/Garcia). *Dejavalse*. *Boris the Spider*

(Entwistle). *Graceful Ghost* (Bolcom). *Friend of the Devil* (Hunter/Dawson/Garcia). *Fantasy in C minor* (J.S. Bach). *Dark Star* (Hunter/Grateful Dead). Joined by Merl Saunders and the Rainforest Band: Merl Saunders, D-60 digital keyboard; Steve Kimock, guitar; Fred Campbell, bass; and Peewee Johnson, drums. Rejoining the Rainforest Band: *Sugaree* (Hunter/Garcia) plus Papa John Creach, violin. Encores: *Tongue 'n Groove* (Anton, Kimock, Fierro, Banana, Kahn).

August 16. New Britain, Connecticut. The Sting (CP-70/1200). With Kingfish: Barry Flast, Fred Campbell, Barry Sless, and David Nelson, guitars and vocals: *Friend of the Devil* (Hunter/Dawson/Garcia). *Truckin'* (Garcia/Weir/Lesh/Hunter). T.C. solo set: *Friend of the Devil* (Hunter/Dawson/Garcia)/*Boris the Spider* (Entwistle). *Dejavalse*. *Presto* from *Sonata in E* (Haydn). *Goin' Home* (Jagger/Richard). *Mountains of the Moon* (Hunter/Garcia). *Dark Star* (Hunter/Grateful Dead). Joined by Merl Saunders and the Rainforest Band: Merl Saunders, D-60 digital keyboard; Steve Kimock, guitar; Fred Campbell, bass; and Peewee Johnson, drums. Rejoining the Rainforest Band: *Sugaree* (Hunter/Garcia) plus Papa John Creach, violin. Encores: *Merl's Piece* (Saunders).

August 17. San Francisco, California. KQED-FM: 'West Coast Weekend', with Sedge Thomson (Life on the Water/Steinway). Rebroadcast of March 9, 1991 show.

August 17. Warwick, Rhode Island. Rocky Point Amusement Park (CP-70/5000). Kingfish set. T.C. solo set: *Friend of the Devil* (Hunter/Dawson/Garcia)/*Boris the Spider* (Entwistle). *I've Just Seen a Face* (Lennon/McCartney). *Mountains of the Moon* (Hunter/Garcia). *Dark Star* (Hunter/Grateful Dead). Joined by Merl Saunders and the Rainforest Band: Merl Saunders, D-60 digital keyboard; Steve Kimock, guitar; Fred Campbell, bass; and Peewee Johnson, drums. Rejoining the Rainforest Band: *Sugaree* (Hunter/Garcia) plus Papa John Creach, violin.

August 18. Portland, Maine. Raoul's Roadside Attraction (KORG SG-1 Sampling Grand/200). With Kingfish: Barry Flast, Fred Campbell, Barry Sless, and David Nelson, guitars and vocals: *Friend of the Devil* (Hunter/Dawson/Garcia). *Truckin'* (Garcia/Weir/Lesh/Hunter). *Candyman* (Hunter/Garcia). T.C. solo set: *Friend of the Devil* (Hunter/Dawson/Garcia)/*Boris the*

*Spider* (Entwistle). *Dejavalse. Presto* from *Sonata in E* (Haydn). Bizet Story. *Rialto Ripples* (Gershwin/Donaldson *via* Kovacs). *Goin' Home* (Jagger/Richard). *Mountains of the Moon* (Hunter/Garcia). *Dark Star* (Hunter/ Grateful Dead). Joined by Merl Saunders and the Rainforest Band: Merl Saunders, D-60 digital keyboard; Steve Kimock, guitar; Fred Campbell, bass; and Peewee Johnson, drums. Rejoining the Rainforest Band: *Sugaree* (Hunter/Garcia) plus Papa John Creach, violin. Encores: *Blues for the Rainforest* (Saunders). *Tongue 'n Groove* (Anton, Kimock et al). *We Bid You Goodnight* (Traditional) – Piano solo.

August 20. Baltimore, Maryland. Steeltown (Roland EP-7 Digital Piano/450). With Kingfish: Barry Flast, Fred Campbell, Barry Sless, and David Nelson, guitars and vocals: *U. S. Blues* (Hunter/Garcia). T.C. solo set: *Friend of the Devil* (Hunter/Dawson/ Garcia)/*Boris the Spider* (Entwistle). *Dejavalse. I've Just Seen a Face* (Lennon/ McCartney). *Mountains of the Moon* (Hunter/Garcia). *Dark Star* (Hunter/Grateful Dead). Joined by Merl Saunders and the Rainforest Band: Merl Saunders, D-60 digital keyboard; Steve Kimock, guitar; Fred Campbell, bass; and Peewee Johnson, drums. Rejoining the Rainforest Band: *Sugaree* (Hunter/Garcia) plus Papa John Creach, violin. Encores: *Merl's Piece* (Saunders). *Feel Like Dynamite* (Saunders).

August 21. Ocean City, Maryland. Scandal's (KORG DSS-1/400). With Kingfish: Barry Flast, Fred Campbell, Barry Sless, and David Nelson, guitars and vocals: *Cumberland Blues* (Hunter/Garcia/Lesh). *Dire Wolf* (Hunter/ Garcia). *Off to the Rodeo* (?). *I Know You Rider* (Traditional). T.C. solo set: *Friend of the Devil* (Hunter/Dawson/Garcia)/*Boris the Spider* (Entwistle). *Presto* from *Sonata in E* (Haydn). *I've Just Seen a Face* (Lennon/ McCartney). *Dark Star* (Hunter/Grateful Dead). Joined by Merl Saunders and the Rainforest Band: Merl Saunders, D-60 digital keyboard; Steve Kimock, guitar; Fred Campbell, bass; and Peewee Johnson, drums. Rejoining the Rainforest Band: *Sugaree* (Hunter/Garcia) plus Papa John Creach, violin. Encores: *Tongue 'n Groove* (Anton, Kimock et al). *Save the Planet* (Saunders) plus Papa John Creach, violin.

August 22. New York, New York. The Bottom Line (Yamaha/175/180). First Show, with Kingfish: Barry Flast, Fred Campbell, Barry Sless, and David Nelson, guitars and

vocals: *Dire Wolf* (Hunter/Garcia). *Truckin'* (Garcia/Weir/Lesh/Hunter). T.C. solo set: *Friend of the Devil* (Hunter/Dawson/ Garcia)/*Boris the Spider* (Entwistle). *Dejavalse. Graceful Ghost* (Bolcom). *Mountains of the Moon* (Hunter/Garcia). *Dark Star* (Hunter/Grateful Dead). Joined by Merl Saunders and the Rainforest Band: Merl Saunders, D-60 digital keyboard; Steve Kimock, guitar; Fred Campbell, bass; and Peewee Johnson, drums. Rejoining the Rainforest Band: *Sugaree* (Hunter/Garcia) plus Papa John Creach, violin.

Second Show. With Kingfish: Barry Flast, Fred Campbell, Barry Sless, and David Nelson, guitars and vocals: *Ripple* (Hunter/ Garcia). *Walkin' Blues* (Johnson). *Friend of the Devil* (Hunter/Dawson/Garcia). *Truckin'* (Garcia/Weir/Lesh/Hunter). T.C. solo set: *Mountains of the Moon* (Hunter/ Garcia). *Boris the Spider* (Entwistle). *Dejavalse. Presto* from *Sonata in E* (Haydn). *Fake Fue Elise. Dark Star* (Hunter/Grateful Dead). Joined by Merl Saunders and the Rainforest Band: Merl Saunders, D-60 digital keyboard; Steve Kimock, guitar; Fred Campbell, bass; and Peewee Johnson, drums. Rejoining the Rainforest Band: *Sugaree* (Hunter/Garcia) plus Papa John Creach, violin.

August 23. Boston, Massachusetts. The Channel (Roland 300s Digital Piano/325). Kingfish set. T.C. solo set: *Friend of the Devil* (Hunter/Dawson/Garcia)/*Boris the Spider* (Entwistle). *Dejavalse. I've Just Seen a Face* (Lennon/McCartney). *Praeambulum, Partita #5* (J. S. Bach). *Mountains of the Moon* (Hunter/Garcia). *Dark Star* (Hunter/Grateful Dead). Joined by Merl Saunders and the Rainforest Band: Merl Saunders, D-60 digital keyboard; Steve Kimock, guitar; Fred Campbell, bass; and Peewee Johnson, drums. Rejoining the Rainforest Band: *Sugaree* (Hunter/Garcia) plus Papa John Creach, violin. Encores: *Tongue 'n Groove* (Anton, Kimock et al). *Feel Like Dynamite* (Saunders)plus Papa John Creach, violin.

August 24. San Francisco, California. KQED-FM: 'West Coast Weekend', With Sedge Thomson (Life on the Water/Steinway). Rebroadcast of April 13, 1991 show.

August 24. Rochester, New York. Red Creek (KORG Digital Keyboard/150/200). First Show. Kingfish set. T.C. solo set: *Friend of the Devil* (Hunter/Dawson/Garcia)/*Boris the Spider* (Entwistle). *I've Just Seen a Face* (Lennon/McCartney). *Mountains of the*

*Moon* (Hunter/Garcia). *Dark Star* (Hunter/Grateful Dead). Joined by Merl Saunders and the Rainforest Band: Merl Saunders, D-60 digital keyboard; Steve Kimock, guitar; Fred Campbell, bass; and Peewee Johnson, drums. Rejoining the Rainforest Band: *Sugaree* (Hunter/Garcia) plus Papa John Creach, violin. Second Show. With Kingfish: Barry Flast, Fred Campbell, Barry Sless, and David Nelson, guitars and vocals: *Candyman* (Hunter/Garcia). *Goin' Down the Road Feelin' Bad* (Traditional). *Dire Wolf* (Hunter/Garcia). T.C. solo set: *Friend of the Devil* (Hunter/Dawson/Garcia)/*Boris the Spider* (Entwistle). *I've Just Seen a Face* (Lennon/McCartney). *Mountains of the Moon* (Hunter/Garcia). *Dark Star* (Hunter/Grateful Dead). Joined by Merl Saunders and the Rainforest Band: Merl Saunders, D-60 digital keyboard; Steve Kimock, guitar; Fred Campbell, bass; and Peewee Johnson, drums. Rejoining the Rainforest Band: *Sugaree* (Hunter/Garcia) plus Papa John Creach, violin. Encores: *We Bid You Goodnight* (Traditional) – Piano solo. *Save the Planet* (Saunders). *F Blues*.

August 25. Parksville, New York. Arrowhead Ranch (KORG Sampling Grand/500). With Kingfish: Barry Flast, Fred Campbell, Barry Sless, and David Nelson, guitars and vocals: *Dire Wolf* (Hunter/Garcia). *Cumberland Blues* (Hunter/Garcia/Lesh). *I Know You Rider* (Traditional). *Ripple* (Hunter/Garcia). *Truckin'* (Garcia/Weir/Lesh/Hunter). T.C. solo set: *Friend of the Devil* (Hunter/Dawson/Garcia)/*Boris the Spider* (Entwistle). *Dejavalse. Presto* from *Sonata in E* (Haydn). *Mountains of the Moon* (Hunter/Garcia). *I've Just Seen a Face* (Lennon/McCartney). *Dark Star* (Hunter/Grateful Dead). Joined by Merl Saunders and the Rainforest Band: Merl Saunders, D-60 digital keyboard; Steve Kimock, guitar; Fred Campbell, bass; and Peewee Johnson, drums. Rejoining the Rainforest Band: *Sugaree* (Hunter/Garcia) plus Papa John Creach, violin. Encores: *Feel Like Dynamite* (Saunders).

August 26. Buffalo, New York. Melody Fair (K. Kawai 7'/1500). With Kingfish: Barry Flast, Fred Campbell, Barry Sless, and David Nelson, guitars and vocals: *Fire on the Mountain* (Hunter/Hart). *Ripple* (Hunter/Garcia). *Cumberland Blues* (Hunter/Garcia/Lesh). *Truckin'* (Garcia/Weir/Lesh/Hunter). *Deep Elem Blues* (Traditional). *Dire Wolf* (Hunter/Garcia). *U. S. Blues* (Hunter/Garcia). T.C.

solo set: *Friend of the Devil* (Hunter/Dawson/Garcia)/*Boris the Spider* (Entwistle). *Dejavalse. Graceful Ghost* (Bolcom). *Presto* from *Sonata in E* (Haydn). *Prelude, Op. 23 #6* (Rachmaninoff). *Mountains of the Moon* (Hunter/Garcia). *Dark Star* (Hunter/Grateful Dead). Joined by Merl Saunders and the Rainforest Band: Merl Saunders, D-60 digital keyboard; Steve Kimock, guitar; Fred Campbell, bass; and Peewee Johnson, drums. Rejoining the Rainforest Band: *Sugaree* (Hunter/Garcia) plus Papa John Creach, violin. Encores: *Tongue 'n Groove* (Anton, Kimock et al). *Feel Like Dynamite* (Saunders).

August 27. Toronto, Ontario. Rock 'n Roll Heaven (Roland 250s/1200). With Kingfish: Barry Flast, Fred Campbell, Barry Sless, and David Nelson, guitars and vocals: *Cumberland Blues* (Hunter/Garcia/Lesh). *Ripple* (Hunter/Garcia). *Friend of the Devil* (Hunter/Dawson/Garcia). *Candyman* (Hunter/Garcia). *Truckin'* (Garcia/Weir/Lesh/Hunter). *U. S. Blues* (Hunter/Garcia). T.C. solo set: *Friend of the Devil* (Hunter/Dawson/Garcia)/*Boris the Spider* (Entwistle). *Dejavalse. I've Just Seen a Face* (Lennon/McCartney). *Mountains of the Moon* (Hunter/Garcia). *Dark Star* (Hunter/Grateful Dead). Joined by Merl Saunders and the Rainforest Band: Merl Saunders, D-60 digital keyboard; Steve Kimock, guitar; Fred Campbell, bass; and Peewee Johnson, drums. Rejoining the Rainforest Band: *Sugaree* (Hunter/Garcia) plus Papa John Creach, violin. Encores: *Tongue 'n Groove* (Anton, Kimock et al). *Feel Like Dynamite* (Saunders). *We Bid You Goodnight* (Traditional) – Piano solo.

August 30. Cleveland, Ohio, WNCX – FM 98.5. Interviewed with Merl Saunders by Bill Louis.

August 30. Cleveland, Ohio. Agora Theatre (Rhodes Mark 1 Stage Piano/900). With Kingfish: Barry Flast, Fred Campbell, and Barry Sless, guitars and vocals: *Goin' Down the Road Feelin' Bad* (Traditional). *Ripple* (Hunter/Garcia). *Don't Ease me In* (Traditional) plus backup vocal. *I Know You Rider* (Traditional). *Dire Wolf* (Hunter/Garcia). *Deep Elem Blues* (Traditional). *Friend of the Devil* (Hunter/Dawson/Garcia). *Fire on the Mountain* (Hunter/Hart) plus backup vocal. *Truckin'* (Garcia/Weir/Lesh/Hunter) plus backup vocal. *New New Minglewood Blues* (Noah Lewis). *U. S. Blues* (Hunter/Garcia). T.C. solo set: *Friend of the Devil*

(Hunter/Dawson/Garcia)/*Boris the Spider* (Entwistle). *I've Just Seen a Face* (Lennon/McCartney). *Presto* from *Sonata in E* (Haydn). *Mountains of the Moon* (Hunter/Garcia). *Dark Star* (Hunter/Grateful Dead). Joined by Merl Saunders and the Rainforest Band: Merl Saunders, D-60 digital keyboard; Steve Kimock, guitar; Fred Campbell, bass; and Peewee Johnson, drums. Rejoining the Rainforest Band: *Sugaree* (Hunter/Garcia) plus Papa John Creach, violin. Encores: *Tongue'n Groove* (Anton, Kimock et al). *Feel Like Dynamite* (Saunders).

August 31. San Francisco, California. KQED-FM: 'West Coast Weekend', with Sedge Thomson (Life on the Water/Steinway). Rebroadcast of May 4, 1991 show.

August 31. Chicago, Illinois. Cubby Bear (CP-80/600/600). First Show. With Kingfish: Barry Flast, Fred Campbell, and Barry Sless, guitars and vocals: *Don't Ease me In* (Traditional) plus backup vocal. *Deep Elem Blues* (Traditional). *Dire Wolf* (Hunter/Garcia). *Dark Hollow* (Traditional). *I Know You Rider* (Traditional) plus backup vocal. *Ripple* (Hunter/Garcia). *Fire on the Mountain* (Hunter/Hart) plus backup vocal. *Walking Blues* (Robert Johnson). *Truckin'* (Garcia/Weir/Lesh/Hunter) plus backup vocal. T.C. solo set: *Friend of the Devil* (Hunter/Dawson/Garcia)/*Boris the Spider* (Entwistle). *Dejavalse. Presto* from *Sonata in E* (Haydn). *Mountains of the Moon* (Hunter/Garcia). *Dark Star* (Hunter/Grateful Dead). Joined by Merl Saunders and the Rainforest Band: Merl Saunders, D-60 digital keyboard; Steve Kimock, guitar; Fred Campbell, bass; and Peewee Johnson, drums. Rejoining the Rainforest Band: *Sugaree* (Hunter/Garcia) plus Papa John Creach, violin.

Second Show. With Kingfish: Barry Flast, Fred Campbell, and Barry Sless, guitars and vocals: *Goin' Down the Road Feelin' Bad* (Traditional). *When I Paint my Masterpiece* (Dylan). *Truckin'* (Garcia/Weir/Lesh/Hunter) plus backup vocal. *Friend of the Devil* (Hunter/Dawson/Garcia). *Deep Elem Blues* (Traditional). *New New Minglewood Blues* (Noah Lewis). *Ripple* (Hunter/Garcia). *Fire on the Mountain* (Hunter/Hart) plus backup vocal. *U. S. Blues* (Hunter/Garcia). *Don't Ease me In* (Traditional) plus backup vocal. T.C. solo set: *Mountains of the Moon* (Hunter/Garcia). *I've Just Seen a Face* (Lennon/McCartney). *Dejavalse. Praeambulum, Partita #5* (J. S. Bach). *Boris the Spider* (Entwistle). *Dark Star* (Hunter/Grateful

Dead). Joined by Merl Saunders and the Rainforest Band: Merl Saunders, D-60 digital keyboard; Steve Kimock, guitar; Fred Campbell, bass; and Peewee Johnson, drums. Rejoining the Rainforest Band: *Sugaree* (Hunter/Garcia) plus Papa John Creach, violin.

September 7. San Francisco, California. KQED-FM: 'West Coast Weekend', with Sedge Thomson (Life on the Water/Steinway). *{Don't Know What You've Got till it's Gone* (Mitchell)/*Dejas. Mountains of the Moon* (Hunter/Garcia). *The Asra* (Rubinstein – excerpt). *Rockin' Promenade.* Nixie Comment. *BBC News* (Varon) Outro. *Audience Adventure Boogie.*

September 8. Las Vegas, Nevada. Terry Ryan Studio (Knabe). *Mountains of the Moon* (Hunter/Garcia). *I've Just Seen a Face* (Lennon/McCartney). *Romance, Op. 118 #5* (Brahms).

September 9. Las Vegas, Nevada. Terry Ryan Studio (Knabe). *Etude #25* (Chopin). *Romance, Op. 118 #5* (Brahms). *Mountains of the Moon* (Hunter/Garcia).

September 14. San Francisco, California. KQED-FM: 'West Coast Weekend', with Sedge Thomson (Life on the Water/Steinway). *{Let me be there.(?)/Dejas. Fa-la-la Good Thee Bye. Urban Geographer* Intro/Outro. *Play the Game* (McShee/Portman-Smith) 6/8 version. *Audience Adventure Boogie.* Anne Lamott Intro/Outro. *Rockin' Promenade.*

September 16. San Francisco, California. Life on the Water soirée (K. Kawai). *Graceful Ghost* (Bolcom). *Friend of the Devil* (Hunter/Dawson/Garcia)/*Boris the Spider* (Entwistle). *Prelude, Op. 23 # 6* (Rachmaninoff). *Romance, Op. 118 #5* (Brahms). *Mountains of the Moon* (Hunter/Garcia). *I've Just Seen a Face* (Lennon/McCartney). *Praeambulum, Partita #5* (J. S. Bach). *Etude, Op. 25 #6* (Chopin).

September 21. San Francisco, California. KQED-FM: 'West Coast Weekend', with Sedge Thomson (Life on the Water/Steinway). *{Hail, Hail, the gang's all here (?)/Dejas. De Falla* Bridge. *Jazzoid* Bridge. *Astronaut* M. Hughes-Fulford Intro/Outro. *Urban Geographer* Intro/Outro. *BBC News* (Varon) Outro. *Hurdy Gurdy Man* (Leitch). *Audience Adventure Boogie.* Author Julie Smith Intro/Outro. *Green Piece. Rockin' Promenade.*

September 22. Oakland, California. Piedmont Piano Co. (Yamaha). *Earplay Seventh Annual Gala.* Waltz Project Celebration. *Sentimental Waltz* (Ashforth). *A Waltz for Evelyn*

*Hinrichsen* (Harrison). *Dejavalse*. With Jerry Kuderna, Barbara Shearer, Marvin Tartak, Naomi Sparrow, Karen Rosenak, Louise Bidwell, George Thomson, and Elizabeth Davidson.

September 28. San Francisco, California. KQED-FM: 'West Coast Weekend', with Sedge Thomson (Life on the Water/ Steinway). *{Webern Op. 27 opening/Dejas. Modern Love Waltz* (Glass) Bridge. Space Bridge. *Urban Geographer* Intro/Outro. *Audience Adventure Boogie. Rockin' Promenade.*

September 27, 30. San Francisco, California. Hank Smith Productions. *Simple Gifts* (Traditional).

September 29. San Pablo, California. Grateful Dead Documentary (Pease). Steve Steinberg, Producer. *Mountains of the Moon* (Hunter/Garcia). *Dark Star* (Hunter/Grateful Dead). *Dejavalse.*

October 5. San Francisco, California. KQED-FM: 'West Coast Weekend', With Sedge Thomson (Life on the Water/Steinway). *{Anniversary Waltz* (?)/*Dejas. Twin Peaks* Bridge. *One Toke over the Line* (Brewer/ Shipley) Bridge. *Rockin' Promenade. BBC News* (Varon) Outro. *Audience Adventure Boogie. Urban Geographer* Intro/Outro

*GRATEFULLY YOURS: THE SECOND TOUR*

October 10. Solana Beach, California. Belly Up Tavern (KORG Sampling Grand)/487). With acoustic Kingfish: Barry Flast, guitar and vocals, Matthew Kelly, harmonica, guitar, and vocals; Barry Sless, guitar and pedal steel; and Fred Campbell, guitar and vocals; plus David Nelson, guitar, mandolin, and vocals; and Papa John Creach, violin and vocals: *Cumberland Blues* (Hunter/ Garcia/Lesh). *Truckin'* (Garcia/Weir/ Lesh/Hunter). Piano solo: *St. Stephen* (Hunter/Garcia)/*A Day in the Life* (Lennon/ McCartney). *Friend of the Devil* (Hunter/ Dawson/Garcia)/*Boris the Spider* (Entwistle). *Dejavalse. Presto* from *Sonata in E* (Haydn). *Hurdy Gurdy Man* (Leitch). *Mountains of the Moon* (Hunter/Garcia). *Dark Star* (Hunter/Grateful Dead). Joined in progress by electric Kingfish: Barry Flast, keyboard and vocals, Matthew Kelly, harmonica, guitar, and vocals; Barry Sless, guitar and pedal steel; Fred Campbell, bass and vocals; and Eric Parker, drums; plus David Nelson, guitar and vocals: *I Know You Rider* (Traditional)/*Hand Jive* (Otis)/*The Eleven* (Hunter/Lesh). *New New Minglewood Blues* (Weir/Lewis)/*New Minglewood Blues*

(Lewis). *Althea* (Hunter/Garcia). Plus Papa John Creach, violin and vocals: *Down Home Blues* (Creach). *Pop's Boogie* (Creach). *U. S. Blues* (Hunter/Garcia). Encores: *Juke* (Kingfish). *Knockin' on Heaven's Door* (Dylan).

October 11. Los Angeles, California. KPFK-FM: 'Thursday Lunch.' With Tom Norton and Bob Young (Mason and Hamlin). *Mountains of the Moon* (Hunter/Garcia). *Dejavalse. Presto* from *Sonata in E* (Haydn). *Boris the Spider* (Entwistle). *Prelude, Op. 32 #1* (Rachmaninoff). *Dark Star* (Hunter/Grateful Dead).

October 12. San Francisco, California. KQED-FM: 'West Coast Weekend', with Sedge Thomson (Life on the Water/Steinway). *{On the Road Again* (Traditional)/*Dejas. Waltz for Evelyn Hinrichsen* (Harrison). *Modern Love Waltz* (Glass) Excerpt. A. A. Milne reading by Sedge Thomson Bed. *Urban Geographer* Intro/Outro. *Mountains of the Moon* (Hunter/Garcia). *Audience Adventure Boogie. Rockin' Promenade.*

October 12. North Hollywood, California. The Palomino (CP-80/279). With acoustic Kingfish: Barry Flast, guitar and vocals, Matthew Kelly, harmonica, guitar, and vocals; Barry Sless, guitar and pedal steel; and Fred Campbell, guitar and vocals; plus David Nelson, guitar, mandolin, and vocals; and Papa John Creach, violin and vocals. *Oh, Babe it ain't no lie* (Cotten). *Cumberland Blues* (Hunter/Garcia/Lesh). *Truckin'* (Garcia/Weir/Lesh/Hunter). Piano solo: *St. Stephen* (Hunter/Garcia)/*A Day in the Life* (Lennon/McCartney). *Friend of the Devil* (Hunter/Dawson/Garcia)/*Boris the Spider* (Entwistle). *Dejavalse. Mountains of the Moon* (Hunter/Garcia). *The Ballad of Shane Muscatell. Presto* from *Sonata in E* (Haydn). *Dark Star* (Hunter/Grateful Dead). Joined in progress by electric Kingfish: Barry Flast, keyboard and vocals, Matthew Kelly, harmonica, guitar, and vocals; Barry Sless, guitar and pedal steel; Fred Campbell, bass and vocals; and Eric Parker, drums; plus David Nelson, guitar and vocals: *I Know You Rider* (Traditional)/*Hand Jive* (Otis)/*The Eleven* (Hunter/Lesh). *Althea* (Hunter/ Garcia). Plus Papa John Creach, violin and vocals: *Down Home Blues* (Creach). *Pop's Boogie* (Creach). *U. S. Blues* (Hunter/Garcia). Kingfish Segment. *Deal* (Hunter/Garcia). *Around & Around* (Berry).

October 13. Isla Vista, California. The Anaconda (Roland ep-7 digital piano/ca 200). With acoustic Kingfish: Barry Flast, guitar and vocals, Matthew Kelly, harmonica, guitar, and vocals; Barry Sless, guitar and pedal steel; and Fred Campbell, guitar and vocals; plus David Nelson, guitar, mandolin, and vocals; and Papa John Creach, violin and vocals. *Friend of the Devil* (Hunter/Dawson/Garcia). *Truckin'* (Garcia/Weir/Lesh/Hunter). Piano solo: *Friend of the Devil* (Hunter/Dawson/Garcia)/*Boris the Spider* (Entwistle). *Dejavalse. I've just seen a Face* (Lennon/McCartney). *Presto* from *Sonata in E* (Haydn). *Mountains of the Moon* (Hunter/Garcia). *Dark Star* (Hunter/Grateful Dead). Joined in progress by electric Kingfish: Barry Flast, keyboard and vocals, Matthew Kelly, harmonica, guitar, and vocals; Barry Sless, guitar and pedal steel; Fred Campbell, bass and vocals; and Eric Parker, drums; plus David Nelson, guitar and vocals: *Mission Impossible* (Schifrin) Vamp. *Woman Smarter* (Span)/*Iko Iko* (Traditional)/*Althea* (Hunter/Garcia). *Dark Star* (Hunter/Grateful Dead). Encores: *Panama Red* (Rowan). *Deal* (Hunter/Garcia). *Knockin' on Heaven's Door* (Dylan). *One More Saturday Night* (Weir).

October 15. New York, New York. Wetlands Preserve (KORG SG-1D sampling grand/ca 300). With acoustic Kingfish: Barry Flast, guitar and vocals, Matthew Kelly, harmonica, guitar, and vocals; Barry Sless, guitar and pedal steel; and Fred Campbell, guitar and vocals; plus David Nelson, guitar, mandolin, and vocals. *Cumberland Blues* (Hunter/Garcia/Lesh). *Truckin'* (Garcia/Weir/Lesh/Hunter). Piano solo: *St. Stephen* (Hunter/Garcia)/*A Day in the Life* (Lennon/McCartney). *Friend of the Devil* (Hunter/Dawson/Garcia)/*Boris the Spider* (Entwistle). *Prelude, Op. 32 #1* (Rach-maninoff). *Dejavalse. Presto* from *Sonata in E* (Haydn). *Mountains of the Moon* (Hunter/Garcia). *Dark Star* (Hunter/Grateful Dead). Joined in progress by electric Kingfish: Barry Flast, keyboard and vocals, Matthew Kelly, harmonica, guitar, and vocals; Barry Sless, guitar and pedal steel; Fred Campbell, bass and vocals; and Eric Parker, drums; plus David Nelson, guitar and vocals: *New New Minglewood Blues* (Weir/Lewis)/*New Minglewood Blues* (Lewis). Joined by Danny Kalb, guitar and vocals. *E Blues.* Kingfish Segment: *Althea* (Hunter/Garcia). Joined by Willi Jones, vocals. *Love me like a Man* (?). *I Know You Rider* (Traditional)/*Deal* (Hunter/Garcia)/*Hand Jive* (Otis). *The Eleven* (Hunter/Lesh)/*Woman Smarter* (Span)/*Iko* 

*Iko* (Traditional)/*Woman Smarter* (Span).

October 16. Springfield, Virginia. Zaxx (KORG SG-1D sampling grand/ca 35). Piano solo: *Friend of the Devil* (Hunter/Dawson/Garcia)/*Boris the Spider* (Entwistle). *Dejavalse. Presto* from *Sonata in E* (Haydn). *I've just seen a Face* (Lennon/McCartney). *Prelude, Op. 28 #10* (Chopin). *Mountains of the Moon* (Hunter/Grateful Dead). *Dark Star* (Hunter/Grateful Dead). Joined in progress by electric Kingfish: Barry Flast, keyboard and vocals, Matthew Kelly, harmonica, guitar, and vocals; Barry Sless, guitar and pedal steel; Fred Campbell, bass and vocals; and Eric Parker, drums; plus David Nelson, guitar and vocals: *I Know You Rider* (Traditional)/*Deal* (Hunter/Garcia). *Goin' down the Road Feelin' Bad* (Traditional). *New New Minglewood Blues* (Weir/Lewis)/*New Minglewood Blues* (Lewis). *Althea* (Hunter/Garcia). *Panama Red* (Rowan). *Hand Jive* (Otis).

October 17. York, Pennsylvania. WHTF-FM: *The Mike Tyler Show.* Interviewed with Barry Flast and David Nelson.

October 17. Lancaster, Pennsylvania. The Village (Clavinova/328). With Acoustic Kingfish. *Cumberland Blues* (Hunter/Garcia/Lesh). *Truckin'* (Hunter/Garcia/Weir/Lesh). Piano solo: *St. Stephen* (Hunter/Garcia)/*A Day in the Life* (Lennon/McCartney). *Friend of the Devil* (Hunter/Dawson/Garcia)/*Boris the Spider* (Entwistle). *Presto* from *Sonata in E* (Haydn). *Dejavalse. Mountains of the Moon* (Hunter/Garcia). *Prelude, Op. 28 #10* (Chopin). *Dark Star* (Hunter/Grateful Dead). Joined in progress by electric Kingfish: Barry Flast, keyboard and vocals, Matthew Kelly, harmonica, guitar, and vocals; Barry Sless, guitar and pedal steel; Fred Campbell, bass and vocals; and Eric Parker, drums; plus David Nelson, guitar and vocals: *Goin' down the Road Feelin' Bad* (Traditional)/*Althea* (Hunter/Garcia). *I Know You Rider* (Traditional). *New New Minglewood Blues* (Weir/Lewis)/*New Minglewood Blues* (Lewis). *Juke* (Kingfish)/*Panama Red* (Rowan)/*Hand Jive* (Otis)/*Woman Smarter* (Span)/*Iko Iko* (Traditional)/*Woman Smarter* (Span).

October 18. Philadelphia, Pennsylvania. Chestnut Cabaret (Roland A-80 MIDI controller/ca 200). With acoustic Kingfish: Barry Flast, guitar and vocals, Matthew Kelly, harmonica, guitar, and vocals; Barry Sless, guitar and pedal steel; and Fred Campbell, guitar and vocals; plus David

Nelson, guitar, mandolin, and vocals. *Truckin'* (Garcia/Weir/Lesh/Hunter). Piano: *Friend of the Devil* (Hunter/Dawson/Garcia)/*Boris the Spider* (Entwistle). *Dejavalse. Presto* from *Sonata in E* (Haydn). *Mountains of the Moon* (Hunter/Garcia). *Dark Star* (Hunter/Grateful Dead). Joined in progress by electric Kingfish: Barry Flast, keyboard and vocals, Matthew Kelly, harmonica, guitar, and vocals; Barry Sless, guitar and pedal steel; Fred Campbell, bass and vocals; and Eric Parker, drums; plus David Nelson, guitar and vocals: *U. S. Blues* (Hunter/Garcia)/*Deal* (Hunter/Garcia). *Goin' Down the Road Feelin' Bad* (Traditional)/*Next Time You see me* (?)/*Panama Red* (Rowan). *Hand Jive* (Otis)/*The Eleven* (Hunter/Lesh)/*Hand Jive* (Otis). Encore: *Around and Around* (Berry).

October 19. Virginia Beach, Virginia. Peppermint Beach Club (KORG SG-1D sampling grand/427). With acoustic Kingfish: Barry Flast, guitar and vocals, Matthew Kelly, harmonica, guitar, and vocals; Barry Sless, guitar and pedal steel; and Fred Campbell, guitar and vocals; plus David Nelson, guitar, mandolin, and vocals. *Cumberland Blues* (Hunter/Garcia/Lesh). *Truckin'* (Garcia/Weir/Lesh/Hunter) with Eric Parker, drums. Piano solo: *St. Stephen* (Hunter/Garcia)/*A Day in the Life* (Lennon/McCartney). *Friend of the Devil* (Hunter/Dawson/Garcia)/*Boris the Spider* (Entwistle). *Dejavalse. I've just seen a Face* (Lennon/McCartney). *Prelude, Op. 32 #1* (Rachmaninoff). *Mountains of the Moon* (Hunter/Garcia). With Barry Flast, vocal. *Dark Star* (Hunter/Grateful Dead). Joined in progress by electric Kingfish: Barry Flast, keyboard and vocals, Matthew Kelly, harmonica, guitar, and vocals; Barry Sless, guitar and pedal steel; Fred Campbell, bass and vocals; and Eric Parker, drums; plus David Nelson, guitar and vocals: *I Know You Rider* (Traditional)/*Candy Man* (Hunter/Garcia). *U. S. Blues* (Hunter/Garcia)/*Althea* (Hunter/Garcia). *Goin' down the Road Feelin' Bad* (Traditional). *Panama Red* (Rowan). *Hand Jive* (Otis)/*The Eleven* (Hunter/Lesh)/*Hand Jive* (Otis). *One More Saturday Night* (Weir). Encore: *Woman Smarter* (Span)/*Iko Iko* (Traditional)/*Woman Smarter* (Span).

October 20. Baltimore, Maryland. Steeltown (Roland ep-7 digital piano/ca 100). With acoustic Kingfish: Barry Flast, guitar and vocals, Matthew Kelly, harmonica, guitar,

and vocals; Barry Sless, guitar and pedal steel; and Fred Campbell, guitar and vocals; plus David Nelson, guitar, mandolin, and vocals. *Friend of the Devil* (Hunter/Dawson/Garcia). *Truckin'* (Garcia/Weir/Lesh/Hunter). Piano solo: *Mountains of the Moon* (Hunter/Garcia). *Friend of the Devil* (Hunter/Dawson/Garcia)/*Boris the Spider* (Entwistle). *I've just seen a Face* (Lennon/McCartney). *Presto* from *Sonata in E* (Haydn). *Dark Star* (Hunter/Grateful Dead). Joined in progress by electric Kingfish: Barry Flast, keyboard and vocals, Matthew Kelly, harmonica, guitar, and vocals; Barry Sless, guitar and pedal steel; Fred Campbell, bass and vocals; and Eric Parker, drums; plus David Nelson, guitar and vocals: *Deal* (Hunter/Garcia)/*I Know You Rider* (Traditional)/*Althea* (Hunter/Garcia). *U. S. Blues* (Hunter/Garcia). NRPS Segment: *Panama Red* (Rowan). *Hand Jive* (Otis)/*The Eleven* (Hunter/Lesh). *Knockin' on Heaven's Door* (Dylan). Plus Dave Jacobsen, guitar. *Promised Land* (Berry). *Woman Smarter* (Span).

October 22. Knoxville, Tennessee. WUTK-FM. Interviewed with Barry Flast by Kent DuMont.

October 22. Knoxville, Tennessee. Orpheus (KORG Concert 4000/ca 100). With acoustic Kingfish: Barry Flast, guitar and vocals, Matthew Kelly, harmonica, guitar, and vocals; Barry Sless, guitar and pedal steel; and Fred Campbell, guitar and vocals; plus David Nelson, guitar, mandolin, and vocals. *Fire on the Mountain* (Hunter/Hart). *Cumberland Blues* (Hunter/Garcia/Lesh). *Truckin'* (Garcia/Weir/Lesh/Hunter). Piano solo: *Friend of the Devil* (Hunter/Dawson/Garcia)/*Boris the Spider* (Entwistle). *Dejavalse. I've just seen a Face* (Lennon/McCartney). *Presto* from *Sonata in E* (Haydn). *Mountains of the Moon* (Hunter/Garcia). *Dark Star* (Hunter/Grateful Dead). Joined in progress by electric Kingfish: Barry Flast, keyboard and vocals, Matthew Kelly, harmonica, guitar, and vocals; Barry Sless, guitar and pedal steel; Fred Campbell, bass and vocals; and Eric Parker, drums; plus David Nelson, guitar and vocals: *Woman Smarter* (Span)/*Deal* (Hunter/Garcia)/*Althea* (Hunter/Garcia). *Big Boss Man* (Smith/Dixon)/*Goin' down the Road Feelin' Bad* (Traditional). NRPS Segment: *Panama Red* (Rowan). *Hand Jive* (Otis)/*The Eleven* (Hunter/Lesh). *I Know You Rider* (Traditional). Encore: *U. S. Blues* (Hunter/Garcia).

October 23. Nashville, Tennessee. 328 Performance Hall (Roland RD-1000 digital piano/ca 100). With acoustic Kingfish: Barry Flast, guitar and vocals, Matthew Kelly, harmonica, guitar, and vocals; Barry Sless, guitar and pedal steel; and Fred Campbell, guitar and vocals; plus David Nelson, guitar, mandolin, and vocals. *Goin' down the Road Feelin' Bad* (Traditional). *Fire on the Mountain* (Hunter/Hart). *Ripple* (Hunter/Garcia). *Cumberland Blues* (Hunter/Garcia/Lesh). *Truckin'* (Garcia/Weir/Lesh/Hunter). Piano solo: *St. Stephen* (Hunter/Garcia)/*A Day in the Life* (Lennon/McCartney). *Friend of the Devil* (Hunter/Dawson/Garcia)/*Boris the Spider* (Entwistle). *Dejavalse. Presto from Sonata in E* (Haydn). *Mountains of the Moon* (Hunter/Garcia). *Dark Star* (Hunter/Grateful Dead). Joined in progress by electric Kingfish: Barry Flast, keyboard and vocals, Matthew Kelly, harmonica, guitar, and vocals; Barry Sless, guitar and pedal steel; Fred Campbell, bass and vocals; and Eric Parker, drums; plus David Nelson, guitar and vocals: *Woman Smarter* (Span)/*Deal* (Hunter/Garcia)/*Big Boss Man* (Smith/Dixon). *Candy Man* (Hunter/Garcia)/*Althea* (Hunter/Garcia). Kingfish Segment: *Panama Red* (Rowan). *Hand Jive* (Otis)/*The Eleven* (Hunter/Lesh)/*Hand Jive* (Otis). Encore: *U. S. Blues* (Hunter/Garcia).

October 24. Athens, Georgia. Georgia Theatre (Suzuki SE-88 digital piano/254). With electric Kingfish: Barry Flast, keyboard and vocals, Matthew Kelly, harmonica, guitar, and vocals; Barry Sless, guitar and pedal steel; Fred Campbell, bass and vocals; and Eric Parker, drums; plus David Nelson, guitar and vocals: *I Know You Rider* (Traditional)/*Deal* (Hunter/Garcia)/*Althea* (Hunter/Garcia). *Panama Red* (Rowan). *Next Time You see me* (?). *Dark Star* (Hunter/Grateful Dead)/*Fire on the Mountain* (Hunter/Hart). *Hand Jive* (Otis)/*The Eleven* (Hunter/Lesh)/*Hand Jive* (Otis). *Woman Smarter* (Span)/*Iko Iko* (Traditional)/*Woman Smarter* (Span). Encores: *Around and Around* (Berry). *Knockin' on Heaven's Door* (Dylan).

October 25. Tallahassee, Florida. The Moon (Yamaha KX-88/Roland/ca 250). With acoustic Kingfish: Barry Flast, guitar and vocals, Matthew Kelly, harmonica, guitar, and vocals; Barry Sless, guitar and pedal steel; and Fred Campbell, guitar and vocals; plus David Nelson, guitar, mandolin, and vocals. *Cumberland Blues* (Hunter/

Garcia/Lesh). *Truckin'* (Garcia/Weir/Lesh/Hunter). Piano solo: *St. Stephen* (Hunter/Garcia)/*A Day in the Life* (Lennon/McCartney). *Friend of the Devil* (Hunter/Dawson/Garcia)/*Boris the Spider* (Entwistle). *Dejavalse. Prelude, Op. 32 #1* (Rachmaninoff). *Mountains of the Moon* (Hunter/Garcia). *Dark Star* (Hunter/Grateful Dead). Joined in progress by electric Kingfish: Barry Flast, keyboard and vocals, Matthew Kelly, harmonica, guitar, and vocals; Barry Sless, guitar and pedal steel; Fred Campbell, bass and vocals; and Eric Parker, drums; plus David Nelson, guitar and vocals: *Fire on the Mountain* (Hunter/Hart)/*Deal* (Hunter/Garcia)/*Althea* (Hunter/Garcia). *New New Minglewood Blues* (Weir/Lewis)/*New Minglewood Blues* (Lewis). *Goin' down the Road Feelin' Bad* (Traditional). Kingfish Segment: *Juke* (Kingfish). *Groupie* (Kingfish). *Hand Jive* (Otis)/*The Eleven* (Hunter/Lesh)/*Woman Smarter* (Span). *Iko Iko* (Traditional)/*Woman Smarter* (Span)/*Hand Jive* (Otis). Encores: *U. S. Blues* (Hunter/Garcia). *Knockin' on Heaven's Door* (Dylan).

October 26. Ft. Lauderdale, Florida. Summers on the Beach (KORG SG-1D sampling grand/513). With acoustic Kingfish: Barry Flast, guitar and vocals, Matthew Kelly, harmonica, guitar, and vocals; Barry Sless, guitar and pedal steel; and Fred Campbell, guitar and vocals; plus David Nelson, guitar, mandolin, and vocals. *Cumberland Blues* (Hunter/Garcia/Lesh). *Truckin'* (Garcia/Weir/Lesh/Hunter). Piano solo: *St. Stephen* (Hunter/Garcia)/*A Day in the Life* (Lennon/McCartney). *Friend of the Devil* (Hunter/Dawson/Garcia)/*Boris the Spider* (Entwistle). *I've just seen a Face* (Lennon/McCartney). *Mountains of the Moon* (Hunter/Garcia). With Barry Flast, vocal. *Dark Star* (Hunter/Grateful Dead). Joined in progress by electric Kingfish: Barry Flast, keyboard and vocals, Matthew Kelly, harmonica, guitar, and vocals; Barry Sless, guitar and pedal steel; Fred Campbell, bass and vocals; and Eric Parker, drums; plus David Nelson, guitar and vocals: *Fire on the Mountain* (Hunter/Hart)/*Althea* (Hunter/Garcia). *I Know You Rider* (Traditional)/*Deal* (Hunter/Garcia)/*Don't Ease me in* (Traditional). Kingfish Segment: *Panama Red* (Rowan). *Knockin' on Heaven's Door* (Dylan). *Hand Jive* (Otis)/*The Eleven* (Hunter/Lesh)/*One More Saturday Night* (Weir). Encore: *Around and Around* (Kingfish).

October 27. St. Petersburg, Florida. Jannus Landing (Roland RD-300s digital piano/ 418. With acoustic Kingfish: Barry Flast, guitar and vocals, Matthew Kelly, harmonica, guitar, and vocals; Barry Sless, guitar and pedal steel; and Fred Campbell, guitar and vocals; plus David Nelson, guitar, mandolin, and vocals. *Cumberland Blues* (Hunter/Garcia/Lesh). *Truckin'* (Garcia/ Weir/Lesh/Hunter). Piano solo: *St. Stephen* (Hunter/Garcia)/*A Day in the Life* (Lennon/ McCartney). *Friend of the Devil* (Hunter/ Dawson/Garcia)/*Boris the Spider* (Entwistle). *I've just seen a Face* (Lennon/McCartney). *Mountains of the Moon* (Hunter/ Garcia). *Dark Star* (Hunter/Grateful Dead). Joined in progress by electric Kingfish: Barry Flast, keyboard and vocals, Matthew Kelly, harmonica, guitar, and vocals; Barry Sless, guitar and pedal steel; Fred Campbell, bass and vocals; and Eric Parker, drums; plus David Nelson, guitar and vocals: *Althea* (Hunter/Garcia). *Deal* (Hunter/Garcia). *Woman Smarter* (Span)/*Iko Iko* (Traditional)/ *Woman Smarter* (Span). Kingfish/NRPS tunes. *Panama Red* (Rowan). *Candy Man* (Hunter/Garcia). *Hand Jive* (Otis)/*The Eleven* (Hunter/Lesh)/*Hand Jive* (Otis). Encore: *U. S. Blues* (Hunter/Garcia).

October 29. Tuscaloosa, Alabama. The Ivory Tusk (Roland RD-1000 digital piano/220). With acoustic Kingfish: Barry Flast, guitar and vocals, Matthew Kelly, harmonica, guitar, and vocals; Barry Sless, guitar and pedal steel; and Fred Campbell, guitar and vocals; plus David Nelson, guitar, mandolin, and vocals. *Cumberland Blues* (Hunter/ Garcia/Lesh). *Truckin'* (Garcia/Weir/ Lesh/Hunter). Piano solo: *St. Stephen* (Hunter/Garcia)/*A Day in the Life* (Lennon/ McCartney). *Friend of the Devil* (Hunter/ Dawson/Garcia)/*Boris the Spider* (Entwistle). *Prelude, Op. 32 #1* (Rachmaninoff). *Mountains of the Moon* (Hunter/Garcia). With Barry Flast, vocal. *Dark Star* (Hunter/ Grateful Dead). Joined in progress by electric Kingfish: Barry Flast, keyboard and vocals, Matthew Kelly, harmonica, guitar, and vocals; Barry Sless, guitar and pedal steel; Fred Campbell, bass and vocals; and Eric Parker, drums; plus David Nelson, guitar and vocals: *Althea* (Hunter/Garcia)/ *Deal* (Hunter/Garcia). *New New Minglewood Blues* (Weir/Lewis)/*New Minglewood Blues* (Lewis). *I Know You Rider* (Traditional). *Candy Man* (Hunter/Garcia). *Goin' down the Road Feelin' Bad* (Traditional). *Juke* (King-

fish). *Friend of the Devil* (Hunter/Dawson/ Garcia). *Fire on the Mountain* (Hunter/Hart). *Panama Red* (Rowan). *Woman Smarter* (Span)/*Iko Iko* (Traditional)/*Woman Smarter* (Span).

October 30. Montgomery, Alabama. Coconut Bay (Yamaha CP-20/ca 350). With acoustic Kingfish: Barry Flast, guitar and vocals, Matthew Kelly, harmonica, guitar, and vocals; Barry Sless, guitar and pedal steel; and Fred Campbell, guitar and vocals; plus David Nelson, guitar, mandolin, and vocals. *Cumberland Blues* (Hunter/Garcia/ Lesh). *Truckin'* (Garcia/Weir/Lesh/ Hunter). Piano solo: *Friend of the Devil* (Hunter/Dawson/Garcia)/*Boris the Spider* (Entwistle). *I've just seen a Face* (Lennon/ McCartney). *Mountains of the Moon* (Hunter/Garcia). With Barry Flast, vocal. *Dark Star* (Hunter/Grateful Dead). Joined in progress by electric Kingfish: Barry Flast, keyboard and vocals, Matthew Kelly, harmonica, guitar, and vocals; Barry Sless, guitar and pedal steel; Fred Campbell, bass and vocals; and Eric Parker, drums; plus David Nelson, guitar and vocals: *Althea* (Hunter/Garcia)/*I Know You Rider* (Traditional)/*Deal* (Hunter/Garcia). *Candy Man* (Hunter/Garcia). *Fire on the Mountain* (Hunter/Hart). *New New Minglewood Blues* (Weir/Lewis)/*New Minglewood Blues* (Lewis). *Big Boss Man* (Smith/Dixon). *Goin' down the Road Feelin' Bad* (Traditional). Kingfish Tunes. *Panama Red* (Rowan). *Woman Smarter* (Span)/*Iko Iko* (Traditional)/*Woman Smarter* (Span).

October 31. Charlotte, North Carolina. 1313 Club (KORG M1 digital workstation/177). With acoustic Kingfish: Barry Flast, guitar and vocals, Matthew Kelly, harmonica, guitar, and vocals; Barry Sless, guitar and pedal steel; and Fred Campbell, guitar and vocals; plus David Nelson, guitar, mandolin, and vocals. *Cumberland Blues* (Hunter/ Garcia/Lesh). *Truckin'* (Garcia/Weir/ Lesh/Hunter). Piano solo: *Friend of the Devil* (Hunter/Dawson/Garcia)/*Boris the Spider* (Entwistle). *I've just seen a Face* (Lennon/ McCartney). *Mountains of the Moon* (Hunter/Garcia). With Barry Flast, vocal. *Dark Star* (Hunter/Grateful Dead). Joined in progress by electric Kingfish: Barry Flast, keyboard and vocals, Matthew Kelly, harmonica, guitar, and vocals; Barry Sless, guitar and pedal steel; Fred Campbell, bass and vocals; and Eric Parker, drums; plus David Nelson, guitar and vocals: *Althea*

(Hunter/Garcia)/*I Know You Rider* (Traditional)/*Deal* (Hunter/Garcia). *Candy Man* (Hunter/Garcia)/*Fire on the Mountain* (Hunter/Hart). *New New Minglewood Blues* (Weir/Lewis)/*New Minglewood Blues* (Lewis). *Big Boss Man* (Smith/Dixon). Kingfish Tunes. *Panama Red* (Rowan). *Hand Jive* (Otis)/*The Eleven* (Hunter/Lesh)/*Woman Smarter* (Span). *Iko Iko* (Traditional)/*Woman Smarter* (Span). *We Bid You Goodnight* (Traditional) – Piano solo.

November 1. Birmingham, Alabama. Simpson Hall. Birmingham Southern College. (CP-70/ca 350). With acoustic Kingfish: Barry Flast, guitar and vocals, Matthew Kelly, harmonica, guitar, and vocals; Barry Sless, guitar and pedal steel; and Fred Campbell, guitar and vocals; plus David Nelson, guitar, mandolin, and vocals. *Cumberland Blues* (Hunter/Garcia/Lesh). *Truckin'* (Garcia/Weir/Lesh/Hunter). Piano solo: *Friend of the Devil* (Hunter/Dawson/Garcia)/*Boris the Spider* (Entwistle). *Presto* from *Sonata in E* (Haydn). *Mountains of the Moon* (Hunter/Garcia). With Barry Flast, vocal. *Dark Star* (Hunter/Grateful Dead). Joined in progress by electric Kingfish: Barry Flast, keyboard and vocals, Matthew Kelly, harmonica, guitar, and vocals; Barry Sless, guitar and pedal steel; Fred Campbell, bass and vocals; and Chris Cuelo, drums; plus David Nelson, guitar and vocals: *Althea* (Hunter/Garcia)/*I Know You Rider* (Traditional)/*Deal* (Hunter/Garcia). *Candy Man* (Hunter/Garcia)/*Fire on the Mountain* (Hunter/Hart). *New New Minglewood Blues* (Weir/Lewis)/*New Minglewood Blues* (Lewis). *Big Boss Man* (Smith/Dixon). *Panama Red* (Rowan). *Hand Jive* (Otis)/*The Eleven* (Hunter/Lesh)/*Woman Smarter* (Span). *Iko Iko* (Traditional)/*Woman Smarter* (Span). Encore: *U. S. Blues* (Hunter/Garcia).

November 2. Memphis,Tennessee. 616 Club (Roland RD-1000 Digital piano/316). With acoustic Kingfish: Barry Flast, guitar and vocals, Matthew Kelly, harmonica, guitar, and vocals; Barry Sless, guitar and pedal steel; and Fred Campbell, guitar and vocals; plus David Nelson, guitar, mandolin, and vocals. *Friend of the Devil* (Hunter/Dawson/Garcia). *Walkin' Blues* (Johnson). *Ripple* (Hunter/Garcia). *Cumberland Blues* (Hunter/Garcia/Lesh). *Truckin'* (Garcia/Weir/Lesh/Hunter). Piano solo: *St. Stephen* (Hunter/Garcia)/*A Day in the Life* (Lennon/McCartney). *Boris the Spider* (Entwistle).

*Dejavalse. Presto* from *Sonata in E* (Haydn). *Mountains of the Moon* (Hunter/Garcia). With Barry Flast, vocal. *Dark Star* (Hunter/Grateful Dead). Joined in progress by electric Kingfish: Barry Flast, keyboard and vocals, Matthew Kelly, harmonica, guitar, and vocals; Barry Sless, guitar and pedal steel; Fred Campbell, bass and vocals; and Chris Cuelo, drums; plus David Nelson, guitar and vocals: *Althea* (Hunter/Garcia)/*Goin' down the Road Feelin' Bad* (Traditional). *New New Minglewood Blues* (Weir/Lewis)/*New Minglewood Blues* (Lewis). *Fire on the Mountain* (Hunter/Hart). *Big Boss Man* (Smith/Dixon). Kingfish Segment: *Panama Red* (Rowan). *Hand Jive* (Otis)/*The Eleven* (Hunter/Lesh)/*Woman Smarter* (Span)/*Iko Iko* (Traditional)/*Woman Smarter* (Span). Encores: *U. S. Blues* (Hunter/Garcia). *One More Saturday Night* (Weir).

November 4. Solana Beach, California. Belly Up Tavern (KORG Sampling Grand/ca 250). 'Dead Head Night.' With Heartstrings: Darryl Cifarelli and Karen Luisi. and members of Bordertown: David Beldock, Glenn Goodwin, Bo Wade, and Randy Renner. *Love is the Sun* (Cifarelli). Piano solo: *St. Stephen* (Hunter/Garcia)/*A Day in the Life* (Lennon/McCartney). *Friend of the Devil* (Hunter/Dawson/Garcia)/*Boris the Spider* (Entwistle). *Dejavalse. Prelude, Op. 32 #1* (Rachmaninoff). *Mountains of the Moon* (Hunter/Garcia). *I've just seen a Face* (Lennon/McCartney). *Dark Star* (Hunter/Grateful Dead). Joined in progress by Travel Agents: Mike Kim, guitar and vocals; Paul Kelly, guitar, and vocals; Bob Rosencrans, bass and vocals;. David Chesavag, keyboard and vocals; and Frank Lazzaro drums; and Hal Seenor, congas. *Tangled up in Blue* (Dylan). *China Cat Sunflower* (Hunter/Garcia)/*I Know You Rider* (Traditional). *Trip Song* (Rosencrans). *Boogie on Reggae Woman* (Wonder). *Bird Song* (Hunter/Garcia)/*Eyes of the World* (Hunter/Garcia). Encores: *Hard to Handle* (Redding/Jones/Isabell). With Sandy Troy, vocal. *Lovelight* (Scott-Malone). *Knockin' on Heaven's Door* (Dylan). Piano solo: *We Bid You Goodnight* (Traditional).

November 8. Arcata, California. KHSU-FM. Interviewed with Barry Flast and David Nelson by Bob White.

November 8. Arcata, California. Van Duzer Theatre; Humboldt State University. (Roland A-80 MIDI controller/ca 300). With acoustic Kingfish: Barry Flast, guitar and vocals, Matthew Kelly, harmonica, guitar, and vocals; and Fred Campbell, guitar and vocals; plus David Nelson, guitar, mandolin, and vocals. *Ripple* (Hunter/Garcia). *Walkin' Blues* (Robert Johnson). *Cumberland Blues* (Hunter/Garcia/Lesh). *Truckin'* (Garcia/Weir/Lesh/Hunter). Piano solo: *St. Stephen* (Hunter/Garcia)/*A Day in the Life* (Lennon/McCartney). *Friend of the Devil* (Hunter/Dawson/Garcia)/*Boris the Spider* (Entwistle). *Dejavalse. Presto* from *Sonata in E* (Haydn). *Mountains of the Moon* (Hunter/Garcia). With Barry Flast, vocal. *Dark Star* (Hunter/Grateful Dead). Joined in progress by electric Kingfish: Barry Flast, keyboard and vocals, Matthew Kelly, harmonica, guitar, and vocals; Fred Campbell, bass and vocals; and Ernest 'Boom' Carter, drums; plus David Nelson, guitar and vocals: *Fire on the Mountain* (Hunter/Hart)/*I Know You Rider* (Traditional). *Althea* (Hunter/Garcia)/*Deal* (Hunter/Garcia). *New New Minglewood Blues* (Weir/Lewis)/*New Minglewood Blues* (Lewis). *Candy Man* (Hunter/Garcia). Kingfish Segment: *Knockin' on Heaven's Door* (Dylan). *Panama Red* (Rowan). *Hand Jive* (Otis)/*Woman Smarter* (Span)/*Iko Iko* (Traditional)/*Woman Smarter* (Span).

November 9. San Francisco, California. KQED-FM: 'West Coast Weekend', with Sedge Thomson (Life on the Water/Steinway). *{Sloop John B (Wanna go Home) (?)/Dejas. Prelude, Op. 28 #10* (Chopin). *E Tag. Rockin' Promenade. George Cudahay* (Talen) Intro. *Mountains of the Moon* (Hunter/Garcia). *Audience Adventure Boogie.*

November 16. San Francisco, California. KQED-FM: 'West Coast Weekend', with Sedge Thomson (Life on the Water/Steinway). *{Hotel California* (Eagles)/*Dejas. Walk Don't Run* (?) Tag. *Urban Geographer* Intro/Outro. *BBC News* (Varon) Outro. *Concerto, Op. 3 #7/1st Mvt.* (Vivaldi/arr. J. S. Bach). *Audience Adventure Boogie. Lilias* Tag. *Rockin' Promenade.*

November 20. Cambridge, Massachusetts. WMBR-FM: *Lost and Found.* With Chris Cowles and Eli Polansky. Phone interview.

November 22. Oakland, California. Chabot Planetarium (Yamaha SY77). Benefit for Oakland Schools' Science Program. Improvisation with Henry Kaiser. Wise words of Kingsley Wightman.

November 23. San Francisco, California. KQED-FM: 'West Coast Weekend', with Sedge Thomson (Life on the Water/Steinway). *{Ninja Turtles* (?)/*Dejas. Prelude,*

*Op. 32 #11* (Rachmaninoff). *Urban Geographer* Intro/Outro. *Funeral March for a Marionette* (Gounod). *Audience Adventure Boogie. Rockin' Promenade.*

November 23. Oakland, California. Chabot Planetarium (Yamaha SY77). Benefit for Oakland Schools' Science Program. Improvisation with Henry Kaiser, guitar; and Lukas Ligeti, drums. Wise words of Kingsley Wightman.

November 25. Berkeley, California. Fantasy Studios (Studio A/Yamaha). Vince Wojno, Engineer. *We Bid You Goodnight* (Traditional). *I Know you Rider* (Traditional).

November 26. San Mateo, California. B Street Studios (Roland A-80 MIDI controller). Grape Session; George Rivas, Engineer. *Paint the White House Blue* (Lashley). *Blowin'* (Lashley). *With a Tear and a Smile* (Lashley).

November 30. San Francisco, California. KQED-FM: 'West Coast Weekend', with Sedge Thomson (Life on the Water/Steinway). *{Brahms Piano Concerto #2 opening/Dejas.* With Third Ear: Kaila Flexer and Julian Smedley, violin; and Joe Preussner, bass. *Imagine* (Lennon) plus vocal. *Entertainment Tonight* Bridge. *Urban Geographer* Intro/Outro. *BBC News* (Varon) Outro. *I Know you Rider* (Traditional). *Audience Adventure Boogie. Green Piece* Intro/Outro. *George Cudahay* (Talen) Intro/Outro.

December 4. Pacifica, California. Pacifica Cable Channel 8. 'The Bruce Latimer Show' (Baldwin upright). First Segment: *I Know You Rider* (Traditional). *Presto* from *Sonata in E* (Haydn). *Imagine* (Lennon) plus vocal. Second Segment: *Romance, Op. 118 #5* (Brahms). *Dejavalse. Mountains of the Moon* (Hunter/Garcia).

December 7. San Francisco, California. KQED-FM: 'West Coast Weekend', with Sedge Thomson (Life on the Water/Steinway). *{Let's Get Together* (Young)/*Dejas.* Two Meditative Interludes. *Urban Geographer* Intro/Outro. *Audience Adventure Boogie. Rockin' Promenade.*

December 14. San Francisco, California. KQED-FM: 'West Coast Weekend', with Sedge Thomson (Life on the Water/Steinway). *{Tidings of Comfort and Joy/Dejas. Elizabethan Farewell. I Know you Rider* (Traditional). *Audience Adventure Boogie. Different Drummer Boy. Wexford Carol* (Traditional). *Un Flambeau, Jeannette, Isabella* (Provençal carol). *Rockin' Promenade.*

December 16. Solana Beach, California. Belly Up Tavern (KORG SG-1D/ca 200). 'Dead

Head Night.' With Bordertown: Cici Porter, David Beldock, Dan Conner, Glenn Goodwin, Bo Wade, Larry Groupe, and Randy Renner, plus Hal Seenor: *Sugar Magnolia/Sunshine Daydream* (Weir/Hunter). Piano solo: *I Know you Rider* (Traditional). *Dejavalse. Sonata #15. III mvt* (Beethoven). *Friend of the Devil* (Hunter/Dawson/Garcia)/*Boris the Spider* (Entwistle). *Oriental (Spanish Dance #2)* (Granados). *Mountains of the Moon* (Hunter/Garcia). *Dark Star* (Hunter/Grateful Dead)/*The Eleven* (Hunter/Lesh). Joined in progress by Travel Agents: Mike Kim, guitar and vocals; Paul Kelly, guitar, and vocals; Bob Rosencrans, bass and vocals;. David Chesavag, keyboard and vocals; and Frank Lazzaro, drums. *Trip Song* (Rosencrans). *Shakedown Street* (Hunter/Garcia). *Althea* (Hunter/Garcia). *Think* (McCracklin). *Scarlet Bego-*

*nias* (Hunter/Garcia)/*Fire on the Mountain* (Hunter/Hart). *Deal* (Hunter/Garcia). Encore: *Morning Dew* (Dobson).

December 21. San Francisco, California. KQED-FM: 'West Coast Weekend', with Sedge Thomson (Life on the Water/Steinway). *(Turn, Turn, Turn* (Byrds)/*Dejas. Xmas Song/Kinderszene.* Anne Lamott Intro/Outro. *BBC News* (Varon) Outro. *Audience Adventure Boogie. Green Piece* Intro/Outro. *Rockin' Promenade/Urban Geographer* Intro/Outro.

December 28. San Francisco, California. KQED-FM: 'West Coast Weekend', with Sedge Thomson (Life on the Water/Steinway). *(Them Changes* (?)/*Dejas. Prelude, Op. 28 #10* (Chopin). *Entertainment Tonite* (?) *Bridge. Audience Adventure Boogie. Ashokan Farewell* (Ungar) Tag. *Speaking* (Forrester).

Printed by Thomson-Shore, Inc., Dexter, Michigan